SOCIAL
CONFLICTS

2nd Edition

SOCIAL CONFLICTS

LOUIS KRIESBERG
Syracuse University

PRENTICE-HALL, INC.   Englewood Cliffs, N.J. 07632

Library of Congress Cataloging in Publication Data

KRIESBERG, LOUIS.
  Social Conflicts.

  (Prentice-Hall series in sociology)
  Previously published as: The sociology of
social conflicts. 1973.
  Includes bibliographies and indexes.
  1. Social conflict. 2. Social problems.
3. Negotiation. I. Title. II. Series.
HM136.K77 1982   303.6   81-7343
ISBN 0-13-815589-5   AACR2

*Editorial/production supervision and interior
design by Linda Schuman
Cover design by Zimmerman/Foyster
Manufacturing buyer: John Hall*

Prentice-Hall Series in Sociology
Neil Smelser, Editor

Printed in the United States of America

10 9 8 7 6 5 4 3 2 1

PRENTICE-HALL INTERNATIONAL, INC., *London*
PRENTICE-HALL OF AUSTRALIA PTY. LIMITED, *Sydney*
PRENTICE-HALL OF CANADA, LTD., *Toronto*
PRENTICE-HALL OF INDIA PRIVATE LIMITED, *New Delhi*
PRENTICE-HALL OF JAPAN, INC., *Tokyo*
PRENTICE-HALL OF SOUTHEAST ASIA PTE. LTD., *Singapore*
WHITEHALL BOOKS LIMITED, *Wellington, New Zealand*

Contents

2

The Bases of Social Conflicts   23

3

The Emergence of Social Conflicts   66

4

Pursuing Conflict Goals   114

8

Consequences of Social Conflicts   291

9

Essentials, Settings, and Implications   317

Author Index   337

Subject Index   344

Preface to the First Edition

As a teacher of social conflicts and as a partisan and observer of them, I have long felt the need for a comprehensive study of conflicts. I felt it was necessary to bring together the main ideas pertaining to each aspect of a struggle or, better yet, to relate these ideas consistently. This might mean disproving some, reinterpreting others, and specifying and synthesizing still others.

I have tried to meet these needs in this book by presenting a comprehensive analysis of all kinds of group conflicts. Instead of describing certain kinds of conflicts or particular aspects of struggles, this book provides a framework for analyzing all kinds of disputes, struggles, fights, and contentions. The framework is relevant for conflicts between groups in organizations, communities, societies, and even between national governments. For illustrative purposes, the discussion focuses upon some recent struggles: women's liberation, the cold war, the Arab-Israeli conflict, collective bargaining, student protests, and the fight for racial equality.

In presenting a comprehensive framework, I hope to raise important and neglected questions. We shall ask about deescalation as well as escalation, outcomes as well as bases, and noncoercive as well as coercive means of conducting struggles. We will ask why fights differ in consequences, in origins, and in violence.

In answering these questions I have tried to be systematic and specific. Nevertheless, competing ideas and interpretations have not been excluded. I have sought to counterpose plausible ideas and to assess them. I have tried to be honest and open about the theoretical and evidential difficulties with the positions taken.

Rather than gloss over the problems, I have directly discussed them and given my best current judgment.

The general orientation of this work is sociological, but I have not hesitated to draw upon theoretical and empirical work from political science, anthropology, economics, psychology, and history. I have also examined and analyzed sample surveys, newspaper accounts, census, and other kinds of data to probe some of the ideas examined in the illustrative cases.

The comprehensive scope of this effort necessarily leaves out many details. More significantly, many issues are inadequately resolved. I hope that my efforts will stimulate and facilitate the work of others to overcome those failures. I hope to continue in that endeavor myself.

Preface to the Second Edition

The first edition of this book presented a comprehensive and systematic framework for analysing the major aspects of a variety of social conflicts and provided a sound and valuable way of examining all their stages. The second edition retains the framework but has benefited from the broadening of my knowledge and experience and from the recent developments in the study of social conflicts.

Six changes should be noted. First, a new chapter on conflict intermediaries and mediation has been added; only a few pages were devoted to this topic in the first edition. Second, the chapter on terminations and outcomes has been completely restructured. Third, the various chapters and sections of chapters are more thoroughly integrated; for example, the discussion about outcomes of conflicts and negotiating their termination has been more clearly related to the bases of conflicts and their interlocking character. Fourth, the literature cited has been brought up to date and the range of material used has been expanded. The first edition drew largely from sociology, but in revising the work I have drawn even more than before from many other disciplines. Therefore, I changed the title of the second edition from *The Sociology of Social Conflicts* to simply, *Social Conflicts*. Fifth, I have added discussions of class conflict and revolutions to this edition. Finally, the book has been largely rewritten and the phrasing clarified.

The additions and changes derive from new developments in the study of social conflicts, my own work experience, and reactions to the first edition. Areas that I noted in the first edition as particularly lacking in research have become the subject of more analysis: notably, alternative ways of conducting struggles, the outcomes of conflicts, and ways of mitigating conflicts. I can now discuss these matters on the basis of a significantly larger research base.

Some of the added material was not previously used because I was unfamiliar with it. Continued reading, teaching, and research have expanded my knowledge beyond sociology and deepened my understanding and familiarity with current theoretical and substantive issues. My recent work has focused on the use of noncoercive inducements as well as coercive ones in international conflicts, especially the struggles between the U.S. and Soviet governments and Israeli and Arab governments and groups. This research has informed several topics in this book. In addition, I have been associated with organizations involved in social conflicts and their mitigation. Among the organizations are: the Consortium on Peace Research, Education and Development (COPRED); the National Peace Academy Campaign; the International Peace Academy; Reevaluation Counseling; American Professors for Peace in the Middle East; and the American Association of University Professors. I learned much by explaining and applying the ideas developed in this book to persons engaged in social conflicts. I have also learned a great deal by observing and listening to persons in these organizations.

Finally, I have heard from students and colleagues who have used the book in their classrooms and research. Their comments have shown me where presentations were unclear or needed elaboration and suggested many avenues for future work. I incorporated comments that were generally consistent with the approach I had chosen for the book.

I enjoyed rewriting this book since I was able to improve significantly my treatment of a topic of great concern to me. The analysis of social conflicts is intellectually challenging and exciting. Moreover, practical implications of a better understanding of conflicts are immensely and increasingly important. I am concerned that as we enter a period of greater scarcity, conflicts are likely to multiply and intensify. The means of violence are increasingly effective so that more people can be more quickly destroyed. Resorting to violence in the pursuit of disputed goals often produces greater than anticipated damage. Meanwhile, as I cannot forget, we live with the incredible threat of a nuclear war and the immense costs of preparing to wage one. At the same time, I recognize the necessity of struggle—it is needed to liberate people, preserve freedom, increase equity, and loosen rigidities. I want to contribute to understanding how conflicts can be pursued with minimal violence. I believe the analysis presented in this book provides a basis for exploring a variety of ways to mitigate the coercive aspects of waging social conflicts.

I wish to acknowledge the help of many persons in preparing this edition of *Social Conflicts.* Fortunately, I have continued benefiting from discussions with most of the people I thanked in the first edition. I want to thank here the other persons who commented on the first edition, reviewed one or more chapters of this revision, or responded to my requests for information and assistance. In particular, I wish to thank M. Richard Cramer, Jerry Jacobs, Ross A. Klein, Harry Murray, Anthony Oberschall, Donald B. Straus, Ralph Turner, and Paul Wehr. Finally, I have benefited from my association with practitioners of conflict management: James Laue, Irving Goldaber, Neil Katz, John E. Mroz, and Major General Indar Jit Rikhye. In preparing this volume, as in the past, I have appreciated and enjoyed the support and professionalism of the people at Prentice-Hall, particularly Edward Stanford. The indices were prepared by Harry Murray.

SOCIAL
CONFLICTS

1

Variations
and
Stages

Social conflicts are all around us. They are inherent in human relations. But this does not mean that every social relationship is entirely or even partly conflicting all the time. Nor does it mean that every underlying conflicting relationship will be expressed with the same degree and kind of hostility or violence. Conflicts vary in their bases, duration, means, outcomes, and consequences. This book is about these variations. It focuses on the development and course of specific social conflicts, fights, and struggles, rather than on the conflicting aspects of social life. It is about contentions between groups of people, not between individuals acting alone. Finally, we are more concerned here with struggles in which coercion and violence are likely or possible than with ones that are so highly regulated that coercion and violence do not occur.

The major questions we seek to answer are within these realms. We ask what conditions produce violent fights. We want to know what makes groups believe that they have incompatible goals. We want to know how aggrieved groups seek justice. We ask why some groups do, and others do not, attain what they seek. We want to learn the consequences of conflict for the contending parties and for the larger system of which they are a part, even if those consequences are not desired or anticipated by any of the parties.

In trying to answer these and related questions we assume that all conflicts have some things in common. We assume it is possible and even useful to consider the similarities as well as the differences among class, community, international, and industrial struggles. Having said that, we must also point out that there is a wide variety of social conflicts. In order to answer the questions we have raised, it is necessary to distinguish among the different types of conflict and stages in the course of a struggle. Before beginning to do that, a few observations about different evaluative orientations toward conflicts should be made.

EVALUATIONS OF SOCIAL CONFLICTS

Conflicts are exciting. People are drawn to study them because of that stimulation as well as from intellectual curiosity. Persons also may be drawn to study social conflicts because they want help in deciding what stand to take on an issue. In addition, partisans in a social conflict want to know how to wage their struggle better. Whatever the stimulus or incentive to study conflicts, two major evaluative orientations may be discerned among students of social strife.

Some persons are concerned about the disruption or violence of fights. They see a larger collectivity or system that is threatened or injured by the conflict and wish to discover ways of mitigating its disruptive character. They may be troubled by the prospects of international wars or interracial violence; they tend to evaluate conflicts negatively. Other persons are concerned about the injustice or repression of some category of persons and, siding with that collectivity, are interested in learning how such people may form conflict groups and successfully end or reduce their oppression. These persons tend to view such struggles as necessary and even desirable.

I have suggested two positions students of social conflict may take: that of the larger system to which the partisans belong or that of one of the partisans (Gamson 1968). I have also suggested that the latter students would consider conflict necessary or even admirable, while the former would consider it regrettable or even evil. A strong evaluative position may be a powerful motivation for study and analysis, but it also may distort the analysis. The dangers of evaluations corrupting the analysis can be lessened if one keeps in mind alternative viewpoints and a wide range of conflicts.

Even if one takes a partisan perspective, it is possible to regard conflict as undesirable. It depends upon who is causing the trouble. Consider the shifting evaluations of community strife. During the early 1950s in the United States many persons concerned with community conflict felt it unhealthful and dangerous. The prototypical conflict seemed to be attacks from the political right upon the liberal establishment, which was being innovative in the schools or was trying to introduce fluoridation into the cities' water systems (Coleman 1957). In the 1960s community conflicts more often referred to the attempts of the poor and the blacks to gain greater influence in decision making (Haggstrom 1964). People who were unsympathetic to the community controversies of the 1950s are likely to have been sympathetic to those of the 1960s. Consider, too, international conflict. Partisans of countries relatively satisfied with the status quo are likely to view international war as reprehensible: They would not accept the legitimacy of a "war of national liberation."

Even those who take a system perspective need not regard conflict as harmful and evil (Coser 1956; Simmel 1955; Sumner 1952). Many persons believe that conflict, properly institutionalized, is an effective vehicle for discovering truth, for attaining justice, and for the long-run benefit of a society as a whole. For example, the American judicial system is based upon the adversary principle. The struggle between the lawyer for the prosecution and the lawyer for the defense, conducted within the court, is considered to be the best way of obtaining justice. Similarly, both management and trade unions in the United States now generally feel that the struggle between them, conducted through collective bargaining, serves the interests of the entire society, as well as their own.

Evaluations of conflict in general or of specific struggles depend upon many considerations: upon the unit with which one identifies, upon the issue in contention, and upon the means used in attaining a given outcome, to name a few. To accept without question a particular evaluation of a struggle handicaps analysis and understanding of it. One safeguard against such implicit assumptions is to keep in mind the many grounds of evaluation and consequently the alternative judgments of the conflict. We cannot simply put aside our own evaluations, but we can avoid ignoring alternative assessments. Another way to avoid some of the risks of examining conflicts from too narrow a point of view is to use a comprehensive framework of analysis. One of the tasks of this book is to provide such a framework.

Every fight is unique. Yet they all have some qualities in common. One way to bring these two truths together is to recognize the several dimensions along which conflicts vary. In this chapter we consider four ways in which conflicts differ: the issues in contention, the characteristics of the contending parties, the relations between the parties, and the means they use to conduct the struggle. Each of these aspects will be discussed in considerable detail and in many different contexts later in the volume. At this point, fundamental issues pertaining to each will be examined in order to provide the basis for the detailed analysis that follows.

ISSUES IN CONTENTION

Conflicts are generally about something. The antagonists have, or believe they have, incompatible goals. For our immediate purpose, two kinds of variations are related to the issue in contention: How realistic is the conflict and to what extent are the conflicting interests mixed with cooperative ones?

Realistic or Unrealistic

Most writers about social conflict regard an essential element in its definition that the parties are aware that they are in contention (Coser 1956, p. 8; Weber 1947, pp. 132–133). Thus Park and Burgess state:

Conflict is always conscious. Indeed it evokes the deepest emotions and strongest passions and enlists the greatest concentration of attention and of effort. Both competition and conflict are forms of struggle. Competition, however, is continuous and impersonal. Conflict is intermittent and personal. (Park and Burgess 1924, p. 574)

This formulation is also followed by Boulding who defines conflict as a form of competition in which the competing parties recognize that they have mutually incompatible goals (Boulding 1962).

Social conflict may also be defined objectively; that is, in terms of the "real" incompatibility of the people in the situation. Dahrendorf (1959), for example, asserts that in an imperatively coordinated organization, such as a factory, persons without power are in a conflict relationship with those who have power. Conflict, so defined, may encompass awareness by the people in the situation, but it does not require it. The existence of an objective conflict, then, must depend on the observer's judgment that a real incompatibility of interests exists. This judgment is based on a theoretical understanding of the situation.

Even formulations of social conflict that emphasize its subjective character often assume that there is an underlying objective conflict situation. The relationship between presumed objective conflict and the belief among adversaries that they are in conflict is complex (Bernard 1957). On the one hand, writers who discern an objective conflict may refer to groups who do not recognize their antagonistic interests as having "false consciousness" (Marx 1963). On the other hand, writers who think they can discern an objective conflict may decide that there is none even when adversaries believe they are in conflict; in those cases the observers would assert that the conflict is "unrealistic."

False consciousness may occur for different reasons. One or more objectively antagonistic groups may be unwilling to recognize the antagonism because they fear the consequences of doing so. Or one or more groups may have been socialized to believe in the legitimacy of the situation, even if they are "oppressed" in it, and therefore fail to recognize their true interests. Or the protagonists may have many common and cooperative interests that they regard as more important than the conflicting ones and therefore tend to ignore the conflicting ones.

Now let us consider why people may seem to think they are in conflict when an observer would say they are not and the conflict is unrealistic. Basically, in these cases, one or more adversaries are acting antagonistically due to internal reasons rather than ones pertaining to their relationship. Thus, anger and hostility may be displaced from a powerful, frustrating, competitor to a more vulnerable antagonist, and the fight with that weaker antagonist would be regarded as unrealistic. Or, certain groups within a large collectivity may benefit by developing coercive strength; although this is done for domestic reasons, it becomes the basis for taking provocative or aggressive actions against other collectivities. Or, defensive actions by one side are misperceived as threatening due to past, but irrelevant, experiences and the other side prepares for attack; the side that had taken defensive actions views this as threatening and prepares even more for an anticipated attack. The spiral of mutual defensiveness and fear may be viewed as a conflict by the protagonists while an observer may think the whole matter is unrealistic.

The theoretical and policy implications of considering a conflict unrealistic or thinking that antagonists have false consciousness are profound. If one believes that adversaries are engaged in an unrealistic conflict, better communication between them would probably dissolve the antagonistic struggle. Intermediaries would seek to convince the antagonists of their true interests. Longer run preventive action would entail reducing the domestic or internal sources of hostile feelings and aggressive actions.

If an observer thinks that a group is unaware of an important conflicting relationship, he or she may want to raise its members consciousness so that the group can fight for its own interests. Leaders of oppressed groups may agitate in order to end each group's false consciousness. Such persons might then go on to argue that leadership and organization are necessary to make the potential partisans aware of their conflicting relations. The success of such leaders in mobilizing the partisans and bringing the conflict to the desired outcome, however, still depends upon the leaders' correctness in interpreting the objective situation. As Lenin said in *Left-Wing Communism, an Infantile Disorder*:

> . . . in order that actually the whole class, that actually the broad masses of toilers and those oppressed by capital may take up such a position, propaganda and agitation are not enough. For this the masses must have their own political experience. (Lenin 1940, p. 74)

Some students of social conflict tend to think that most social conflicts are expressions of objective conflicts. They argue that conflicts naturally arise from the inevitable incompatibility of interests that are readily perceived by the antagonists (Madison 1937). Other analysts emphasize that social conflicts frequently involve large unrealistic components. Adversaries are aroused by emotional symbols, displaced feelings of hostility, or the gratifications of expressing anger and even injuring others.

But how do we decide whether the partisans are "correctly" perceiving the objective conflict, are suffering from false consciousness, or are engaged in an unrealistic struggle? Such assessments all depend on the observer's ability to know what the objective conflicting relation really is. The observer or analyst needs to have a theory that not only asserts when an objective conflict exists but also the conditions in which the principal actors will or will not believe they are in conflict. There is no consensus about such a comprehensive theory. As we proceed in this book, we will examine various elements of different theoretical approaches that may contribute to such a theory.

In general, we assume that in all conflicts realistic and unrealistic components are both present. Specific fights or struggles vary in the mixture of these components. We assume that there are innumerable objective conflicts. In Chapter 2, we specify the variety of objective or underlying conflicts. Since there are so many different kinds of conflicts, it is always possible to find some realistic elements in every fight once it has begun. In Chapter 3 we examine the conditions that affect the adversaries' becoming aware of objective conflicts and also what factors may generate beliefs and conduct that produce unrealistic components of conflicts.

Pure or Mixed

Parties with some bases for conflict between them also have common and complementary interests and, therefore, could engage in cooperation or exchange as well as in conflict (Kriesberg 1968). Given enough time or large relational context, some nonconflicting relations can always be found. For example, union and management negotiators may come to regard their common interests in the firm's share of the market and its profit as more or less compelling. Parties to a dispute always have varying *proportions* of conflicting and nonconflicting interests; therefore, disputes are more or less pure. This can be illustrated in the language of game theory (von Neumann and Morgenstern 1944).

In pure conflict, we speak of a zero-sum game. That is, what one side loses, the other side wins. Suppose two persons, Dan and Joe, agree to play a game of matching pennies; if the pennies match, either both heads or both tails, Joe gives Dan a penny; if the pennies do not match, Dan gives Joe a penny. The payoff matrix of this game is shown in Figure 1.1. We follow the convention that the actor identified on top of the figure has his payoff written first in each box. In this payoff matrix, the sum within each box is constant. The payoffs add up to zero; it is indeed a zero-sum game.

The other major kind of matrix is nonconstant sum; one interesting variety of this is the mixed motive game. A frequently used example is that of the prisoners' dilemma (Rapoport 1960). In this case, two men have been arrested upon suspicion of committing a serious crime. They are guilty, but there is insufficient evidence for conviction on the serious offense but enough for a lesser one. They are not allowed to communicate with each other. They have the following possi-

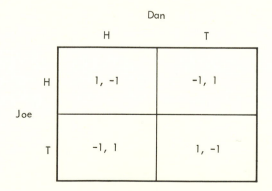

Figure 1.1

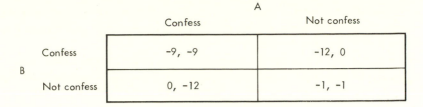

A

	Confess	Not confess
Confess	-9, -9	-12, 0
Not confess	0, -12	-1, -1

B

Figure 1.2

bilities. If they both confess, they will be convicted of the serious offense, but their sentence will be reduced slightly for their cooperation. If one confesses, he gets off without punishment and his confederate gets the maximum sentence of twelve years. If they both hold out and do not confess, they can be convicted only of the lesser offense and sentenced for one year. The payoff matrix based on years in prison is diagramed in Figure 1.2.

This payoff matrix poses a dilemma for the prisoners because if each tries to maximize his own gain, he will confess and implicate his confederate. If they both do that they will be worse off than if they both held out and did not confess. Yet, if each one considers what he should do, regardless of what the other does, he should confess. Thus, if B confesses, A is better off if he too confesses; if B does not confess, A is again better off if he confesses. The dilemma can be resolved only if the prisoners trust each other, follow a criminal code of never cooperating with the police, or identify with each other to such a degree that the confederate's payoff in some degree is his own.

Some conflicts embody such dilemmas. Consider two countries in an arms race; each fears the other. If one government does not increase its arms expenditures, it is at a military disadvantage and becomes subject to domination by the other side. Each side sees only the alternatives of submission or increasing its arms. It is as if they see cells (b) and (c) in Figure 1.3 as the only alternatives. Let us also assume that if both sides continue to increase their expenditures, both suffer some loss in that they cannot use their resources for other purposes and yet neither gains relatively from their arms. Finally, assume that if both halt their

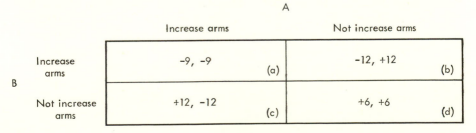

A

	Increase arms	Not increase arms
Increase arms	-9, -9 (a)	-12, +12 (b)
Not increase arms	+12, -12 (c)	+6, +6 (d)

B

Figure 1.3

arms expenditures, they will both have some gains. The payoff matrix is presented in Figure 1.3. Again, if each side pursues its own interest, they will both be worse off than if they acted cooperatively.

Obviously, real-life conflict situations are much more complex than such simple payoff matrices, but the matrices reveal how individual, reasonable calculations can result in aggregate losses. We will consider various aspects of this dilemma and some of its dynamics in later chapters. At this time, let us discuss the extent to which conflicts are actually zero sum.

Pure zero-sum conflicts always can be transformed into variable-sum conflicts. Consider standard games with rules such as chess or poker. The players of one of these games have many social relations with each other that transcend the game. Within that larger social context, *how* each player wins or loses and whether or not each pursues a set of games until the players all agree the series is concluded is important to all the players. In other words, the players have an interest in playing the game through and doing so properly and honestly. All would suffer some loss if the game were not correctly played to a conclusion. In that sense, playing the game is part of a larger payoff matrix that has the quality of a mixed motive game. The counterpart of all this in natural conflicts is that the parties to a conflict have greater or fewer common ties and interests. They also may be more or less integrated with each other and more or less interdependent and implicated in exchange relations. If the parties are highly integrated or have many common interests, the issue in contention will not be viewed as a pure zero-sum situation.

What seems like pure conflict may also be transformed when the issue in contention is fractionated (Fisher 1964); that is, the disputed matter is broken up into many components. Some may be traded off against others. Instead of one side's winning and the other side's losing the entire fight, the fight is thought to include many components; one party may lose one and not another part. For example, the payoff in a game of poker is not just in the winning or losing of money but also in the winning or losing of prestige and honor. These can be gained without necessarily winning money, depending upon the skills used in handling a poor hand of cards, in interpreting the events of the game, and in reacting to the other's winning and losing money.

This point can also be illustrated by what might be regarded as a simple zero-sum international dispute such as contention over a boundary. The conflict may be considered zero sum if each party regards control over the disputed territory as total, in which one side or the other has absolute control. It is possible, however, to consider the variety of specific referents of possible control. One government may have the right to have the people pay taxes to it, the other to ensure that the people study in schools in which their language is used. Both governments may agree that the people in the disputed territory have complete freedom of movement across any borders they draw. They may agree that one side will have sovereign rights over the territory, but neither will station any military forces there.

Furthermore, conflicts always involve many parties. Every adversary has many groups within it, and there are many groups outside who are or might be induced to become allies. In addition, there are entities that cross-cut and transcend the adversaries. Thus, in a national union-management conflict, the union consists of national elected leaders, staff persons, local union officials, and rank-and-file members at varying pay scales; management consists of the labor relations department heads and staff, sales, production, and advertising departments, and overall heads. In addition, each group has ties with political parties, government officials, consumers, stockholders, and affirmative action organizations serving women and minorities. A conflict over wages might seem to be pure zero sum: What the workers get, managers do not retain for profit. But given all these parties any conflict between any two parties can be seen to be embedded in interlocking conflicts. Consequently, each dispute can be seen as a mixed motive game, in which various benefits can be gained from some parties by making concessions to others. The implications of the interlocking character of conflicts will be elaborated in regard to many topics in this book.

In short, the purity of a conflict depends upon the whole set of relations between the parties in conflict. It also depends upon the degree to which the issue in dispute may be broken down into smaller issues. These characteristics of a struggle depend in part upon the way the parties to the conflict view it: (1) to what extent is it isolated from common interests or embedded in a wide range of common interests, and (2) how do the various conflict parties interlock with one another. These perceptions are likely to change in the course of a struggle. The purity of the conflict, in turn, affects its intensity and the choice of ways to reach collective agreement.

CHARACTERISTICS OF THE PARTISANS

Most typologies of conflicts are made in terms of the units involved. Analysis is often limited to disputes within or between particular units: communities, classes, races, religions, nations, factories, or universities. At this point we will consider the characteristics of adversaries in terms of two dimensions particularly relevant to social conflicts: boundary clarity and degree of organization. Attention to such general dimensions facilitates studying the aspects of social conflicts comparatively.

Boundary Clarity

The boundaries of each conflict party may be more or less visible to the members of the social system containing the antagonists. Boundaries may be more or less permeable to persons from other parties and open to interaction and communication between people on both sides. Furthermore, the boundary between the parties may involve more or less of the lives of the members of each party—that is, it may vary in comprehensiveness. Each of these variations may be briefly illustrated. In a collective bargaining dispute between labor and management, the membership in each party is relatively visible and clear, not readily permeable, and not very comprehensive.

The units of an underlying conflict must be considered in terms of their potential emergence as adversaries. The boundaries between social categories that are potential conflict units also vary as conflict parties do. Thus, the difference between males and females is visible and generally recognized; it is not permeable in the sense that persons change membership from one category to another (although it is permeable in the sense that there is considerable interaction across the boundary) and is comprehensive in the sense that many aspects of persons' lives are affected by their belonging in one category rather than another. The boundaries in some self-conscious conflict groups are not as high as in others. Within the women's liberation movement, for example, there are a variety of organizations. Females and males vary considerably in their involvement in one or another organization, in the women's movement generally, or as antagonists to the movement.

It is important to keep in mind that being limited by boundaries is a matter of degree. In the political world today, on the one hand, nation-states are particularly highly bounded. There is general agreement that everyone belongs to one or another nation-state, and there are formal procedures for determining membership. Furthermore, interaction is channeled by such membership, and many aspects of a person's life are determined by membership in a nation-state. Even in this case the boundaries are not impermeable and total. Not all transnational interactions are controlled and directed by the national governments. Ideas, goods, and people cross political borders; people feel commonalities with persons of similar ages, occupations, religions, and ideologies in other political jurisdictions. On the other hand, in local community conflicts the contending groups are relatively unbounded. It is even difficult to distinguish the social categories that serve as the recruiting ground for active participants in opposing groups. People shift back and forth, tend to interact with one another, and have many interrelations despite what an observer might determine to be the boundaries between adversary groups. Again, even in such local cases there is some boundedness. Members of a community have some shared understandings about what kinds of people are likely to be on each side of particular issues.

Disputes between parties with varying degrees of boundedness tend to be studied differently. In the case of relatively unbounded conflict units, as in community struggles, we usually give special attention to how potential participants in conflict groups become aware of their grievances, what the underlying grievances may be, and how people are mobilized and organized to engage in conflicting behavior. In the case of fights between relatively bounded units, as in international or industrial conflicts, the mobilization of members is taken as less problematic and the emphasis tends to be upon the means used in pursuit of conflicting goals. One value of studying many kinds of social conflicts and developing a paradigm for a whole range of conflicts is that it makes us more ready to consider something problematic that we might otherwise take for granted. Thus, it is worthwhile to consider how governments actually mobilize and maintain constituent support for conflicts with other governments. The Vietnam War has certainly helped remind us of the pertinence of this matter. Comparably, it is worthwhile to consider variations in how conflicts are pursued in fights among less clearly bounded parties, such as in women's liberation or black liberation movements.

Degree of Organization

Related to the boundedness of the parties to a conflict is their degree of organization. At one extreme are two social categories that an observer regards as the recruiting ground for two conflict groups. The members of those categories may have no sense of common identity and little or no organization. At the other extreme are highly bounded groups with members of each group conscious of their adherence. In the more organized groups there tends to be considerable differentiation among the members as they play different roles in the maintenance of the organization. What concerns us here is the degree of differentiation for external affairs. In every social group there is likely to be some differentiation such that particular roles are more implicated in relations with nonmembers. For most groups this differentiation also takes the form of some degree of specialization in conflicting relations with external groups and with particular kinds of external groups.

The nation-state again can serve as a prototype. There is considerable differentiation within the society and special agencies dealing with "foreign affairs." Those agents are further specialized so that they deal with cooperative and exchange as well as with conflict relations. They tend to be specialized to deal with comparable counterparts; thus, foreign ministries deal with foreign ministries and armies with armies. In a conflict between a nation-state and an international religious or ideological movement or between an army and a guerrilla force, there are peculiar difficulties.

Trade unions, too, have developed specialized agencies for dealing with their regular adversaries. Some conflict groups are much less organized. Thus, university students protesting some aspect of their lives in the university are usually not highly organized.

One of the important implications of the degree of organization and differentiation is the variation in the position of leaders. In more organized and differentiated conflict groups the leaders tend to claim, and tend to have acknowledged, the authority and legitimacy to represent the entire group. They are likely to be so recognized by the other side, and their role as spokespersons is accepted by the adversary. They are also more likely to be able to commit the group as a whole and control and direct their conflicting behavior effectively.

The degree of organization of conflict groups is affected by a number of factors. As the examples suggest, larger and more autonomous groups tend to be more organized. Furthermore, the longer a conflict relationship persists, the more organized the parties become. The degree of organization of each conflict group affects the degree of organization of its adversary. Union-management relations illustrate this development. The point is also illustrated by the efforts of university administrators during a student strike to find leaders who represent the students and, therefore, with whom they can negotiate. The students themselves, however, may resist any formalization in which some of them are leaders. If the struggle persists in an active form and with conflicting behavior, such differentiation and organization cannot be completely resisted.

This discussion of organization should raise a general question that may have been evoked by the previous discussion of boundedness. Who are the parties to a conflict? Are they the large categories of potential partisans or the self-conscious groups purporting to represent that larger category? Are they those groups that consciously try to coerce one another and regard one another as adversaries, or are they the opposing leaders or the entire groups? For example, consider only one side in the American conflict about equality between whites and blacks. One side might be all American blacks, those whites and blacks favoring greater equality, the National Association for the Advancement of Colored People (NAACP), the Southern Christian Leadership Conference (SCLC), the Black Panthers, the Congress of Racial Equality (CORE), some combination of the organizations, or the leaders of some of them.

If analysis is to be cumulative and effective, it is necessary to be explicit about the units that are involved in the disputes being studied. The answer to the question, then, depends upon the issue in contention and the time period used to delimit the conflict. For example, are we considering a conflict about full racial equality in America or about discrimination by a local bus company? Are we considering a three-day confrontation or a decade of struggle? There is no right or wrong answer to these kinds of questions; they should suggest some of the factors that affect deciding what groups are in contention.

ADVERSARY RELATIONS

Conflicts also vary in the kinds of relations between adversaries: the degree of integration between them, the degree and content of shared norms and beliefs, and their relative power. At this point, we focus on power inequality and system context.

Power Inequality

Power is a fundamental concept and is variously defined (Weber 1947, pp. 324–329; Wrong 1979; Baldwin 1971). It may refer to the ability to influence or to control others or to the actual influencing or controlling of others. It may rest on coercion, authority, relative access to positive sanctions, or manipulation. In this work, we use the term *power* more restrictively. It refers to a person's or group's use (actual or threatened) of negative sanctions (coercion) to induce others to act as the power wielders wish. That is, we are concerned with the force that one side can exert against another, aside from the other side's evaluation of the legitimacy of that force. We might think of force or strength as the resources available to be directed at an adversary (Aron 1966, pp. 48–50). Power depends upon the strength one side has relative to the other side. Power is specific to a given relationship; that is, great force applied against a much greater force turns out to be little power. It is also specific to a particular purpose.

Since power is relative, it can be assessed only in terms of the specific relationship and issue in contention. This relativity has several components. First, there is the cost to each side of exercising coercion against the other side. In exercising force against another party, or even organizing to do so, costs are incurred. The magnitude of such costs relative to the resources remaining for other purposes for each party affects their power relative to each other. Second, the costs to each side of enduring the other's coercion varies for each. The costs depend upon the nature of the coercion and the total resources of the side subject to the coercion. Furthermore, the costs and the willingness to exercise coercion and to absorb the coercion of the adversary depend in good measure upon the importance of the issue at stake. The costs are meaningful only in relation to what is being sought by each side.

All this should indicate why it is so difficult for partisans in a conflict to assess their power. Consequently, a direct test or confrontation is often necessary for the parties to assess their relative power and how valuable the matter in contention is to each of them. Noting these components of power should also make explicable how it is possible for one party with an apparently small force to withstand or even defeat a much larger force. This may be seen in international affairs especially in the breaking of colonial bonds. For the people in a colony, their national independence may appear so important that they are willing to suffer great losses, while the colonial power is unwilling to endure much discomfiture for an objective that is not central to it.

The degree of power differences can affect the awareness of the conflict by both parties, how the parties try to reach an agreement to terminate the conflict, what that outcome is likely to be, and even whether an underlying conflict exists. These effects will be examined in the course of the book. At this point it is appropriate simply to note that the implications of power differences are not the same for all aspects of social conflict and indeed can appear to be contradictory. Large power differences, for example, can be a source of grievance to the less powerful but can deter overt expression of the grievance. The less powerful may yield to threats of coercion, and so coercion will be exercised infrequently; but the more powerful may tend to seek further gains because of the tempting weakness of the less powerful and may provoke fights.

If the power differences are small, a different set of contradictory implications can be suggested. If the parties are equally powerful it may be that allocations of valued and contestable matters between them will be equitable and neither would have serious grievances. But being equal, either may misjudge its power and think a marginal advantage can be obtained with only a little effort. If the parties are equal, they may deter each other so that coercion is not exercised, but, in order to maintain the equality, they may engage in a power race that evokes fear and hostility in each until coercion is used preemptively by one side.

When so many contradictory but plausible implications of power differences can be suggested, they cannot be used alone to explain the emergence and expression of social conflicts. Obviously power relations are of central importance in struggles; the consequences of differing degrees of power inequality, however, depend upon many other circumstances. Extended discussion must await later chapters.

System Contexts

Another major variation in the relations between adversary units is the social system that they constitute or to which they belong (Angell 1965). The conflict units may be independent of each other and of any unit superordinate to them; or both units may be within a larger entity; or one unit may be *part* of the other unit that claims jurisdiction over it. For example, nation-states are relatively autonomous and unsubordinated, unions and management are under some governmental control, and a black caucus may be a faction in a trade union.

Although as an observer one may decide what the systematic relationship is between the conflicting units, the participants themselves may not concur. Indeed, they are likely to contend with one another about the nature of their place in the system. A government claiming jurisdiction over some segment of the society is often attacked by the segment as being the agent of an opposing one and not representative of the total society. For example, the government may be viewed as the instrument of large business corporations, of whites, of the rich, or of the elderly. The government may contend it is for all the people; business management may assert it is above the conflict between workers, supervisors, and other segments within the company; and university administrators may argue that they represent and mediate all the interests of the university community and do not themselves constitute a separate interest.

These contentions are important aspects of social conflict; in part they are efforts to persuade the adversary and potential allies about the nature of the struggle, and in part they are efforts to mobilize support and gain allies to coerce the adversary. As the illustrations suggest, the superordinates in any system are more likely to claim to represent all parties than are the subordinates. Sometimes the subordinates, being relatively numerous, may claim to be the total system and their adversary an exploitive, unnecessary appendage.

The possible contentious quality of any characterization of the system of adversary units should be kept in mind by us as students of social conflicts. We must be thoughtful in making assertions about the system relations among units. Keeping in mind the discrepancies of the views of the conflicting units should help prevent us from making an implicitly partisan assumption.

In the light of these considerations, it seems advisable to consider potential and actual conflict units as autonomous, but with varying degrees and kinds of integration between them and within social contexts in which other units have varying degrees of involvement. That is, the conflict units have complementary and cooperative relations as well as conflicting ones. These complementary and cooperative relations may be institutionalized in the form of shared organizational structures, or they may simply be expressed in the transactions of members of the two units, as individuals or as collectivities. For example, consider a university. A variety of units can be discerned by an analyst of social conflict; for the present, consider only students and administrators. The members of these two units have a variety of relations that make them interdependent and in conflict. The administrators in some ways can and do act in the name of the collectivity of the university, including the students. The same is true of the students. The extent to which each does this depends upon understandings between them and the expectations and prescriptions of many other people. In short, for any units in conflict, the actual systemic relations are matters of degree. We have suggested three major dimensions of possible systemic relations: (1) the degree of subordination to third parties, (2) the degree of integration or autonomy from each other, and (3) the degree to which one unit claims and the other acknowledges an authority relationship based upon representing an entity broader than (but including) the other unit.

CONFLICT INTENSITY AND REGULATION

The most visible variation in social conflicts is the way in which the adversaries conduct them. To what extent do they do violence to each other and to what extent are issues quietly resolved are the questions of absorbing attention. At this point, we will consider intensity and regulation, two dimensions of this aspect of conflict variation.

Intensity

The intensity of feelings or behavior of the partisans in the conflict may vary. Feelings may be more or less intense depending upon how strongly committed the partisans are to the goals they wish to reach, how hostile they feel toward each other, and how much they want to harm each other. The intensity of behavior depends upon the means the parties use to attain their aims. They may try to coerce each other and they may use more or less severe forms of coercion. Some observers restrict the term social conflict to disputes in which parties kill or physically harm their adversaries or threaten to do so.

It might seem reasonable to assume that feelings and behavior are parallel in intensity. One might expect that if one party wants to injure its adversary, it will and that as the emotional desire to hurt another party increases, so does its use of coercion in expressing that desire. Conversely, great violence is not usually employed without great anger. A little reflection, however, should reveal the inadequacy of such assumptions. There are times when one or both parties to a conflict feel intense hostility and yet do not try to injure the other. On the one hand, they may be deterred by the fear of countercoercion or by the belief that coercion will not be effective in getting what they want from the adversary. On the other hand, in some circumstances great injury may be inflicted upon an adversary with little or no hostile feeling accompanying the violence. This is most likely when large collectivities are engaged in the conflict; the violence is committed through complex technologies, and there is great division of labor in the conduct of the struggle and the use of violence. Such circumstances are especially apparent in international wars where high altitude bombing is employed. Even among infantry combat soldiers, however, "hatred of the enemy, personal and impersonal, was not a major element in combat motivation," the authors of the study of American soldiers in World War II concluded (Stouffer and others 1949, p. 166). Dispassionate killing may seem particularly repugnant, but intense hatred can be the cause of that personally conducted indiscriminate violence, which we call atrocities.

Although behavioral and attitudinal aspects of conflicts can be independent of each other, each may be determined by similar conditions and hence be associated with the other. Feelings and behavior also affect each other; consequently, as a matter of fact, we do expect some association between these two aspects of conflict intensity.

Regulation

Conflicts vary in the degree to which they are regulated and institutionalized. Regulation varies in comprehensiveness and precision. Regulation usually includes rules about the means used in pursuing incompatible goals to reach a joint decision. It certainly includes rules about the kinds and degree of coercion that can be exercised. Established procedures may also delimit the conditions under which force is legitimately exercised and prescribe what degrees and forms of coercion are legitimate. Thus, laws define legitimate and illegitimate force in collective bargaining in the United States.

Regulation is institutionalized insofar as the rules (1) have been internalized by the participants, (2) are expressed in tradition, formal writing, or some other embodiment external to the participants, and (3) are enforced by sanctions (Blau 1964, pp. 273–276). Rules may have more or less effect in prescribing and proscribing conduct. The control of conduct is greater to the extent that participants believe in the rules and that violating them makes the violators feel guilty. The existence of rules in a form that is external to the participants constrains the actors since they are less able to modify the rules by reinterpretation. Finally, the rules are more likely to be followed when violators are known to be punished. Tittle (1969), for example, found that crime rates are lower when the certainty of punishment is higher.

Certain kinds of conflicts may be so highly regulated and institutionalized that the participants do not even regard themselves as in conflict. Participants in a legal proceeding, partisans in a legislative body, or parties in established electoral races are seeking mutually incompatible goals by procedures that may be so well accepted by all the participants that violence is eschewed and hostility is minimal. The partisans are then in a contest that may even take on the spirit of a game being played for the fun of it. The rules that regulate conflict, then, differ in content, specification, and degree of institutionalization. The bases and consequences of conflict regulation and institutionalization are analyzed in Chapter 4.

DEFINITION AND STAGES OF CONFLICT

Having discussed many dimensions of social conflict and some of the characteristics of units that may be in contention, we may state more meaningfully how the term *social conflict* will be used here. *A social conflict exists when two or more parties believe they have incompatible objectives.* The phenomena included and excluded by this definition should be noted.

The incompatibility of goals refers to the subjective judgment of each party that the attainment of its goals is hampered or prevented by the other side's attainment of its goals. The term *parties* refers to groups and individuals who purport to represent larger collectivities, such as a country, a trade union, blacks, a faction within a political party, or the proletariat.

We often think of conflicts as involving attempts by adversaries to threaten, injure, or otherwise coerce each other. Some writers include such conduct in defining social conflict (Coser 1956). We will be paying attention to conflicts in which coercion is an important way in which contending parties seek to gain their objectives. Analytically, however, we can distinguish the situation in which parties believe they have incompatible goals from what they do about it. A conflict party may try to use coercion to force another party to yield what it seeks, but there are two other inducements to gain goals in a conflict situation: persuasion and reward.

Persuasion involves trying to convince the adversary that it should yield what is being sought. The adversary is urged to agree because agreement would be in its own interest or in conformity with its own values. Reward refers to positive sanctions, to promises that offer the adversary something it values and is made in anticipation of a reciprocating concession (Baldwin 1971). In any actual social conflict all three inducements are mixed together as one party threatens, cajoles, and holds out the promise of benefits to the other. The varieties of coercion, persuasion, and rewards are examined in detail in Chapter 4.

Conflict is related to competition, but the two are not identical. Competition may or may not involve awareness, while conflict does. Parties in a competition are seeking the same ends, whereas conflicting parties may or may not be in agreement about the desirability of particular goals. In addition, competing units generally seek that which is not already part of or dominated by the competitor. They seek it from third parties rather than directly from each other.

Situations that an observer assesses to be conflicting, but which are not so assessed by partisans, are not social conflicts. We refer to such situations as objective, potential, or latent conflicts. If the parties come to believe that they have incompatible goals, however, a social conflict has emerged. The objective conflict situation underlies a dispute and persists regardless of the partisans' awareness of it. Once the parties believe they have incompatible goals, each or both may try to attain them. They will try coercive and noncoercive means in seeking to reach their goals. After a time, the parties will cease their efforts, and there will be an outcome. Such terminations and outcomes may be more or less permanent and accepted by the participants. A general ongoing conflict relationship can continue while several disputes are terminated and begun in a never-ending, overlapping series. Often it is the observer who decides for purposes of his own analysis when a specific conflict is terminated.

Social conflict refers to a situation in which parties believe that they have incompatible goals. The term also refers to the interactional sequence in which the parties contend with each other; it is a war, fight, strike, struggle. A comprehensive analysis of social conflicts should include the objective conditions underlying a conflict situation and the processes that lead to groups believing they have incompatible goals. A comprehensive analysis would also examine the pursuit of conflicting goals, the termination and outcomes of social conflicts, and the consequences of those outcomes.

These distinctions suggest a series of possible stages in the course of struggles, as diagramed in Figure 1.4. Some of the relations between parties are objectively conflicting; *some* of the underlying conflicts become manifest; and only in some of the manifest conflicts do the parties actively pursue their conflicting goals. Even then coercion is not always used.

Although all conflicts do not go through every step, it will prove helpful to consider social conflicts in a series of stages including ones that precede and follow the conflict itself. A simplified diagram of this entire range is shown in Figure 1.5.

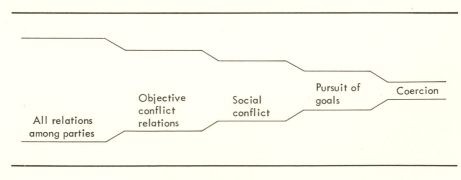

Figure 1.4

The series of arrows forming the circle indicates that one conflict emerges, escalates, deescalates, terminates, and results in an outcome that becomes the bases for another conflict. The small arrows entering from inside and outside of the circle indicate that factors that are internal to an adversary as well as social environmental factors affect each stage in addition to preceding stages of the conflict. In this way the *belief* among adversaries that they are in a conflict is affected by factors internal to each of them and only partly relevant to the relationship between them. This view is another way of denoting the mixture of unrealistic and realistic components in a specific fight. The primary circle of arrows indicates the processes linking each stage of a conflict and shows that each affects the succeeding ones. One or another alternative followed in one stage affects the alternative followed in the next. Moreover, anticipation of alternatives in later stages sometimes affects the choices made in earlier stages.

The book is organized to follow the flow of stages before, during, and after specific conflicts. This format permits us to ask precise questions about social conflicts and consider different answers to the same question, rather than compare writers whose arguments go past each other as they seek to answer different

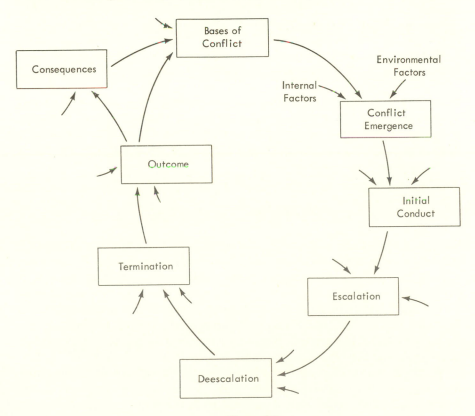

Figure 1.5

questions. In Chapter 2 we examine objective conflict situations and the bases of social conflicts. In Chapter 3 we consider how conflicts emerge, focusing upon the conditions and processes leading to awareness. In Chapter 4 we analyze the various means of pursuing conflicting goals and what affects the means used. In Chapter 5 we examine the changes in the means used as the parties each seek to gain their ends, attending to escalation and deescalation of the struggle. In Chapter 6 we discuss the termination and possible outcomes of social conflicts and what affects the outcomes. Chapter 7 turns aside from this sequence to examine intervention and mediation. In Chapter 8 some of the consequences of different outcomes and modes used are examined; special attention is given to the consequences for other conflicts. In Chapter 9 we consider the peculiarities of social conflicts in such different settings as organizations, whole societies, and the world of nation-states; the chapter also provides a review and synthesis of the major themes of the book and discusses the policy implications of the approach taken here.

As we go along we use several social conflicts as cases to illustrate and test the ideas presented. We consider conflicts within industrial and university organizational settings. We consider society-wide conflicts based on race and on sex and rebellious challenges to political rulers. At the world level we examine the Arab-Israeli and the U.S.-U.S.S.R. conflicts.

By juxtaposing conflicts in diverse contexts such as women's liberation, trade union strikes, the cold war, and political revolt, we shall see how useful an examination of social conflicts in general actually is. Perhaps at the present stage of knowledge, or because of the nature of the phenomena, it is not illuminating to examine the processes and conditions of social conflicts in general. Obviously in writing a book about social conflicts, I believe that there are enough commonalities in all struggles that it will advance our understanding of each to have an approach that is applicable to all.

SUMMARY AND CONCLUSIONS

We have discussed the many ways social conflicts vary in order to make possible systematic comparisons and to provide guidelines for generalizing. We have seen that the issues in contention can be more or less purely conflicting and vary in the extent of unrealistic components. We have noted that conflicting parties differ in their degree of organization and the degree to which their boundaries are clear. We discussed the relations between adversaries in terms of power inequality and the contexts of different systems. Finally, we examined the ways in which conflicts can vary in intensity and in regulation.

We noted, too, certain commonalities among social conflicts. We defined them to include beliefs about incompatible goals but not to limit their conduct to coercive means. We noted that several stages in the course of a social conflict could be analytically distinguished: the underlying bases, the emergence into awareness, initial efforts, escalation, deescalation, termination, outcome, and consequences.

We have argued that social conflicts are social relationships. This means that at every stage of conflict the parties interact socially; each party affects the way the others act, not only as each responds to the others but also as each may *anticipate* the responses of the others. Even the ends each party seeks are constructed in interaction with adversaries.

BIBLIOGRAPHY

ANGELL, ROBERT C., "The Sociology of Human Conflict," in E. McNeil (ed.), *The Nature of Human Conflict* (Englewood Cliffs, N.J.: Prentice-Hall, 1965), pp. 91–115.

ARON, RAYMOND, *Peace and War* (New York: Doubleday, 1966).

BALDWIN, DAVID A., "The Power of Positive Sanctions," *World Politics,* 24 (October 1971), 19–38.

BERNARD, JESSIE, "Parties and Issues in Conflict," *The Journal of Conflict Resolution,* 1 (June 1957), 111–121.

BLAU, PETER M., *Exchange and Power in Social Life* (New York: John Wiley, 1964).

BOULDING, KENNETH E., *Conflict and Defense* (New York: Harper & Row, Pub., 1962).

COLEMAN, JAMES, *Community Conflict* (New York: Free Press, 1957).

COSER, LEWIS A., *The Functions of Social Conflict* (New York: Free Press, 1956).

DAHRENDORF, RALF, *Class and Class Conflict in Industrial Society* (Stanford, Calif.: Stanford University Press, 1959).

FINK, CLINTON F., "Some Conceptual Difficulties in the Theory of Social Conflict," *The Journal of Conflict Resolution,* 12 (December 1968), 412–460.

FISHER, ROGER, "Fractionating Conflict," in R. Fisher (ed.), *International Conflict and Behavioral Science* (New York: Basic Books, 1964).

GAMSON, WILLIAM A., *Power and Discontent* (Homewood, Ill.: Dorsey Press, 1968).

HAGGSTROM, WARREN C., "The Power of the Poor," pp. 205–223 in F. Riessman, J. Cohen, and A. Pearl (eds.), *Mental Health of the Poor* (New York: Free Press, 1964).

KRIESBERG, LOUIS, "Internal Differentiation and the Establishment of Organizations," pp. 141–164 in H. S. Becker and others (eds.), *Institution and the Person* (Chicago: Aldine, 1968).

LENIN, V. I., *Left-Wing Communism, An Infantile Disorder* (New York: International Publishers, 1940). Originally published in 1920.

MADISON, JAMES, "The Federalist No. 10 (1787)," pp. 53–62 in A. Hamilton, J. Jay, and J. Madison, *The Federalist* (Washington, D.C.: Home Library Foundation, 1937). Originally published in 1787.

MARX, KARL, *The Poverty of Philosophy* (New York: International Publishers, 1963). Originally published in 1847.

PARK, ROBERT E. AND ERNEST W. BURGESS, *Introduction to the Science of Sociology* (Chicago: University of Chicago Press, 1924).

RAPOPORT, ANATOL, *Fights, Games, and Debates* (Ann Arbor, Mich.: University of Michigan Press, 1960).

SIMMEL, GEORG, *Conflict and the Web of Intergroup Affiliations* (New York: Free Press, 1955). Originally published in 1908 and 1922.

STOUFFER, SAMUEL A., ARTHUR A. LUMSDAINE, MARION HARPER LUMSDAINE, ROBIN M. WILLIAMS, JR., M. BREWSTER SMITH, IRVING L. JANIS, SHIRLEY A. STAR, AND LEONARD S. COTTRELL, JR., *The American Soldier: Combat and Its Aftermath,* Vol. 2 (Princeton, N.J.: Princeton University Press, 1949).

SUMNER, WILLIAM GRAHAM, *What Social Classes Owe Each Other* (Caldwell, Idaho: Caxton Printers, 1952). Originally published in 1883.

TITTLE, CHARLES R., "Crime Rates and Legal Sanctions," *Social Problems,* 16 (Spring 1969), 409–423.

VON NEUMANN, J. AND O. MORGENSTERN, *Theory of Games and Economic Behavior* (Princeton, N.J.: Princeton University Press, 1944).

WEBER, MAX, *The Theory of Social and Economic Organization,* translated by A. M. Henderson and Talcott Parsons (New York: Oxford University Press, 1947). Originally published in 1921.

WRONG, DENNIS H., *Power: Its Forms, Bases and Uses* (New York: Harper & Row, Pub., 1979).

2

The Bases
of Social Conflicts

The task of this chapter is to assess the underlying conditions of social conflicts. What conditions constitute a potential dispute? In order to answer the question, we must recognize and resolve several difficult conceptual and substantive problems. In the preceding chapter, we defined social conflict as a relationship in which parties believe they have incompatible goals. Potential conflict refers to conditions that underlie and generate beliefs regarding incompatible aims.

Here is the problem. How does one know what those conditions are before they produce the anticipated consequences? One can know them only as theoretical constructs. Empirical indicators must be indirect and depend upon a chain of theoretical links. It is necessary to be clear about this before we proceed. Informally and commonly, we see some conflict behavior, presume a conflict relationship, and then conjecture that there is and was an underlying conflict situation. But not all conflicts are expressed in conflict behavior; the antagonistic parties may be aware of their opposition but neither side attempts to induce the other in order to reach the incompatible goals. Furthermore, of the innumerable potential conflict situations few become manifest. We must also take into account the possibility of "unrealistic" conflict. That is, it might be argued that a coercive act is unrelated to a conflict relationship; it is simply expressive or accidental. It might be argued that a struggle is based upon misunderstandings about the incompatibility of the participants' goals. If such "unrealistic" struggles can exist, it is even more difficult to discern what is a potential or underlying conflict situation.

Ultimately, as analysts, we must attempt to construct a reasonable and consistent theory to explain what we are trying to understand and then see how useful it actually is. This requires making assumptions about phenomena and processes that cannot be directly tested. We can test an interrelated set of ideas if they are ordered so that they could lead to observable results. In discussing the underlying bases of social conflicts, we will be considering theoretical constructs. The bases lie in the mind of the student of social conflict, not necessarily in the minds of the persons observed. This assumption is then tested by seeing whether or not a struggle emerges under conditions specified in the theory.

We begin with the idea that the basis for a conflict is a situation in which two parties are *likely* to come to believe that they have conflicting goals. The term *likely* needs elaboration. Any social situation has the potentiality of conflict under some conceivable circumstances. The emphasis upon likely indicates the advisability of giving special attention to those conditions that, according to the analyst's theory, are most frequently going to be recognized as conflicting by participants in the social situations. The assumption of the existence of an objective conflict is confirmed if either of the following occurs: (1) the participants come to believe that they are in conflict, or (2) they do not, but for reasons specified in the theory. In either case the evidence is consistent with the assumption and in that sense supports it. Given our concerns in the study of social conflict, we are particularly interested in those potential disputes which, when they are actualized, are likely to involve coercion.

APPROACHES

In order to argue that certain situations are likely to have particular consequences, assumptions about human nature and universal social processes are inevitable. How good those assumptions are can be assessed only by comparing their implications. In this section, we focus on two kinds of approaches: one stressing internal, especially personal, factors and one stressing systemic and interactional factors.

Internal

Since social conflicts are ubiquitous, it might seem reasonable to seek the underlying bases of conflicts in an inherent characteristic of the human species. Indeed there is a recurring interest in explanations of social conflicts in terms of biological instincts. A recent formulation of this idea made by Ardrey concerns what he calls the "territorial imperative":

> We act as we do for reasons of our evolutionary past, not our cultural present, and our behavior is as much a mark of our species as is the shape of a human thigh bone. . . . If we defend the title to our land or the sovereignty of our country, we do it for reasons no different, no less innate, no less ineradicable, than do lower animals. (Ardrey 1966, p. 5)

Even in these formulations, room is left for learning what our country is and how it is to be defended. The more open the formulation, to take into account the actual variations in human conduct, the less distinct and meaningful is the idea of instinct.

Take the idea of an aggressive instinct. Presumably that idea is even more open, since we are discussing only a drive. For observers stressing such instinctual drives, aggression is the source of social conflicts. But such writers also recognize other human needs and drives, and obviously they do not say that all persons are constantly and only seeking to harm or kill each other (Freud 1939; Lorenz 1963; Tinbergen 1968). The human species would hardly have survived in that case. The assertion, then, is that aggression is innately gratifying but does not require constant satisfaction and can be expressed in a variety of ways. Accepting such an instinct, one then needs to study what conditions affect its expression in various ways. Some of the ways may be quite ritualistic and not in any way perilous to the physical security of any of the partisans.

Nevertheless, in this work we do not assume that aggression is innate. To do so would be to draw our attention to the inner drives of the struggling partisans; channeling and transforming their drives would be the focus of concern. But conflicts are about something; parties are in contention over matters of importance to them. Conflict management involves developing ways of handling these contentious issues, not simply ritualizing the expression of aggressive instincts. Essentially, conflicts are part of social relations; they depend upon the relationship of groups of people and not upon drives or instincts within a person without reference to others.

There is another implication to an emphasis upon human aggression. It follows from that emphasis that aggression may be free floating or displaced from one target to another. This can be discussed best in considering the frustration-aggression relationship (Dollard and others 1939). It might appear obvious that if persons are frustrated, they will become aggressive, seeking to inflict harm upon somebody or something. If frustration always resulted in aggression and aggression were always caused by frustration, we would have a fundamental premise upon which to base a theory of conflict. It turns out not to be so simple.

Research on frustration and aggression makes it clear that what is frustrating depends upon the goals and intentions of the persons supposedly being frustrated. Those goals may not be evident to the observer. Studies also indicate that aggression depends upon the availability of a target that seems appropriate. The target is attacked partly because of its stimulus quality and not only because of a need of the attacker to express his or her frustration (Berkowitz 1969). In other words, frustration and aggression really involve a social relationship; frustration and aggression involve social interaction.

This does not deny that a person or a group of persons, feeling frustrated, may attack another group that is a safe and exciting target but is unrelated to the frustration. Taking out their anger on an "innocent" party certainly would seem to be a case of unrealistic conflict. That may make it seem impossible to ever develop a theory of social conflict utilizing the concept of underlying or objective conflict situations. Several observations should be made about this matter.

First, if any group acts to injure another, the injured party is likely to respond as if it were being attacked—since it is. The first group may then find that a realistic conflict has begun. For some purposes of analysis, the source of attack may not be important. For any general theory about social conflicts, however, it does matter. The means chosen to pursue goals and the possible outcomes are all affected by the underlying basis for the conflict. As Coser (1956) has argued, in unrealistic conflicts injuring another party is an end in itself. In realistic conflict, conflict behavior is a means and alternative means may be tried; additionally, a readjustment in the relationship may terminate the particular conflict.

The theoretical implications of the possibility that hostility is displaced and, therefore, unrealistic conflict results must be faced more directly. We should acknowledge one fundamental difficulty. Suppose a group attacks another and gives a reason, upon what basis do we call it displacement and unrealistic? We do so only because *we* have a theory about what *really* are the determinants of their distress and the irrelevance of their targets to those determinants. Thus, if a group attacks Jews as exploiters undermining Western civilization, how do we know that it is not a valid explanation of the ills of the world? We think we know better. But take the case of the populists after the American Civil War. When farmers blamed eastern business interests for their economic difficulties, was this a matter of displacement and unrealistic conflict or an expression of the underlying conflict situation and a realistic conflict?

We cannot call something an unrealistic conflict without thinking we know what the realistic conflict is. Furthermore, we can assume that everyone has some free-floating hostility and that it can be directed at a large number of targets. What is interesting for us is the channeling of deprivation into particular social conflicts. For such developments, social processes at the group level will be more important than the human capacity to displace feelings or make erroneous diagnoses of their situation.

The point can be made in another way. Displacement may be a common process among humans and still not help very much to explain intergroup conflicts. For collective action, some shared experience and, therefore, common situation are necessary. In other words, some characteristics of the situation in which a category of people live must underlie the emergence of its members' consciousness of a grievance. Thus a worker's family distress may be displaced and his anger at his wife may be directed at his supervisor. But that is not the basis on which a group of factory workers organize a trade union.

System and Interaction

A very different approach to the bases of social conflicts is represented by analysts who view society as a functionally integrated system (Durkheim 1933; Huntington 1968; Gurr 1970; Johnson 1966). Groups within the societal system are interdependent, and they share values and beliefs. As differentiation occurs, there is a threat of distintegration as consensus is undermined. This approach has been applied particularly to societies in the throes of modernization and economic development. Rapid social change fosters the likelihood of disorder and the possibility of revolution.

This approach is most relevant for societal conflicts, but it is less applicable for the entire range of social conflicts considered in this volume. Furthermore, analysts working within this approach give relatively little attention to specifying how the disintegration of the social system is manifested in the relations between different categories of people.

In this book, we will give attention to the way in which particular groups are differentially affected by changes in a social system. We will draw upon the functionalist approach to conflict, but, in paying attention to groups within society and to value differences among them, we will be drawing more on the work of scholars working in the traditions of Max Weber (1956) and Karl Marx (1852). To analyze the bases of conflicts, we shall consider the conditions underlying possible social conflicts from the perspective of outside observers. But the validation of the analysis must be found in the thoughts and actions of the people in those conditions. It is they who do or do not create a social conflict from the underlying conditions.

Special attention is given in this work to the ways in which conflicts involve many conflict groups whose disputes are intermingled. Adversaries are always multiple, and the antagonists are not mutually exclusive entities. Each party in a fight can be conceived as constituting many subgroups and itself may be part of even larger collective entities. In addition, interests and, hence, possible conflict parties cut across other conflict groups. Often, we give salience to one conflict, the primary or focal one. But the existence of many interlocked conflicts helps explain how the focal conflict escalates and deescalates (Kriesberg 1980). For example, for Iranian government leaders the conflict with the U.S. government in 1979–1980 became less important in the context of a war with Iraq and deescalated.

We distinguish among six ways in which conflicts are interlocked: (1) serial or nested in time, (2) converging or nested in social space, (3) superimposed, (4) cross-cutting, (5) internal, and (6) concurrent. Each kind of interlocked conflict will be briefly characterized.

First, conflicts persist in a series of fights, each succeeding the other. Adversaries may regard a dispute as one battle in an ongoing war. Second, conflicts converge when, for example, some adversaries coalesce as allies against other adversaries. Such coalitions may be based on broadening collective identifications rooted, for example, in ideology or religion. Third, many contentious issues may be superimposed on one another; thus, in the United States, race, class, and regional differences may be superimposed and linked together. Fourth, issues may be cross-cutting, such as divisions by region or class that crosscut religious differences. Fifth, conflicts within adversary parties interact with conflicts between them; note, for example, the struggles within the United States during the Vietnam War. Finally, a conflict party may be engaged concurrently in conflicts with two different and unconnected adversaries.

The interlocking nature of all social conflicts has great pertinence for the distinction between realistic and unrealistic conflicts. Observer-analysts may regard the conflict in which adversaries are engaged as not as important as a cross-cutting one and, therefore, as unrealistic. When World War I erupted, for example, Socialist parties in France and Germany supported their respective governments, and V. I. Lenin argued that the workers of all the capitalist countries should recognize that the international class struggle and not an imperialist war was the primary conflict. Adversaries and observers disagree among themselves about which conflict should be regarded as the focal one and, consequently, about the realistic character of a particular struggle.

In the next chapter, we examine the three components of conflict emergence: self-awareness as a collectivity, a shared sense of grievance, and oppositional goals that offer redress. In this chapter, we discuss the conditions that underlie the emergence of these components. We consider cleavages as an underlying condition for collective identity and analyze consensual and dissensual issues as the basis for grievances and the formulation of oppositional goals.

CLEAVAGES

People may be divided in infinite ways. Almost any division of people into two or more sets can be the basis for collective identification and organization into conflict groups. Here, we note the variety of important possible divisions and the social systems within which they are significant.

Some divisions are well established; they preexist the emergence of any special social conflict. They may have been formed in the course of a long history of conflicts, and the adversary groups are highly organized. Thus, national governments purport to represent their country in external relations. The office holders of a government claim the state they control has jurisdiction over clearly bounded territory and people. The divisions between governments and countries, then, are ready-made cleavages available for conducting struggles. Similarly, in collective bargaining in the United States, there are many established divisions with organizations' claiming to represent various constituencies in conducting conflicts about wages and working conditions of unionized workers.

People may also be divided into groupings that are less clearly bounded and articulated. People make socially recognized distinctions, although consensus about the terms may not be high, and no generally accepted organizations exist to represent them in conflicts. These distinctions involve collective self-definitions and also efforts by some people to define and separate others. Such distinctions based on life styles, religion, ethnicity, age, gender, and ideology are common throughout the world.

Finally, some divisions are based on analytic categories that an observer uses to discern important cleavages. For example, a Marxist observer may regard the distinctions between owning the means of production and working for the owners as the fundamental cleavage in a capitalist social order. Other observers might regard different positions in the labor market or the amount of income a person or household receives as a basis for making significant divisions.

In this book, we examine major cleavages and consider the circumstances in which one or the other division takes on primacy. Very often, the cleavages coincide, and, as we shall see in later chapters, that has important implications for the emergence and conduct of struggles.

Whatever the division to which we give attention, it can have meaning only within the context of a social system. For example, governments exist within a system of states with shared understandings about sovereignty. Many of the other divisions we have noted can be understood only within a societal context: This means noting the complex interdependencies of many institutions and social structures and the power of the state in channeling conflicts. Other divisions, particularly those based on social definitions, should be considered within the context of a common culture and the shared values and beliefs that are part of a culture. Divisions also should be regarded as connections between different groupings; each set of persons is defined in relation to the others. This is the case for socially defined distinctions among ethnic groups; they are often characterized in opposition to one another. It is also true for analytic distinctions, when, for example, employees and employers are jointly defined.

In discussing the bases of conflicts, we will consider large categories of persons and not primarily existing, conflict groups. Here, we are interested in quasi-groups, or categories, that are the recruiting ground for organizations. In the next chapter, we analyze how persons in quasi-groups and how established conflict groups are mobilized.

The boundaries between relevant social categories are not inherent in the categories. The divisions that are particularly important depend in part upon the social definitions of the partisans. In assessing potential conflicts, however, we as observers must gauge what those social definitions will be, how successfully they will be propagated, and under what circumstances given forms of conflict behavior will arise. For example, if we are considering struggles between blacks and whites, should we regard all blacks and all whites in the United States as two categories? Should we compare poor blacks and rich whites, blacks and whites in professional occupations, blacks and whites in different metropolitan areas, or blacks and whites in different regions? Even in international conflicts, the parties are not fixed. In the Arab-Israeli conflict, for example, the parties have varied with different time periods. In 1947–1948 was one of the parties to the conflict composed of all Jews, Jews in Palestine, Jews in refugee camps in Germany, all persons living in Palestine, Jews in Yemen and North Africa, or some combination of these? Was the other side all the countries bordering Israel, all Arab countries, all Muslim countries, all anti-Zionists, or Arab Palestinians? These possibilities could be extended (Kriesberg 1980).

Two kinds of issues underlie social conflicts: consensual and dissensual (Aubert 1963). In the case of consensus, the parties agree about what they want, but a conflict may arise when one side apparently obtains more of what it wants, and the other receives less. Dissensual conflicts exist when the parties differ in norms, values, or beliefs and either the requirements of coordination make those differences incompatible or one side wants the other to accept the values, beliefs, or way of life it professes and thus makes unacceptable claims upon the other.

In this chapter, we examine both types of issues. We consider each type separately for analytic purposes, although particular struggles are based upon both consensus and dissensus. For example, students and administrators in universities value power in determining the actions of the university as a whole and in regard to each of them. This is the basis for a consensual conflict. The students and administrators may also disagree about how each should live, what they should strive for, or what they should learn. Such differences could be the basis for a dissensual conflict. Although these two bases of conflicts are intermingled, it is useful to consider them separately because their origins and consequences are not the same. Furthermore, one or the other basis is usually dominant in disputes.

DISSENSUS

People differ about a wide variety of values and beliefs. Such differences are the bases for dissensual conflicts only if certain other beliefs are also held. Members of two units may, for example, adhere to different religions. If each unit is indifferent to the other's religious convictions, thinks them quaint, or even thinks that it is useful that the other side has them, then no potential conflict exists. If, however, one or both units feel that the other's religious convictions are morally outrageous, then an underlying conflict exists. The outraged persons would want those who hold such improper views to alter them or stop exhibiting them. Or suppose that persons in one unit are so convinced of the virtue and importance of their views that they wish the members of the other unit to agree. In other words, the truth of their views is to be accepted by the others for their own good or for their salvation. In such circumstances, a potential conflict also exists. Or suppose one group feels the members of another are contemptible because of the values they hold. The basis for a conflict would still exist because those scorned would want that view of themselves altered so long as they associated with the other groups. We shall consider both what people differ about and the sources of such differences.

Issues in Contention

People differ about what is worth striving for and how to get what they want. Disagreements about what is desirable are particularly relevant to conflicts that are expressed in violence; we consider these disagreements first and will then consider disagreements about beliefs.

One fundamental value issue concerns the bases of evaluations. People may differ about the criteria or standards by which they judge or evaluate one another. Should we judge others by their actions or intentions? Should we judge others by their beauty, intelligence, moral character, generosity, power, and wealth, or by the degree of consideration they show? Even if we agree upon a criterion, how are we to agree on an appropriate measure of that criterion? Is black more beautiful, just as beautiful, or less beautiful than white? Claims, counterclaims, and the rejection of other people's claims about these values indicate that the actual conflicts are about many things. As analysts, we look at value differences that in themselves are potentially conflicting.

We can consider any of the above differences and note that those who rank high according to one standard are likely to urge its importance, and, therefore, a basis for a dissensual conflict exists for every imaginable criterion. That hardly helps our comprehension of the bases of social conflicts. What helps us decide which criteria are more or less relevant is an understanding of which ones will emerge into awareness and which are likely to be pursued coercively. These bases for criteria are discussed in many parts of this book. For the present, we simply point to value differences from among the cases used illustratively in this book.

Some people may believe it is good to be aggressive, dominating, unexpressive of emotions, risk taking, and physically tough, and they label such characteristics masculine. Then, with a few elliptical steps in reasoning, they argue that feminine means the opposite of masculine, as characterized previously. If males must be "masculine" and females "feminine," then values are likely to be imposed upon people. Some persons in the women's liberation movement, partly on the basis of such imposed value differences, contend that males as well as females are constrained and are denied much of themselves as they are forced and force themselves to be only part of what they might otherwise be. In that case, the liberation of women from the restricted roles they learn and must play would also mean the liberation of men. Other people may insist that indeed there are value differences between men and woman, but they differ in the evaluation of those values. In a male-dominated society, masculine ways of living would be highly valued; if females disagreed and thought expressiveness and consideration of others were to be highly valued, then the value differences would be part of an objective dissensual conflict.

In addition to values involving criteria of evaluation, some values pertain to ways of life or goals that are intrinsically meaningful and valuable. They are ultimate ends. Differences in such values often imply an objective conflict because their believers are likely to make universal claims and seek to convert the non-believers. Such conflicts may be seen in international and national ideological struggles. Believers in political democracy, free elections, a multiparty system, nongovernmental means of expression, and limits on governmental power may come to regard such arrangements as intrinsically valuable, that is, desirable for themselves and for all other people. It is then the obligation of the believers to provide tutelage to others so that they can attain the state in which these arrangements are also theirs. Others may believe that a political party that possesses the truth should not be handicapped in realizing that truth by those with erroneous views. They may also believe in the desirability of people's working together, submerging egocentric personal wishes for collective purposes; equality and solidarity may be prized as ends in themselves.

Thus far we have discussed dissensual conflicts in terms of the values of the potential partisans. Dissensus may also be about beliefs concerning how to reach agreed upon goals. In a sense, every struggle might be defined as one in which contending parties simply disagree on how to reach such an agreed upon goal as salvation, the good of life, or security. But there are such profound disagreements about the meaning of salvation, the good life, and security that to argue that all struggles are over means obscures important differences. Since it is possible that persons share a goal and disagree about how to attain it, the disagreement is a potential conflict if a decision affecting all the parties is needed to pursue the specific goal. Such potential conflicts are not usually given much attention in the study of social conflict, because coercion and violence are not as frequently used as in dissensual value conflicts. This is true because the cooperative aspects of the relationship are more prominent in cases of dissensus over means than in dissensus over ends. Disagreements about means, however, are of special interest in the study of the course of conflict development. The dynamics of conflict escalation and deescalation are affected by disagreements within each party about the best way to attain their goal.

Sources of Issues

People develop values and beliefs from their experiences. Insofar as persons in every social category live in a particular environment, they develop a unique set of values and beliefs. This may be true for members of one society compared to another and for members of an age, sex, ethnic, class, or other social category within a society. Thus, the opportunities and constraints of men, of students, of workers, of blacks, of Israelis, of Americans, or any other entity differ from those not in the same category. Many factors affect the uniqueness of the experiences of the members of a social category and its elaboration into a potential conflict. We are most interested in aspects of the *relations* between the categories that tend to bring the members of the categories into contention.

One element is the degree of isolation of persons in one category from the members of another. Insofar as the members of a category have much to do with others in the same category, to the relative exclusion of others, the elaboration of unique values and beliefs will be facilitated and hastened. The isolation of persons in a category increases the likelihood that peculiar world views will emerge and even a set of beliefs and values so distinctive and interrelated as to constitute a culture.

Such isolation may occur naturally, for example, linguistic or physical barriers between societies reduce communication and interaction between the peoples of the societies. Even within a society, different circumstances produce diverse experiences and, insofar as these experiences are not communicated and shared, further differentiation develops. Such differentiation occurs frequently between rural and urban life and provides a basis for dissensus. The traditional and virtuous life of the village is contrasted with the libertine and worldly cosmopolitan life of the large urban centers by leaders of conservative or reactionary movements. Such dissensus played a role in the Nazi movement in Germany. The rural-urban difference in some societies is augmented by ethnic diversity associated with area of residence. For example, the prohibition struggle in the United States was in part a struggle between rural Protestants and urban Catholics (Siegfried 1927, pp. 70–90).

Isolation between members of social categories occurs for many reasons. Isolation may be self-imposed, as by a religious sect seeking to avoid contamination from a surrounding evil society. Isolation may also be imposed by nonmembers of a social category, as in the cases of discriminatory segregation. Significantly, social isolation may even exist when there is social interaction. The interaction may be so stylized and coerced that little beyond the conduct prescribed by restricted roles is expressed or communicated, as happened in the southern United States. Even before the 1960s, blacks and whites in the South had considerable interaction but with limited understanding of the others' feelings and ideas because racial etiquette dictated the manner of interaction (Dollard 1937; Johnson 1943). True feelings, particularly of blacks, were masked; but behind the masks, distinctive world views could mature. Moreover, the dominant group created conditions that required accommodation by members of the subordinate group. That accommodation often took forms that were ridiculed by the dominant group while becoming part of the rationale for continued subordination. The ways of accommodation involved, rather than confrontation, manipulation, evasiveness, and the appearance of witlessness. These ways are not uncommon among other subordinate groups; the guile of women may be viewed in this way (Myrdal 1944; Bird and Briller 1968, pp. 110–125).

Distinctive values or beliefs are a necessary condition for dissensus conflict, but they are not sufficient. In addition, the differences must be such that the values or beliefs are incompatible. Incompatibility has two basic sources. One is that the persons with the different views be in a social relationship that places the views in opposition. The other source is that persons with one set of views assert objectionable claims upon persons not sharing the views. These two sources need elaboration and illustration.

Although isolation provides the opportunity for different views to develop, it also precludes opposition. There can be no conflict between groups that have nothing to do with one another. When groups of people enter into a social relationship that requires joint action or actions that affect both groups and they hold different views pertinent to that relationship, the basis for a dissensual conflict exists. Such social relationships come about in many ways. People with a distinctive set of views may move into a governmental jurisdiction previously dominated by persons with another set of views. This is the basis of many community conflicts (Coleman 1957). For example, waves of immigrants to New

England villages in the nineteenth century and migrants from the cities to suburban villages during the 1950s provided the basis for community controversies over taxes, churches, and school appropriations. Universities, previously dominated by persons from one social background, may become the setting for an objective dissensual conflict when significant numbers of persons enter them with different views because of their differences in class or ethnic backgrounds. This dissensus can take many forms. Consider a university that is drawing students from the local community and training them for businesses in the community. A new administration may try to change the orientation of the university to the demands of the national market; the selection of students and the competition among them will then be increased despite the objections of the local students and their families. Or consider the changes that a religiously based university undergoes as it becomes secular, or the changes introduced when an elite college broadens its social base. Most potential dissensual conflicts, of course, do not become actualized with the parties' using coercion.

Social relations that require joint action also occur between generations, and the generations may differ in values and beliefs that hamper coordination. Thus, young persons have distinctive experiences as children at home. Some of them may be reared to have values that they then find are inconsistent with adult values when they enter universities or the labor market. This disjunction between the values learned in the family and those of the work-a-day world varies in magnitude in different societies and periods. In economically developing societies the disjunction between traditional family values and the demands of the new society place a strain upon persons who are seeking to find a place in the new society (Eisenstadt 1956; Flacks 1970; Parsons 1962). This strain may be a cause for the creation of student movements in opposition to their governments. As we shall see, there are alternative or supplementary explanations as well (Westby and Braungart 1966; Wood and Ng 1980).

In addition to people's coming together so that they must coordinate their activities, the circumstances affecting potential conflict groups may alter and affect them unequally so that differences in views become incompatible. People may be accommodated to their value and belief differences or to mutual dependence until conditions require more intense coordination; then the value or belief differences will be revealed as imcompatible. For example, the military elites in each society develop special views as a result of their training and experience. A foreign military threat or defeat or a period of economic dislocation may make their differences in orientation and ways of thinking result in incompatible goals. Consequently, those differences may result in a military coup.

Another kind of external change that reveals dissensus and makes it become an objective conflict is the appeal by contending parties for support and assistance. Thus, any disagreement between adversaries can evoke wider dissension among additional groups who differ in relevant ways. For example, students in a university may make demands of administrators; the differences among the faculty will be a potential dissensual conflict insofar as it is expected that the faculty will participate or consciously avoid participating in making a decision about the demands. Or a civil war in Angola may aggravate the ideological dissensus between the United States and the Soviet Union.

The other major source of incompatibility in values or beliefs is the claim by the adherents of one set of views that nonadherents are subject to the same views. One form this takes is the claim that others should share the views held by the adherents of a particular religious or political ideology. Convinced of the moral or spiritual supremacy of their views, one group finds the other group's rejection to be repugnant; the group feels that the true faith must be brought to the nonbeliever. As the language suggests, this kind of claim is most clearly made in reference to religious views; but political ideologies may also assume a similar universal and insistent quality.

Some views, however, cannot be shared. They are part of a culture or identity that is ascribed and not achieved. This produces incompatible values when one party claims superiority for its identity and insists that others acknowledge the claim. The issues can be illustrated by considering the claims of nationalities and ethnic groups. National societies with relatively autonomous governments may be somewhat relativistic; that is, none insists that it is superior and that its superiority be acknowledged by all other peoples. Yet, such insistence has been made. The Nazi ideology proclaimed the racial superiority of "Aryan" Germans over Slavs, Jews, and others. Within each society, racism or sexism may make claims that are not acknowledged by those who are placed in an inferior status. Even religious differences may take on this character. Thus, Protestants and Catholics may regard their religious views as superior and yet not seek or expect conversion by the others. Religious adherence is taken as an ascribed status that cannot be altered.

People throughout the world tend to believe that their own ways of life are admirable and other people's ways are strange and less worthy. Sumner (1906, p. 13) defined ethnocentrism as

> this view of things in which one's own group is the center of everything and all others are scaled and rated with references to it. . . . Each group nourishes its own pride and vanity, boasts itself superior, exalts its own divinities, and looks with contempt on outsiders. Each group thinks its own folkways the only right ones, and it observes that other groups have other folkways, these excite its scorn.

This kind of ethnocentrism has been widely observed (LeVine and Campbell 1972) and is a fundamental basis for social conflicts.

CONSENSUS

In consensually based conflicts, the adversary parties agree about what they want. Consensus, however, can be the basis for cooperation as well as conflict. When two parties want the same thing and each can attain it only or insofar as the other does, the basis for a cooperative relationship exists. This consensus may occur because of a sense of identity by the two parties. It may also exist because the attainment of the goal for each depends upon the other's attainment as well. For example, the control of a communicable disease may require its reduction or elimination in adjoining territorial jurisdictions. Or the effective use of a river for power and irrigation may require the cooperation of parties' sharing the river as a border. Parties within a business corporation or a society also have a basis for a cooperative relationship since increasing the total wealth of the organization or society depends upon each party's getting more wealth.

Consensus, then, underlies social conflict only in conjunction with certain other conditions. In addition, there must be a basis for at least one party to experience or view the distribution of the consensually desired values as unsatisfactory. Furthermore, the basis must exist for one or more parties to believe that the unwanted distribution is attributable to an adversary or at least cannot be altered without a loss to another party. In other words, there must be a basis for viewing the distribution and alterations of it as a zero-sum situation. In this chapter, we consider the kinds of issues that are often involved in consensual conflicts. We also consider the circumstances in which consensually shared values underlie social conflicts.

Issues in Contention

Any value that two parties share can be a basis for social conflict between them. We need to consider the circumstances and beliefs that must accompany consensus in order for it to constitute an objective social conflict. Our attention will be focused upon those values that most frequently provide the basis for consensual conflicts. We begin by analyzing one such value to serve as a prototype of other possible ones.

Consider wealth. Obviously, consensus about the desirability of wealth is widespread among many sets of potential adversaries. What circumstances or beliefs make such consensus the basis for a struggle? One possibility, as we have already noted, is that each party wants more wealth, and each can obtain it only at the expense of the other. The extent to which such a condition actually exists, however, is itself subject to dispute among partisans. Consider a factory with several departments and several levels of hierarchy within each department. If each department is allocated a fixed amount of money by the central management, then the persons at each hierarchical level would seem to be in a position where the gains of one level must balance the losses of another. The levels are in a conflicting relationship. But this reasoning makes assumptions that may or may not be valid. It assumes allocations will be made by levels, that there can be no alteration of the total amount available, and that funds from external sources are not differentially available to various levels. It also assumes that everyone is thinking in terms of the same period, for example, one budgetary year. Given other assumptions, the relationship need not be a conflicting one.

Some values seem to be inherently conflicting when parties share them. Imagine that each party wants to have *more* wealth than the other has. Now what they want is relative to the adversary, and, by definition, both cannot attain their goal simultaneously. Even in this case, however, the conflict need not be pure and zero sum. For the conflict to be zero sum, all the wealth must be possessed by the primary adversaries, and additional wealth can come only from them. In actuality, wealth is likely to be obtainable from outside parties, and it may be increased by the internal actions of each contending party itself. The more autonomous the party, the more likely any increases of wealth will depend on internal developments rather than be at the expense of an adversary. Thus, such possibilities are greater for countries than for segments of organizations.

Some values, however, are necessarily assessed relatively and assume a closed system. Consider, for example, the desire for prestige or deference. How much one unit has can only be measured relative to the amount that others have in the same system. Remember, we are discussing values about which the members of the units are in agreement, they agree about the desirability for attaining deference and are assessing it the same way.

Desiring power is another such value. As discussed in Chapter 1, social power is relative. The amount of force one party has at its disposal does not determine its power, its power depends upon how much it has *compared* to its adversaries. This definition gives a struggle over power a zero-sum quality. It is true that power over subordinates makes it possible for superiors to utilize collective resources more effectively for the welfare of the entire collectivity (Parsons 1951). The increased gains for the collectivity are relative to some other entity and mean that more goods or other gains can be divided within the collectivity; but all this does not alter the zero-sum character of the power relations within the collectivity. This characteristic is one of the reasons why so many social conflicts arise from and about power differences and also why such disputes are so often handled coercively. The inherent nature of power differences within any hierarchical organization or social system is one basis for asserting that conflicts are inevitable. Dahrendorf (1959) defines classes in terms of possession of authority, and, hence, differences in authority underlie class conflicts. Presumably, people with less power are relatively disadvantaged and, under appropriate conditions, recognize that.

Another major reason why consensus about the value of power so often underlies social conflicts, particularly conflicts in which coercion is used, is that power is a means to attain many other resources. Power sought as a means can readily become an end in itself. If conflict were defined as necessarily involving the use of coercion, then a power struggle would be part of every conflict (Weber 1947, p. 132). Given our definition of social conflict, power struggles do not underlie every social conflict. But contentions about power become more common and significant when the conflict becomes manifest and as coercion is used.

In addition to the value of power, prestige, and comparative wealth there may be consensus about resources that are not assessed relatively. These views are usually quite specific, such as Israeli and Jordanian government contentions over Jerusalem or Soviet and U.S. government disagreements about Berlin. Even contentions about these places, insofar as they are consensual conflicts, have large amounts of power and prestige components in them. In the discussion of objective consensual conflicts, we will concentrate on the abstract and generally conflict-pertinent dimensions of power, prestige, and wealth.

For conflicts based upon consensus to exist, people must want the same thing. They may want it as individuals or as members of a collective unit within a larger social system. Our first question is how does the consensus come about? One way is that people in a society are socialized as to what is desirable. As sharers of the same culture, they want the same things. Thus, in American society workers and managers in a factory want money and the things money can buy. Success has many conventional meanings, and we are brought up in each society to know what they are and what is worth striving for. The very consensus essential for social life, then, is also the basis for conflicts.

In each society people are also socialized to "know their place," to be different and want different things. It will prove helpful to assume that despite such variations, there are some universal human experiences and, hence, universal sentiments. One which is particularly relevant for the study of social conflicts is the preference for self-regulation or autonomy (Arendt 1965, pp. 259–278). We shall assume that despite socialization into subordination, even by ascription, people prefer autonomy to subordination; this assumption holds for individuals and for collectivities with which persons identify. That is, it is assumed not only for persons regardless of age, sex, ethnicity, or rank in a hierarchy but also for groups of persons who think of themselves as having a collective entity and seek some control over their own group, as a group, whether this be age, sex, ethnicity, or class.

Some of the issues underlying these assertions can be illustrated by considering very young children. They are perhaps the only category of persons whom others still regard as being incapable of having much control over their own lives. Despite adult claims, however, children do not abandon all claims to controlling their own activities. We need not decide whether children or their adult masters have better judgment about the way children should behave. Clearly, there is no inherent or fully successful inculcation of children's acceptance of adult control. It may be won by coercion or be exchanged for affection and material rewards.

Consensus, then, may be based upon the shared culture of a particular social system. The social system may be a society with extended means of socialization. It may be an organization, such as a factory or university, with much more limited opportunities for socialization into a common culture and with only a rudimentary common culture to share in any case. Consensus may also be the result of universal human experiences (Shibutani 1961, pp. 393–401). These forms of consensus result from being raised by other humans, usually in a family setting, and from the similarity of experiences people have in a variety of social relations, usually within a hierarchical order. Some of these experiences may not be universal, but they can transcend a single social system. An example of this might be the experience of impersonal interaction as it occurs in urban settings or in highly formalized bureaucracies in many different countries.

Sources of Issues

We need to consider the circumstances which, in conjunction with consensus, constitute objective consensual conflicts. As social observers, we must be able to discern a distribution of consensually desired resources that will be unsatisfactory to one or another potential partisan and that is likely to be viewed as a zero-sum relationship between the potential partisans. The task in this chapter is to outline what produces those circumstances.

Whatever the distribution of what is valued, it can conceivably be part of a consensual conflict. Members of a category who have less of what is valued than those in another category are likely to feel they are unjustly deprived. But even people in a category who have more than people in another may believe that they should have even more. We must consider what affects each group's satisfaction with what has been allocated to both.

Satisfaction depends upon the criterion used in evaluating a position and an assessment of how well the standards are being met. For example, members of a category may believe that they should have at least enough money for an adequate living given their training and efforts in their task. What is enough depends partly upon a comparison with others with similar preparation and efforts.

A variety of criteria may be used to evaluate the allocation of consensually desired resources. The criteria may be assessments of efforts or of outputs, of intentions or of consequences, and of being or of doing. They may have built-in comparisons, such as equality, whether of opportunity or of attainment.

For people to assess how well their standards are met, they must have a basis of comparison or a point of reference. Other persons often are the basis for determining how well the criteria have been met; for example, one ethnic group compares itself with another. The point of reference also may be the group's own past; how close they are to meeting their aspirations depends upon how far they were from reaching these standards in the past.

The first step is to consider the differences between parties in what they have or what they agree is desirable. We must reflect, if only briefly, upon possible degrees and kinds of differences. Suppose we consider two categories of people; we can compare them as collectivities or as aggregates of individuals. The members of one category can be compared to another as a group that has more or less wealth than other groups. On the other hand, the members of each category can be compared in terms of the characteristics of their individual members. For example, the People's Republic of China may have a large gross national income, but the per capita income may be much less than in countries with a collectively small income.

The relative position of two categories, even as aggregates, can be compared in several ways, for example, by comparing averages or distributions. A sampling of some distributions is shown in Figure 2.1. Consider A and B to be different ethnic groups within a society or organization. When we compare the distribution of income, we might find that all members of the category have less than every member of the other category. This is depicted in part 1 of Figure 2.1. Or, as shown in part 4 of Figure 2.1, the members of one category may have almost the same distribution of income as do the members of the other category. The average income of A and B is much less different in part 4 than in part 1. The averages are very similar in parts 2 and 3, although the distributions are different. A shared sense of injustice is more likely to arise when the members of the group with the lower average income are not very differentiated, and the distribution among the members is similar (in Figure 2.1, part 2 rather than part 3).

The criteria people use are partly a matter of what they learn is appropriate. There is often consensus about the criteria for the allocation of what is desired as well as about what is desirable. Consensus about the criteria of allocation is less likely to be high than is consensus about what is desirable. People with different experiences develop their own criteria and apply them. When people in different categories do not agree upon the criteria or upon the basis for evaluating their fulfillment, the members of at least one category will feel dissatisfied.

For example, whites in the United States may view the discrepancies in income between blacks and whites and argue that their criterion of equality is being met. They might argue that there is equality of opportunity, and the differences in income are simply a consequence of differences in ability and motivation for which they share no collective responsibility. The blacks, however, might hold that the society should so operate that the distribution of income does not differ between blacks and whites. Viewing the same differences between blacks and whites that the whites observed, they might feel that their criterion of equality is not being met and will feel dissatisfied.

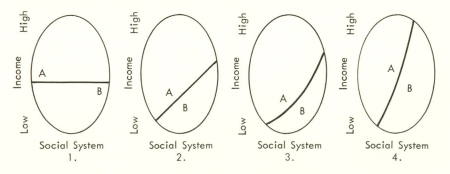

Figure 2.1 Patterns of Distribution.

In addition to feeling dissatisfied, for a social conflict to occur some other set of people must be held responsible. A natural disaster can cause a great deal of dissatisfaction and not a social conflict. The selection or creation of a target is a major topic of concern in the next chapter. Our concern here is with the conditions that tend to make a group of persons believe that they are in a conflict relationship with another group. This concern leaves aside the questions about displacement of feelings of anger that arise from dissatisfaction. In analyzing the bases for social conflicts, we are especially interested in the conditions that underlie two groups' thinking they are essentially in a zero-sum situation.

Three interrelated conditions affect the extent to which groups think they are in a zero-sum relationship. First, people may believe that what is consensually valued is scarce (Stanley 1968). Such beliefs depend upon the nature of what is valued and the sources for its creation. Insofar as what is valued is less than the desired amount and is not increasing, groups are more likely to believe that the increase in one party's share necessarily diminishes the other side's attainment of what is valued. As we noted in discussing power and prestige, their scarcity seems inherent. Now we emphasize that the scarcity of any resource also depends upon the boundedness of the social system. This is the second condition that markedly affects the extent to which the parties are in a zero-sum relationship. Insofar as the parties constitute a closed system and insofar as they are mutually dependent, a change in one group's possession of what is consensually valued will affect the other side. If, in addition, the resource is scarce and changes in its magnitude are confined to the social system that the parties constitute, the parties are in a zero-sum relationship. For example, labor and management may be in a zero-sum relationship within the confines of a given market, but they might, under other market conditions, jointly increase what they get at the expense of third parties.

Finally, insofar as one party has taken by coercion, manipulation, or another illegitimate fashion its share from the other side, the other side will have experienced a zero-sum relationship. It is conceivable that the allocation of values among potential adversary parties might be dictated by impersonal natural forces or processes or that outside parties and external nonsocial factors might seem to have determined the allocation. Of course, whether the allocation is determined by nature (for example, the "natural" differences between the races or sexes) or by exploitation is often a matter of contention among the parties in conflict.

Karl Marx's ideas about class conflict illustrate the form of analysis presented here (Marx 1964). He argued that technological developments resulted in the emergence of large-scale capital investments. Under capitalism the ownership of capital by a few resulted in the relative disadvantage of the workers, those who did not own the means of production. The owners of the means of production gain the advantages of increased industrial productivity. The workers must sell their labor and are compensated only enough to sustain themselves. The capitalists' profits constitute exploitation of the workers according to this analysis. Marx assumed that both the workers and the owners of the means of production valued autonomy, control over the product of their labors, and material benefits. Marx also went on to examine the conditions that were necessary for workers to recognize that they were exploited and that the private ownership of the means of production was the basis for that exploitation. In the next chapter, we discuss the variety of factors that affect the awareness of a conflict.

In summary, we are arguing that there are conditions that underlie consensual conflicts and that the observer selects the aspects he or she believes most pertinent to social conflicts, for example, class or power differences among ethnic, or gender, or ownership categories. Within that context the analyst can discern agreement about the desirability of a particular resource. The analyst conceives of possible contending parties and notes the allocation of the desired resources among the parties and then considers how likely it is that members of the potentially adversary parties are to be dissatisfied with that allocation. Finally, the analyst must assess the likelihood that one party will come to regard another as the cause of the dissatisfaction and the possessor of resources which, if given up, would reduce its own dissatisfaction.

THE MIXED NATURE OF ACTUAL CONFLICTS: SOME CASES

In any specific dispute, the contending parties have both consensual and dissensual bases for conflict. The relative importance of each varies in different conflicts; it also varies among the different segments of each party and probably changes in the course of a struggle. Thus, a religious difference between two groups may be a part of an objective dissensual conflict; the leaders of each religious group may, however, agree about the value of power, and for them a large component of the conflict would be consensual.

Several conflicts will be used illustratively throughout this book. We will consider struggles within organizations (particularly between labor and management and between university students and administrators), and within countries (conflicts of race and gender within the United States and revolutions in Russia and elsewhere), and struggles within the world system (particularly between the U.S. and Soviet governments since World War II and among groups in the Middle East since the establishment of the state of Israel). In the case of university, race, and gender conflicts, we will give particular attention to their manifestations during the 1960s. In this chapter, we look at underlying conditions at the beginning of the decade, and in later chapters we will consider subsequent stages of the conflicts.

Industrial Conflicts

The bases for many conflicts exist within industrial organizations: between workers and managers, line and staff personnel, different departments (for example, marketing and production), different occupations or trades (such as carpenters and electricians). These conflicts occur within a single factory, a corporation with many plants, an industry, a society, and globally. The bases for social conflicts exist in all these settings, but some are more likely than others to become manifest. People organize into a variety of groups in order to wage a struggle; in the contemporary United States a few occupations have craft unions, others are organized into professional associations, other workers have formed industrial unions to bargain collectively, and employers and managers are organized in trade and employer associations.

The many categories of persons and positions in industrial organizations are recruiting grounds for conflict organizations. In this chapter, we describe some features of industrial organizations and of the varying resources accruing to persons in different positions. A wide variety of activities are coordinated within an industrial organization to produce marketable products. Most organizations in the United States are privately owned, and the authority to direct that coordination derives from that ownership. In practice in many large corporations ownership is sufficiently diffuse for managers to have considerable autonomy in making decisions, limited only by the constraints of the political order, the various markets in which the organizations are implicated, and the network of social relations in which the managers are themselves embedded.

The industrial conflicts of the 1930s emerged from underlying conditions quite different from those of the 1960s. Working conditions had deteriorated, and alliances with many groups gained governmental support for union organization and collective bargaining. By the 1960s industrial conflicts between organized workers and employers had become highly regulated. In this section we describe some underlying issues between industrial workers and employers in the 1960s in order to provide a basis for analyzing the course of industrial conflicts. We focus on differences in prestige, power, and income of various groups of members of industrial organizations.

The different occupations and positions within industrial organizations vary considerably in prestige as well as in power and income. We can safely assume that people in every society value prestige. This does not mean that some people would not rather have security, safety, or high income to compensate for low prestige, but prestige is valued. Furthermore, there is considerable evidence that at least within the United States there is high agreement about how occupations are ranked in prestige (Hodge, Siegel, and Rossi 1966; Kriesberg 1979; Reiss 1961). The occupations within any given company have society-wide prestige value. The variations in ranking of the general occupational titles that may be found in companies are presented in Table 2.1. The scores are taken from a national U.S. survey conducted in 1963; the respondents were asked to rate ninety occupations. Scores were compiled for each occupation and ranged from 94 for a Supreme Court justice to 34 for a shoe shiner.

Similarly, within each company and across the society as a whole, material benefits are not equally distributed among different occupational strata. There are many ways of comparing income among different occupations: weekly, monthly, yearly, or lifetime earnings or income before or after taxes. Let us consider the

TABLE 2.1 Prestige Scores of Selected Occupations

Occupation	Score
Member of a board of directors of a large corporation	87
Accountant for a large business	81
Owner of a factory that employs about 100 people	80
Trained machinist	74
Machine operator in a factory	63
Night watchman	50

Source: Data from Hodge, Siegel, and Rossi 1966.

most frequently used measure, namely, annual gross earnings. Table 2.2 shows variations between large heterogenous occupational categories. Even comparing such categories, we can see that in 1969 the median earnings of operatives in manufacturing industries was 49 percent of the median earnings of salaried managers in manufacturing. The variation is much greater if we compare high- and low-ranking persons in the occupations. One indication of the range at the highest managerial levels is shown in Table 2.3.

As discussed earlier in the chapter, what is considered to be a fair allocation of earnings varies with the comparison group. Generally, in the United States workers view higher earnings of others as opportunities for themselves or their children rather than as exploitative. Furthermore, the general increase in earnings in nearly all occupations has meant that if people compare themselves with their past earnings, they experience improvement. For example, the median earnings of operatives increased 27 percent between 1959 and 1969, taking into account inflation. Their earnings relative to managers, however, did not change.

Power differences among occupations are even more difficult to quantify, but they exist. Occupational groups differ in the degree to which members can control their own work activities. In some occupations, neither the mode of work nor its pace are under the workers' control, as for example, on the assembly line (Blauner 1964). Workers have varying amounts of control over their own activities depending on the technology of the occupation and the amount and kind of supervision to which they are subject. Control over one's own work is closely related to power relations with others in relevant occupations. Within a factory or corporation, for example, there may be clear lines of authority associated with different occupational roles, and roles at each rank are superior to some and subordinate to others.

The control may not only refer to the work activities themselves but to claims about the incumbency of the occupational role. In some occupations, particularly in professions, the members largely determine entrance, but once someone has entered, the rights to the position may depend upon customers, colleagues, or superiors. In industrial employment in the past, superiors in authority determined entrance and duration of employment; the major constraints upon the arbitrari-

TABLE 2.2 Annual Earnings of Males in Selected Industrial Occupations in 1959 and in 1969

Occupations	Earnings in 1959	Earnings in 1969
Salaried managers in manufacturing	9,156	14,379
Operatives in manufacturing	4,447	7,059
Laborer in manufacturing	3,623	5,560

Sources: U.S. Bureau of the Census 1965, pp. 231–233 and 1973, pp. 235–237.

ness of such decisions were the nature of the competitive market for each occupation and the customary standards of appropriate notice. With the development of trade unions, unionized workers have gained significant collective control over the terms of employment (Foote 1953; Hildenbrand 1953).

Occupational strata also differ in their power to determine policy for the larger units of which they are a part. Thus, even with unionization, workers as a group have relatively little power in decisions about matters such as investments, mergers, marketing choices, or new product developments of the factory or corporation in which they work. The relative power of workers and managers in formulating policy in the community and society in which they live also affects their bargaining power within factories. On the whole, wage earners are practically unrepresented in the U.S. Congress and hardly represented in state legislatures (Matthews 1954, Table 7). Even considering the occupational origins of political elites, we find that few are children of wage earners (Keller 1963, p. 312; Kriesberg 1979).

TABLE 2.3 Annual Earnings of Males in Selected Occupational Positions

Occupational Position[a]	Annual Salaries, about 1971
Chairman, General Electric	252,250
Chairman and president, International Telephone and Telegraph (ITT)	382,494
Chairman, General Telephone and Electronics	100,000
President, Xerox Corporation	325,063
Cable and pipe repairman, New York Telephone Company	5,460

[a] Does not include expense allowances, stock options, or bonuses. In 1971, the chairman and president of ITT received a bonus of $430,000.

Source: Tetlow 1972.

Differences in power are likely to be the bases of conflicts insofar as the parties with different amounts of power disagree about the decisions to be made. That is, when dissensus about collective values is added to consensus about the desirability of having power, we have the basis for conflict. If workers and managers agreed about what the factories, companies, and society should do, however, then the differences in allocation of power would not be fraught with serious implications for them. In the case of factories or companies, we do not know a great deal about how different the goals of workers and managers actually are for the whole enterprise. There are certainly some differences. Managers, given their identification with the firm and their specific roles within it, are more likely than the workers to be concerned with the firm's size, rate of growth, or percentage of market holdings. But, there is probably considerable consensus, within the society, about the basic aims of the firm.

The dissensual conflicts between workers and managers are generally based upon the incompatible aspects of their social relationship that requires coordination. Conflicts are much less likely to arise from claims about values or life styles made upon each other. The disdain of workers and managers for each other's way of life is not so strongly held in the United States that it would generally lead to efforts to impose their own views.

College and University Conflicts

Unlike the consumers of industrial outputs, the primary consumers of college and university services, students, are also organizational members. Divisions exist between many categories of members: faculty, staff, administrators, students, and trustees or other supervisory units. Members of each of these categories can be further subdivided (for example, by rank or tenure) and are crosscut by discipline, schools, and programs. In this section we focus on the issues that can underlie conflicts between students and administrators and particularly on those conflicts in the 1960s.

Given the nature of students and administrators within colleges and universities, differences in prestige and money are generally not significant conditions underlying conflict. Their relative prestige and money is in great measure derived from their social and economic positions outside of colleges and universities. In societies where attendance at institutions of higher learning is restricted to children of the highest socioeconomic stratum, the prestige of the students is high, and they may be able to maintain a high standard of living as well. In these cases, their prestige and income is not based on their position as students. In countries such as the United States, where attendance is widespread and the students are not drawn from a homogeneously high stratum, the prestige of students has some independent value. Although the prestige of students and administrators has not been assessed in any systematic way, it is probably safe to infer from our own experience that students have lower prestige within the university than faculty and administrators. Given the view of students as uneducated recipients of knowledge and skills from the faculty, the low prestige of students relative to faculty and administration is integral to the setting in which they operate.

Power differences between students and administrators are clearly an inherent characteristic of colleges and universities as organizations. Students usually have relatively little individual power and often lack even collective power. The general difficulties in the assessment of power are compounded because power relations are always in flux, and they vary widely among organizations and in different spheres of organizational life. In curricular matters students have little direct power, but they have influence through aggregate market conduct, namely, the choice of college and the choice of courses and programs of study. They also have some control by their definitions of what is appropriate and necessary work, but this control is handled within powerful constraints which are essentially constructed by the faculty and administration (Becker, Geer, and Hughes 1968). There has been an increase in formal student participation in curriculum decisions since the 1950s (Freidson 1955; McGrath 1970). Furthermore, before the mid-1960s students had little individual or collective control over many spheres of extracurricular activities, such as housing and drinking. Finally, there is the matter of relative power in determining the general policy of the university or college. The issues here relate to the organization's investments, expansion into surrounding neighborhoods, and kinds of research constraints imposed or not imposed. Students generally had little influence in making such decisions, but their numerical expansion in the 1960s could be viewed as a source of collective power.

Dissensus in values between administrators and students is typically present in universities. It arises in part from a generational difference in experience and interest. Furthermore, their respective positions within the university structure result in different perspectives. Finally, differences in social, economic, and ethnic backgrounds accentuate the existing dissensus. These bases of dissensus increased in the early 1960s with the rapid expansion of higher education and its greater openness.

As we noted earlier, dissensus constitutes objective conflict when differences in values and beliefs are incompatible. Incompatibility may arise from the need to act in coordination or from the claims one group makes upon the other regarding their differences. Both kinds of incompatibility exist in universities. Joint coordination is required as the various groups within universities must work together. Actually, much of the work of various categories within a university can and must be done relatively autonomously; close coordination is unnecessary or impossible. This reduces the objective dissensual conflicts. Nevertheless, in the 1960s there was increasing questioning of the way universities affected both the neighborhoods in which they were located and the policies of governmental units as well as questioning of the ways universities invested their endowment.

The kind of relationship in colleges and universities, the age differences, and the societal context all make it likely that dissensus in values will be incompatible because people make unacceptable claims on one another. In a college in which administrators feel responsible for the lives of their students, they make judgments about the students' moral conduct and try to channel it in accord with their own values. Arrangements about such aspects of living as sexual relations, drinking, and dressing can all become issues of contention. As we shall see, one outcome of conflicts about such issues is an alteration in the moral claims people make on one another. To some extent there may have been a decrease in dissensus from the 1960s to the 1980s, but this seeming decline may simply be the result of more tolerance for differences.

Gender Conflicts

Although the physiological differences between males and females are usually unambiguous, the social differences between men and women are not. For some purposes it may be appropriate to consider the lines of cleavage for potential conflict to be those of males and females. But the social meaning of male and female is diverse, and, for purposes of studying social conflict, we have to recognize that a woman's position is dependent not only on her sex but also on the social role of women. That social role is partly defined in relation to male roles. Therefore, in noting possible lines of cleavage by gender, it may be appropriate to consider categories based on age, marital status, and employment in conjunction with sex.

One assumption should be made explicit: There are no innate differences between men and women about what they would consider desirable. Males and females are presumed to be equally capable of valuing power, prestige, and material goods. Aside from differences directly and necessarily involved in human reproduction—conception and pregnancy—we can assume that whatever the differences, they are a matter of degree. Even if there were innate differences on the average between males and females in some human capacity, the overlap in that capacity between men and women is so great that the differences could be socially ignored. The differences that we observe between men and women in values and conduct are largely a product of the social structure that they have created and in which they live (Weisstein 1970). As in all assumptions, the test of this assumption must be in its usefulness for understanding the variations in the genesis and development of conflicts.

As for other quasi-groups, we consider differential allocations of prestige, power, and economic resources. Measures of the relative prestige of men and women, aside from associated characteristics, is not obtainable. There is scattered evidence that men and women agree that men have higher status. One kind of evidence is the degree to which women talk less than men when in groups of men and women (Strodtbeck, James, and Hawkins 1957). Furthermore, girls, asked if they wished they could have been boys, are ten times as likely as boys to say they wished they were of the other sex (Watson, cited in Millett 1970, p. 57). Even among adults, surveys in 1965 and 1970 reveal that women are more likely than men, by 16 percent compared to 4 percent, to admit to having wished that they belonged to the opposite sex (Erskine 1971, p. 290).

The basic peculiarity of men and women as conflict groups is that they live more intimately with each other than among themselves. It is within the family as well as in their relations in the larger society that the objective conflict must be considered. In the 1960s, as later, legal subordination of wives to husbands existed in the United States. In some states a wife did not have any legal claims upon her husband's earnings or property while they are married, aside from the right to be supported (Mead and Kaplan 1965, p. 153). In other states a wife had an interest in the property that was commonly owned, but exclusive authority to manage and control that property generally belonged to the husband. In some states she was not an independent legal agent in a variety of ways (Schulder 1970).

Outside the home women were not equal beneficiaries of the various distribution and ranking systems in the society. In the past women were excluded from higher education. Even in the 1960s there was a remarkable attrition as the levels of education progressed. Thus, in 1965, women constituted 50.6 percent of the high school graduates, 40.7 percent of the B.A. (or first professional degree recipients), and 32.1 percent of the M.A. recipients, and they received only 10.8 percent of the doctoral degrees awarded (Epstein 1970, pp. 57–58). The attrition within one field may be illustrative. In sociology, women made up:

43 percent   of the college seniors planning graduate work in sociology

37 percent   of the master's candidates in graduate school

31 percent   of the graduates who are teaching undergraduates

30 percent   of the Ph.D. candidates in graduate school

27 percent   of the full-time lecturers and instructors

14 percent   of the full-time assistant professors

 9 percent   of the full-time associate professors

 4 percent   of the full-time full professors

 1 percent   of the chairmen of graduate sociology departments

 0 percent   of the 44 full professors in the five elite departments (Rossi, 1970, p. 11).

Women constituted 41.6 percent of professional and technical workers in 1940 and 37.9 percent in 1966. The earnings of full-time employed women did not increase relative to men; indeed, between 1939 and 1966, women earned a smaller percentage of the median income of men in nearly every occupational category. For example, among clerical workers in 1939 the female median income was 78.5 percent of the male median income; in 1966 it was only 66.5 (Knudsen 1969; Mead and Kaplan 1965).

Finally, in terms of political power it should be recalled that in the United States it was not until 1920 that women obtained the right to vote. Even in the 1960s women were very markedly underrepresented at all levels in holding public office. In the actual operations of the legal system, women tended to be treated as less valuable as well as more vulnerable than men and, therefore, in need of extra protection (Nagel and Weitzman 1972).

Dissensus between men and women in values and beliefs is popularly judged to be highly compatible. Men are more oriented toward, and committed to, concerns about physical courage and aggressiveness, to instrumental efforts and rationality while women are directed toward nurturance, expressiveness, intuition, and emotion. As long as each thinks that what the other wants is good for those others and useful for oneself, the dissensus can be complementary and the basis for exchange. Persons in each category may tend to associate with others in their own group, enjoying and developing their own special qualities. Within contemporary American society, there is considerable variation in values and beliefs among men and among women as well as great overlap. Nevertheless, given the differences in socialization and the different social experiences of each, some dissensus is widespread.

For dissensus to be part of the basis of a social conflict, the members of the different categories must think that the differences between them are incompatible. One source of incompatibility arises from the need for coordination. Despite considerable segregation between the sexes, coordination is necessary in many spheres. Most obviously, within each family unit coordination between men and women is needed. The difficulties in achieving a satisfactory level of coordination does not concern us here except insofar as these are seen as part of societally shared difficulties between major social categories requiring social changes and not simply the need for improved interpersonal relations and more love between husband and wife.

Within other institutional spheres, such as the economy or politics, the dissensus generally seems irrelevant to the needs for coordination. It is possible that insofar as there are differences, for example, in aggressiveness, men and women might find it difficult to agree in choosing among policies that differ in possible violence. Thus, it might be that support for goals that might entail violence will be a source of contention between men and women. Later in the book we will consider this possibility further.

The other source of possible incompatibility is that men and women make claims upon the other that are mutually objectionable. Sometimes this takes the form of arguing that the others should hold values and beliefs like their own. Witness the anguished cry from *My Fair Lady:* "Why can't a woman be more like a man?" Thus, too, some feminists argue that men also need liberation—to be freed of the role pressures that they be assertive, domineering, and unemotional (Roszak 1969). As liberated persons, they could be more expressive, more openly loving of their children, and generally freer to develop a wider range of tastes and abilities than now. Sometimes this incompatibility arises from the asserted superiority of one's own group's values, beliefs, and patterns of conduct. Again, this might be clearer if we point to an example from the women's liberation movement. Some members argue that the nonhierarchical, egalitarian solidarity of sisterhood is superior to the more typically hierarchical rankings insisted upon by men.

Dissensual and consensual conflicts can, and often do, exacerbate each other. Sometimes, however, aspects of each can mitigate the other's effects. If men and women agree that power is good and if women demand that men have less power over them, then it follows that if women's demands are met, men must lose something that is desirable. But, women might argue that if men who value autonomy and freedom stop trying to have so much power over women, then they themselves would also be freer. Such inconsistencies do not invalidate the other claim. Rather, different people at different times, and to different audiences, may stress one or the other value. The elaboration and specification of the many claims into an integrated program is what leaders of organizations do in formulating the ideology for a particular conflict group. In considering objective conflicts, we need simply to discern the possible relations between consensual and dissensual conflicts.

Race Conflicts

To illustrate differences among ethnic groups as a possible basis for social conflicts, we will consider blacks and whites in the United States, especially in the 1960s. First, we should note that the differences between blacks and whites are social, not biological. Who is white and who is black is a matter of self and other definitions. We will use the popular and conventional definitions because they have social meaning. Given the nature of certain kinds of data, we will sometimes use information about whites compared to nonwhites; most nonwhites in the United States are blacks.

In discussing objective consensual conflict, we assume there are no genetic differences among the many socially defined "races" relevant to their valuing power, prestige, or material well-being. Persons, regardless of "race," are equally capable of desiring such resources.

In the United States in the 1960s blacks were accorded less prestige or social status than were whites. The assertion that black is beautiful is part of an effort to reduce that status difference, at least in the eyes of the blacks. In the past blacks have acknowledged the status hierarchy that placed them below whites. Their efforts to lighten skin color and straighten hair were indications of this hierarchical difference. It is in this connection that denial of access to public facilities, segregation of public facilities, and unequal provision of public services was particularly oppressive.

The availability of public services and of the goods and services that can be bought on the private market is, of course, intrinsically important. That is, differences in the ability to eat well, have adequate shelter and clothing, and enjoy what people in a given society think appropriate have inherent value to members of a society. The differences between whites and nonwhites in these regards have been, and are, great, as shown in Table 2.4. Thus, in 1959, 18.1 percent of all white persons were living in poverty compared to 56.1 percent of nonwhite persons. The decline in the proportion of persons in poverty, as defined by the U.S. government, in the 1960s and the lack of decline in the 1970s is probably related, in part, to the turbulence and protests in the 1960s (Kriesberg 1979; Piven and Cloward 1979).

TABLE 2.4 Percent of Persons below Poverty Level by Race: 1959 to 1977

Categories	1959	1969	1977[a]
All persons	22.4	12.1	11.6
White	18.1	9.5	8.9
Black and other races	56.2	31.0	29.0

[a] Not strictly comparable with earlier years due to revised procedures.

Source: U.S. Bureau of the Census 1979, p. 463.

The persistence in differences in the incidence of poverty between whites and nonwhites rests on differences in employment rates, family structure, kinds of jobs held, and wages paid for similar employment. Thus, even with equal educational attainment and the same occupations, whites generally earn more money than nonwhites (see Table 2.5). Related to such income differences are inequalities in the distribution of food, housing, health care, and education and in mortality rates.

Finally, we must consider the distribution of power between blacks and whites. Two aspects of power relations are pertinent here—for collectivities and for aggregates of individuals. In both regards, blacks have less power than whites. Individually, for example, blacks have had fewer civil rights than whites; thus, they have tended to receive more severe punishments for similar convictions and until the mid-1960s had been largely disenfranchised in some sections of the country. Collectively, there has been a disproportionately low representation of blacks in various levels of government. After the 1970 congressional elections,

TABLE 2.5 Occupations and Median Earnings of Males 25 to 64 Years Old in the Experienced Civilian Labor Force with Earnings in 1959, by Education and Color

Occupation and Education	Median Earnings in Dollars	
	White	Nonwhite
Accountants and auditors (all)	6,834	5,771
with 4 yrs. or more of college	7,311	6,115
Civil engineers (all)	7,952	6,800
with 4 yrs. or more of college	8,691	7,817
Elementary school teachers (all)	5,471	4,476
with 4 yrs. or more of college	5,601	4,565
Laborers (except farm and mine)	3,871	2,666
Elementary: 0 to 7 yrs.	3,229	2,379
8 years only	3,932	3,044

Source: U.S. Bureau of the Census 1963.

blacks had the highest representation since Reconstruction; yet they constituted 3 percent of the House of Representatives and 1 percent of the Senate.

The extent to which there are potential dissensual conflicts between whites and blacks is more difficult to assess. A way of life different from their own is attributed to blacks by many whites; they allege widespread differences in family life, child rearing, patterns of consumption, and personal moral qualities. Many blacks also see themselves as an ethnic group with its own distinctive way of life, but they see different distinctive characteristics than do many whites. The experiences of oppression are not purely ennobling; if they were, we might all wish to be oppressed. Nevertheless, many blacks perceive an admirable and distinctive style that has developed from the peculiar experiences of blacks in the United States. The distinctive way of life is shown in warmth, spontaneity, solidarity, courage, and "soul" (Rainwater 1970).

In actuality, American blacks and whites generally share fundamental values and beliefs. Their differences in the distribution of certain values and beliefs are in large part attributable to differences in economic class and social status. Still, there are enough differences and beliefs in the differences for objective dissensual conflicts to exist.

Dissensual conflicts depend on the incompatibility of differences in values and beliefs. Such incompatibility arises from the necessity of coordinating programs in education, welfare, and even foreign policy; it arises from the need to coordinate activity in specific organizations, such as factories, schools, and political agencies.

Incompatibility also arises from claims whites and blacks may make on each other in regard to their distinctive values and beliefs. Thus, whites and blacks might feel that the way of life they perceive the others to have is morally outrageous. This might be expressed in avoidance, but it may also be expressed in desires to bring the others to the correct and morally proper way of life. The differences in values and beliefs and the simple sense of collective ethnic identity give added purpose to desires for more power for ethnic collectivities. The power desired may be for control over the other group, or it may be for greater autonomy to assure the opportunity to maintain and pursue the distinctive styles of one's own ethnic group.

Again, we can see that in such specific conflicts as those between blacks and whites, consensual and dissensual components are mixed. The emphasis, however, can and does vary over time and among different segments of each category.

Revolutions

Some writers define revolutions as massive popular participation in extensive violent efforts, and other writers define them as fundamental transformations of the social order they produce. In this volume, we examine alternative means of waging conflicts and regard the outcome as problematic. Therefore, we consider revolutionary efforts that did not succeed and even the absence of such efforts when conditions might seem suitable. The term *revolutionary efforts* refers to actions of large numbers of people in a society that are directed to transform the social and political order by their supporting parties seeking to seize state power. This definition excludes efforts to bring about massive change when introduced "from above," for example by a modernizing elite that seized power through a coup. In this section we will review conditions that might result in revolutionary efforts. In later chapters, we will consider different ways in which revolutionary efforts are pursued and what their outcomes and consequences are.

Several conditions might be expected to result in revolutionary struggle: All pertain to the nature of the cleavages in the society and the issues that divide the potentially antagonistic groups. For a revolutionary situation to exist, the cleavages must be between major groupings in the society. They are often based on class lines, pitting peasants and industrial workers against large landowners and large-scale employers. This cleavage generally coincides with that between persons who have effective political power and those who do not. Thus, the landowners and employers may also effectively control the state to maintain their class interests. Ethnic cleavages may also play a role. In some cases, they support separatist efforts, but when they coincide with class and political cleavages, a revolutionary situation is enhanced.

For example, prior to the Mexican Revolution, which began in 1910, a small landowning oligarchy dominated the government, under the presidency of Porfirio Diaz. Members of the oligarchy were *criollos,* white, powerful, and wealthy; the Indians and *mestizos* (persons of mixed Indian and European parentage) were dark-skinned, poor, and excluded from political power. The situation in Angola prior to the revolutionary nationalist events of the early 1960s presents another illustration.

> The rapid expansion of the coffee export economy between 1950 and 1960 led to the expropriation of African lands and the growth of a migratory labor system, and these economic changes in turn created the possibility of a political coalition between coffee laborers, African coffee farmers, and traditional tribal authorities. The poverty of the Portuguese estate owners and the marginal economic character of the estates themselves made coercion an integral part of the coffee economy. The racial distinctions enforced by colonial rule were necessary to insure land and labor for the estates, but land concessions and forced labor were major sources of African discontent. (Paige 1975, p. 277)

Consensual and dissensual issues generally are mixed together in revolutionary situations, but consensual issues about control of land, industry, and the government are at the core of issues underlying revolutionary efforts. Paige (1975) has analyzed agrarian revolutions by relating them to the organization of agriculture to produce crops for export. He begins with the division between cultivators and noncultivators, with cultivators tending to be subordinate to the noncultivators.

Cultivators draw their income predominantly from either land or wages, noncultivators from land or capital. These two dimensions combine into four major kinds of agricultural organizations: (1) hacienda, (2) sharecropping or migratory labor, (3) small holding, and (4) plantation, as illustrated in Figure 2.2.

In the hacienda system land is divided into domain land and labor subsistence land, with domain land devoted to production for the market. The subsistence farmers owe work on the hacienda owner's domain lands. The system was common in Mexico prior to the 1910 revolution and in the Peruvian highlands until reforms began in 1968. It tends to exist in areas with low-cost land and little market in land. Commercial haciendas exist where the noncultivators draw their income from the crops produced on their land and cultivators draw their income from the parcels of land they own. Where the noncultivators receive their income from the land they own and cultivators from the wages they earn, the agricultural organization is based on sharecropping (tenancy) or migratory labor.

Noncultivators can also receive their income from: financial or industrial capital. In one case "the upper class surrenders control of the direct cultivation to a system of decentralized small farms, while in the other the upper class controls the agricultural enterprise directly, usually through a joint stock corporation" (Paige 1975, p. 14). In the former case the cultivators' source of income is the land they own and the small-holding farming system results; in the latter case the cultivators' source of income is wages and this constitutes the plantation system. Plantations are worked with either wage or slave labor and are most common in producing labor-intensive crops requiring high capital investment on relatively cheap land, as in rubber or sugar cane crops.

Paige reasons and gives evidence that some kinds of agricultural organizations are more likely to result in revolutionary efforts than are others. He convincingly argues that the conflict with the cultivators is more likely to be revolutionary when the noncultivators derive their income from the land than when they derive their income from capital. Conflicts over ownership of the land are less amenable

Noncultivators' Income Sources	Cultivators' Income Sources	
	Land	Wages
Land	COMMERCIAL HACIENDA (coffee, cotton)	SHARECROPPING (cotton, grains) MIGRATORY LABOR (coffee, grapes)
Capital	SMALL HOLDING (coffee, cocoa, cotton, tobacco, fruits and nuts, grains)	PLANTATION (rubber, tea, sugar)

Figure 2.2 Typical forms of agricultural organization and sources of income of cultivators and noncultivators. (*Source:* Paige 1975; adopted from Figure 1.1 and Table 2.1.)

to compromise than conflicts about sharing the income derived from capital; in the latter case reform efforts are more likely. Noncultivators dependent on land for their income must rely on the state to enforce their ownership to a greater extent than noncultivators who derive their income from capital and can rely more on market mechanisms and less on an authoritarian state system.

Dissensual issues also generally underlie revolutionary efforts. These typically take the form of ideological differences about social, political, economic, and national rights. Ideologies about nationalism, liberal democracy, and socialism have varying appeals to different strata in every society. The ideologies are important in creating a revolutionary situation because they provide a basis for alliances among diverse groups. Sometimes agricultural workers, small business people, professionals, and industrial workers can be brought together, for example, under the banner of nationalism or political democracy and civil rights.

The revolution against the czarist government in Russia in 1917 is illustrative. Before the revolution, imperial Russia was intermediate in development between the industrialized countries of Western Europe and the United States and the underdeveloped countries of Asia and Africa. Its agricultural production was oriented toward export, and it imported capital; in many ways its economy was dependent upon that of Western Europe. Production as well as ownership and control were concentrated in the hands of a few. The state was authoritarian and repressive and heavily involved in economic policies.

Imperial Russia was a predominantly agricultural society, less than 10 percent of the population derived their livelihood from industry. In 1861 serfs were emancipated, but they had to make annual money payments to their former owners for forty years, in effect, to ransom themselves off. This payment was compensation to their masters for the services and dues they no longer would be commanded to provide under serfdom (Doob 1948, p. 50). Although there was an increase in the owning of land by peasants, inequality among them grew, and the population increased more rapidly than did available land. The system of authority in the villages was breaking down with the changes in land ownership and usage.

Although the industrial proletariat was a small proportion of the Russian work force, it was highly concentrated. Living conditions of the workers were much worse than in other industrialized countries; many workers lived in crowded, underground, barracklike lodgings. Wages were low. Efforts to take concerted action to improve conditions were repressed.

Of course, important underlying conditions for the 1917 revolution were related to the Russian participation in World War I. Living conditions deteriorated, and masses of workers and peasants were mobilized and sent into combat with inadequate military equipment. The authority of the czarist state was undermined by the failures in waging the war and in maintaining economic conditions.

In many countries of the world, fundamental cleavages exist and large segments of the population suffer from poor economic conditions. Life expectancy is low, and many people are undernourished, ill, and inadequately clothed and housed. They are also politically repressed and have little or no effective participation in forming public policy. That revolutionary efforts break out as infrequently as they do under these circumstances and even more rarely result in fundamental social transformations indicate that additional factors must account for the emergence of revolutionary struggles.

International Conflicts

Governments are ready-made adversaries in international conflicts. Each claims absolute sovereignty, and each has specialized subunits to conduct conflict. The cleavages, however, do not simply pit each government against every other. Governments are linked together into many cross-cutting-alliances, which are based on ideology, economic interests, and military concerns. In addition, many nongovernmental actors play major roles in international conflicts, including transnational organizations based on occupations, political ideologies, religions, and ethnicity. Some groups are would-be governments. The issues that divide these potential international adversaries are consensual and dissensual. Consensual ones pertain particularly to matters of security and autonomy. Dissensual issues pertain to ideology and to some extent to religious and cultural values.

To consider international consensual issues, we must ask whether or not there is consensus among peoples of the world concerning power, status, and material well being for a conflict to exist. There is probably great consensus among government leaders and the populace of societies worldwide about the importance of material wealth and even about how it is measured. Considerable consensus probably also exists about the desirability of status, prestige, and national honor, but less agreement exists about its assessment than about that of material wealth or power. Power is undoubtedly an important value about which there is a high level of consensus. Agreement is even high about its assessment, total military expenditures being a very good indicator of popular perceptions of power (Alcock and Newcombe 1970).

Several conditions must combine for consensual and dissensual issues to underlie a social conflict. We will examine those conditions as they relate to two sets of international conflicts: those in the Middle East and those between the Soviet and U.S. governments.

The Middle East conflicts involve, among many other parties, the governments of Israel and of the neighboring Arab countries, the adherents of Islam, Christianity, and Judaism, the peoples who identify themselves as Arab Palestinians and as Jews, the governments of the United States, the Soviet Union, Great Britain, and France, and the officials of international organizations such as the United Nations. These parties have interacted in a shifting set of conflicts since the British withdrew their military forces from Palestine in 1948. Without general acceptance of the UN plan for the partition of the British-mandated Palestine, Jews there established the state of Israel in a war against the neighboring Arab countries that sought to prevent it. The former Palestinian territory was divided among Israel, Jordan (incorporating the West Bank and the old city of Jerusalem), and Egypt (occupying the Gaza Strip), as shown on the map in Figure 2.3. Between 1948 and 1967 the conflict escalated and deescalated several times, but it did not fundamentally change (Kriesberg 1981; Khouri 1968). In 1967, faced with what the Israeli government leaders thought were threats of imminent destruction, Israel launched a successful attack. As a result of that six-day war, Israeli military forces controlled the Golan Heights, the West Bank, all of Jerusalem, the Gaza Strip, and all of the Sinai. That new structure remained until the surprise attack by Egyptian and Syrian forces in October 1973. After a negotiated disengagement and partial withdrawal of Israeli forces, again there was relative stability until the major initiative by President Anwar Sadat in November 1977 that led to the peace treaty between the Israeli and Egyptian governments. Throughout this period the underlying conditions for the next stage in the struggle shifted. We focus, here, on the major underlying conditions affecting the Egyptian and Israeli governments in the early 1960s.

The per capita income of Israel was much greater than the per capita wealth of Egypt. This difference in itself, however, did not constitute an objective conflict. Undoubtedly, the peoples and governments of each country were dissatisfied with their income, but not because they used each other as reference groups; the United States, other countries of more similar character, and their own past were more significant points of reference. Even more fundamentally, they did not consider that per capita income would be increased at the expense of the other side. Within the nation-state framework, there is little that one country can coerce or take from the other to improve its per capita standard of living. Increased trade or decreased military expenditures would generally benefit both sides. Total income is easier to consider as a constituent of potential struggles. Its relative size is important because it is so closely related to power. Furthermore, it is possible to alter the relative amounts of the gross national product (GNP) two neighboring countries have by taking some land and resources from one country and adding them to the other. This difference over land and resources was a basis for consensual conflict between Israel and its neighbors (Khouri 1968).

Status differences were another source of potential consensual conflicts between Israeli and Egyptian leaders and peoples. Thus, Egyptians, especially those most directly involved in military relations with Israel, felt a loss of status as a result of the military defeats of 1948, 1956 and 1967. Status was of particular importance to President Nasser, given his effort to be the leader of Egypt and also of the Arab alliance against Israel.

The final basis of consensual conflicts to be considered here pertains to power. Given the nature of the units involved and the nation-state system of which they are parts, the relative power of the adversaries constituted objective conflicts. Neither Israel nor its adversaries, the Arab Palestinians organized in the Palestine Liberation Organization (PLO) and the surrounding countries, had enough power relative to the other to feel secure, given the magnitude of the issues in contention between them. Each side's relative power could be increased only at the expense of the other within the context of a simple dyadic system.

The Israeli-Arab differences in religious, social, and political views were great, but they did not entail universal claims on each other. Yet many Israelis and Arabs feared the destruction of their way of life by the actions of the other. Value

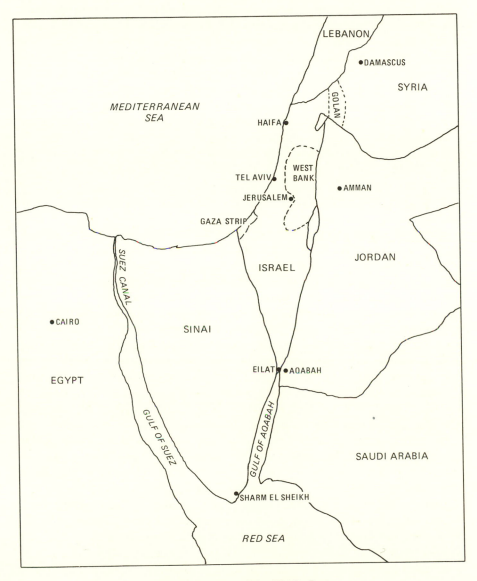

Figure 2.3 Map of the Middle East.

differences among Islam, Judaism, Western civilization, Zionism, nonalignment, and Arab traditions were alien to different sets of leaders and peoples among the potentially adversary groups.

The underlying conflicts between the Soviet and U.S. governments could be examined from the establishment of the Soviet government during the Russian Revolution of 1917. For our purposes here, we will focus attention on the 1960s. The United States was the dominant economic and military power and the leader of a coalition of other countries, organized as a counterforce to the Soviet Union. The Soviet government, too, was the leader of a coalition. In the early 1960s those coalitions were weakening and the tight bipolar world of the cold war of the 1950s was lessening: The French government was pursuing a somewhat independent policy, and the Chinese People's Republic was in the process of breaking away from the Soviet government. The military capability of the Soviet Union was increasing but, in strategic terms, was not yet equal to that of the United States.

In the 1960s, a number of disputes escalated and deescalated, including the Cuban missile crisis of 1962. By the end of the decade, the war in Vietnam had escalated and although the U.S. military forces were directly engaged in fighting against the North Vietnamese government, which the Soviet Union aided, the war was relatively isolated from other relations between the U.S. and Soviet governments.

The governments and peoples of the United States and the Soviet Union may have been more conscious of each other as standards of comparison for living standards, but, like Israel and its neighbors, gains were not likely to be seen as coming at the expense of the other. Differences in gross national product were less able to be altered at the expense of the other side than they were for Israel and the surrounding Arab countries. Control over other countries might, conceivably, affect trade and investment opportunities. Insofar as each major power is economically exploitative of territories it dominates, then the denial of such territories to the other side increases its wealth at the expense of the other side. Any assessment of wealth is complicated by the ambiguity about the composition of the adversaries. Is the Soviet Union pitted against the United States, the North Atlantic countries, or the capitalist world? The relative wealth of two sides in a potential conflict obviously varies with the composition of the two sides.

Objective consensual conflicts regarding status were present in the relationship between the United States and the Soviet Union. Being regarded as equals was important for Soviet leaders; U.S. leaders and government leaders in other countries generally did not accord the Soviet Union equality in status.

Power differences are fundamental issues between national governments. Within the nation-state system, governments and their constituencies generally regard military capability as paramount to maintaining autonomy. In the cold war period of the 1950s and early 1960s, the U.S. and Soviet governments tended to consider increases in the military and political power of one as resulting in decreases of the other. The possibility of mutual losses as a result of war emerged most sharply in conjunction with the 1962 Cuban missile crisis (Schlesinger

1965). The importance of entities that were nonaligned and would be independent of the U.S. and Soviet conflict was growing, but Soviet and U.S. government leaders still tended to regard the world system as primarily dyadic, with themselves as superpowers (Kissinger 1960).

Objective dissensual conflict was present between many segments of the Soviet and American societies. Not only did they have differing views associated with Marxism-Leninism and Communism or Americanism and capitalism, but many people espousing their views made universal claims (Kennan 1961). There were important similarities, however, among some elites in both countries (Angell 1964).

SUMMARY AND CONCLUSIONS

Objective conflicts have varying proportions of both consensual and dissensual issues. Neither consensus nor dissensus can underlie social conflicts, however, unless a set of related conditions are also present. Consensus underlies social conflict when there are bases for one or more parties to view the distribution of what is desired as unsatisfactory and to believe that they can reach a more satisfactory position at the expense of the other side. Dissensus underlies social conflicts when it is the source of incompatibility. This condition may arise from the requirements for social coordination or when the differences in values and beliefs are accompanied by other views that would lead one group to make unacceptable claims upon another.

In specific conflicts consensual and dissensual components are combined in varying proportions. Consensual elements may be more important to some segments of each party to a potential struggle than to others, as in the case of leaders compared to those in the rank and file. The proportions are also likely to vary as a fight runs its course.

As students of social conflicts, we should be sensitive to the objective conditions that underlie manifest conflicts and the variety of objective conflicts that may be part of what appears to be a single fight. This sensitivity should help us understand the likely course and outcome of specific conflicts. It should help us discern important differences within what might appear to be a single struggle.

This may mean that the "same" people engaging in conflict behavior may or may not be expressing the "same" underlying issue. Students demonstrating at a college may, for example, do so for a variety of underlying reasons. For some students in relations with some administrators, the issue is essentially consensual —a struggle over power and autonomy; while for other contending parties, dissensus about life styles is more central. Furthermore, there is the possibility that one party in the struggle misunderstands the goals that another is pursuing.

Even when partisans are struggling for the same goals, the underlying conflicts may be different for the many segments constituting each party. This is particularly apparent when we consider groups that are allied during a specific conflict.

For example, in the civil rights struggle for equal material well-being and power between blacks and whites in America, the underlying conflict may be viewed quite differently by the various groups struggling to that end. Consider even the variety of underlying bases for whites to be allied with blacks. For some there may be dissensual bases for the conflict with other whites: The commitment to values about equality is compelling. They feel that their own moral character is corrupted by being part of a system in which they are oppressing other humans, in which they can feel superior for no reason except belonging to a large social category by accident of birth. Other whites may agree that material well-being is a primary value but believe that their own material interests would best be served by adding the possible contribution blacks could make to the collective output. Finally, other whites may feel in ultimate agreement with whites and blacks about the value of power but believe that their political party or faction would have more power with the support of blacks as allies than they would by turning aside such support.

We have suggested a wide range of possible bases for social conflicts. This should sensitize us to the complexities of any particular struggle. The clinical diagnosis of a specific fight requires much detailed information, but that information must be combined with an understanding of the processes and conditions common to all kinds of social conflicts.

Thus far, we have considered the conditions that constitute objective conflicts. Clearly, the conditions are manifold and many different ones combine to underlie social conflicts. Not all potential conflicts are actualized. How objective conflicts become manifest is the topic of the next chapter. As we proceed, we shall see the implications of different kinds of objective conflicts in the way social conflicts emerge, how incompatible goals are pursued, and what the outcomes are.

BIBLIOGRAPHY

ALCOCK, NORMAN, Z. AND ALAN C. NEWCOMBE, "The Perception of National Power," *Journal of Conflict Resolution*, 14 (September 1970), 335–343.

ANGELL, ROBERT C., "Social Values and Foreign Policy of Soviet and American Elites," *Journal of Conflict Resolution*, 8 (December 1964), 329–385.

ARDREY, ROBERT, *The Territorial Imperative* (New York: Dell Pub. Co., Inc., 1966).

ARENDT, HANNAH, *On Revolution* (New York: Viking, 1965).

AUBERT, VIHELM, "Competition and Dissensus: Two Types of Conflict and Conflict Resolution," *Journal of Conflict Resolution*, 7 (March 1963), 26–42.

BECKER, HOWARD S., BLANCHE GEER, AND EVERETT C. HUGHES, *Making the Grade: The Academic Side of College Life* (New York: John Wiley, 1968).

BERKOWITZ, LEONARD, "The Frustration-Aggression Hypothesis Revisited," pp. 1–28 in Leonard Berkowitz (ed.), *Roots of Aggression* (New York: Lieber-Atherton, Inc., 1969).

BIRD, CAROLINE WITH SARA WELLES BRILLER, *Born Female: The High Cost of Keeping Women Down* (New York: D. McKay, 1968).

BLAUNER, ROBERT, *Alienation and Freedom: The Factory Worker and His Industry* (Chicago: The University of Chicago Press, 1964).

COLEMAN, JAMES, *Community Conflict* (New York: Free Press, 1957).

COSER, LEWIS A., *The Functions of Social Conflict* (New York: Free Press, 1956).

DAHRENDORF, RALF, *Class and Class Conflict in Industrial Society* (Stanford, Calif.: Stanford University Press, 1959).

DOLLARD, JOHN, *Caste and Class in A Southern Town* (New Haven, Conn.: Yale University Press, 1937).

DOLLARD, JOHN, LEONARD W. DOOB, NEAL E. MILLER, O. H. MOWRER, AND ROBERT R. SEARS, *Frustration and Aggression* (New Haven, Conn.: Yale University Press, 1939).

DOOB, MAURICE, *Soviet Economic Development Since 1917* (London: Routledge & Kegan Paul, 1948).

DURKHEIM, EMILE, *The Division of Labor in Society* (New York: Macmillan, 1933).

EISENSTADT, SAMUEL N., *From Generation to Generation* (New York: Free Press, 1956).

EPSTEIN, CYNTHIA FUCHS, *Woman's Place: Options and Limits in Professional Careers* (Berkeley: University of California Press, 1970).

ERSKINE, HAZEL, "The Polls: Women's Role," *Public Opinion Quarterly*, 35 (Summer 1971), 275–290.

FLACKS, RICHARD, "Social and Cultural Meanings of Student Revolt: Some Informal Comparative Observations," *Social Problems*, 17 (Winter 1970), 340–357.

FOOTE, NELSON N., "The Professionalization of Labor in Detroit," *The American Journal of Sociology*, 58 (January 1953), 371–380.

FREIDSON, ELIOT (ed.), *Student Government, Student Leaders, and the American College* (Philadelphia: United States National Student Association, 1955).

FREUD, SIGMUND, "Why War," pp. 13–30 in John Rickman (ed.), *Civilization: War and Death* (London: Hogarth Press, 1939). Originally published in 1932.

GURR, TED ROBERT, *Why Men Rebel* (Princeton, N.J.: Princeton University Press, 1970).

HILDENBRAND, GEORGE H., "American Unionism, Social Stratification, and Power," *The American Journal of Sociology*, 58 (January 1953), 381–390.

HODGE, ROBERT W., PAUL M. SIEGEL, AND PETER H. ROSSI, "Occupational Prestige in the United States: 1925–1963" in R. Bendix and S. M. Lipset (eds.), *Class, Status, and Power* (New York: Free Press, 1966).

HUNTINGTON, SAMUEL P., *Political Order in Changing Societies* (New Haven, Conn.: Yale University Press, 1968).

HUREWITZ, J. C., *Middle East Politics: The Military Dimension* (New York: Frederick A. Praeger, Inc., 1969).

JOHNSON, CHALMERS, *Revolutionary Change* (Boston: Little, Brown, 1966).

JOHNSON, CHARLES S., *Patterns of Negro Segregation* (New York: Harper & Row, Pub., 1943).

KELLER, SUZANNE, *Beyond the Ruling Class* (New York: Random House, 1963).

KENNAN, GEORGE F., *Russia and the West Under Lenin and Stalin* (Boston: Little, Brown, 1961).

KHOURI, FRED, J., *The Arab-Israeli Dilemma* (Syracuse, N.Y.: Syracuse University Press, 1968).

KISSINGER, HENRY A., *The Necessity for Choice: Prospects of American Foreign Policy* (New York: Harper & Row, Pub., 1960).

KNUDSEN, DEAN D., "The Declining Status of Women: Popular Myths and the Failure of Functionalist Thought," *Social Forces,* 48 (December 1969), 183–193.

KRIESBERG, LOUIS, *Social Inequality* (Englewood Cliffs, N.J.: Prentice-Hall, 1979).

———, "Interlocking Conflicts in the Middle East," pp. 99–118 in Louis Kriesberg (ed.), *Research in Social Movements, Conflicts and Change,* Vol. 3 (Greenwich, Conn.: JAI Press, 1980).

KRIESBERG, LOUIS, "Noncoercive Inducements in International Conflicts," *Peace and Change: A Journal of Peace Research,* September 1981.

LEVINE, ROBERT A. AND DONALD T. CAMPBELL, *Ethnocentrism: Theories of Conflict, Ethnic Attitudes, and Group Behavior* (New York: John Wiley, 1972).

LORENZ, KONRAD, *On Aggression,* translated by Marjorie Kerr Wilson (New York: Bantam, 1967). Originally published in 1963.

McGRATH, EARL J., *Should Students Share the Power?* (Philadelphia: Temple University Press, 1970).

MARX, KARL, "The Eighteenth Brumaire of Louis Bonaparte," pp. 436–525 in Robert C. Tucker (ed.), *The Marx-Engels Reader* (New York: W. W. Norton & Co., Inc., 1972). Originally published in 1852.

———, *Selected Writings in Sociology and Social History,* translated by T. B. Bottomore. T. B. Bottomore and M. Rubel (eds.). (New York: McGraw-Hill, 1964). Originally published in 1844–1873.

MATTHEWS, DONALD R., *The Social Background of Political Decision-Makers* (New York: Doubleday, 1954).

MEAD, MARGARET AND FRANCES BAGLEY KAPLAN, *American Women, The Report of the President's Commission on the Status of Women and other Publications of the Commission* (New York: Scribner's, 1965).

MILLETT, KATE, *Sexual Politics* (New York: Doubleday, 1970).

MYRDAL, GUNNAR, "A Parallel to the Negro Problem," pp. 1073–1078 in *An American Dilemma,* Appendix 5 (New York: Harper & Row, Pub., 1944).

NAGEL, STUART AND LENORE J. WEITZMAN, "Double Standard of Justice," *Society,* 9 (March 1972), 62–63.

PAIGE, JEFFERY M., *Agrarian Revolution: Social Movements and Export Agriculture in the Underdeveloped World* (New York: Free Press, 1975).

PARSONS, TALCOTT, *The Social System* (New York: Free Press, 1951).

———, "Youth in the Context of American Society," *Daedalus,* 91 (Winter 1962), 97–123.

PIVEN, FRANCES FOX AND RICHARD A. CLOWARD, *Poor People's Movements* (New York: Vintage, 1979).

RAINWATER, LEE (ed.), *Soul* (Chicago: Aldine, 1970).

REISS, ALBERT J., JR., *Occupations and Social Status* (New York: Free Press, 1961).

RIDDELL, DAVID S., "Social Self-Government: The Background of Theory and Practice in Yugoslav Socialism," *British Journal of Sociology,* 19 (March 1968), 47–75.

ROSSI, ALICE S., "Status of Women in Graduate Departments of Sociology," *The American Sociologist,* 5 (February 1970), 1–12.

Roszak, Betty, "The Human Continuum," pp. 297–306 in B. Roszak and T. Roszak (eds.), *Masculine/Feminine* (New York: Harper & Row, Pub., 1969).

Schlesinger, Arthur M., *A Thousand Days* (Boston: Houghton Mifflin Co., 1965).

Schulder, Diane B., "Does the Law Oppress Women?" pp. 139–157 in Robin Morgan (ed.), *Sisterhood Is Powerful* (New York: Vintage, 1970).

Shibutani, Tamotsu, *Society and Personality: An Interactionist Approach to Social Psychology* (Englewood Cliffs, N.J.: Prentice-Hall, Inc., 1961).

Siegfried, Andre, *America Comes of Age* (New York: Harcourt, Brace, and Co., 1927).

Stanley, Manfred, "Nature, Culture and Scarcity: Foreword to a Theoretical Synthesis," *American Sociological Review,* 33 (December 1968), 855–870.

Strodtbeck, Fred, Rita M. James, and Charles Hawkins, "Social Status in Jury Deliberations," *American Sociological Review,* 22 (December 1957), 713–719.

Sumner, William Graham, *Folkways* (Lexington, Mass.: Ginn, 1906).

Tetlow, Karin, "How Much Can a Person Make for a Job Like That?" *New York,* 5 (May 1972), 28–35.

Tinbergen, N., "On War and Peace in Animals and Man," *Science,* 160 (June 28, 1968), 1411–1418.

U.S. Bureau of the Census, *U. S. Census of Population: 1960 Subject Reports: Occupations by Earnings and Education.* Final Report PC (2)-7B (Washington, D.C.: U.S. Government Printing Office, 1963).

———, *Statistical Abstract of the United States: 1965,* 86th ed. (Washington, D.C.: U.S. Government Printing Office, 1965).

———, *Statistical Abstract of the United States: 1973,* 94th ed. (Washington, D.C.: U.S. Government Printing Office, 1973).

———, *Statistical Abstract of the United States: 1979,* 100th ed. (Washington, D.C.: U.S. Government Printing Office, 1979.

Weber, Max, *The Theory of Social and Economic Organization,* translated by A. M. Henderson and T. Parsons (New York: Oxford University Press, 1947).

———, *Wirtschaft und Gesellschaft* (Tübingen: J. C. B. Mohr, 1956). Originally published in 1921. (English translation: Guenther Roth and Claus Wittich (eds.), *Economy and Society,* 3 vols.). [New York: Bedminster Press, 1968].

Weisstein, Naomi, " 'Kinder, Kuche, Kirche' as Scientific Law: Psychology Constructs the Female," pp. 205–220 in Robin Morgan (ed.), *Sisterhood is Powerful* (New York: Vintage, 1970).

Westby, David L. and Richard G. Braungart, "Class and Politics in the Family Backgrounds of Student Political Activists," *American Sociological Review,* 31 (October 1966), 690–692.

Wood, James L. and Wing-Cheung Ng, "Socialization and Student Activism: Examination of a Relationship," in Louis Kriesberg (ed.), *Research in Social Movements, Conflicts and Change,* Vol. 3 (Greenwich, Conn.: JAI Press, 1980).

3

The Emergence
of Social Conflicts

For social conflicts to exist, groups of people must believe that they have incompatible goals. In this chapter we analyze what makes people have such beliefs. In the last chapter, we discerned circumstances that could and probably would lead to social conflicts. But most potential conflicts do not emerge into awareness. Despite all the reasons for social conflict, why do some, but not others, emerge?

For social conflicts to become manifest, three components are needed. First, the groups or parties to the conflict must be conscious of themselves as collective entities, separate from others. Second, one or more groups must be aggrieved with their position relative to other groups. Finally, they must think that they can reduce their dissatisfaction by another group's acting or being different; that is, they must have aims that involve another group's yielding what it would not otherwise yield. Before trying to explain how these subjective states emerge, we shall discuss each in more detail.

A group's self-awareness of being a collective entity in opposition to another group is formed and transformed in the course of a conflict. For example, class consciousness emerges from class struggle and ethnic identity from others' hostility and prejudice. Nevertheless, some awareness is necessary at the struggle's outset. Awareness may be expressed in social movements or in organizations within a social movement. We should keep in mind the problematic character of conflict groups. As noted in the first chapter, parties to a conflict may be more or less clearly bounded. The members of a group themselves determine that they are an entity with boundaries and, therefore, exclude some kinds of people and include others. Conceptions of collective self-identity, therefore, generally entail conceptions of other collectivities, as when class consciousness includes characterizations of class structure (Kriesberg 1979, pp. 302–313). Even in the case of nation-states, the parties should not be taken for granted. In a dispute between the United States and the Soviet Union, are the contending parties the two governments, the people supporting each government's goals, all the citizens of the two countries, or all the supporters of each side's general ideology? The mobilization of people from categories or quasi-groups into self-conscious groups that are in opposition to one another is a primary aspect of any social conflict. Without self-conscious groups, discontented persons may express their dissatisfaction individually but not engage in a social conflict. Discontented workers in a factory, for example, may be absent frequently or may leave after a short time on the job; such a factory would have a high absentee or turnover rate but not necesarily a high degree of social conflict.

The second component of a social conflict is that members of one or more groups have a grievance. As used here, grievance includes being dissatisfied, judging that dissatisfaction is unjustified, and believing it is correctable. Dissatisfaction entails members' feeling they have less than they want of a consensually valued resource or that the values they hold are not being adequately respected or supported by other groups. In order for such feelings to constitute a grievance, the inadequacy must be evaluated as unjust, and the members of the group must believe that they are entitled to more; the members must, therefore, have a standard by which they judge the adequacy of what they have. In addition, a grievance entails the belief that redress is possible, that people think they need not continue to suffer from the inadequacy. It means that they do not think that they have less than they deserve because of unalterable limits or because it is God's unshakable wish.

The third component of a social conflict is that the aggrieved conflict parties develop oppositional goals. These can be more or less inchoate. What is essential is that one group believes that another collectivity is responsible for its grievances. The aggrieved party believes that if another group would act or be different, its dissatisfaction would be lessened. Its leaders may even formulate specific demands of another group. Whether clearly formulated or not, the other group must reject the claims of responsibility and the implications that it behave differently or change its ways of thinking. In other words, the parties must have incompatible goals. We discuss the formulation, transformation, and implications of different conflicting aims in other chapters of the book. At this time we will outline the major kinds of aims.

We can distinguish two sets of conflicting goals: to terminate the relationship of the groups or to alter it. The aim of terminating a relationship may involve either withdrawal or the obliteration of the other unit. Thus, in the case of consensual conflicts a group may seek to flee from the claims made by another or may hope to destroy or exterminate the other party as an adversary (to do so may mean the destruction of it as an organized group or killing all its members or its leading segments). In the case of dissensual conflicts, the relationship may be terminated by secession or by converting the other party so that it no longer exists as a dissensual conflict group.

More commonly the goal of a conflict group is to alter the relationship with its adversary. The alteration may involve changing the policy of the adversary, changing who occupies certain positions in the relationship, or changing the structure of the relationship (Tilly 1978). Seeking to change the adversary's policy may entail changes toward groups outside the primary conflict, as when the U.S. government tried in 1980 to change the Soviet government's policy in Afghanistan. It may also entail changes in policies among the adversaries in the primary conflict, as happens when organized workers strive for wage increases from their employers. Such alterations in policy are generally over the allocation of resources that are divisible and, hence, compromises are possible and even likely. Efforts to change the policy of the adversary are frequent in consensual issues but also occur in dissensual conflicts (when, for example, a minority group is seeking such a civil right as the freedom to practice its religion without hindrance from the majority).

Seeking to change the people who occupy particular positions is more frequently associated with consensual issues. One group might wish to occupy the dominant positions and displace the current holders in a palace revolution, for example, or they may seek acceptance as legitimate participants in general decision making. A variety of goals involve changing the structure of the relationship in consensual conflicts. As an example, a revolutionary group may seek to end private ownership of large agricultural estates. Such goals are unitary and not easily divisible and are, therefore, less subject to compromise (Paige 1975). An adversary seeking to induce others in the total social system to conform to some of its religious or ideological views, however, exemplifies changing their relationship and is a dissensual conflict.

In this chapter we are primarily concerned with understanding how conflict groups become conscious of themselves as groups, come to perceive that they have grievances, and formulate goals that would lessen their dissatisfaction at the apparent expense of another party. These three components of a manifest conflict are highly interdependent. Who we are, what we have to complain about, and who is to blame for it are all related and help determine one another. For example, if we are women and subjugated, it must be men doing the subjugation. If capitalists are in charge and we are underpaid, we are proletarians.

We must account for variations in these subjective states in order to explain changes in the intensity and extensiveness of conflicts. To account for the alterations in subjective states, we study variations in the proportion of persons within a given category who are organized into conflict groups and the proportion who are mobilized to support the goals of the organizations; we study variations in how intense the feeling of grievance is among the members of the movement or organizations in conflict; and, finally, we consider variations in the radicalism of the aims pursued. That is, are the goals relatively minor modifications of the current relationship or a fundamental restructuring? The measure of this is likely to be how the other side regards the goals.

The bases for consensual and dissensual issues help account for the extent and intensity of manifest conflicts. But they cannot provide a complete explanation. Additional factors must be introduced: (1) the characteristics of the units, (2) the relations between adversaries, and (3) the adversaries' environment or context. As we discuss each set of factors we will try to see how they relate to the conditions underlying conflict to produce or not produce manifest conflicts.

We depend upon empirical evidence to support the contention that a particular condition makes conflict more or less likely or more or less intense and radical. The evidence, however, is more available about the conflict behavior of units than about their subjective states. Yet the state of mind that defines the existence of a social conflict may not be expressed in conflict behavior. As we shall see in the next chapter, still other factors must be taken into account to explain how parties in conflict conduct their struggle. We should hesitate, therefore, to test the ideas about values and beliefs by referring to conduct rather than direct measures of what people are thinking and feeling.

UNIT CHARACTERISTICS

It might be argued that whether or not a group enters into conflict with another depends entirely on their interrelationship. Alternatively, it might be contended that some units, or their members, are basically aggressive or hostile and such characteristics account for social conflicts. On the whole, however, we emphasize the relationship between parties as the explanation for their disputes. But we also need to recognize the role of internal or domestic factors that affect the emergence of conflicts.

Collective Identity

We begin considering unit factors by examining how characteristics of the people in a social category affect the likelihood that they (or some of them) come to view themselves as having a collective identity. What about people leads them to think that they share a common fate and that they have more in common with one another than with members of other social categories?

A prerequisite for a sense of common identity is communication among the members of the category. Insofar as communication among members is hindered while communication with nonmembers is not, so is the likelihood that the development of a sense of common identity and collective identity will be hindered. Many factors affect the ease of communication. The proximity and density of the members of a category, their absolute number, the social and nonsocial barriers between them, and the social and technical skills the members possess all affect the rate of communication (Kriesberg 1979, pp. 305–313).

The factors that bring persons of a social category into large concentrations facilitate their communication with one another and the development of common perspectives. For example, industrial employment in large factories provides such opportunities; in czarist Russia although the industrial proletariat was small, "it was disproportionately concentrated both in large-scale industrial enterprises and in major industrial centers" (Skocpol 1979, p. 92); this contributed to the emergence of the 1917 Russian Revolution. Similarly, the concentration of ethnic or racial groups in particular regions or parts of a city provides the opportunity for developing shared experiences and recognizing that they are shared. Less physically concentrated people are handicapped in developing collective self-awareness. For example, women in this society are not concentrated in any particular locations.

Communication does not depend entirely on physical distance. Access to the technology of communication and the possession of the social skills for communication are more critical. Social categories that have members with such resources more readily develop collective self-consciousness and express this awareness in organizational form. One of the factors that accounts for the order in which trade unions have been established is the ability of the workers to communicate and organize; printers, shoemakers, and other skilled craftsmen were the first to form trade unions.

Significantly, when we consider consensual conflicts it is those who have more status, power, or material wealth who are also most likely to have more of the requisite skills and resources for communication (Parkin 1971). Furthermore, those with more power may use their power to limit the development of communication skills in the groups with less power. For example, in the United States education had been forbidden to or limited for slaves, and even since slavery, American blacks have not had equal access to education. Women, too, have not had equal educational opportunities (Flexner 1959, pp. 23–40).

The availability of the means of extensive communication also favors the dominant groups. Thus, the mass media generally convey the perspectives of whites, of males, and of upper-white-collar occupations (see, for example, Johnson, Sears, and McConahay 1971). Similarly, within organizations, newspapers are often controlled by the dominant groups in the organization (witness the traditional pattern of control even over student-run college publications). Members of subdominant categories, then, have less opportunity to develop a collective identity. In the case of dissensual conflicts, however, the restrictions of media often help the growth of in-group solidarity. This feeling of solidarity may be reinforced by language differences, like those between societies or between ethnic groups within a society.

Communication is also affected by the size of the units under consideration—but in contradictory ways. The larger the unit, the greater is the difficulty to reach common understandings and a sense of common interest. The chances are better, however, that interaction in larger units will be contained within the unit rather than with outside persons, as illustrated by the finding that the ratio of intrasociety transactions to intersociety transactions increases with the population size of societies (Sawyer 1967).

Homogeneity of the members in a social category tends to facilitate communication and the growth of a sense of solidarity and common fate (Hodge and Treiman 1968). For example, Landecker (1963) found that class consciousness was more frequent among persons with high status crystallization than among those with low status crystallization. One of the frequently observed difficulties in the formation of worker solidarity in the form of trade union membership or of class consciousness in the United States has been the extensive immigration and ethnic heterogeneity of the American workers (Perlman 1928, pp. 162–169; Bok and Dunlop 1970, p. 30). This may also be seen in variations among different occupational groups or within organizations. For example, in a study of teachers and administrators in twenty-eight high schools, it was found that incidents of disputes among teachers were correlated with heterogeneity of the faculty (Corwin 1969). The occupational differentiation among workers also hinders the development of working class solidarity (Form 1976).

Solidarity among women as a conflict group is also handicapped by their heterogeneity. Not only do they have the diversity of men in terms of ethnicity, region, and occupation, but their marital status and their husband's positions have great importance to them as well. In dissensual conflicts some homogeneity in values must exist within each of the conflict groups, but it may be relatively trivial compared to the differences within and the similarities across group lines. Groups in dissensual conflict often seek to create a homogeneity based upon past experience. National and ethnic groups emphasize, therefore, a common historical origin or basic experience that distinguishes them from nonmembers.

The boundedness and degree of organization of the category affect the growth of group solidarity. The more clear and unchanging are the boundaries of a social category, the more likely are its members to develop a sense of common fate. Members of a caste are more likely (everything else being equal) to think of themselves as a collective group with a common interest than are members of a social class. Social categories based upon ascribed and unchanging status, such as race or sex, are conducive to solidarity. We have already noted some, however, and will note additional factors associated with lower rank that operate in a contrary direction. National societies are highly bounded and internally organized, which helps explain why their members have a relatively high sense of common interest and solidarity with their compatriots.

Networks are crucial in the development of collective identity in conflict entities (Oberschall 1973; Tilly 1978). People within each are linked through many interconnected groups. These preexisting groups facilitate mobilization as the news of emerging contention spreads along interpersonal channels. Persons in churches, trade unions, informal friendship networks, and so on can be more readily joined together than isolated persons or persons in another set of networks. Groups that were allied in previous fights can be rallied against former adversaries, even as new divisive issues arise (Leahy and Mazur 1978).

The more highly interdependent and integrated are the members of a category, the more likely they are to see themselves as a collectivity with common interests. This self-image can be seen in variations among members of different occupations (see, for example, Kriesberg 1953; Seidman, London, Karsh, and Tagliacozzo 1958). Miners, for example, are vitally interdependent in their work activities and historically have had a high sense of solidarity compared to other occupational groups (Gouldner 1954). Of course, the solidarity of the miners is reinforced by many factors, such as isolation and concentration.

Finally, the more highly organized the group is and the more it precedes and transcends a particular conflict, the less problematic is mobilizing support for any particular conflict. In many ways, self-consciousness of the group is less important; it can be taken for granted. Thus, in conflicts between established conflict groups (for example, governments or trade unions), acquiescence or support of a constituency is generally assumed.

Sense of Grievance

The aspect of social conflict that has received the most attention among students of conflict is the degree of discontent or dissatisfaction among the members of a partisan group. This is understandable. When a group pursues an aim that is incompatible with another group's desired position, it seems natural to ask what is making the group do that and to look for the answer in the members' dissatisfaction. Even if that dissatisfaction is not a comprehensive explanation for the emergence of social conflicts, it is an essential element.

The sense of grievance must reside among the members of one, or both, adversary groups, but the sources of the grievance may reside in the relations of the two parties in contention, in their environment, or in the characteristics of the members themselves. We will consider the third source first. The analytic view of a sense of grievance is that it entails people's having less than they think they should have and conceivably could have. Stated this generally, the formulation is appropriate for dissensual conflicts as well as consensual ones. But, in discussing and illustrating the sources of the discrepancies, we concentrate upon consensual conflicts.

It might seem reasonable that feelings of grievance or discontent are at the opposite end of a continuum from happiness or a sense of well being. Research has revealed the inaccuracy of this idea (Bradburn 1969; Bradburn and Caplovitz, 1965). The research indicates that self-assessed happiness or well being is based upon the balance of positive and negative feelings. Furthermore, positive and negative feelings are not necessarily associated with each other; that is, a person may have a lot of both, a lot of one and little of the other, or little of either. In addition some factors contribute to satisfying or positive feelings, while others contribute to negative or dissatisfying ones.

These findings suggest that we should not interpret indicators of satisfaction or dissatisfaction alone as the measure of a general sense of grievance or level of discontent. For a particular social conflict, however, specific dissatisfactions probably have special pertinence. Unfortunately, there is little research or even speculation about the components and structure of feelings of discontent as an aspect of social conflict. The complexities are mentioned here because they can help to reconcile what otherwise would be inconsistent findings.

There are several formulations of the bases of a sense of inequity (Goodman and Friedman 1971; Homans 1961). We will discuss three approaches to sources of discontent. The first approach emphasizes the absolute magnitude of the deprivation the members of a group endure and the number of spheres in which the people are deprived (Dahrendorf 1959). The second approach stresses the inconsistent ranks at which people perform or appear among different ranking systems (Lenski 1954; Goffman 1957). The third approach emphasizes the changes over time in what people have or think they should have (Gurr 1970; Davies 1962).

Deprivation. According to the deprivation approach, there is sufficient agreement in consensual struggles that the more deprived people are, the worse they feel. They do not need any particular insight to know that they are deprived; lacking power or material resources is inherently undesirable (Blau 1964; Dahrendorf 1959). In any case, other groups of people are readily available for comparison; reference groups can always be found. The important corollary of this idea is that people who are low ranking in several dimensions are more deprived, and feel that they are, than are persons who are high in some ways even if they are low in others.

There are additional reasons why we might expect that insofar as groups are deprived, and uniformly so, they will be dissatisfied. First, the homogeneity of the members of the group facilitates their interaction and the likelihood that they view themselves as a collective entity.

In addition, if members of a category do not share other positions with persons in adversary groups, conflict lines will be superimposed. Instead of being bound together by cross-cutting ties, they will find that each conflict issue reinforces the other. Feelings of dissatisfaction will not be muted. Suppose all poor people live in one region of the country, are of the same low status ethnicity, and have little political power. Then, in the event that a conflict along income lines should arise, all the other bases of cleavage would be drawn into the struggle. If these various categories were not superimposed, then people of low income might be of different ethnic, regional, or political positions and have ties, based on friendship or calculative interest, with people who see them as allies at another time, on another issue.

Furthermore, persons who are deprived in one sphere, without satisfactory redress, tend to generalize their dissatisfaction from one area of discontent to another. They have fewer compensating satisfactions. In short, the more deprived people are, the more likely are they to have general feelings of frustration.

On the basis of these arguments, we expect that lower ranking persons will be more likely to be dissatisfied and to feel their dissatisfaction more intensely than higher ranking persons. There is evidence consistent with these expectations. Inkeles (1960) reviewed data from many societies and found that persons of lower occupational or economic levels tend to be generally dissatisfied as indicated by responses to several different kinds of questions. Similarly, occupational studies generally find that the lower the prestige, income, or work autonomy of an occupation, the more likely are its incumbents to be dissatisfied with it and wish to leave it (see, for example, Blauner 1964; Friedmann and Havighurst 1954).

We also expect that the more spheres in which people are ranked low, the more likely they are to feel dissatisfied. In studies of happiness the findings generally indicate that education and income are each directly related to being happy and to having a higher ratio of positive to negative feeling (Bradburn 1969, p. 95; Bradburn and Caplovitz 1965, pp. 10–11). Furthermore, these two variables generally have cumulative effects.

There are other reasons, however, to expect that greater deprivation is not directly related to greater sense of grievance. First, people who rank low on a consensually valued dimension tend to think poorly of themselves and wish to avoid identifying themselves in terms of that dimension. They would, therefore, avoid interacting with others similarly placed or at least avoid making any collective identification. The absence of solidarity, then, interferes with collectively recognized and experienced dissatisfaction.

If deprivation is severe, persons will be preoccupied with the day-to-day private efforts at coping rather than with developing shared discontent. Even moderate deprivation can be mentally restricting. Buchanan and Cantril (1953, pp. 20–22) in a public opinion study in nine countries found that workers in comparison with middle-class respondents were less likely to identify with persons of their nation not of their own class and less likely to identify with persons of their own class in other countries. Related to this finding is the fact that if deprivation is severe the deprived tend to accommodate to the deprivation. This accommodation may take the form of suppression and denial of hostile feelings and of placating and ingratiating behavior (Karon 1958; Parker and Kleiner 1970). These reactions do not aid in the development of a collective sense of grievance. Another related point deserves mention. Severe deprivation may make people despair of changing the conditions, and, as an accommodation to such despair, even the self-recognition of collective discontent may not occur. All these arguments indicate that the issues in contention, the stage in the course of a struggle, and other aspects of social conflict must be taken into account to assess the impact of deprivation.

Another apparent difficulty with the degree of deprivation as an explanation of discontent must be considered. In many struggles the party that seems to initiate pursuit of contentious goals is the relatively advantaged party. It is the stronger, the richer, or the higher status group that seeks an increasingly unequal distribution of what is consensually valued. It may be that these groups are not so much more discontented than the others but are more able to pursue their desires. We need to consider other possible sources of discontent and their consequences before making a judgment on this matter.

Rank Disequilibrium. Another major theme in contemporary discussions of sources of discontent is rank disequilibrium, status inconsistency, or rank incongruence. The idea is that persons who are high in some rank dimensions and low in others will be particularly dissatisfied. There are several reasons offered for this. First, it is argued that people within social systems tend to have approximately equivalent ranks in different hierarchies; therefore, a person who is high on some ranks and low on others is odd, is treated as odd, and feels odd. Social interaction is uncomfortable, and this discomfort is communicated to the persons with inconsistent ranks (Hughes 1944; Lenski 1954). Consequently, rank disequilibrium is experienced as a source of strain.

This strain is compounded by the tendency of others to try to relate to people in disequilibrium in terms of their low ranks and the persons in disequilibrium themselves to relate to others in terms of their high ranks (Galtung 1964). This kind of ranking might be seen in a male worker "putting down" a woman supervisor for being just a woman and the supervisor treating the worker as just a subordinate. Relations among workers in restaurants abound in such problems (Whyte 1948). Note that these strains can be diffuse and, hence, relatively easily displaced from one target to another. Such strain, then, can be the source of unrealistic conflicts (Lipset and Raab 1970).

The third major reason that status inconsistency is a source of grievance is that it makes people feel that their low rank is particularly objectionable. This feeling is partly because people treat them in terms of their low rank when that is not the major way they see themselves. It is also the case because if they use the high rank as a reference or comparison level, the low rank is more objectionable than if they used the low rank as the reference level. The low rank is also particularly grievous because the high rank provides a claim for an equal level on that ranking. Moreover, the high rank makes it credible that the same level be attained on other ranking dimensions. As noted earlier, having less than people would like is not enough to make a grievance; people must also think that it is possible for them to have what they think they should have.

A final consideration deserves noting. If people have high ranks along some dimensions, they are likely to have resources and skills that give them reason to think that they might alter their circumstances, at least compared to those who are uniformly deprived. The sense of competence or possible efficacy would make it easier for persons to admit, recognize, and collectively acknowledge their dissatisfaction.

Not all patterns of rank incongruencies have the same consequences. Thus, persons ranked high on ascribed dimensions (for example, ethnicity) or dimensions that are considered investments (such as, education) but low on achieved or reward dimensions (for example, occupational status or income) may be called underrewarded. They will experience failure and disappointment (Jackson 1962; Geschwender 1967). They are likely to feel anger. On the other hand, persons ranked low on ascribed or investment dimensions and high on achieved or reward dimensions should feel a sense of success and not be discontented; but some may feel guilt.

There is evidence consistent with these arguments. Geschwender (1968) studied unrest among male manual workers; unrest was indicated by questions about job satisfaction, neighborhood satisfaction, participation in voluntary associations, and several other activities. He found that those with inconsistent ranks who were underrewarded tended to exhibit symptoms of individual unrest. Similarly, there is some indication from the happiness studies that other persons with high education but low income are less likely to be happy than one would expect from a simple additive model (Bradburn 1969, p. 96; Bradburn and Caplovitz 1965, pp. 10–11). Presumably among young persons the possibility of raising their income to the appropriate level for their education is viewed as still available. The concept of relative deprivation and reference groups is related to another specification of rank disequilibrium (Hyman 1942; Merton and Kitt 1950; Runciman 1966), namely, that people judge how well they are doing by reference to some groups to which they may or may not belong. This sphere of reference is applicable to any explanation of a sense of grievance since that depends upon a discrepancy between what people think they should have and what they do have.

The idea's particular relevance for rank disequilibrium can be briefly noted. Each status category to which people belong can serve as a reference group. The basic difficulty with reference group theory is that it does not tell us which of the many possible groups will be selected as the reference group. Thus, among status inconsistents, people could choose a high status as their reference and feel deprived, but it is also possible for them to choose a low rank and, using that as a standard, feel relatively well off. Analysts of status inconsistency usually presume that people choose their high ranks as standards, and that is why those with inconsistent ranks would generally be more dissatisfied than those with consistent ranks. Other students of the matter argue that statuses that entail investments serve as the standard. Another line of reasoning stresses that certain statuses have particular importance in each society or group and are the "master" status (Hughes 1944). In American society occupation is salient, and we use it to locate each other socially. Consequently, we would expect that a person would use his or her occupation as the standard of reference. Thus, the manual/nonmanual occupational distinction is a fundamental one in this society; the distinction is a kind of boundary behind which each group conducts important social relations. Assessments of income or of work role are made relative to oneself and one's friends as manual workers. Therefore, high income manual workers might be expected to think they are not doing so badly compared to others who are socially relevant to them and, hence, would be satisfied. There is evidence that lends credence to this reasoning (Runciman 1966, pp. 188–208; Bradburn 1969, p. 196). It might be expected by the same reasoning that low-income white-collar workers would be especially dissatisfied. The same studies do not indicate any such effect. Apparently these conditions are relevant to satisfactions but not (at least in the same manner) to dissatisfactions.

Although the reasoning by which status inconsistency is a source of discontent and, therefore, a basis for the emergence of social conflict seems plausible and evidence can be cited in support of it, there are methodological and substantive considerations that limit its utility as an explanation for the emergence of social conflict. First, consider an important methodological issue, called the identification problem by Blalock (1967a and 1967b). The difficulty arises from trying to distinguish an interaction effect from an additive effect of two or more variables. In an additive model each variable affects the dependent variable independently of the other; hence one can simply add together their effects. In an interaction model the effects of each variable depend on the other. The difficulty may be more easily understood by discussing some illustrative (and hypothetical) data.

Suppose we were interested in the effects of earnings and job autonomy on work satisfaction. We might expect that high job autonomy and high earnings would each provide for work satisfaction, regardless of the other. In that case, we would expect results, such as the hypothetical data presented in Table 3.1. The sums of the consistent and inconsistent cells each add up to 100; they are equal and this indicates no interaction effects. Suppose, however, that the results are those shown in Table 3.2. Now the sum of the inconsistent cells (60 + 70) is greater than the sum of the consistent cells (20 + 80). This indicates that an interaction effect does exist. We might interpret Table 3.2 to mean that being high on either earnings or autonomy and being low on the other dimension is about as dissatisfying as being low on both because the discrepancy between being high in one way and low in another is very distressing; this interpretation is in accord with the general discussion of status inconsistency.

The identification problem arises because other possible combinations of additive and interaction effects could produce the table. Thus, in Table 3.3, we can

TABLE 3.1 Percent Feeling Dissatisfied

| Power of | Earnings | |
Autonomy	High	Low
High	20	50
Low	50	80

TABLE 3.2 Percent Feeling Dissatisfied

| Power of | Earnings | |
Autonomy	High	Low
High	20	60
5 Low	70	80

see a variety of possible interaction effects. The significance and meaning of the main effects of the independent variables also vary depending on the presumed contribution made by the interaction of the two variables. In the case of combination C, for example, it appears that earnings do not markedly affect satisfaction and that persons with high power and low earnings are particularly outraged—presumably feeling that they are particularly underpaid given their power.

Clearly, an infinite number of possible combinations of additive and interaction components can be constructed to yield the hypothetical results shown. Several implications follow from this identification problem. First, it demonstrates that contentions between deprivation and status inconsistency approaches should not be thought of as mutually exclusive. Empirical findings can be consistent with both ideas at the same time. Second, the identification problem cannot be solved by any methodological device (Hornung 1972). It is necessary to develop precise theoretical statements about the impact of each variable. That is, in order to argue that there is an interaction effect one should be very clear about the expected main effects of the independent variables under specific conditions and at particular magnitudes. Third, since there is considerable ambiguity about interpreting any single set of empirical findings, it is advisable to choose the simpler explanation as long as it is plausible; this is the additive model (Blalock 1967b). Another alternative is to develop a comprehensive set of specific interpretations and consider a wide variety of empirical findings to assess the usefulness of the set of interpretations. It is this latter course that we will be trying to chart.

So far in discussing the limits to status inconsistency as an explanation for the emergence of social conflict, we have only considered the ambiguity of interpreting empirical findings. There also are substantive reasons for expecting that rank disequilibrium does not account for the emergence of conflict or more specifically a sense of grievance. Some of the reasons are the ones offered to explain why consistent deprivation can be a basis for discontent. First, being high in some hierarchies could compensate for being low in others. Second, belonging to incongruent statuses subjects people to inconsistent claims and directives. A general reaction to such cross pressures is to reduce attention and withdraw interest from the issues in contention among the status groups (Lazarsfeld, Berelson, and

TABLE 3.3 **Results and Possible Components**

				Possible Components					
		Results			Additive			Interaction	
	H	L							
H	20	60	=	20	50	+	0	10	A
L	70	80		50	80		20	0	
			=	20	40	+	0	20	B
				60	80		10	0	
			=	20	30	+	0	30	C
				70	80		0	0	

Gaudet 1944; Kriesberg 1949). This may have more relevance for expressing the grievance or in formulating conflicting objectives, but lack of certainty in these areas might also dampen self-acknowledgment of discontent. Finally, experiencing rank disequilibrium could result in feelings of self-inadequacy or failure rather than in a grievance directed at another group. Thus, Jackson (1962, p. 476) found that "persons whose inconsistency is due to high racial-ethnic status and low occupational or educational status tend to respond to their stress" with high levels of psycho-physiological symptoms. These inconsistents are "underrewarded" and would be expected to be dissatisfied. Worrying and having symptoms of anxiety are related to dissatisfaction but as such do not seem to be a direct stimulus for collectively defined grievances.

In considering deprivation and rank disequilibrium we presented evidence that each is the basis for the feelings of discontent that are components of a conflict situation, but we also saw that these factors have contradictory implications. Before proceeding further, it is advisable to try to integrate the two sets of ideas. The integration is tentative, but it will serve as a basis for elaboration.

On the whole, within a common culture we expect that persons will feel dissatisfied in relation to the number of areas in which they are deprived or have low ranks. The additive model is assumed to be fundamental for discontent. Empirical comparisons of additive and interaction models have usually been consistent with the additive model; it seems to explain more of the variance in the dependent variable than the interaction model (Treiman 1966; Lauman and Segal 1971; Laslett 1971; Goffman 1957; Hornung 1972). Certain kinds of inconsistencies under specific conditions have interacting effects upon particular aspects of the sense of grievance. The belief in the ability to improve one's condition, for example, is supported by being high in some regards or at least not being generally very low.

Landecker (1970) has suggested that rank disequilibrium is a source of disturbance in the small group where it affects face-to-face interaction, but in a larger social system, such as the society at large, the resulting cross-cutting ties would be integrative. It is true that the presumption of strain resulting from status inconsistencies is dependent upon certain kinds of social interactions. The gross measures of status inconsistency at a societal level include many people who normally do not experience strain as a result of "status inconsistency." Status categories are necessarily very broad at the societal level. A wide range exists within each status category and many persons, therefore, do not experience status inconsistency in day-to-day social interaction. Within organizations, status categories are narrower; measurement of inconsistency should be closer to incumbents' experiences. The effects of status inconsistency, then, should be greater within organizations than within entire societies.

Related to the size of the unit being studied is the nature of the boundaries among the status categories within the unit. For example, the distinction between manual and nonmanual workers is still socially significant in Great Britain, and this distinction affects the patterns of social interaction and the bases of reference (Parkin 1971). These observations are pertinent to the findings that higher paid manual workers in England are somewhat more satisfied with their income than one would expect on a purely additive model (Runciman 1966). We should also expect that higher income American blacks would tend to be more satisfied with their income than equally well off whites or poorer blacks, but it is not so. At every income level, blacks are more dissatisfied than whites (see Table 3.4). It is possible that the results are partly due to blacks' having less income than whites within each broad income stratum. Indeed within much narrower income categories, blacks are not consistently more likely to be dissatisfied than whites. In addition, perhaps the blacks are using the whites as a comparison group and given their own education, occupation, and other status characteristics at each income level, evaluate their income as inequitable (see Table 2.3). They do not seem to evaluate themselves only within the black community and say in effect, "I'm doing fine for a black."

Changes in Attainments and Expectations. The third major source of grievance arises from a decline in what people have or an increase in what they expect. Dissatisfaction rises as people have less of what they feel they should and could have. This discrepancy is argued to be the fundamental basis for revolts and other kinds of turmoil and violence (see, for example, Gurr 1970; Feierabend, Feierabend, and Nesvold 1969; Davies 1962; Tanter and Midlarsky 1967). We need to elaborate on this deceptively simple idea.

A variety of changes in either expectations or attainments can increase an unwanted discrepancy between them. Figure 3.1 presents the basic types. Type A is the most obvious; the members of a society or an organization or a segment of a society have decreasing amounts of what they previously possessed. This might be due to a bad growing season and a poor harvest, or it might be due to another group's reducing the autonomy, income, or honor of these people. The

TABLE 3.4 Percent Dissatisfied with Family Income, by Race and Income, 1980

| *Annual* | *Race* | |
Family Income	White	Black
$ 7,999 or less	34 (266)	44 (61)
8,000 to $14,999	35 (258)	50 (28)
15,000 to $24,999	26 (384)	43 (21)
25,000 or more	10 (310)	47 (15)

Question: "On the whole, would you say you are satisfied or dissatisfied with your family income?"

Source: National U.S. sample survey, conducted by the National Opinion Research Center.

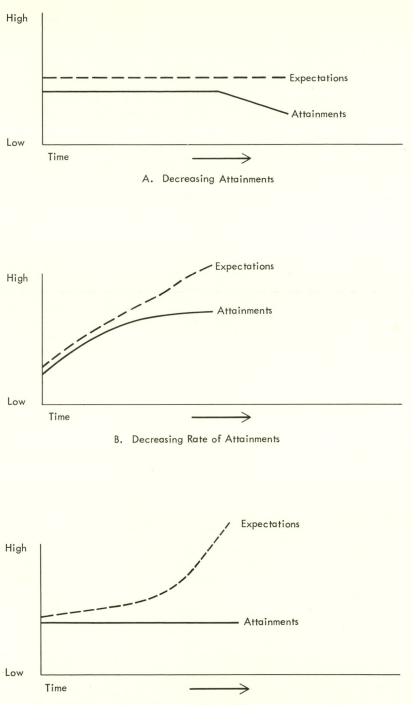

A. Decreasing Attainments

B. Decreasing Rate of Attainments

C. Rising Expectations

Figure 3.1 Types of Changes.

expectations persist, at least for a while. Having attained a certain level, that level is felt to be appropriate, desirable, and certainly attainable. A *fall in actual attainments,* then, would produce dissatisfaction and a sense of grievance.

Type B is stressed in many studies of revolutions (see, for example, Davies 1962; Brinton 1955). It accounts for revolutions' occurring not after a long period of constantly bad times but as conditions improve. It is *improving conditions which then deteriorate* that particularly create a sense of grievance. Expectations continue to advance at the rate that past experience dictates. Even a leveling off of progress, but certainly a fall in attainments, is experienced as a deprivation. This line of reasoning is appropriate to precipitants of conflict as well as to general discontent underlying a social conflict. Thus, the precipitating incident for the student protest at the Berkeley, California, campus in 1964 was the university administration's decision to forbid the continued use of an area then being used for political activities (Lipset and Wolin 1965).

The third source of discrepancy arising from changes in expectations and attainments, type C, is *rising expectations.* For a variety of reasons, people may raise their expectations about what they could and should have and hence discover that what they have is intolerably inadequate. The phrase "revolution of rising expectations" refers to this idea particularly in regard to economically underdeveloped countries. The peoples in these societies become increasingly dissatisfied with their conditions as they become familiar with what is available to some people and what people in economically advanced societies already have. Within every society leaders may promise gains and even begin programs that raise expectations, which are then unmet. For example, in the United States, the expectations of the blacks and of the poor were raised in regard to racial equality and to the ending of poverty by federal governmental actions and words in the early 1960s.

Evidence for these arguments is indirect. Studies have related revolutionary efforts, violence, or domestic turmoil to changes in previous conditions; the feelings of dissatisfaction and of grievance are inferred (Snyder 1979). We have already seen that dissatisfaction can arise from other sources than changes in attainments or expectations, and dissatisfaction may not always be expressed in conflict behavior or in coercion. Even if groups are pursuing conflicting goals, they may seek to pursue them by noncoercive means or through nonviolent coercion. The emergence of a conflict relationship and a group's choice of how to pursue its aims depend on many other factors than feelings of dissatisfaction and having a grievance. Finally, conflict behavior may be undertaken, not because dissatisfaction has grown, but because redress seems feasible.

Changes in expectations and conditions have limits as explanations of discontent leading to conflict behavior. First, poor conditions may be made endurable by the promise of improvements in the future. The raised expectations of a glorious future often have made people willing to accept current sacrifices. It is also conceivable that if conditions have been improving, people are more able to absorb a setback with less bitterness than they would a more consistently deprivational condition. Under still other circumstances, a new deprivation may be experienced as a failure that induces guilt or self-hate such that an outwardly directed grievance does not even emerge. Or, the deprivation may lessen positive feelings and yet not increase negative ones (Bradburn 1969), which, in balance, would make people feel less happy, but not appreciably raise the level of conflict-relevant discontent. Finally, the improvement of conditions may be large enough to satisfy rather than intensify appetites. For example, European immigrants found American industrial employment much better than their previous conditions and were, therefore, much less dissatisfied than American-born workers (Ellsworth 1952).

These possibilities indicate that the level of deprivation and the degree of equilibrium among different ranks affect how changes in attainments and expectations are related to conflict-relevant grievances. For example, a fall in economic well being from an already low level may impose such severe burdens that expectations quickly fall also. If high levels in other rank systems were sustained, however, the reaction to the fall in that sphere might be very great.

This discussion of sources of discontent suggests that we could find reasons for any group anywhere to be dissatisfied. And, as a matter of fact, everybody can report grievances. No one and no group can be without any. In order for grievances to be pertinent to the emergence of social conflicts the discontent must be intense, shared by a significant number of persons, and channeled into the pursuit of an end that is opposed by some other social group.

Discontent varies in intensity. It may be useful to assume that simple deprivation is the best predictor of the intensity of feeling dissatisfied. But expressing such dissatisfaction depends on the belief that improvement is possible. It is in this regard that status inconsistency, relative deprivation, and changes in expectations and actual conditions have particular pertinence.

For example, consider the findings about the level of satisfaction in different societies as related to socioeconomic conditions in those societies (Cantril 1965; Stone 1970). A cross section of persons in fourteen countries was interviewed using a self-anchoring-ladder rating technique. In this technique each respondent is asked to imagine his or her future in the best possible light and then in the worst possible light. The respondent then describes each. Taking these two points as extremes on a ten-step ladder, the respondent is asked to rate where he or she stands now, stood five years ago, and where he or she expects to be in five years.

Cantril found that the rank correlation between the socioeconomic level in the countries and the average present rating of the people in the countries is $+.67$. In other words, the general level of deprivation in the society is strongly related to the level of satisfaction. Stone then examined the relationship of these data to the degree of inequality in the societies based on the distribution of agricultural land and found that inequality is not highly related to present self-ratings. Inequality, however, is significantly related to ratings of the future; the correlation is $+.53$, and the correlation between the inequality and the degree of shift from the present to the future is $+.59$. In other words, in societies with much inequality people tend to expect greater improvements in their lives than in countries with more equality. Nevertheless, even in this study the current socioeconomic level in the society was just as strongly related to expectations of improvement; the poorer the country, the greater was the expectation of change.

The different explanations also have varying pertinence for different segments of a conflict party. Thus, as we noted earlier, there is evidence that in status systems with clearly marked boundaries, those toward the top of a low-ranking stratum tend to be relatively satisfied. We noted this for higher income manual workers (Runciman 1966). Yet, it is usually from these levels that the leaders of mass organizations of the entire stratum emerge (see, for example, Lipset 1950, pp. 179–198). This is partly due to the higher ranking persons within each stratum having the social status and skills that make them likely to be leaders in their stratum. It may also be that they are particularly responsive to changes in expectations and conditions. Furthermore, such persons are in some ways marginal; they do not fit clearly in the low-ranking or high-ranking strata. Marginality can be a source of insight and facilitate a questioning posture, useful for a leader (Shibutani and Kwan 1965, pp. 351–361).

Of course the leaders or would-be leaders play a critical role in arousing discontent and making people aware of their grievances. Some issues are more dependent than others on the interpretation of leaders or a vanguard. For example, Rossi and Berk (1970) found in their study of black neighborhoods that popular discontent with the police could be accounted for without recourse to the role of black community leaders, but feelings of economic exploitation by people in the business community were more dependent upon leaders.

The selection of the particular grievance whose redress is sought is influenced by leaders. Therefore, the leaders' own special circumstances may affect the basis of discontent that becomes paramount. We assume that the leader can increase sensitivity to grievances but not, at least in the first instance, create the grievance. Leaders may help to increase awareness or raise the consciousness of the members of a social category and, in doing so, may emphasize deprivation or the discrepancies that the people themselves feel in their status; or the leaders may emphasize the people's deprivation compared to others or their own past. Leaders play a special role in the analysis of what is wrong and what is to be done.

In every social conflict some persons who "belong" to one side of the conflict ally themselves with an adversary group. Explanations for such "traitors" may well be different than for most members of the adversary group. Thus, status inconsistencies and changes in expectations or conditions may be particularly important explanations for the whites who join with blacks in the struggle for racial equality, for nonmanual workers who ally themselves with manual workers, or for faculty who are sympathetic to student protests. For example, Donald (1956) found that the white abolitionists of the 1830s were from old and prominent Northeastern families who were being displaced in leadership by urban manufacturers.

The three approaches to grievances arising from internal characteristics of the conflict unit pertain to consensual conflicts. They may contribute to dissensual conflicts as additional issues in contention or by the displacement of feelings. The sources of grievances in dissensual conflicts are best considered later when we examine grievances as they arise from the relationship between conflict groups.

Goals

For a social conflict to emerge, groups must believe that they hold incompatible goals. Not all aims sought to redress grievances are oppositional and incompatible with those of a potential adversary. A working-class goal of other worldly salvation, for example, may be compatible with managerial goals, although an observer might regard the two groups as being in a potential conflict relationship. In this section we examine group characteristics that affect the formulation of incompatible aims. Before doing so, we should note aspects of goals that are particularly relevant to social conflicts.

A necessary component of any goal is the belief that it is attainable or at least that the present unhappy conditions can be altered in the direction of the desired future position. In other words, for a group to have a grievance and pursue an aim to rectify it against the wishes of an adversary, the group must expect that its efforts will reduce the grievance. Without such hope or belief, rectification of grievances will rarely be attempted and the grievance itself may not be admitted into awareness. The belief may vary from complete confidence to desperate hope.

All goals are ideas about what might be; they are mental constructs of a future condition that is desired. As such they are embedded in a set of ideas about the present plight and what can be done about it. These ideas may be more or less well articulated. When they are explicit and elaborated we refer to them as an ideology. They may also be so unformulated that they are implicit and must be inferred from indirect verbal expressions and actions. Hobsbawm (1959, pp. 108–116) observed that although the classical city mobs were a prepolitical phenomenon, some ideas were manifested in their actions. For example, participants in mobs expected to achieve something, assumed that the authorities would be sensitive to their actions, and directed their activities selectively against the rich and powerful. In this book we are concerned especially with sustained conflict behavior, and that behavior generally entails relatively explicit goals.

As noted at the beginning of the chapter, the content of goals varies. We distinguish between seeking to terminate the relationship with an adversary and seeking to alter the relationship. Termination may be attained by withdrawal, as in secession or group migration, or by obliterating adversaries by killing them or destroying the basis for their existence (for example, doing away with the landlord class by ending private ownership of large agricultural estates). The relationship may be altered by inducing policy changes or preventing an undesired change that would otherwise be made. This alteration may entail workers' seeking a raising of the minimum wage by the employers or one government's seeking another government's military withdrawal from contested land. The relationship may also be modified by exchanging incumbency of leading positions, as when a coup occurs and a new military junta seizes state power. In addition, a challenging group may seek not to displace the adversaries, but to join them in making decisions that affect them all, as when feminists struggled for suffrage (Gamson 1975). Finally, the relationship may be altered through restructuring, such as changing the rules governing union-management relations by the establishment of collective bargaining rights. These different kinds of goals are interrelated and are mixed together in concrete struggles.

Goals differ in other ways, cross-cutting as well as coinciding with these differences. First, conflict goals may be more or less radical in the sense of seeking fundamental changes. Certainly, seeking to terminate a relationship or to restructure it is a more basic goal than seeking to modify existing or prospective policies or changing who participates in making decisions for the social system in which the adversaries belong. The latter goals are generally viewed as reformist rather than radical.

Goals also differ in their collective or aggregate character. That is, some goals pertain to the unit or group as a collective entity, which wishes to advance or defend its power and prestige. Other goals pertain to opportunities of members of the unit as individuals. These two kinds of goals are related, but they represent different emphases. Thus a women's liberation organization may be seeking to improve the status of women in general or their political power as a group, or they may be seeking greater educational and occupational opportunities for women in relationship to men. This distinction is related to, but not the same as, Paige's (1975) distinction between divisible and unitary goals. He notes that some goals can be readily divided and others cannot be; thus the abolition of private ownership of large agricultural estates is a unitary goal while an increase in the wages by 10 percent is readily divisible. Collective goals are more likely to be unitary than are aggregate goals. But these characteristics of goals should be viewed as dimensions along which goals vary rather than as sharply distinct types.

Finally, goals are often described as being "left" or "right." These dimensions refer to various kinds of modifications desired by adversaries in a relationship. Seeking to restructure the relationship or to modify a policy is generally considered left insofar as the objective is to increase equality in class, status, or power differences (Lipset 1960). Another way of characterizing the variations along this dimension is to note who is making claims on whom; when the underclass, in economic or political terms, is making claims against the wealthier or dominant class, their objectives are considered leftist; if, on the other hand, a group that is part of the dominant or ruling stratum seeks to maintain themselves in that position when they are losing it, they are generally characterized as rightists (Tilly 1978, p. 203). Thus, ethnic groups whose primacy is being threatened may seek to prevent new groups from entering the legitimate governing class, or they may even pursue policies that are intended to return to an earlier period of even greater dominance. Such goals are generally referred to as reactionary.

Now we turn to consider selected aspects of the adversary units that shape the unit's goals. We examine the role of leaders, the bases of the unit's grievances, mobilization of resources, and other unit characteristics.

Although focused on articulated goals, these factors affect vaguely expressed ones as well.

Leaders. Leaders of a conflict group play a primary role in formulating aims. Discontent may be dormant and fester; unhappiness may appear to be a necessary part of the human condition, and often it is. But leaders can point to possible changes and future conditions in which the grievances would lessen or disappear.

Goals differ in the anticipated time and effort needed for their realization and the certainty of their attainment. Thus a group may hope in some future generation to achieve a grand purpose but meanwhile may seek only a limited goal for the next year. In order to reach a great end, it currently seeks what is viewed as a prerequisite. In other words, there are strategic and tactical goals.

For a conflict organization to mobilize support and sustain itself, let alone expand, the succession of goals must be closely related to the group's capacities. An appropriate balance must exist between the aims to be attained and the effort needed to attain them.

Particularly for emerging conflict organizations, the choice of immediate goals is important in building support for the organization (Haggstrom 1968). The organization, as part of a larger social category and social movement, must choose goals whose support will increase group awareness and sense of grievance if it is to grow. To say that the sense of grievance must be increased for the movement to succeed sounds strange. There is a paradox here. In one sense the organization must succeed in meeting the demands of the supporters, but success obviates the basis for support of the organization. Leaders, the opposition, and fortuitous circumstances, may or may not conjoin to yield a combination of distant goals and immediate achievements that sustain the emerging conflict organization. Some cases will illustrate the paradox.

Organizers of the poor in community action programs during the 1960s found that organization building was more successful if demands were met with initial resistance and later yielding by the opposition. Resistance is important because it seems to confirm the validity of the analysis that claims that a conflict organization is necessary. Yet failure to attain any benefit would also reveal the invalidity of the diagnosis of the problem or the way of solving it.

Leaders also play an important role in forming coalitions of diverse interests. For example, George Wallace, in 1968, like Barry Goldwater in 1964, may have appealed to white fears about racial integration and "crime in the streets." But Wallace combined this fear with expressions of concern about the welfare of the workers and of the "little people." Wallace received a larger measure of support from workers and trade union members than Goldwater (Lipset and Raab 1970, pp. 362–367).

The dynamics of events in the social movement may make if difficult for the leadership to establish itself or develop goals that meet the paradoxical requirements. For example, consider the May 1970 university student strikes following the U.S. invasion of Cambodia and the killing of students at Kent State and Jackson State. The wave of protests had many purposes reflecting a variety of student interests. One immediate aim came to be "no business as usual." Many students could be mobilized for that goal, but for different reasons. For some it was the beginning of a national strike in which all business would be stopped, the Vietnam War ended, and a radical social transformation of the society brought about. For others it was an opportunity to educate other students and the community about the war and other social issues. For still others it was a way to bring pressure upon the federal government to end the war. For some it was pressuring the local university administrators to give students greater power in the university. For some others it was a way to end the semester early without final examinations and with no academic penalty. This mixture of interests and goals made it sometimes seem that all students were trying to make a revolution and still get good grades.

Some universities did shut down, which meant that dormitories and university facilities were closed, and students had no base from which to work and left the campus. In other universities, after a few days of interruption in normal procedures, business as usual returned. At still other universities a compromise was reached: Classes were to continue as usual for students who wanted to attend, and, for those who wanted to engage in special activities, workshops and community action could be conducted and grades would be given by arrangement with the instructor, usually on the basis of work already done. After a few days of activity, students began to drift away once arrangements for grades had been made and as the momentum of a massive social action disappeared.

In the labor movement one can trace a variety of formulas that leaders constructed to build a viable conflict organization. During the nineteenth century in the United States many national trade unions began but did not survive: the Knights of Labor, the National Labor Union, and the Industrial Workers of the World (Perlman 1928). The "pure and simple trade unionism" of the American Federation of Labor provided a set of immediate and long-term goals, which were always partially attainable. Thus, when the founder-leader, Samuel Gompers, was asked what the workers wanted, he answered, "more, more, more, and more."

In elaborating goals, beliefs about the past as well as the present and the future are promulgated. Certain beliefs about the past can make ends seem more legitimate and attainable. Leaders can argue that the desired future position is attainable because such a position once existed. Land and other property were once communally owned; in early human history women were socially superior to men and were worshipped by them (Steinem 1971); or our ethnic group once had an autonomous and high culture compared to the barbarians of the time.

Beliefs about the contemporary events are relevant when they indicate the possibility of attaining the sought-for ends. Thus, leaders often seek to convince the supporters that the adversary is weak or weakening while the supporters are strong and getting stronger. For example, Palestinian Arab leaders claimed many victorious guerrilla attacks after the Six-Day War of June 1967 in order to promote the growth of the Arab Palestinian movements (Peretz 1970).

Leaders agitate, then, not only by trying to increase discontent, but also by holding out a better and attainable future. There is another paradox here. To depict how exploited and victimized people are seems to contradict the possibility of such a weak group's bettering itself against the desires of the group doing the victimizing. One way out of the paradox is to use the power of weakness. People who really have nothing are invulnerable to threats and coercion. Having nothing, they can lose nothing. Thus, the Communist Manifesto exhorted the workers to unite in struggle, since "you have nothing to lose but your chains" (see Blau 1964, pp. 230–231).

Leaders not only organize others' interests, but also advance their own interests. We must consider the relationship between persons in authority and their constituencies, followers, and competitors. In large conflict entities the complexity of relationships among the many subgroups constituting the entity is an important factor affecting the formation of conflict goals.

We do not expect those in authority always to be either more or less aggressive than the rank-and-file constituency in establishing conflict goals. Many conditions affect the relative assertiveness of different subgroups within any conflict unit. On the one hand, leaders may greatly identify with the collectivity as a whole and seek its glory, even at the expense of the sacrifices the constituents must make to seek that glory, and the constituencies making sacrifices may value collective glory much less and hence support more modest goals. On the other hand, leaders may have to negotiate regularly with opposition leaders and recognize the limits that their counterparts face, while the supporters may be less constrained by the possible limits in gaining radical goals.

The implications of leaders' and followers' having different interests also vary depending upon the autonomy the leaders have in determining policy for the collectivity. Leaders generally seek to maintain themselves in power, and in many conflict groups doing so means paying attention to what their followers want, even catering to them rather than being attentive to the interactions with an adversary collectivity. Thus, government leaders may take ultranationalistic positions out of a feeling that they would otherwise lose their leadership role rather than because they believe the international situation calls for it. The nature of the leadership challenges may also affect the assertiveness of the policies pursued. For example, Wolfe (1979) argues that the Democratic party in the United States has generally acted vigorously anti-Soviet since World War II because its leaders feel vulnerable to challenges and threats from traditionally rightist elements and from the Republican party. The Republican leaders, secure from such competitive challenges, can in practice be less assertive in challenging the Soviet Union.

Bases of Grievance. The character of a conflict goal is shaped by the kind of grievance it is intended to redress. Considering how the previously discussed sources of discontent affect aims will help to resolve the apparent contradictions in the ideas about the sources.

People who are deprived or whose conditions have deteriorated are more likely to support radical goals than are people with status inconsistency or improved conditions. For example, during periods of severe economic depression in the United States, relatively radical aims have been voiced by some, albeit small, groups within the labor movement; but during the economic upswing after the depression, trade union organizations, with much more reformist goals, expanded (Dunlop 1951). Or we might consider blacks in the United States during the 1960s. Blacks with higher education and income tended to be conventional militants, while those who were more uniformly worse off tended disproportionately to support black separatist objectives (Marx 1969, esp. pp. 57, 117). Among persons who are not greatly deprived, however, status inconsistency is related to utopian goals. For example, in the 1960s college students with status inconsistency tended to belong to organizations with utopian goals, while those with more consistent backgrounds tended to belong to more conventional political groups (Braungart 1979).

The direction of goals, whether to the left or right, toward increasing or decreasing inequalities, also depends on the nature of the discontent. Deteriorating conditions for the formerly high-ranking persons, even if the deterioration is only relative to those lower than themselves, makes them favor aims that restore previous inequalities. It is from such groups that reactionary political movements have drawn disproportional support. We also expect status inconsistents, with ascribed or investment statuses that are higher than achieved or reward statuses, to support conservative or reactionary goals, while persons with overrewarded kinds of inconsistencies would support more liberal or egalitarian aims (Schmitt 1965; Broom and Jones 1970; Braungart 1979).

The pattern of status inconsistency also affects the content of the goal. People will try to raise themselves along the dimensions in which they have relatively low status and, therefore, will be challenging those who are above them on that dimension. This challenge helps determine the goal and the adversary. Thus, persons with low ethnic status and high occupational and income levels might try to raise the status of their ethnic category and challenge those who presume to have higher ethnic status, or individuals may try to "pass" and deny their ethnicity.

The content of the grievance profoundly affects the goal. If economic deprivation is experienced, then efforts usually will be directed at improving those conditions, for example in trade union action. But how that is to be done and who is the opponent depends in part on the leaders' ideas, as previously noted, and also upon the resources of the group and the prevailing ideas among its members.

Resource Mobilization. What benefits members of a unit believe they can attain sets the limits of what they seek. What they think they can get is based on the resources they have, are able to control, and are willing to use against their adversaries. It also depends on their resources, relative to those of their adversaries, as discussed in a later section of this chapter. At this point, we consider the components of resource mobilization and how a group's mobilization of resources affects the conflict goals it forms.

In recent years several students of social conflicts and of social movements have analyzed and stressed the crucial role resources play in the emergence of social movements and conflicts (Oberschall 1973; Zald and Ash 1966; Tilly 1978). Rather than stress the discontent that people feel as the basis for revolutions, violence, and other forms of conflict behavior and social movement activity, they stress the ability of the members of a discontented category to act. They argue that dissatisfaction is prevalent; whether or not people try to better their lot depends upon their ability to do so rather than on their level of dissatisfaction. In this work, we draw from both emphases and, in addition, examine the interaction between adversaries in order to account for the course of social conflicts. In examining interaction between adversaries, their relative mobilization of resources is especially important.

People are the fundamental resource to be mobilized: It is they who demonstrate, give financial support, vote, strike, and serve in military forces. They are resources insofar as they are willing and able to act in particular ways for a particular conflict goal. They are assets of the leaders insofar as they are committed to performing those actions when called upon in pursuit of shared purposes.

Mobilization of resources occurs when people have been committed to act in specified ways for a particular set of ends. It means people have made a commitment to others to obey and provide certain services when called upon to do so. Such commitment is limited to certain kinds of actions for certain purposes. A revolutionary leader may be able to mobilize supporters for armed resistance to the government forces or for a march in a one-day demonstration protesting a government policy, but the numbers of people who obey one command for one purpose may not be mobilized for another. Similarly, a president or shah may call upon regular military forces to suppress a demonstration, even if this entails shooting unarmed civilians. If they refuse, the ruler lacks the resources to suppress the demonstration (Sharp 1973).

Conflict units differ in the resources they can readily mobilize and, therefore, they differ in the goals they can set. Governmental leaders can generally count on having armies and soldiers ready to obey, even at the risk of killing others or being killed themselves. These accessible resources open up the possibility of government leaders' pursuing goals not considered by leaders of other organizations. Tilly (1978, p.75) reasons that the differences in resources of the poor and powerless as compared to the rich and powerful result in the different kinds of goals they set. Thus, he argues that the rich mobilize to take advantage of new opportunities to maximize their interest, but the poor cannot afford to do that. He distinguishes between defensive and offensive goals and points out that:

> The poor and powerless tend to begin defensively, the rich and powerful offensively. The group whose members are rich can mobilize a surplus without threatening a member's other amusements and obligations. A group with a poor consitituency has little choice but to compete with daily necessities. The group whose members are powerful can use the other organizations they control—including governments—to do some of their work, whereas the powerless must do it on their own. The rich and powerful can forestall claims from other groups before they become articulated claims, and can afford to seize opportunities to make new claims on their own. The poor and the powerless often find that the rich, the powerful, and the government oppose and punish their efforts at mobilization. (The main exception, an important one, is the powerless group which forms a coalition with a rich, powerful patron; European Fascists of the 1920s mobilized rapidly in that fashion.) As a result, any mobilization at all is more costly to the poor and powerless; only a threat to the little they have is likely to move them to mobilize. The rich and powerful are well defended against such threats; they rarely have the occasion for defensive mobilization.

Continuously organized conflict groups enjoy a mobilization advantage over emergent conflict parties, as is the case between governments and protesters or revolutionaries, and their continuous mobilization also makes it easy for even small grievances to be the basis of a manifest conflict. But this is limited by at least two different kinds of circumstances. Continuously organized conflict groups may exercise sufficient domination that their grievances are quickly redressed, but in confrontations with similarly mobilized adversaries, they may inhibit one another from seeking redress in ways that make an underlying conflict emerge.

Other Unit Characteristics. Many unit attributes have significance relative to the adversary and will be considered in that context. For example, the size of a group is significant in large part in relationship to the size of its adversary. But the size of a social category in itself has consequences for the formation of explicit goals. Thus, articulating aims is facilitated by interaction among a sufficient number of persons; a critical mass of similarly thinking persons must be present. The concentration of a large number of possible supporters also gives a sense of power (even if inaccurate when compared to the adversary) that strengthens the belief that a grievance can be redressed and, therefore, that a goal of a better future can be formulated. These are part of the reasons why the size of the student body is the best predictor of student protest demonstrations in universities (Scott and El-Assal 1969). Similarly, a comprehensive study of racial disturbances in the United States in the 1960s found that the number of blacks in a city was highly related to disorders (the correlation was .59) (Spilerman 1970, 1971). Snyder

(1979) has specified this relationship by finding that riots could be more adequately explained by the availability of persons, times, places, and occasions to assemble.

Olson (1968) has raised several significant issues about the way group size affects collective action. In his analysis of organizations that are expected to further the common interests of their members, a central issue that concerns him is the "free rider" problem. If an organization advances the common interests of a category of people, it is in the self-interest of each individual in that category not to expend his or her resources in participating in the organization as long as others in that category are expending their resources on the organization. Thus, the individual will freely derive the gains from the collective effort. Olson further reasons that the larger the group, the farther it will fall short of providing enough of the common good, or shared benefits, to make participation worthwhile. In order to induce individuals to participate in large organizations, then, private incentives or side payments may have to be offered. For example, a large professional organization lobbying to advance the interests of the profession may offer its members a group life insurance policy. This reasoning suggests that large conflict groups will tend to have multiple goals, some of which are directed at simply maintaining membership.

In actual conflict groups, however, many other factors affect the readiness of individuals to participate in struggles to advance collective interests. There are social norms about participation, and social pressure is a form of coercion to induce participation. Individuals may also derive some gratification from participation itself, for example, the joy of marching with friends in a just cause. They may also have erroneous conceptions about the implications of participating and receiving the collective benefits that induced them to participate. In a variety of ways, people are mobilized to participate by building solidarity and raising the consciousness of common interests (Fireman and Gamson 1979). As Tillock and Morrison (1979) conclude from their empirical testing of Olson's theory, some people believe that not to attain certain kinds of collective goods is a public evil, for example, not avoiding but experiencing a nuclear war. They cannot as *individuals* obtain the good or escape the evil. Finally, we should note that in many circumstances the larger the number of persons taking part in a collective action, the smaller the cost each participant in the action has to bear in order to gain the collective good, the greater the likelihood of attaining it, and, therefore, the greater the readiness of individuals to join the collective action (Oberschall 1980). Mobilization and demobilization, therefore, can proceed rapidly in loosely structured conflicts.

In addition to size, the experience that the members of a group have had with previous efforts at redressing grievances also affects goal formulation. A history of failure may inhibit formulating any goals of a better future; but if one is made, it is likely to be more radical than for groups with a history of past success.

Within any social category persons vary considerably in their inability to imagine radical transformations, to desire collective solidarity, or to hold other values and beliefs that are relevant to the nature and direction of aims. Thus, a small percentage within every large social category might support radical goals, but widespread support requires the convergence of many appropriate conditions. Therefore, organizations may be able to find a smaller number of members to support extreme goals, but as members join the aims are likely to become less extreme; moderate goals may even be formulated in order to attract popular support. Units may also differ in the proportion of persons with given personality traits. For example, people differ in the degree to which they are intrapunitive or extrapunitive. That is, some people tend to blame themselves, while some people tend to blame other persons when things go wrong. Groups with many extrapunitive members tend to believe that their dissatisfactions are attributable to an adversary and, therefore, they formulate goals that are incompatible with the other group's aims (Gurr 1970, pp. 164–168).

Many unit characteristics interact to affect the ends to be pursued. Goals, however, are not merely the expression of the inner desires of the members of a social category or a group. We also must take into account the relations between the adversaries and the context in which the parties confront each other.

RELATIONS BETWEEN ADVERSARIES

Relations between adversaries strongly affect collective identity, the sense of grievance, and the formulation of goals.

Collective Identity

Groups wittingly and unwittingly define one another as well as themselves. Qualities become salient in relationship to other persons. Within the United States being an American is not a salient identification, but it is when an American is in another country. Identity is partly established in contrast to others (Voegelin 1940; Shibutani and Kwan 1965, pp. 383–391). Thus, there is evidence that persons living in ethnically heterogeneous neighborhoods take their ethnicity more seriously than do those in ethnically homogeneous neighborhoods (Borhek 1970; also see Barth 1969).

Not only the awareness, but also the content of collective identity are established in interaction. Each self-conscious collectivity defines nonmembers. If a group is relatively powerful, it will try to impose its definitions upon other groups. Where whites are dominant they seek to define who is nonwhite. The criteria and variety of nonmembers may be more or less clearly delimited and imposed. The Nazis' attempt to define Jews and other groups stands as one of the most grotesque efforts of this kind. The definitions may entail trying to assert how the other group acts and thinks as well as who is and who is not a member. Thus, men say what women are like; university officials define what students are; and whites say how blacks behave.

In cases with illegitimate power inequalities, the subordinate group will try to reject the definitions imposed by superordinates. What ensues is a struggle over who has a right to define membership and the qualities of each group. But, interestingly, if there has been long experience of mutual involvement, even when the subordinate group rejects the definition of the superordinate, it may accept the terms of evaluation. This is the self-hatred syndrome in which members seek to deny that they are different in the ways the dominants assert. Under circumstances of more autonomy, the subordinated group may reject the criteria of evaluation and assert the superiority of its own way as compared to that of the superordinants. Even then, however, its own way may be defined in opposition to the way of the dominants.

To illustrate: In some circumstances students, blacks, and women have tried to refute allegations that they are less responsible, hard working, or committed than administrators, whites, or men; at other states of collective identity, some segments of the group may argue that they really have the characteristics attributed to them, but that these are good (being black, for example, may then entail being appropriately expressive and warm in human relations). The matter gets even more complicated when one group tries to define the other as a way of arguing to itself about what it should be. In the women's liberation movement, some persons feel that the masculine way of life is so wrong, with hierarchy and domination, for example, that efforts should be made to avoid taking over its qualities. As some feminists put it:

> In order to assert our principles and prevent their co-optation by the male power structure, we must, within the movement, fight the development of a class system based on skills which are not available to everyone. We must fight the ascendancy of leaders in order to encourage the development of leadership skills in all women. We fear that the artificial creation of leaders, as has always been the case in male-dominated societies, will inevitably suppress the initiative of the majority. (The Feminists from New York City, 1970)

From this interplay of assertion, repudiation, acknowledgment, and reinterpretation of one's own group as viewed by others and of others from the perspective of one's own group, identities with new content emerge.

Nationalist identification often emerges in the face of coercive treatment by foreign armies. Thus Johnson (1962) argued that the Chinese peasant masses were mobilized by the 1937 Japanese invasion. The Japanese troops took ruthless action against the entire rural population, and consequently the Chinese developed intense anti-Japanese feelings. The invasion and subsequent occupation raised the Chinese peasants' sense of citizenship and their interest in bettering the Chinese state. The Japanese invasion and occupation helped generate sentiments in the peasantry that played a crucial role in the rise of the Communist party.

Sense of Grievance

Many aspects of the relations between adversaries profoundly affect the emergence of discontent, the judgment that it is unjustified, and the belief that it can be reduced. We will discuss two major sets of factors: the degree of integration between the adversaries and the balance of resources between them.

Integration. Relations between groups vary in degree and content. Members of one group may interact a great deal or very little with members of another group, and conflicting relations may constitute a large or a small proportion of all their interactions. We will use the term integration to refer to both dimensions of interaction. High integration means that intergroup interactions are high and relatively nonconflicting. Since the degree and content of the interaction need not be associated with each other, we will also consider each separately.

On the whole, we expect that with larger proportions of nonconflicting relations, any particular objective conflict is less likely to become manifest. Presumably the cooperative relations compensate for the conflicting ones; therefore, an issue in contention is not felt to be as grievous as it would be if unmitigated by common and complementary relations (Morris and Jeffries 1968).

As diagrammed in Part A of Figure 3.2, this reasoning yields a linear inverse association between the likelihood of recognizing a conflict and the proportion of nonconflicting relations between adversaries. Thus, differences of interest between allies are less likely to be perceived as conflicts than similar differences between antagonists.

Integration also involves the extent of the relationship—the number of ways in which people interact and relate to one another. Everything else being equal, the more groups have to do with one another, the more they have to quarrel about. If they have nothing to do with one another, they have no basis for a social conflict. We also presume, however, that the proportion of nonconflicting relations increases as the extent of interaction increases. Consequently, we would expect a curvilinear association between the likelihood of becoming aware of a conflict and the number of relations between the parties. This is illustrated in Part B of Figure 3.2.

On the whole, integration above a low level inhibits recognition of conflicts. See Part C of Figure 3.2. With increasing integration, cross-cutting ties of conflict as well as cooperation bind people together and tend to inhibit open acknowledgement of each particular conflict (Coser 1956). At a more interpersonal level, people with social relations across conflict-group boundaries are less likely to perceive issues as contentious. For example, in one community allegations about Jews were raised in a local election. Jews with cross ties with gentiles tended not to respond with ethnocentrism, especially if they spoke about the issue with gentiles (Weinberg and Williams 1969).

There is even an additional possibly inhibiting mechanism. The more emotionally involved people become with one another, the more reluctant they are to admit that they have issues of contention with them. Coser (1956, p. 62) writes, "The closer the relationship, the greater the affective investment, the greater also the tendency to suppress rather than express hostile feelings." In less interpersonal, psychological terms, the tendency to suppress hostile feelings and the awareness of conflict may be due to shared identification. That is, insofar as groups feel that they are part of the same larger entity, they tend to deny the issues

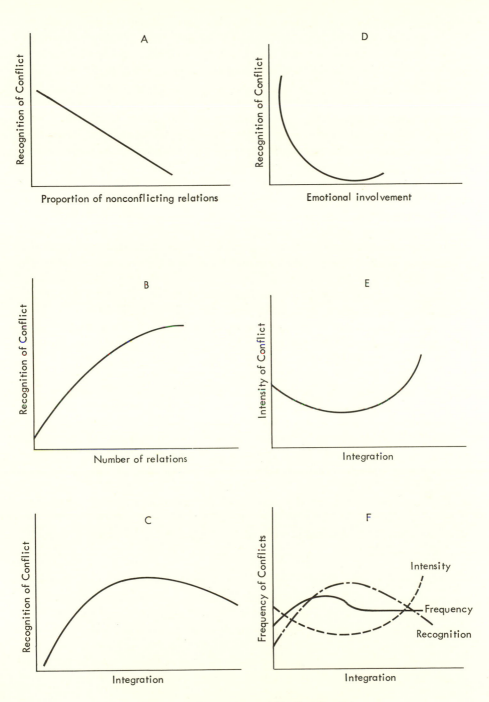

Figure 3.2 Integration and Manifest Conflict.

that divide them. At very high levels of involvement, however, there may be higher demands made of each other for responsiveness that are likely to be unmet and hence provoke disappointment. The result is a somewhat curvilinear relationship between involvement and conflict recognition, as shown in Part D of Figure 3.2.

Herein arises another paradox. If hostility is suppressed and if diverse issues are unrecognized, the intensity of the hostility and the gravity of the issue grow. The grievance then can burst forth in greater magnitude than if the issues had been recognized earlier. For example, repressive governments may be ignorant of and unresponsive to popular wishes so that once a revolution breaks out, the rage of the people may seem surprisingly great. As illustrated in Part E of Figure 3.2, we posit that at low levels of integration, intense hostility and a sense of grievance can be acknowledged, unchecked by other considerations, and at high degrees of integration, once a conflict becomes manifest, it will also be of great intensity. There is another mechanism that helps account for this. It is particularly relevant in dissensual conflicts. People feel particularly outraged about disagreements with others who are supposed to be close. This is one of the reasons for the intensity of feeling often noted in conflicts regarding what seem like small doctrinal differences when factions break away from larger political or religious groups. This potentially intense sense of grievance adds to the chances that a struggle will emerge.

All of these factors affect the frequency of disputes. Since they do not have the same effect upon the frequency of conflicts, however, there is not a linear association, not even a simple curvilinear one, as may be seen in Part F of Figure 3.2. The resultant line may also help make it clear why social conflicts do not disappear with integration.

The extent of nonconflicting relations between collectivities can also be viewed as interdependency, and this has another set of implications (Baldwin 1978; Blau 1964). Parties who are mutually dependent have the basis for influencing and being influenced by the other. The influence can be based upon the threat of withholding what the other side has come to expect and depend upon. The influence can also derive from the promise of continued or increased provision of desired goods or services. Hence, mutual dependency is closely related to inequality in resources.

Resource Inequality. Conflict groups vary in the resources they have available to them that they can use as coercive, rewarding, or persuasive inducements. These inequalities affect the likelihood of conflict emergence. We will consider such effects for inequality in coercive resources or power differences.

If one group has much more power than another, the more powerful may suppress the weaker to such an extent that the weaker neither acknowledges its dissatisfactions nor formulates a goal that challenges the stronger. Repression and intimidation may make any such formulation seem futile and self-defeating. Of course the intimidation and repression in themselves are sources of discontent among those experiencing it, and additional repression may be needed to suppress that discontent. Herein lies one check upon continued aggrandizement by the superordinate.

Superior power, particularly in large and total social systems like a society, can also be used to convince the weaker that they are not deprived and have no grounds for grievance. Formal and informal means of education or indoctrination convince the weaker that the existing allocation of what is consensually valued conforms with standards of equity and legitimacy (Mann 1970). Interestingly, arguments in terms of such standards also become restraints upon the superordinates. Suppose, it is argued, that the subordinates owe obedience because of the benefits being given them by the superordinates or, in other words, a fair exchange exists. In that case, the superordinates are constrained to honor the terms of the exchange in order to maintain their claims against the subordinates.

The degree of power inequality also affects the likelihood of a grievance's becoming manifest because it is related to the magnitude of the grievance. The weaker one side is, the more reason its members have to complain. For example, Schuman and Gruenberg (1970) found that the smaller the proportion of blacks in a city, the more likely are blacks to feel dissatisfied; presumably where blacks are a smaller proportion of the city population, they are less politically effective.

This finding implies that a deprived group will use whatever power it has to press its demands and it needs power to do so. On the whole, then, great power inequalities increase dissatisfaction at the individual level but for this dissatisfaction to be collectively recognized, some expectation of improvement by one's own efforts in opposition to an adversary is necessary. Thus, trade union organizations were first developed among the most strategically located workers in each industry—locomotive engineers in the railroad industry, loom fixers in textiles, molders in casting, and cutters in the garment industry (Dunlop 1951, pp. 49–50).

Changes in relative power, therefore, are often the source of newly emerged consciousness of grievance. Revolutionary situations, for example, typically arise when the governmental power has been eroded, often as a result of external wars that have strained the capacity of a government and made its weaknesses apparent. Skocpol's analysis of the great revolutions of France, Russia, and China reveals that the state in each case had been strained beyond its capacity by the international situation in which it was involved. Laqueur (1968, p. 501) summarizes many of the reasons that war has been decisive in the emergence of revolutionary situations in modern times. He observes:

> Most modern revolutions, both successful and abortive, have followed in the wake of war (the Paris Commune of 1871, the Russian revolution of 1905, the various revolutions after the two World Wars, including the Chinese revolutions). These have occurred not only in the countries that suffered defeat. The general dislocation caused by war, the material losses and human sacrifices, create a climate conducive to radical change. A large section of the population has been armed; human life seems considerably less valuable than in peacetime. In a defeated country authority tends to disintegrate and acute social dissatisfactions receive additional impetus

from a sense of wounded national prestige (the Young Turks in 1908, Naguib and Nasser in 1952). The old leadership is discredited by defeat, and the appeal for radical social change and national reassertion thus falls on fertile ground.

Goals

Each side helps shape the other side's purposes. One way this happens is a conflict party responds to how it is being defined and what is being sought from it. The other way is that a conflict party shapes its goals in terms of the anticipated responses of its antagonists.

Reactions. A collectivity shapes its goals in response to an adversary by imitation or by contrast. In consensual conflicts the members of a collectivity deny the differences attributed to them, and their aim is to attain the conditions that make that denial valid. In dissensual conflicts the members of a collectivity may exaggerate the differences along the very lines stressed by the adversary. Some illustrations should make these possibilities clearer.

The intensified persecution of Jews in Russia toward the end of the nineteenth century spurred and helped shape Zionist aims. Seeking a national home and a normal social and economic life, with emphasis upon productive work and especially labor on the land, was one kind of response to anti-Semitic allegations and persecutions. Zionism was based partly on the argument that the Jews should be like other people; if they could not be accepted as Russians or as Germans because they were Jews, then they were indeed Jews who also had a national identity and needed a national homeland. Similarly, U.S. college students who argue against the *in loco parentis* doctrine contend that they are responsible and can control themselves just as well as adults or others living away from a college.

The response can also be one of contradiction. If the other side alleges immorality, looseness, lack of discipline, and hedonism, then the response is the glorification of spontaneity, warmth in human relations, soul, and a counterculture. Sometimes people emphasize a presumed goal of the other side pertaining to themselves as a way of directing their own collectivity. Thus, some people stress the antireligious elements in Soviet ideology as a way of arguing that America has religious and specifically Christian goals.

The demands one party makes on another sets the guidelines of the other party's counterclaims. And each party's demands and counterclaims reflect its location in a particular situation and structure. For example, a government facing heavy international burdens may seek to raise taxes or even resort to internal coercion in mobilizing its resources. Such actions may be viewed by the populace as violations of understandings, and they reduce the legitimacy they accord to government leaders. Such withdrawal could readily lead to revolutionary goals.

The goals that different classes seek against each other are based upon their particular class relations and the opportunities available to them. In Paige's (1975) analysis of agrarian revolutions, he demonstrates how certain structural class conditions generate particular sets of conflicting goals and, therefore, different kinds of revolutionary efforts or nonrevolutionary struggles for reforms. For example, consider the class relations where the noncultivators derive their income from the ownership of the land and the cultivators derive their income in the form of wages, as migratory workers. Revolutionary nationalist movements are likely to occur in such migratory estate systems in colonial areas. Several other conditions must converge for this to emerge. Although migratory workers may generally feel aggrieved, they usually lack the resources for organizing to seek redress. But if migratory workers are thrown back to village subsistence holdings when the harvest season is over, the traditional tribal or peasant leadership could provide the resources needed for organization. Whether or not the traditional village authorities join with the members of their village who have labored as migratory workers on the estate depends upon their own economic circumstances. They are willing to join the migratory workers "only when their own economic base of support is being ended by the same estate system that is exploiting the poor laborers" (Paige 1975, p. 36). This has occurred in Vietnam and Angola.

Anticipation. A conflict party can affect its adversary's aims by making clear what it will, and will not, allow its adversary. This situation is most likely to occur when the conflict party is relatively strong. In some cases, it allows individuals to "let off steam," "gripe," "bitch," or ridicule what they do not like (Coser 1956, p. 41), which may reduce some pressure and make the party seem more human. It may even provide a way of communicating challenges and desires for change that would not otherwise be communicated. Such vents may even be institutionalized as in the office party when people can get drunk and tell the boss off or in skits when students lampoon the faculty. These methods may dissipate rather than generate collective goals.

In order to understand how anticipated reactions affect the development of conflicting purposes, we need to recall one of the fundamental components of an emerging social conflict: A dissatisfied party must believe it is possible to improve one's lot, to get closer to what is desired, at the expense of some other party. There are several ways in which the other party gives credence to such beliefs. If the other side seems weak and incompetent, it may be giving evidence that indeed it is not only responsible for the unsatisfactory conditions but that it is also subject to pressure and to change. Students of revolutions generally agree that one of the immediate causes of revolts against the authorities is the appearance of hesitancy, uncertainty, and self-doubt among the authorities. These sentiments may be signaled by verbal signs of panic and by defections. Such signals invite more radical formulations of goals; they may indicate that fundamental restructuring of authority relations rather than reforms seems possible and necessary.

Aside from such signs of collapse by the adversary, a group or its leaders may try to formulate its goals for maximum impact upon the opponent. An ideology is not only directed at the constituency to make them believe that an aim is desirable and attainable, it is also directed toward the adversary. If the adversary can be convinced of, or at least question, the morality and justice of its position, then chances of inducing defections, uncertainty, and guilt in the adversary increase. That in turn would yield further evidence to the members of the group that they can get what they want from the adversary. Consequently, aims are often formulated in terms of shared values of freedom, justice, and equality. For example, leaders of national independence movements lay claim to the rights of a people to rule themselves.

This direction of goals also means that immediate aims may be chosen from among the array of possible goals partly in terms of which one is most likely to be yielded by the adversary. Consider white opposition to the different possible integration aims of blacks in the 1960s. According to a 1963 national survey, about 80 percent of the whites conceded that Negroes ought to have as good a chance as white people to get any kind of job; about three-fourths favored equal access to public facilities; about 60 percent thought white and Negro students should go to the same schools; but less than half disagreed with the statement that white people had a right to keep Negroes out of their neighborhoods if they wanted to (Sheatsley 1966, p. 224). On that basis, striving for equal jobs might seem to be a most promising goal for blacks. Support for legal and political equality probably would be even more generally found (Williams and Wienir 1967). But the vulnerability of those who control these different spheres of life, the kinds of tactics available to the blacks, and considerations of the major dissatisfactions and organizational needs of blacks and their leaders also dictate the choice of a goal.

Finally, we should note that the utility of pursuing a particular goal is affected by how the group feels about the other side and its reaction to yielding a particular goal. This has been called "vicarious utility" (Valavanis 1958). For example, if one group has strong animosity toward another, it will derive extra pleasure from pursuing an aim that humiliates its adversary. Vengeance can be sweet. Without such feelings a less extreme end might be chosen. On the other hand if there is a high mixture of positive feelings or common interests, a goal may be chosen that will minimize the harm to the opponent, even if it fails to maximize the group's own values independently of considering the vicarious value of the other side's satisfaction.

The gratifications of getting retribution and humiliating the enemy may sometimes lead a group to pursue aims that would otherwise seem to be self-defeating or would inflict self-losses not commensurate with what might be won. To that extent, an observer would view the conflict as partly unrealistic.

ENVIRONMENT OF ADVERSARIES

In addition to the characteristics of each unit and the relations between them, the social context within which the conflict parties exist helps shape their identities, grievances, and goals.

Collective Identity

The prevailing ways of thinking at any given time profoundly affect the categories in which people think of themselves. Identification in terms of religious beliefs, class relations, ethnicity, or ways of life may be more or less salient in different times and places. For example, class consciousness is generally more prevalent in European societies than in the United States.

Such prevailing ways of thought have significance beyond the way parties think of themselves. They define each other in terms of prevailing categories. Moreover, people who are not immediate actors in the conflict recognize and support actors in terms of the shared understandings of which categories are important. Thus there is often popular support to claims for separatism and national autonomy by ethnic groups. Yet governments are reluctant to support such movements because they themselves are vulnerable to secessionist movements. Nevertheless, appeals for support in terms of nationality or of political liberty have some built-in audience, as can be seen in the support Jews received in recognition of a claim for a homeland and more recently that Palestinian Arabs have received in their claims (Avineri 1970).

Sense of Grievance

The social context in which the parties to a conflict exist is not only a source of their discontent but also helps provide the criteria for evaluating conditions and possible changes. The available alternatives and their relative salience help explain why some conditions become manifest grievances at certain times and not others.

Two kinds of contextual effects on the level of dissatisfaction deserve attention: diffuse feelings of discontent and specific responses to structural conditions. The first effect is stressed by theorists of the mass society (Kornhauser 1959). They observe that in large, industrial, urban societies, many people are isolated and alienated. They lack the informal, primary group relationships that would provide emotional support and a sense of community. They live and work in large bureaucratic organizations and interact impersonally in segmented roles rather than as whole humans. Consequently, free-floating distress is generated and is available to be channeled against a variety of targets. This condition is particularly evident in societies undergoing rapid change, either in economic development or as a result of economic depressions or inflation. Demagogues can seek to mobilize people against vulnerable groups who would serve as scapegoats. This kind of analysis has been used in accounting for the rise of totalitarian movements and governments, as in Nazi Germany. But this approach underestimates the continuing links that people have to family, work groups, ethnic and religious identifications, and organizations. It underestimates the continuing importance of interests resulting from economic and social positions that are differentially advantaged or disadvantaged by the rapid socioeconomic change (Halebsky 1976).

The social context also structures relations between adversaries so that particular dissatisfactions are likely to emerge. Hierarchical organizations and societies pit particular categories of people against each other. Subordinates are controlled by superordinates, and the inherent conflicts of interest between members of each category result in discontent of each with the other. Large-scale organizations are particularly conducive to engendering resentments in such circumstances because relations are likely to be guided by impersonal rules. Rapid changes in the scale of operation may especially aggravate feelings of antagonism. Thus, in the 1960s, colleges and universities expanded relatively quickly, and the numbers of students in institutions of higher learning greatly increased. This growth was a source of discontent for the students, as they experienced more impersonal treatment, and it also increased the number who could see they had new capability to redress grievances.

As previously discussed, for a social conflict to emerge from an objective conflict relationship, at least one party must feel that the condition is not satisfactory according to its standards. Its standards of equity, however, are drawn from the prevailing tone, from the Zeitgeist. We are now experiencing a worldwide increase in the value of equality (Beteille 1969). Leaving aside the sources of this emerging standard, its rise makes less tolerable those inequities based upon age, race, nation-state, or sex.

Related to this general increase is the example that each group provides every other group with a standard for what is acceptable. Deprivations accepted as legitimate are questioned, if others reject what they had accepted as proper. Thus, the increase in claims for equity by blacks, by the poor, by women, by youth—each reverberates upon the other and confirms to each that they have a right to be dissatisfied.

Finally, standards may be directly raised by actions and words of others who are not immediate partisans to a conflict. For example, the 1954 U.S. Supreme Court decision (*Brown* v. *Board of Education*) declaring segregated schools unconstitutional raised the hopes of many blacks in the United States (see, for example, Bell 1968, p. 6; The National Advisory Commission on Civil Disorders 1968, p. 226). Second-class citizenship was not good enough.

In addition to raising evaluative standards, a sense of grievance can become manifest when objectionable conditions become viewed as unnecessary. That is, people come to believe that it is possible for improvements to be made. Here, too, the gains others are making elsewhere raise expectations. The mass media certainly help to quickly spread the word about what is possible. But, as already reviewed, there are many self-insulating factors that inhibit people from feeling aggrieved, although they do not individually or collectively have what some others do.

A basic component of a sense of grievance is that a collectivity can improve its position at the expense of another collectivity. Viewing the relationship as one that has a zero-sum payoff is crucial for the emergence of a social conflict. Such views are dependent upon the actual limits of the system within which the parties are operating and upon the parties' perceptions of the limits. For example, Gurr (1970, pp. 125–126) reports several studies indicating that believing limits are fixed, that what one group gets another must lose, is particularly widespread in

Latin America. That expanding limits reduce the belief that contending parties are in a zero-sum relationship is also indicated by the finding that European states had fewer wars with each other when colonial empires were expanding than during other historical periods (Rosecrance 1963). The expanding U.S. economy and the open frontier, even if exaggerated in their effects, probably have mitigated the sense of grievance.

The degree to which conflict regulation is institutionalized also significantly affects the emergence of manifest social conflicts. If there are generally supported and well-understood procedures for handling disputes, matters of possible contention tend to be viewed as competitive, and not conflicting, or as part of a larger exchange relationship, and not simply as a zero-sum relationship.

The availability of allies and possible coalition partners also affects the likelihood of seeking to redress grievances. If the potentiality of mobilizing widespread support from the environment appears to exist, the belief in the ability to redress grievances will be strengthened and, hence, the likelihood of a conflict emerging will be enhanced.

Goals

The formulation of goals is channeled by the contexts within which the contending parties exist. First, the terms in which aims are formulated depend upon the contemporary way of thinking, analysis of problems, and the solutions that are available. In much of the world today, for example, issues are politicized (Gurr 1970, p. 179), and grievances are often diagnosed as pertaining to power and authority. One of the influential books in the women's liberation movement is titled *Sexual Politics,* and, indeed, the theme is that women are oppressed in a power relationship (Millett 1970, pp. 125–127). Even within the politicized realm, societies may differ in styles of analysis and hence solutions. In the United States extremist and populist thought is sufficiently widespread that this can affect the formulation of goals for a variety of grievances. Analyses of the McCarthyism of the 1950s in the United States testify to this (Shils 1956, pp. 98–185). Nationalism is a widespread way of thinking and can help mobilize and channel conflict efforts. Revolutionary challenges to a government can be aided when robed in nationalistic claims. The government can be charged with failing to defend national interests. Effectively, this played a role in the Russian Revolution (Skocpol 1979, p. 98). Sometimes the government may be charged with being an instrument of foreigners, as has been charged in revolutionary struggles in many third-world countries, including the revolution against the Shah of Iran's government.

The formulation of goals is dependent upon the current way of thinking, but what is current changes. There are fashions in what is the appropriate kind of solution to grievances. Insofar as this is the case, leaders of conflict groups or those with more access to the surrounding social world will tend to keep up with these changes more than the rank-and-file constituency. These varying views can be a source of discrepancy in goals within a conflict unit and may explain why leaders can sometimes appear to be more radical than their followers.

Which goals are chosen depends upon possible adversaries who are believed able to redress grievances. The social environment, in this sense, provides targets for displaced dissatisfactions. In general, the environment helps each conflict group determine who the adversary can and ought to be. We observed that issues are currently often viewed as involving power and authority relations and requiring political solutions. This is also true in the sense that the government itself tends to be viewed as the place to find redress for grievances. Thus, in societies where the government is the major employer of university graduates, dissatisfactions of underemployed intellectuals or of university students are directed at the government.

The visibility and salience of different groups in a society make them more or less likely adversaries. Some groups, like governments, make themselves available as targets by presuming to be responsible for a wide range of social and economic as well as political conditions. But societies vary in the ethnic groups, the kinds of economic institutions, family structures, and so on, in ways that make different groups more or less likely as adversaries. For example, in a study of revolutions in Latin America, Midlarsky and Tanter (1967) report evidence indicating that hostility toward the United States increased with higher levels of U.S. aid and investment. This seemed to be true, however, only in counties with nondemocratic governments; presumably in these countries, the United States could be readily viewed as co-opting the local government.

Third parties and their likely evaluations also affect the way in which conflict groups formulate their goals. Taking into account how others feel may not be readily compatible with the group's own requirements and hopes. For example, Arab Palestinian organizations have disagreed about their aims. Recognizing that asserting their goal to be "throwing the Jews into the sea" has done "grave damage" to the Arab position, debate has focused upon the goal of creating a "democratic Palestinian state" in which Arabs and Jews will live in peace (Circular of the Popular Democratic Front for the Liberation of Palestine 1970, p. 63). But opposition to that aim by some Arab factions "was based on the claim that the slogan contradicts the Arab character of Palestine and the principle of self-determination which was established in the National Covenant of the (Palestine) Liberation Organization, and that it also advocates a peaceful settlement with the Jews of Palestine."

Finally, the degree and form of the institutionalization of conflict regulation affect the formulation of goals, particularly their radicalism. Units that are part of a larger system with institutionalized means of reaching collective decisions tend to formulate reformist goals.

SUMMARY AND CONCLUSIONS

The collective identities of conflict units, their grievances, and their oppositional goals are based upon underlying conflicts. The cleavages and issues of the objective conflict in the long run shape the identities, grievances, and goals in social conflicts. The preceding discussion suggests which cleavages and issues are particularly important. Cleavages which persist over many generations provide an enduring basis for collective identities. Where people are socialized into conceptions of themselves as members of a particular ethnicity, race, religion, or class, these identities are readily able to be mobilzed for conflicts. Where such groups also have agencies specialized to wage struggles, obviously, the mobilization essential to social conflict is already present. Issues based on profound interests are likely to be the source of major grievances. Differences in power, status, and material resources are interests of fundamental importance in consensual conflicts.

Manifest conflicts are not simply determined, however, by the underlying conflict. Additional factors affect the salience of collective identities, grievances, and oppositional goals. For example, we noted that feelings of alienation or hostility may be aroused in one setting and displaced toward targets selected because of their availability and vulnerability. Such processes add unrealistic components to social conflicts.

In this chapter we analyzed three major elements of every social conflict: collective identity, sense of grievance, and incompatible goals. We discussed the conditions and processes that lead a category of people to think of themselves as a collectivity with a common identity and the factors that affect the content of their collective identity. We examined what makes people think they do not have that which is appropriate for them to have and possible for them to have—that is, how people come to feel aggrieved about not attaining what they think they should and could get. Finally, we studied what determines the formulation of goals that would be objectionable to another collectivity. We discussed what conditions and processes made one group believe that its grievances could be reduced by another group's yielding something or altering its conduct. Knowing how adversaries perceive their conflict reveals its structure; diagnosing the structure is critical to assessing its course and outcome.

As we move from underlying manifest conflict, we give increased attention to leaders and to the aware segments of the social categories in contention. Not all members of a conflict unit exhibit consciousness of the social conflict. Most university students are not generally in a manifest conflict relationship with administrators. Most Americans are indifferent to the pursuit of the majority of foreign policy aims of the U.S. government. Consequently, the persons who believe there is a conflict play a crucial role in mobilization of conflict parties.

In examining the determinants of collective identity, sense of grievance, and incompatible goals, we considered three sets of factors: unit characteristics, relations between the adversaries, and the social environment of the units. The various determinants are complexly related to each other and to the various components of a social conflict. It is significant that each factor does not have the same effect upon every aspect of a struggle. The forces do not all operate in the same direction.

Change in conditions may have contradictory effects upon the probability of a dispute's emerging from an objective conflict situation. For example, consider a social category in which power is deteriorating relative to another social category that has been, and still is, superior. As the magnitude of the deterioration increases, we would expect the sense of grievance and the degree of dissatisfaction to do so also. The belief that something can be done about it, that it is possible to improve one's position, may also rise as conditions deteriorate but only up to a point: then further deterioration may weaken such beliefs. Thus studies of unemployed workers reveal that many become apathetic (Sheppard, Ferman, and Faber 1960; Lazarsfeld-Jahoda and Zeisel 1933; Kornhauser 1959, pp. 163–167). These studies also indicate that with deteriorating conditions workers are increasingly isolated from one another, avoid social contacts, and generally exhibit less solidarity. Finally, as conditions deteriorate, the nature of the goals change; the goals are likely to be more radical. These various consequences are diagrammed in Figure 3.3.

This means that the actual behavioral outcome of a deteriorating condition will depend on the responses of the adversary and the social context within which antagonists are contending. It is also likely that a variety of conflict organizations, following different modes of action, will coexist. One of them may become more dominant than the others, depending on the appropriateness of the strategy it follows, given the constituency, the opponents, and the developing circumstances. This discussion of deteriorating conditions serves as a transition to the next chapter. Dissatisfaction is not simply and directly translated into conflict behavior. Other factors must be taken into account in order to understand the recourse to coercion and to violence. Discussion of these factors is the task of the next chapter.

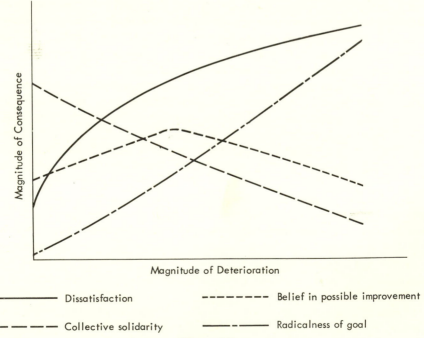

Figure 3.3

BIBLIOGRAPHY

AVINERI, SHLOMO, "Israel and the New Left," *Transaction,* 7 (July/August 1970), 79–84.

BARTH, FREDERICK (ed.), *Ethnic Groups and Boundaries* (Boston: Little, Brown, 1969).

BALDWIN, DAVID A., "Power and Social Exchange," *American Political Science Review,* 72 (December 1978), 1229–1242.

BELL, INGE POWELL, *CORE and the Strategy of Non-Violence* (New York: Random House, 1968).

BETEILLE, ANDRE, "The Decline of Social Inequality?" pp. 362–380 in Andre Beteille (ed.), *Social Inequality* (Baltimore, Md.: Penguin, 1969).

BLALOCK, H. M., JR., "Status Inconsistency, Social Mobility, Status Integration and Structural Effects," *American Sociological Review,* 32 (October 1967a), 790–801.

————, "Status Inconsistency and Interaction: Some Alternative Models," *American Journal of Sociology,* 73 (November 1967b), 305–315.

BLAU, PETER M., *Exchange and Power in Social Life* (New York: John Wiley, 1964).

BLAUNER, ROBERT, *Alienation and Freedom: The Factory Worker and His Industry* (Chicago: The University of Chicago Press, 1964).

BOK, DEREK C. AND JOHN T. DUNLOP, *Labor and the American Community* (New York: Simon & Schuster, 1970).

BORHEK, J. T., "Ethnic-Group Cohesion," *American Journal of Sociology,* 76 (July 1970), 33–46.

BRADBURN, NORMAN M., *The Structure of Psychological Well-Being* (Chicago: Aldine, 1969).

BRADBURN, NORMAN M. AND DAVID CAPLOVITZ, *Reports on Happiness* (Chicago: Aldine, 1965).

BRAUNGART, RICHARD G., "The Utopian and Ideological Styles of Student Political Activists," paper presented at the 2nd Annual Meeting of the International Society of Political Psychology, Washington, D.C., 1979.

BRINTON, CRANE, *The Anatomy of Revolution* (New York: Vintage, 1955). Originally published in 1938.

BROOM, LEONARD AND F. LANCASTER JONES, "Status Consistency and Political Preference: The Australian Case," *American Sociological Review,* 35 (December 1970), 989–1001.

BUCHANAN, WILLIAM AND HADLEY CANTRIL, *How Nations See Each Other* (Urbana, Ill.: University of Illinois Press, 1953).

CANTRIL, HADLEY, *The Pattern of Human Concerns* (New Brunswick, N.J.: Rutgers University Press, 1965).

CIRCULAR OF THE POPULAR DEMOCRATIC FRONT FOR THE LIBERATION OF PALESTINE, 1969, cited in Yehoshafat Harkabi, "Liberation or Genocide?" *Transaction,* 7 (July/August 1970), 63.

CORWIN, RONALD G., "Patterns of Organizational Conflict," *Administrative Science Quarterly,* 14 (December 1969), 507–520.

COSER, LEWIS A., *The Functions of Social Conflict* (New York: Free Press, 1956).

DAHRENDORF, RALF, *Class and Class Conflict in Industrial Society* (Stanford, Calif.: Stanford University Press, 1959).

DAVIES, JAMES C., "Toward a Theory of Revolution," *American Sociological Review,* 27 (February 1962), 5–19.

DONALD, DAVID, "Toward a Reconsideration of Abolitionists," pp. 19–36 in David Donald, *Lincoln Reconsidered, Essays on the Civil War Era* (New York: Knopf, 1956).

DUNLOP, JOHN T., "The Development of Labor Organizations," pp. 48–56 in Joseph Shister (ed.), *Labor Economics and Industrial Relations* (Philadelphia: Lippincott, 1951).

ELLSWORTH, J. S., JR., *Factory Folkways* (New Haven, Conn.: Yale University Press, 1952).

FEIERABEND, IVO K., ROSALIND L. FEIERABEND, AND BETTY A. NESVOLD, "Social Change and Political Violence: Cross-National Patterns," pp. 632–687 in Hugh Davis Graham and Ted Robert Gurr (eds.), *Violence in America* (New York: Bantam, 1969).

THE FEMINISTS FROM NEW YORK CITY, "Kate Millet Please Understand," reprinted in *It Ain't Me Babe* (October 8, 1970).

FIREMAN, BRUCE AND WILLIAM A. GAMSON, "Utilitarian Logic in the Resource Mobilization Perspective," pp. 8–44 in Mayer N. Zald and John D. McCarthy (eds.), *The Dynamics of Social Movements* (Cambridge, Mass.: Winthrop Publishers, 1979).

FLEXNER, ELEANOR, *Century of Struggle* (Cambridge, Mass.: Harvard University Press, 1959).

FORM, WILLIAM H., "Conflict within the Working Class: The Skilled as a Special-Interest Group," pp. 51–73 in Otto N. Larsen (ed.) *The Uses of Controversy in Sociology* (New York: Free Press, 1976).

FRIEDMANN, EUGENE A. AND ROBERT J. HAVIGHURST, *The Meaning of Work and Retirement* (Chicago: University of Chicago Press, 1954).

GALTUNG, JOHAN, "A Structural Theory of Aggression," *Journal of Peace Research,* 2 (1964), 95–119.

GAMSON, WILLIAM A., *The Strategy of Social Protest* (Homewood, Ill.: Dorsey Press, 1975).

GESCHWENDER, JAMES A., "Continuities in Theories of Status Consistency and Cognitive Dissonance," *Social Forces,* 46 (December 1967), 160–171.

————, "Status Inconsistency, Social Isolation, and Individual Unrest," *Social Forces,* 46 (June 1968), 477–483.

GOFFMAN, IRWIN, W., "Status Consistency and Preference for Change in Power Distribution," *American Sociological Review,* 22 (June 1957), 275–281.

GOODMAN, PAUL S. AND ABRAHAM FRIEDMAN, "An Examination of Adams' Theory of Inequity," *Administrative Science Quarterly,* 16 (September 1971), 271–288.

GOULDNER, ALVIN W., *Patterns of Industrial Bureaucracy* (New York: Free Press, 1954).

GURR, TED ROBERT, *Why Men Rebel* (Princeton, N.J.: Princeton University Press, 1970).

HAGGSTROM, WARREN C., "Can the Poor Transform the World?" pp. 67–110 in Irwin Deutscher and Elizabeth J. Thompson (eds.), *Among the People* (New York: Basic Books, 1968).

HALEBSKY, SANDOR, *Mass Society and Political Conflict* (Cambridge, Eng.: Cambridge University Press, 1976).

HOBSBAWM, E. J., *Primitive Rebels* (New York: W. W. Norton & Co., Inc., 1965). Originally published in 1959.

HODGE, ROBERT W. AND DONALD J. TREIMAN, "Class Identification in the U.S." *American Journal of Sociology,* 73 (March 1968), 535–547.

HOMANS, GEORGE CASPAR, *Social Behavior: Its Elementary Forms* (New York: Harcourt Brace Jovanovich, 1961).

HORNUNG, CARLTON ALBERT, "Status Consistency: A Method of Measurement and Empirical Examination," unpublished Ph.D. dissertation, Department of Sociology, Syracuse University, 1972.

HUGHES, EVERETT C., "Dilemmas and Contradictions of Status," *American Journal of Sociology,* 50 (March 1944), 353–359.

HYMAN, HERBERT H., "The Psychology of Status," *Archives of Psychology*, no. 269 (1942).

INKELES, ALEX, "Industrial Man: The Relation of Status to Experience, Perception, and Value," *American Journal of Sociology,* 66 (July 1960), 1–31.

JACKSON, ELTON F., "Status Consistency and Symptoms of Stress," *American Sociological Review,* 27 (August 1962), 469–480.

JOHNSON, CHALMERS A., *Peasant Nationalism and Communist Power* (Stanford, Calif.: Stanford University Press, 1962).

JOHNSON, PAULA B., DAVID O. SEARS, AND JOHN B. McCONAHAY, "Black Invisibility, the Press and the Los Angeles Riot," *American Journal of Sociology,* 76 (January 1971), 698–721.

KARON, BERTRAM P., *The Negro Personality* (New York: Springer Publishing Co., 1958).

KORNHAUSER, WILLIAM, *The Politics of Mass Society* (New York: Free Press, 1959).

KRIESBERG, LOUIS, "Customer Versus Colleague Ties Among Retail Furriers," *Journal of Retailing,* 29 (Winter 1953–1954), 173–176.

———, *Social Inequality* (Englewood Cliffs, N.J.: Prentice-Hall, 1979).

KRIESBERG, MARTIN, "Cross-Pressures and Attitudes," *Public Opinion Quarterly,* 13 (Spring 1949), 5–16.

LANDECKER, WERNER S., "Class Crystallization and Class Consciousness," *American Sociological Review,* 28 (April 1963), 219–229.

———, "Status Congruence, Class Crystallization, and Social Cleavage," *Sociology and Social Research,* 54 (April 1970), 343–355.

LAQUEUR, WALTER, "Revolution," *International Encyclopedia of the Social Sciences,* 13 (1968), 501–507.

LASLETT, BARBARA, "Mobility and Work Satisfaction: A Discussion of the Use and Interpretation of Mobility Models," *American Journal of Sociology,* 77 (July 1971), 19–35.

LAUMAN, EDWARD O. AND DAVID R. SEGAL, "Status Inconsistency and Ethnoreligious Group Membership as Determinants of Social Participation and Political Attitudes," *American Journal of Sociology,* 77 (July 1971), 36–61.

LAZARSFELD, PAUL F., BERNARD BERELSON, AND HAZEL GAUDET, *The People's Choice* (New York: Columbia University Press, 1944).

LAZARSFELD-JAHODA, MARIE AND HANS ZEISEL, *Die Arbeitlosen von Marienthal* (Leipzig: Verlag von S. Hirzel, 1933).

LEAHY, PETER AND ALLAN MAZUR, "A Comparison of Movements Opposed to Nuclear Power, Fluoridation, and Abortion," pp. 143–154 in Louis Kriesberg (ed.), *Research in Social Movements, Conflicts and Change,* Vol. 1 (Greenwich, Conn.: JAI Press, 1978).

LENSKI, GERHARD E., "Status Crystallization: A Non-Vertical Dimension of Social Status," *American Sociological Review,* 19 (August 1954), 405–413.

LIPSET, SEYMOUR MARTIN, *Agrarian Socialism* (Berkeley and Los Angeles: University of California Press, 1950).

———, "Fascism—Left, Right, and Center," pp. 131–176 in S. M. Lipset, *Political Man* (New York: Doubleday, 1960).

LIPSET, SEYMOUR MARTIN AND EARL RAAB, *The Politics of Unreason: Right Wing Extremism in America 1790–1970* (New York: Harper & Row, Pub., 1970).

LIPSET, SEYMOUR MARTIN AND SHELDON S. WOLIN (eds.), *The Berkeley Student Revolt* (New York: Anchor Books, 1965).

MANN, MICHAEL, "The Social Cohesion of Liberal Democracy," *American Sociological Review,* 35 (June 1970), 423–439.

MARX, GARY T., *Protest and Prejudice* (New York: Harper & Row, Pub., 1969).

MERTON, ROBERT K. AND ALICE S. KITT, "Contributions to the Theory of Reference Group Behavior," pp. 70–105 in R. K. Merton and P. F. Lazarsfeld (eds.), *Studies in the Scope and Method of "The American Soldier"* (New York: Free Press, 1950).

MIDLARSKY, MANUS AND RAYMOND TANTER, "Toward a Theory of Political Instability in Latin America," *Journal of Peace Research,* 3 (1967), 209–226.

MILLETT, KATE, *Sexual Politics* (New York: Doubleday, 1970).

MORRIS, RICHARD T. AND VINCENT JEFFRIES, "Violence Next Door," *Social Forces,* 46 (March 1968), 352–358.

NATIONAL ADVISORY COMMISSION ON CIVIL DISORDERS (KERNER COMMISSION), *Report of the National Commission on Civil Disorders* (New York: Bantam, 1968).

OBERSCHALL, ANTHONY, *Social Conflict and Social Movements* (Englewood Cliffs, N.J.: Prentice-Hall, 1973).

————, "Loosely Structured Collective Conflict: A Theory and an Application," pp. 45–68 in Louis Kriesberg (ed.), *Research in Social Movements, Conflicts and Change,* Vol. 3 (Greenwich, Conn.: JAI Press, 1980).

OLSON, MANCUR, JR., *The Logic of Collective Action* (New York: Schoken Books, 1968).

PAIGE, JEFFERY M., *Agrarian Revolution: Social Movements and Export Agriculture in the Underdeveloped World* (New York: Free Press, 1975).

PARKER, SEYMOUR AND ROBERT J. KLEINER, "The Culture of Poverty," *American Anthropologist,* 72 (June 1970), 516–527.

PARKIN, FRANK, *Class Inequality and Political Order* (New York: Praeger, Inc., 1971).

PERETZ, DON, "Palestine's Arabs," *Transaction,* 7 (August 1970), 43–49.

PERLMAN, SELIG, *A Theory of the Labor Movement* (New York: Augustus M. Kelley, 1928).

ROSECRANCE, RICHARD N., *Action and Reaction in World Politics* (Boston: Little, Brown, 1963).

ROSSI, PETER H. AND RICHARD A. BERK, "Local Political Leadership and Popular Discontent," *The Annals* (September 1970), 111–127.

RUNCIMAN, W. G., *Relative Deprivation and Social Justice* (Berkeley and Los Angeles: University of California Press, 1966).

SAWYER, JACK, "Dimensions of Nations: Size, Wealth, and Politics," *American Journal of Sociology,* 73 (September 1967), 145–172.

SCHMITT, DAVID R., "An Attitudinal Correlate of the Status Congruency of Married Women," *Social Forces,* 44 (December 1965), 190–195.

SCHUMAN, HOWARD AND BARRY GRUENBERG, "The Impact of City on Racial Attitudes, *American Journal of Sociology,* 76 (September 1970), 213–261.

SCOTT, JOSEPH W. AND MOHAMMED EL-ASSAL, "Multiversity, University Size, University Quality and Student Protest: An Empirical Study," *American Sociological Review,* 34 (October 1969), 702–709.

SEIDMAN, JOEL, JACK LONDON, BERNARD KARSH, AND DAISY L. TAGLIACOZZO, *The Worker Views His Union* (Chicago: The University of Chicago Press, 1958). 1

SHARP, GENE, *The Politics of Nonviolent Action* (Boston: Porter Sargent Publisher, 1973).

SHEATSLEY, PAUL B., "White Attitudes Toward the Negro," *Daedalus*, 95 (Winter 1966), 217–238.

SHEPPARD, HAROLD L., LOUIS A. FERMAN, AND SEYMOUR FABER, *Too Old to Work—Too Young to Retire: A Case Study of a Permanent Plant Shutdown* (Washington, D.C.: Government Printing Office, U.S. Senate Special Committee on Unemployment Problems, 1960).

SHIBUTANI, TAMOTSU AND KIAN M. KWAN, *Ethnic Stratification* (New York: Macmillan, 1965).

SHILS, EDWARD A., *The Torment of Secrecy* (New York: Free Press, 1956).

SKOCPOL, THEDA, *States and Social Revolutions: A Comparative Analysis of France, Russia, and China* (Cambridge, Eng.: Cambridge University Press, 1979).

SNYDER, DAVID, "Collective Violence Processes: Implications for Disaggregated Theory and Research," pp. 35–61 in Louis Kriesberg (ed.), *Research in Social Movements, Conflicts and Change*, Vol. 2 (Greenwich, Conn.: JAI Press, 1979.)

SPILERMAN, SEYMOUR, "The Causes of Racial Disturbances: A Comparison of Alternative Explanations," *American Sociological Review*, 35 (August 1970), 627–649.

———, "The Causes of Racial Disturbance: Tests of an Explanation," *American Sociological Review*, 36 (June 1971), 427–442.

STEINEM, GLORIA, "A New Egalitarian Life Style," *The New York Times* (Aug. 26, 1971), p. 37.

STONE, PHILIP J., "Expectations of a Better Personal Future," *Public Opinion Quarterly*, 34 (Fall 1970), 346–359.

TANTER, RAYMOND AND MANUS MIDLARSKY, "A Theory of Revolution," *Journal of Conflict Resolution*, 11 (September 1967), 264–280.

TILLOCK, HARRIET AND DENTON R. MORRISON, "Group Size and Contributions to Collective Action," pp. 131–158 in Louis Kriesberg (ed.), *Research in Social Movements, Conflicts and Change*, Vol. 2 (Greenwich, Conn.: JAI Press, 1979).

TILLY, CHARLES, *From Mobilization to Revolution* (Reading, Mass.: Addison-Wesley, 1978).

TREIMAN, DONALD J., "Status Discrepancy and Prejudice," *American Journal of Sociology*, 71 (May 1966), 651–664.

VALAVANIS, STEFAN, "The Resolution of Conflict When Utilities Interact," *Journal of Conflict Resolution*, 2 (June 1958), 156–169.

VOEGELIN, ERIC, "The Growth of the Race Idea," *Review of Politics*, 2 (1940), 283–317.

WEINBERG, MARTIN S. AND COLIN J. WILLIAMS, "Disruption, Social Location and Interpretive Practices: The Case of Wayne, New Jersey," *American Sociological Review*, 34 (April 1969), 170–182.

WHYTE, WILLIAM F., *Human Relations in Industry* (New York: McGraw-Hill, 1948).

WILLIAMS, J. ALLEN, JR. AND PAUL L. WIENIR, "A Reexamination of Myrdal's Rank Order of Discrimination," *Social Problems*, 14 (Spring 1967), 443–454.

WOLFE, ALAN, *The Rise and Fall of the "Soviet Threat": Domestic Sources of the Cold War Consensus* (Washington, D.C.: Institute for Policy Studies, 1979).

ZALD, MAYER N. AND ROBERTA ASH, "Social Movement Organizations: Growth, Decay, and Change," *Social Forces*, 44 (March 1966), 327–341.

4

Pursuing
Conflict Goals

If two parties are in a struggle, it might seem necessary to them to use coercion. How else could one side induce the other to yield what it does not wish to? In a purely zero-sum conflict that may be the case. But, as we noted in Chapter 1, by extending the time range, widening the number of issues in contention, fractionating the single conflict issue, or otherwise shifting the focal conflict, the zero-sum payoff is transformed into a variable-sum payoff. As we shall see in more detail in this chapter, even in an intense conflict there are alternatives and supplements to coercion.

We shall discuss the many ways in which conflicting parties pursue their aims and what affects the choice of alternatives. The use of the word *choice* should not be interpreted to mean that all alternatives are consciously weighed by each party and that, after due calculation, a course of action is selected. Rather, we are concerned with the factors that influence and constrain the course followed. As observers we may consider even those alternatives that were not thought of or were quickly rejected by the participants. It may be that the constraints are generally so great that little thought is given to the selection. The conflicting parties may appear to be doing only the obvious and taking unreflective action.

The point is that conflict behavior is a means to move toward a desired goal. We are not simply interested in expressive action, even violence. Again, this is not to deny that some modes have expressive elements; people do use coercion because it feels good to express hostility or to hurt someone else. We must consider such actions and their determinants, but they are not conflict behavior.

For the coercive action to be conflict behavior, there must be an intention to induce the other side to yield what the coercer wishes to obtain. The choice of a specific alternative may seem counterproductive to an observer; or the coercer's intention may not be recognized by the opponent, to whom it would appear irrational and simply expressive, although it may not appear that way to the coercer. For example, blacks, but not whites, generally viewed the 1960s riots in the ghettos as protest actions that would affect white policies (Brink and Harris 1969, p. 264; Feagin and Sheatsley 1968; Erskine 1968, p. 524; Sears and Tomlinson 1968).

ALTERNATIVE MODES

We will examine alternative modes used in conducing a conflict in terms of the types of inducements applied and the degree to which the application of the inducements is regulated.

Types of Inducements

A conflict party has three basic ways to induce adversaries to move toward the position it desires: It may try to persuade, coerce, or reward the opponents. These three kinds of inducements have been distinguished, with somewhat varying content and designations, by several writers. Deutsch (1973) refers to influence, threats, and promises; Etzioni (1961) speaks of normative, coercive, and utilitarian bases of compliance; Gamson (1968) discusses persuasion, inducements, and constraints; and Turner (1970) distinguishes among persuasion, coercion, and bargaining. Other writers stress the difference between threats and promises or between negative and positive sanctions (Singer 1963; Baldwin 1971). We discuss each kind of inducement separately; but in actual conduct, as we shall see, they are combined in varying proportions.

Persuasion. As used here, persuasion refers to influencing others by communicating arguments or appeals that alter the other's perception of the contentious issue in the manner the persuader intends (Wrong 1979). Pure persuasion is unconstrained by promises or threats. The persons being persuaded weigh the arguments and appeals in terms of their own values and goals.

Several kinds of arguments and appeals are used in attempts to influence opponents. One kind of persuasive effort takes the form of an actor's asking the adversary to take its role. The adversary, for example, is assured that what is being sought is necessary for national security and is not intended to be used aggressively or as a threat. For example, during Egyptian and Israeli peace treaty negotiations, Israeli military officers took Egyptian officers on tours of the West Bank to demonstrate Israeli vulnerability to attack if an armed enemy occupied certain positions.

A second kind of argument points out complementary interests that would be enhanced by yielding what is sought. Thus, during negotiations prior to the 1955 State Treaty, resulting in the withdrawal of Soviet, U.S., British, and French occupation forces from Austria, Austrian leaders sought to convince Soviet leaders that Austria wanted to be and would remain neutral (Allard 1970). They argued how neutrality was in their interests and how it would be beneficial to the Soviet Union as well.

A third kind of persuasive argument tries to turn a divisive issue into a problem that is shared and needs a mutually satisfactory solution. Discussions about arms control often take this form: Each side points out that a war would severely damage all parties, and war, therefore, constitutes a common problem. Proposals to reduce or limit certain kinds of military developments, then, are presented as reducing a shared problem. In discussions of nuclear weapons testing, particularly testing in the atmosphere, in the 1960s adversaries stressed the common damage that radioactivity released into the atmosphere generated. In addition, Soviet and U.S. leaders could argue that public outcries and protests by other governments constituted a common problem shared by Soviet and U.S. government policy makers.

A fourth kind of argument pertains particularly to the interlocking character of conflicts. One actor may try to convince its adversary that they have a common antagonist against whom they can work together. In the 1963 discussions in Moscow to negotiate the partial nuclear test ban agreement, for example, some suggestions were made by U.S. officials of the advantages of limiting the nuclear club and the advantage of adding pressure to inhibit China from developing its nuclear weapons capability (Schlesinger 1965).

Finally, many persuasive arguments are phrased in terms of appeals to common values and norms. For example, appeals are made to fundamental values of freedom, national self-determination, and norms of fairness and equity. The persuading party argues that the adversary should comply because what is sought is consistent with its own interests and values. The appeal is made to abstract principles, shared identifications, or previously neglected values.

These appeals can be advanced in a variety of arenas. The persuasive efforts may be more or less explicit. They may be done mutually in varying degrees; that is, one party may make such efforts with or without the acceptance of an opponent. If done against the wishes of the advocate speaking for one side, these efforts are called subversive. In that case the appeals may be hidden or conducted with subterfuge. Persuadors also vary greatly in the degree to which they utilize symbolic means of communication or try to convince the other side by deeds and demonstrations. Thus, efforts by missionaries, or less obviously by members of each group in a dissensual conflict, may be to convince the other side of the rightness of their own views by what must be recognized as exemplary conduct and rich reward.

Coercion. Coercion involves trying to make the other side yield by reason of fear or actual injury. In attempting to coerce the opponent, the coercer is trying to change the reality in which the opponent exists so that it believes that the pains of not complying will be greater than those of complying. Coercion is punishing and is also conditional in that it depends upon the conduct of the other side; compliance obviates the need to coerce.

Coercion, too, has many forms and arenas. One significant distinction between types of coercion is whether they are threatened or implemented. Given its conditional character, coercion generally is threatened before being applied, in the hope that the threat will suffice. The threat must, however, be convertible to action. The threat may be implicit in the relationship and hardly evoked to induce compliance. In that case, however, we are back at the objective conflict stage.

Coercion also varies in the content of the negative sanctions that may be applied. They include interpersonal efforts at shame and ridicule. In this book, however, we are especially concerned with negative sanctions that involve physical harm to adversaries; these sanctions include nonviolent economic sanctions in the form of withdrawal of goods or services and violent actions that physically prevent or impede opponents from doing what they wish. We use the term *violence* to refer to actual efforts at coercion that involve the immediate and direct physical damage to people or their possessions. This definition is a conventional meaning of the word *violence* and more appropriate for the theoretical position taken in this work. Some writers in the 1960s have broadened the term to include any actions or inactions by people that prevent others from living a complete life (Galtung 1969). In this sense the deaths from malnutrition due to inequitable distribution of the resources of a society are violence. Although this extension of the meaning of violence is inapplicable to the theoretical stance of this work, the definition used here does include actions not always popularly covered by the term (Blumenthal, Kahn, Andrews, and Head 1972, pp. 71–95). Thus, when a state's military forces fire upon a group challenging the state's authority, that is violence as defined here.

Reward. Rewards are obvious inducements, but they may seem strange in relationship to social conflicts. The idea is that one side offers the other a reward for compliance rather than a punishment for not complying. There is extensive literature about the differences between punishment and rewards as inducements to learning and to socialization in general (see, for example, Hilgard and Bower 1966; Becker 1964). The implications for using rewards rather than punishments in handling conflicts, however, has been relatively neglected (Baldwin 1979).

Rewards, like punishments, must be conditional upon the action of the other side, if they are to serve as inducements. It must cost something to a party to offer rewards, otherwise they might be given even if the other side did not comply. Given freely, as in love and identification, the rewards are not an inducement to follow a particular and objectionable course of action.

Rewards, or positive sanctions, can take a variety of forms. Commodity exchanges are the clearest example. In these cases, one group will offer money, land, or payments of another kind in exchange for obtaining what it seeks. The positive sanction may also involve nontangible positive sanctions, such as approbation or deference.

Negative and positive sanctions have several intriguingly different properties (Baldwin 1971). If a conflict party seeks to influence an opponent by a promise, the opponent's compliance obligates the conflict party to give a reward, while the failure to comply does not require any action. On the other hand, a conflict party using threats will act when there is no compliance and plans for such noncompliance. Consequently, "promises tend to cost more when they succeed, while threats tend to cost more when they fail" (Baldwin 1971, p. 28). Promises and threats differ in the circumstances in which they are appropriate and effective as well as in their consequences, as we note in later sections of this book.

Combinations

In any concrete case, these types of inducements are mixed together. Inducements may be explicitly combined, for example, when one government promises benefits and threatens punishment to get compliance. The combination is also often implicit. Thus threats to an adversary are usually cloaked in justifications, and those might have a persuasive effect.

In Figure 4.1 the three dimensions of inducements are diagrammed, and we can imagine the variety of actual means taken as different points within that field. One such set of points will be discussed here because they are often neglected in analyses of social conflict—that is, the variety of nonviolent means of pursuing objectives.

Sharp (1959) has outlined nine different types of nonviolence and action. These range from nonresistance (in which people withdraw into their own purity) to nonviolent revolution (*a* and *i,* respectively, in Fig. 4.1). Between these are: active

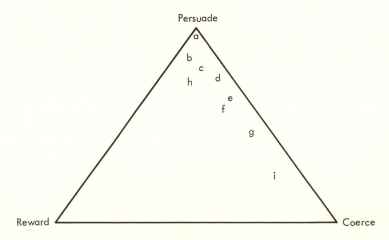

Figure 4.1 Means of Inducement.

reconciliation (*c*), such as engaged in by Quakers; passive resistance or noncooperation (*e*); nonviolent direct action, in which people intervene to disrupt unacceptable procedures (*g*); and satyagraha as formulated by Gandhi (*h*). These types vary in the degree of coercion, but all involve some persuasive components although, again, in varying degrees. Some include rewards in the sense that there is promised a better life, a more ethical life, a closer approach to God by compliance; some are buttressed by elaborate reasoning; and some are almost spontaneously impulsive acts of people in response to conditions that they will not accept. Satyagraha or "truth-force," as developed by Gandhi, is one of the most influential applications and theoretical analyses of nonviolence as a way of bringing about a desired change against the opposition of others (Gandhi 1940; Bondurant 1965).

Three concepts are fundamental in satyagraha: truth, nonviolence, and self-suffering. For Gandhi, truth is God; it is an end that we seek, but since we cannot know absolute truth, its pursuit excludes the use of violence. Nonviolence does not imply the negative action of not harming, but positive love, of doing good to the evil-doer; it does not mean acquiescence to the wrong, but resistance to the wrong-doer, even if that injures the wrong-doer. Self-suffering means inviting suffering upon oneself, not out of weakness but out of courage and refraining from violence when it is possible to use violence. It is directed at moral persuasion; it is a means.

Expedient and coercive arguments are associated with other forms of nonviolence. Coercion is a fundamental aspect of many kinds of nonviolent actions. Passive resistance and noncooperation raise the other side's costs of pursuing its goals. The costs are those of diverting resources to overcome the resisters and of bearing the moral burden of repression. Sharp (1973) provides a comprehensive analysis of the many methods by which nonviolent action is waged.

In actual struggles violent and nonviolent actions occur together (Tilly and Snyder 1972). Once a conflict has begun, violent action by one side may be used to repress nonviolent efforts. Furthermore, in large-scale struggles, different groups within each major adversary coalition are likely to resort to different mixtures of conflict modes.

Institutionalization of Conflict Regulation

Another dimension of the means used to pursue conflicting goals cuts across the three kinds of inducements already discussed: This is the degree to which conflict behavior is regulated and the regulations are institutionalized. Conflict behavior is generally conducted within a set of norms or rules. The norms prescribe what inducements are legitimate for what purposes. Thus, there are even rules of war. The norms may state what forms of various combinations of inducements are appropriate for different conflicting parties. A government, for example, is allowed to use violence in circumstances that are not allowed to nongovernmental actors. Rules vary in scope and specificity among different arenas of conflict.

These rules may be more or less institutionalized. Institutionalization is great insofar as the rules seem to have an external existence—that is, independent of the actors, insofar as they are internalized within the actors and insofar as they are supported by sanctions (Blau 1964, pp. 273–277). Each aspect of institutionalization warrants discussion.

Rules embodied in written form or orally transmitted beyond one generation take on an independent quality that helps maintain them and constrains adherence to them. Codification by precedent or by law makes the rules less vulnerable to each conflict unit's partisan interpretations.

Such externality is not incompatible with the internalization of the rules through socialization. People learn rules and, if they accept them as legitimate, they may become so internalized that violation would be shunned in order to avoid the feelings of guilt or shame that would follow violation.

Sanctions to punish violations of the rules are crucial for their maintenance. Such sanctions vary in magnitude and in the certainty that they will be imposed. The likelihood that they will be enforced depends greatly upon its being in somebody's interest that they be imposed. Since the content of the rules generally is in accord with the interests of the dominants in a relationship, the dominants are the ones who are most interested in maintaining the rules and have the resources to do so. In other words, rules that favor the dominants will be maintained by the dominants, and these are the generally extant rules.

To illustrate: American trade unions were considered illegal conspiracies until the middle of the nineteenth century. At the turn of the century a standard procedure was the labor injunction by which workers intending to strike were issued a restraining order forbidding it; and when the Sherman Antitrust Act was enacted in 1890 it was implemented against the trade unions (Leek 1952; Taft 1964). In this example the employers, the dominants, enlisted the power of the state to maintain rules that would perpetuate the existing pattern of labor-management conflict.

Variations in Conflict Regulation. Each kind of inducement can be more or less regulated. Let us first consider regulation of persuasive inducements. In relations between parties with great power differences, the regulations are likely to facilitate ways in which the dominants can take persuasive actions against the subdominants and protect themselves from persuasive incursions from the other side. Between relatively equal parties, the rules generally permit mutually persuasive efforts. These rules may take the form of mutual agreement not to interfere with each other, as governments do when they agree to limit the access of the people of each country to the persuasive efforts of the other. Where there is also a relatively high integration and many shared understandings, the rules may proscribe too high levels of subterfuge.

The regulation of coercion, too, varies in degree and content. Even in wars, coercion may be very limited and reduced to a ritual. In the past European governments have engaged in warfare under more restrictions about the use of violence than has recently been the practice. In the wars of the seventeenth and eighteenth centuries, fighting was halted to gather harvests; it did not involve the populace at large; and there were restraints upon exploitation of technological innovations (Nef 1950). Even in contemporary wars, certain restraints can be found. For example, bacteriological weapons have not been employed; and chemical warfare has been restricted to defoliating agents used against plants and to chemical agents such as those used for domestic riot control purposes. The scope of military operations has been limited; in the Korean War the United States did not bomb extensively north of the Yalu River. Of course, in such cases it is difficult to argue that these restraints were due to adherence to rules. Rather, they could spring from calculations of self-interest. The limited character of wars may, therefore, depend upon mutual deterrence. For example, bombing China north of the Yalu was eschewed, and the Chinese did not interfere with the movement of supplies between Japan and Korea. The assessment of whether or not rules are adhered to because of acceptance of their legitimacy or because of self-interested calculations is certainly very difficult in any single case. In the long run, theoretically and empirically, the two conditions are highly related.

Rewards, too, may be more or less regulated. Rules tend to be about what is a fair exchange and what the terms of the exchange should be. The economic marketplace is controlled by a complex set of rules, adhered to from common understandings, self-interest, and high levels of institutionalization. On the whole, there is relatively little regulation about rewards in conflict relations. The exchange seems to be worked out by bargaining, with persuasive and coercive inducements also used. There may be extensive regulations, however, about the procedures to be followed in the negotiations through which the bargain is made.

Intermediaries play vital roles in conflict regulation. They may act to enforce rules or to mediate disputes within clear and explicit rules. The various roles of intermediaries, particularly mediators, are examined in Chapter 8; at this point only a few observations need to be made.

Many conflicts are conducted under the supervision or through the actions of a social unit that encompasses the contending parties. There may be arbitration of labor-management conflicts by the government; student and administrator conflicts may be appealed to, and settled by, the university board of trustees; and contending organizations of blacks and whites may petition Congress for legislation to advance their respective aims. Obviously, the partisans to such conflicts do not always accept the neutrality of the intermediary adjudications.

The adjudication of social conflicts is one of the ways in which intermediaries participate in conflicts. The would-be adjudicator may be considered a potential or real ally of one of the contending parties. Within that framework, each conflict group will try to persuade, reward, or even coerce an intermediary to support it in the pursuit of its goals.

This perspective does not rule out the possibility of the third party's playing an impartial role in conflict management. Usually, in such cases, the conflict behavior is highly regulated and institutionalized. The contending parties are likely to emphasize persuasive inducements as they contend they are correct in terms of generally shared principles.

The point is, however, that the neutrality of the intermediary party is not to be taken for granted or to be regarded as absolute. It is more likely to result from a power equilibrium than anything else. The extent to which it exists also depends on the nature of the issue in contention, the character of the units in conflict, and, most importantly, the general context within which the parties exist.

One final observation should be made. Sometimes one of the parties to a conflict claims to be above the conflict, but this claim is not recognized by the others. They argue that the claimant is an adversary. In the perspective used in this book, we will have to regard all of the parties' contentions as persuasive efforts.

Bases of Regulation and Institutionalization. Perhaps the most fundamental factor underlying the content of the rules governing conflict behavior and the institutionalization of the rules are the recurrent practices preceding explicit rules. Repeated practices come to be expected, and after a while deviations become not only violations of expectations but illegitimate (Sumner 1906, pp. 2–30). The way things are done is the way they should be done because that is the way they have been done. There is a kind of social logic to that statement since rules grow from expectations.

Anticipated continuing relations also promote the regulation of conflict behavior. If the parties expect that they will be in contention over and over again, they develop understandings about how they should each pursue their objectives (Sayles and Strauss 1953). Certain kinds of inducements may come to be regarded as out of bounds. It also follows, all things being equal, that patterns that are stable and are anticipated to remain stable are more likely to become institutionalized than are those patterns that are rapidly changing.

Other aspects of the relationship between the parties greatly affect the development of rules regarding conflict behavior. In general, insofar as the parties are integrated and have shared understandings, conflict behavior will be regulated. The way in which the relative power of the contending parties affects the regulation and institutionalization of conflict behavior is more difficult to assess. Presumably if the parties are relatively equal, rules about conflict behavior will be more equitable and adherence to them will be more acceptable to all parties. It is only with the increased power of the trade unions, for example, that collective bargaining has become highly regulated and institutionalized. On the other hand, if power inequalities are great, it may be possible for the dominant to impose rules about conflict behavior.

Characteristics of the parties to a conflict and their general context also greatly affect the degree of institutionalization and regulation. Insofar as the conflicting parties are clearly bounded and autonomous, institutionalization of conflict behavior will be impeded. The lack of conflict regulation among nation-states provides a clear example of this. If the parties are within a larger social system that has the ability to impose sanctions and guide conduct, however, then the conflict behavior between the contending parties will be regulated.

Finally, the kind of issues in contention affects the degree to which conflict behavior will be regulated. The elaboration and institutionalization of ways of handling conflicts are more likely in cases in which the contending parties are dealing with issues that they think require speedy and definite resolution. That is, some issues can be left to simmer, others come to a boil quickly. For example, Wright (1957) studied the kinds of markets that did and did not have commercial arbitration. He analyzed those commodity exchanges, such as fabric makers selling to clothing manufacturers, to see in which ones the buyer and seller made agreements that any disputes would be handled by arbitration rather than through the usual legal procedures of suing through the courts. He found that one factor was very highly related to the use of commercial arbitration: the perishability of the commodity. Presumably, for goods that quickly lose their value, such as fish or vegetables, it is important to reach a speedy decision about a dispute, and almost any decision is better than no decision. In addition, issues that are viewed as crucial to the actors are less likely to be regulated than are issues that are not so viewed.

A variety of factors, then, affects the content and degree of regulation of conflict behavior and the extent to which the regulations are institutionalized. In this work, however, we will usually take the level of regulation and institutionalization as given. The parties in any particular conflict do not modify them greatly. Only in the chapters discussing the outcomes of conflicts and their consequences will we consider the levels of regulation and institutionalization as something to be explained rather than as part of an explanation.

SELECTING THE MODE

As soon as a conflict unit begins to move toward its goal, some way of inducing the other side to yield has been chosen. There always are alternatives and a selection among them must be made. The choice may not be a matter of much reflection by anyone, or it may be the result of long and extensive deliberation. We will examine four sets of factors that jointly affect the selection of means used: the goal, the characteristics of the conflict unit, the relations between the conflict-ing units, and the environment of the units.

The mode chosen in pursuing an aim is a blend of all the inducements with varying degrees of regulation and institutionalization. But the choice is made and remade as long as the struggle continues. Each party shifts its modes of pursuing its goals as it changes, as the other side responds, and as the environment alters, partly as a response to previous choices.

The Goal

The basic factor that affects how a conflict party pursues its goal is the goal itself. How people try to get what they want depends upon what they want. Or that is what they wish were so. Actually there is often much dissension within a conflict unit about the appropriateness of a given means for the end sought. Some means, if utilized, may be counterproductive, indeed may deny the attainment of what is desired. As Kennan (1961, pp. 390–391) writes regarding international conflicts, "Outright war is itself too unambivalent, too undiscriminating a device to be an appropriate means for effecting a mere change of regime in another country. You cannot logically inflict in another people the horrors of nuclear destruction in the name of what you believe to be its salvation, and expect it to share your enthusiasm for the exercise." He even goes on to say:

> . . . modern warfare in the grand manner, pursued by all available means and aimed at the total destruction of the enemy's capacity to resist, is, unless it proceeds very rapidly and successfully, of such general destructiveness that it ceases to be useful as an instrument for the achievement of any coherent political purpose. Such warfare . . . involves evils which far outweigh any . . . purpose at all . . . short of sheer self-preservation, and perhaps not even short of that. (p. 391)

Yet wars continue to be threatened and waged as if for some political goal. This is most likely, for limited wars for limited aims (Blechman 1966).

Several aspects of goals are related to the ways in which they are pursued. Efforts at persuasion are more frequently and extensively exercised in dissensual than in consensual conflicts. After all, what is often sought in dissensual conflicts is an alteration in the values or beliefs of the adversary. In that case, some degree of conversion of the opponent is needed. There is a psycho-logic that compels a party to emphasize either persuasion or coercion, depending on its analysis of the conflict. For example, consider the alternative approaches that black liberationists or women's liberationists might take. If the consensual nature of the conflict is stressed, then it is argued that both sides want the same thing and the other side is getting more of it at the expense of the exploited, deprived side. If that is the case, the other side would not be induced to make concessions and reduce the exploitation without some coercion. But if the dissensual nature of the conflict is stressed, then it must be argued that the other side is not gaining by the deprived position of women or blacks. The analysis and the argument must then be that both sides are suffering and that they have common interests. The possibility of mobilizing one's own side in terms of its exploitation is weakened.

The magnitude of the incompatibility of the goals in a consensual conflict significantly affects the mode chosen. If what is being sought is a fundamental change, then rewards and bargaining are not likely to seem adequate, and in this society, at least, neither is persuasion. Bell (1968, p. 59) in her study of CORE observed that the choice of nonviolence was based on the liberals' belief that discrimination rested on isolated attitudes that were not very deeply rooted.

Lammers (1969) studied strikes and mutinies and distinguished two main goals: (1) promotion of interests, or (2) secession or seizure of power. In the former case he found that the main weapon was a work stoppage, and in the latter case it was violence: imprisonment or killing of superiors.

The degree and nature of coercive violence also varies with the magnitude of the change being sought. In an analysis of civil strife in over a hundred nations in the early 1960s, Gurr (1969, Table 17.7) found that turmoil (strikes, riots, demonstrations) was disproportionally associated with promoting or opposing a specific governmental policy, conspiracy was disproportionately associated with the seizure of political power, and internal war was especially likely when there were several, or diffuse, political aims.

Goals also differ depending upon whether one side wants the adversary to initiate a policy or action that it is not pursuing or wants to prevent it from doing something. In the former case, rewards would typically be more appropriate than threats of punishment. In the latter case, threats of punishment are likely to appear more suitable to deter actions of an enemy. Rewards as an inducement not to act can too easily seem like paying blackmail and a never-ending cost.

Aims also tend to be collective or aggregate; that is, the benefits may be sought for the group as an entity or for the constituent members. Persuasion and conversion or reward and exchange are possible and likely to be tried for the latter aims. But for collective goals, coercion is more likely because collective goals require more open acknowledgment from the adversary, and once a struggle has begun, coercion is likely to seem necessary.

Finally, the very content of the goal may seem to dictate the means used. To some extent a party may try to attain its aim by demonstrating its movement toward the goal. If the end is equality and respect from the other side, one might seek that by presuming it already exists. Or, for example, if group members seek a way of life in which people act spontaneously—if they seek to overthrow what they regard as rigid social conventions—then acting freely themselves might seem a way of bringing that change about. Even the provocation of using obscenities seems appropriate. Indeed the use of obscenity as a way of pursuing a conflicting goal is a kind of social invention. It both coerces the other side and serves as a way of demonstrating what is being sought; it may even be persuasive by demonstrating how much one can get away with. By being so outrageous it casts doubts upon many conventions, even upon the legitimacy of authority. Or so it might seem to those using this technique at the end of the 1960s.

Similarly, people who want to attain self-respect and lose fear may think that one way of doing so is to act tough and intimidate the opposition. Fanon (1966) has argued that committing violence against oppressors gives people a new sense of power and self-respect. If the aim becomes simply to remake onself, then there is no longer social conflict. The other side is treated as an object upon which one acts in order to change oneself. In social conflicts this is never the only reason a mode is used.

The Partisans

In popular thinking the way in which a conflict unit pursues its goals is attributed to the character of that party. We think of some groups as being aggressive and of others as being peaceful. The internal or domestic character of a party is a determinant of the mode used, but not the sole one. The nature of a conflict party limits the range of modes it uses and affects the chances that each will be used under specified conditions. We now turn to consider how this may be so.

Preferences. Members of conflict parties may have cultural traditions, historical experiences, or shared personality characteristics that predispose them to prefer some conflict modes rather than others. They may have preferences about different kinds of conduct that affect the choice made in any particular conflict. If such predispositions are very powerful, they may lead members of one party to choose conflict modes that may be inappropriate given the goals they are pursuing and the adversary they oppose.

Previous usage of a particular mode of pursuing conflicting goals increases the likelihood of its usage again. Thus, in a study of civil disorder in 114 nations during the 1960s, the magnitude of current civil strife was correlated (.29) with historical levels of such strife, within each nation (Gurr 1969, Table 17.12). But it may be that the conditions that produced civil strife in earlier times simply persisted.

Within a society different categories of people may be predisposed to favor some modes rather than others. A 1969 national survey of American men found that more highly educated men were less likely to favor violence either for social control or for social change than were men with fewer years of schooling (Blumenthal, Kahn, Andrews, and Head 1972). It has been suggested that middle class distaste for violence helps account for the use of nonviolence by CORE when there was a high proportion of middle-class persons participating in CORE activities (Bell 1968, p. 80). Presumably the involvement of lower-class blacks in organizations striving to better the conditions of blacks makes the use of coercion and of violence more likely. There is some evidence that persons of lower education, income, or occupational status are more willing than others to resort to violence in pursuit of their ends (McCord, Howard, Friedberg, and Harwood 1969, p. 95). A national survey of blacks conducted in 1963 reveals the same finding. When the survey questions were repeated in 1966, however, there was no longer any difference outside the South by strata; the higher-income blacks were just as likely (21 percent) as those with low incomes to say that blacks will have to use violence to win their rights (Brink and Harris 1969, p. 260). In the 1966 survey, the respondents were asked for the first time whether they would join in something like riots; low-income blacks outside the South were more likely to say they would not than were middle- and upper-income respondents.

Such changes over time help explain the differences by socioeconomic strata in the willingness to use violence. Even if a difference is found, at a given time for a given sample, the meaning is not self-evident (Kriesberg 1970, pp. 5–24). If low-status persons are more ready to use coercion and violence, it may mean that they are pursuing goals that seem amenable to attainment by no other means, and they may have fewer resources needed for other modes. It may not mean that coercion and violence have inherent gratifications, are gratifying because they provide an outlet for more generalized and displaced frustrations, or that persons of different social strata are socialized in ways that make some modes seem proper and others improper (Marx and Wood 1975; Portes 1971). The evidence does not support the thesis of a subculture of violence (Erlanger 1974).

Similar differences exist between men and women. Men generally are more likely to favor and to use coercion and violence in the pursuit of conflicting goals than are women. Some of the ambiguities in interpreting this difference are like those outlined for the differences by socioeconomic rank. The immense cultural component in sexual roles, however, would argue for a difference in socialization and cultural expectations in explaining the differences between men and women in this regard. Typically, in this and many other societies, masculinity includes being physically tough in the sense of being able to take and give bodily pain. The cult of masculinity, or *machismo,* emphasizes physical bravery, inducing and accepting challenges to fight, and risking bodily injury. There is also some evidence that an emphasis upon this kind of masculinity is disproportionately found in the lower socioeconomic strata (McKinley 1964) and also varies by society.

On way of testing these ideas is to look at preferences of different strata and sexes regarding pursuing the same goals. A problem here is that goals have different import to people of different strata and sexes. To reduce this problem we can look at views within one society about a conflict with another country. According to cultural interpretations suggested above, we expect men and lower socioeconomic persons to tend to favor more aggressive pursuit of foreign policy aims and the difference between men and women should be greater among the lower than the higher socioeconomic strata.

Israelis in 1962 were asked, "To what extent would you prefer a policy of 'aggression' [toughness] on the part of the Israeli government toward the Arab states" (see Table 4.1). Men tended to favor a more aggressive or activist policy. Moreover, the less educated, the poorer, those with lower status occupations, and those of lower ethnic status tended to favor a more aggressive policy. The differ-

TABLE 4.1 Percent of Israelis Who "Very Much" Prefer a Policy of "Aggression" (Toughness) toward the Arab States, by Sex and Ethnicity, 1962

Country of Father's Birth	Sex		
	Male	Female	Difference
Russia, Poland, Romania, Galicia	15.5	10.7	4.8
U.S., Germany, Great Britain, etc.	9.5	10.0	–0.5
Palestine	24.0	16.3	7.7
Bulgaria, Greece, Yugoslavia, etc.	26.8	20.9	5.9
Egypt, Syria, Lebanon, Yemen, etc.	40.1	26.8	13.3
Morocco, Algeria, Tunisia, Libya	35.7	25.8	9.9

Source: Secondary analysis of 1962 national survey, probability sample of 1170 cases and an additional sample of 300 kibbutz members. In this analysis, the kibbutz members are included with appropriate weighting. The study was conducted by the Israel Institute of Applied Social Research as part of comparative studies under the direction of Hadley Cantril (1965). The data were made available by The Roper Public Opinion Research Center.

ence between the men and women was greatest in the skilled worker stratum and among persons with less than a secondary education. The pattern was particularly clear and supportive of a cultural explanation in the case of ethnic differences. In Israel the national backgrounds of the Jews are ranked, with the European Jews having higher status than the Oriental Jews. In Table 4.1 we see that the differences by sex are particularly great in the lower status and more traditional ethnic groups.

In the United States in 1964 support for a stronger stand in Vietnam, even if it meant invading North Vietnam, was also more likely among men than among women, and the differences between them were greater in the lower socio-economic strata (see Table 4.2). Unlike Israel, however, support for a stronger war stand was expressed more frequently by respondents with more income, higher occupational status, and more years of formal education (Hamilton 1968).

Even if there is a tendency for males and lower socioeconomic strata to favor more coercive conflict modes, clearly, these are not powerful determining factors (Kriesberg and Klein 1980). In the United States in 1964 the higher socioeco-

TABLE 4.2 Percent of Americans Who Support "Taking a Stronger Stand" in Vietnam, by Sex and Education, 1964

	Sex		
Education	Male	Female	Difference
Less than 8 yrs.	44.4 (45)	8.3 (24)	36.1
8 yrs.	46.2 (39)	21.7 (46)	24.5
9–11 yrs.	55.0 (80)	31.6 (95)	23.4
12 yrs.	62.8 (86)	43.9 (123)	18.9
12 yrs. and some college	62.6 (131)	50.4 (123)	12.2
College completed or more	60.8 (74)	50.0 (56)	10.8

The question was: "Which of the following do you think we should do now in Vietnam?" 1. Pull out of Vietnam entirely, 2. Keep our soldiers in Vietnam but try to end the fighting, 3. Take a stronger stand even if it means invading North Vietnam. The question was asked of those interested enough to have opinion; those uninterested in the issue are not included in this table.

Source: Secondary analysis of Survey Research Center, 1964 election survey. National, cross-section sample of voting age citizens; 1,571 interviews were completed. The data were kindly made available for analysis by the Survey Research Center.

nomic strata tended to support a stronger stand in Vietnam because they tend to be more attentive to and supportive of official leadership (Rosi 1965; Gamson and Modigliani 1966). Taking stronger action seemed to be closer to governmental policy than the other alternatives offered in the question, and the Republican party's opposition was in favor of taking stronger action. The sex differences can also be reversed on issues of greater significance to women than men, or the differences may disappear within particular groups at particular times. For example, consider sex differences among blacks in the United States. In a 1964 national survey men appeared to be more militant than women (Marx 1969, pp. 53–54), and in 1966 in Houston men were less likely than women to say that violence was never justified; but in 1967 in Watts informal interviews did not reveal any differences between men and women (McCord, Howard, Friedberg, and Harwood 1969, pp. 74, 91–93). In the 1967 Milwaukee riot women were less often arrested for rioting, but among those arrested and among an inner city sample, men and women were equally likely to admit to having participated (Flaming 1971). In certain revolutionary situations women may be in the forefront of violent action, as during the French Revolution in the march on Versailles of October 1790 and in later food riots (Coser 1967, p. 68).

An analysis of political protest orientations among black and white adults provides additional specification. Isaac, Mutran, and Stryker (1980) report an analysis of a 1969 survey done in Gary, Indiana. Respondents were asked if they thought various types of collective protest ("sit-ins," mass demonstrations, civil disobedience, and use of violence) were appropriate for members of dissatisfied groups to employ. Isaac, Mutran, and Stryker compared three different kinds of explanations for the variations in approval of unconventional means: mass society, relative deprivation, and differential socialization.

According to the mass society approach, political extremism results from group and personal isolation from primary and secondary relations and also from primitivism, that is, the lack of education and information. In the relative deprivation approach, radical political orientations and protest activity result from the discrepancy between an individual's expectations and achievement; presumably approval of nonconventional political means would also result. According to the differential socialization approach, radical political orientations are "the outcome of exposure to a structurally oriented political ideology learned over a period of time through a variety of interactional or information sources" (Issac, Mutran, and Stryker 1980, p. 195).

Issac, Mutran, and Stryker concluded that the impact of primary group isolation or integration depends on the social context and political orientation of the primary groups. They found that whites who were integrated tended to be conservative in their orientation toward political means, while blacks who had ties with other blacks who see their interests as requiring unconventional political means tended to support a radical political orientation. On the whole, Issac, Mutran, and

Stryker interpret their findings as supporting the differential socialization approach. This finding is consistent with those about the differential participation of students in protest activity during the 1960s; at least initially, they had parents who tended to have similar political orientations (Wood and Ng 1980).

In summary, there is evidence that groups differ in their preferences for the use of coercion and violence. These variations may rest partly on cultural and subcultural differences, but the evidence also indicates that such variations may be relatively unimportant in accounting for preferences for using violence in specific fights. The goals being sought, the nature of the adversary, and the availability of alternative conflict modes all affect the preference and the choices. These other factors generally are more significant and channel cultural determinants. Tradition often seems to be an important determinant because it is consistent with and supported by many other relevant factors, but specific ways of pursuing conflict goals are sometimes developed by conflict subgroups and transmitted informally and formally.

Ideology. A group's ideology embodies prescriptions and proscriptions about how to pursue its goals more specifically than culture or historical precedents do. In general, the elaboration of an ideology tends to objectify the struggle and the adversary, which makes the conflict seem more impersonal. Greater militancy and more severe sanctions can, therefore, be imposed upon the adversary (Coser 1956, pp. 115–116). But, if we think of ideology as the explicit and elaborated ideas about what is wrong, what would be a solution, and how one can attain the desired goal, then the content of the ideology is more important than its mere existence.

Thus, the nonviolent ideology of the civil rights movement in the United States during the 1950s and early 1960s helped to divert efforts toward integration, equality, and freedom and away from violence. The availability of the ideology of nonviolence, as interpreted and applied by Martin Luther King, Jr., undoubtedly affected the choice of method to pursue conflicting aims. King's leadership was important in this regard, but it should be recognized that CORE was using nonviolent direct action for many years prior to the Montgomery, Alabama, bus boycott led by King. Yet, the prior existence of the ideas and tactics of nonviolent direct action by and for blacks in America did not produce or sustain widespread action using such means. Many other conditions had to be present for the wider participation in the civil rights movement of the early 1960s.

There have been, and are, defenders and even praisers of violence. They seem to revel in the heroics and solidarity of those who would indulge in it; they see it as an expression of profound ideas and emotions and as the way to bring about apocalyptic transformations. Advocating a general strike Sorel (1950, p. 302) wrote:

The conception of the general strike, engendered by the practice of violent strikes, admits the conception of an irrevocable overthrow. There is something in this which will appear more and more terrifying as violence takes a greater place in the mind of the proletariat. But, in undertaking a serious, formidable, and sublime work, Socialists raise themselves above our frivolous society and make themselves worthy of pointing out new roads to the world.

Sorel, although intellectually influential, was not a leader of any social conflict groups. Adolf Hitler was. He wrote in *Mein Kampf* (1941, p. 784):

The lack of a great, new, creative idea means at all times a limitation of the fighting power. The conviction of the justification of using even the most brutal weapons is always dependent on the presence of a fanatical belief in the necessity of the victory of a revolutionary new order on this globe. A movement which does not fight for such highest aims and ideals will therefore never take the ultimate weapon.

Nazism, according to Hitler, was such an idea; therefore, terror and violence, domestically and internationally, was possible, justified, proper, and even a kind of evidence for the idea (Arendt 1951, pp. 334–428).

Ideologies that include beliefs and preferences about alternative ways of conducting struggles are common; persistent conflict groups have their own traditions about how fights are to be conducted. Within larger conflict entities, the specialized units that engage in struggle may even have special academies to train their members to engage in conflicts. This is true for military, police, diplomatic, and labor-management groups.

Interestingly, attention is given to the varieties of coercion that can be employed—violent and nonviolent, threatened and implemented. But there is relatively less attention given to noncoercive inducements to conducting conflicts. When there is consideration given to the role of persuasion and reward, it is generally in the context of conducting negotiations.

Social Organization. Many aspects of a conflict group's social structure may predispose it to use one rather than another conflict mode. We limit this discussion to the relations between leaders and followers and the diversity of subgroups and members in the conflict unit.

The development of an ideology embracing violence or nonviolence, or any other means, requires the presence of ideological leaders or ideologists close to the leaders. This is one basis for leadership variation in preference to coercive ways of pursuing collective goals. Certainly, there are times when leaders seem to be cautioning and constraining their followers not to employ violence or, at any rate, only a moderate amount. But at other times leaders seem to be urging reluctant followers to forego persuasive efforts or bargaining and to strike violently. No simple and constant difference between leaders and followers, in these regards, exists, but some conditional regularities may be suggested.

Generally, in conflicts that are highly regulated and institutionalized, leaders are more likely to support the rules than are their constituencies. This means that the followers, or a faction of them, are more often in favor of extreme modes of pursuing their ends than are the leaders. On the other hand, when the conflicts are not as regulated and institutionalized, particularly if the conflict parties are just getting mobilized, the leaders will tend to support more coercive means than the rank and file. This is still too crudely stated. There is more differentiation than simply between leaders and followers. One should, at least, distinguish between active leaders at different levels, active rank-and-file members, nominal members, the constituency or possibly active rank and file, and potential leaders. With these additional specifications, we can suggest further regularities in the relations between kinds of participation in the conflict group and selection of ways of pursuing goals.

In highly institutionalized conflict relations, such as collective bargaining in the contemporary United States, the highest trade union leaders tend to be less militant than lower ranking union officials. There is some evidence that lower ranking officials are more suspicious of management intentions (Mills 1948, p. 141), presumably because the national leaders are more deeply involved in negotiations and other interactions with management and, therefore, develop mutual dependence and understanding. Rank-and-file members probably are less militant than the local leaders, except at the outset of direct coercive action, but union members are undoubtedly more supportive of militant action than nonmembers even of similar economic status. For example, union members are much more likely to support the idea of sympathy strikes than are nonmembers, even if they are poor or have low education (Cantril and Strunk 1951, p. 828).

Conflict units that are large and have persisted over long periods of time generally are complexly organized. This organization entails subgroups or distinctive organized components of the larger collectivity that are specialized in supporting or conducting specific means of waging a struggle. The collusion and competition among these groups, then, may significantly affect the choice of conflict modes. This possibility is particularly evident when we study governments with their special military, political, police, and diplomatic agencies and associated voluntary associations and corporations. One important area in which studies have been made pertains to the military-industrial complex.

President Dwight D. Eisenhower, in his farewell address to the nation in 1961, noted that the "conjunction of an immense Military Establishment and a large arms industry is new to the American experience." He went on to warn: "In the councils of government we must guard against the acquisition of unwarranted influence, whether sought or unsought by the military-industrial complex" (Melman 1970, Appendix B). Eisenhower's use of the term military-industrial complex and his warning about it attracted attention. The speech stimulated inquiries into the relations between the military establishment and industry.

Undoubtedly, the influence of the military in forming collective decisions has grown greatly in the cold war period (Rose 1967; Mills 1956). What is of particular relevance for us in the present context is how different groups within a larger collectivity jointly affect the choice of a conflict mode. Several studies have focused on decision making in the area of foreign policy and military expenditures. Most observers agree that relatively few persons are involved in making decisions in those spheres. Nevertheless, they disagree about how few they are, whom they consult or consider in making decisions, and who they are.

In major U.S. foreign policy and defense decisions, top government office holders formally choose the policy to be pursued. But questions can be raised about the class and status interests they share, whom they listen to, and who influences them. One kind of pertinent research has examined the possibility that members of Congress tend to vote for defense appropriations and support a relatively belligerent foreign policy insofar as defense expenditures are relatively high in their home districts. Grey and Gregory (1968) and Russett (1967) found a weak relationship, as hypothesized, but Cobb (1973) did not. There is not a clear strong relationship. It may be that support for defense expenditures and the belief in their importance is so widely shared in the United States that military expenditures in any given district do not significantly effect hawkishness. Perhaps, when there is less consensus about the salience of military defense and a hawkish foreign policy, a stronger relationship between support for such policies and expenditures in home districts will be found.

Other research has tried to explain choices about military procurement. How is the decision made to develop or not to develop a weapon system such as the Polaris nuclear submarine system, the F-111 plane, or the Minuteman missile system? Kurth (1971) examined several decisions about major aerospace procurement and found that major procurement decisions were timed to keep major production lines in operation and to aid corporations in financial trouble. Other writers stress the competition among bureaucracies, for example, the armed forces competing among themselves for funds and each promoting weapons systems that enhance its own budget (Wolfe 1979). Kantor and Thorsen (1973) examine a variety of alternative and complementary explanations, and their research supports the contention that the timing of major procurement contracts is not determined by strategic military needs. The existence of a particular capability is a prerequisite for its use; it can even become a reason for its use when the people who would be in charge of employing that capability are also major participants in deciding how to conduct a struggle. The role of the CIA in planning and implementing the Bay of Pigs effort in Cuba illustrates this possibility. Similarly, the use of antiinsurgency forces by the Kennedy administration in Vietnam was partly a result of the build up of that capability in an effort to reduce dependence on nuclear weapons (Halberstam 1973).

The diversity or heterogeneity of the conflict group can, in itself, affect the mode selected for the pursuit of goals. A mode must be found that is acceptable to the diverse members. If the group is long established and has consensus about what are the appropriate means, then the diversity may not be an important inhibitor, just as it does not inhibit national governments in their pursuit of foreign goals. But in less clearly bounded and in newly emerging organizations, diversity usually results in less coercive means. For example, in the civil rights movement during the late 1950s and early 1960s blacks and whites of different social strata and of different regions worked together. It is true that there was considerable selectivity within each group. Still, the diversity made attractive the emphasis upon nonviolence within CORE, the Student Nonviolent Coordinating Committee (SNCC), and SCLC and the emphasis on such traditional procedures as persuasive attempts in direct conversations with leaders and adversary proceedings within established legal rules.

Particular Resources. People's preferences for a specific mode are also affected by the costs they have to bear to use one mode rather than another. Every mode involves peculiar risks and expenditures. In general, violence is risky because there is often a good likelihood that it will be reciprocated. Particularly in challenging superior power, there is the risk of having to absorb heavy sanctions. It is partly for such reasons that youth are so often found to be involved in violent disruptions (Coser 1967, pp. 65–71; National Advisory Commission on Civil Disorders 1968, p. 172; Sears and McConahay 1969). Young people not only tend to feel invulnerable because of their age, but they actually have fewer assets that are hostage to those with superior power. They are less likely to have children and spouses to whom they would feel an obligation "to be careful." Their careers do not yet seem so fragile. Even as students they are generally less vulnerable to sanctions wielded by authorities than are employed persons. These reasons explain, in part, why students are so often reported to be involved in civil turmoil (Gurr 1969, Table 17.5) and in civil disobedience and why in the 1960s they were so disproportionately represented in organizations like CORE (Bell 1968; pp. 76–70). Young people are usually less dissatisfied with their own condition than are older persons because they still anticipate improvements. This hope and the freedom to take risks can mean greater participation in conflict behavior despite dissatisfaction's being less widespread among them.

Being free of encumbering commitments facilitates people's participation in conflict behavior apart from, or as well as, its being a motivating source. The socially isolated and those lacking ties of family and friendship may be particularly likely to support extremist objectives (Ringer and Sills 1952–1953), belong to conflict organizations with more provocative tactics, and themselves be particularly likely to engage in conduct with risks of heavy sanctions against them. For example, during the 1967 Detroit riot, neighborhoods in which residents had little social interaction with one another had more severe rioting than other neighborhoods in the riot area (Wanderer 1969).

Since each mode has special requirements, some groups have the appropriate resources to utilize one mode and others do not. Let us consider the implications of the numerical size of the conflict group as a resource.

Conspiracies or terrorism can be carried out by relatively few people. Indeed, for conspiracies to succeed, the number of persons cannot be large. In order to wage internal warfare, however, large social strata must become engaged. Similarly, nonviolent direct action requires a large number of participants to be effective, and a goodly number is also needed for mutual support and protection.

Rioting, too, requires a large number of participants; this gives each person a sense of security and support.

Spilerman (1970) studied racial disorders in the United States between 1961 and 1968 and found that the absolute number of nonwhites in a city was by far the single most important factor in accounting for disorders. Community variables were not markedly related to the disorders. Presumably, the grievances of blacks were sufficiently diffuse in the society and rioting a widely enough accepted form of expression that the more blacks there were available, the more incidents that might trigger a riot would occur and the more people there were available for rioting. Riots, depending in part on milling and contagion, require congeries of people. Streets filled with people who are young enough to take a little risk can begin engaging in an activity that draws in other participants. What is crucial is the number of persons appropriate for a given mode. There may be many elderly persons in a society, but old age inhibits engaging in a variety of coercive actions. Despite the grievances that the elderly may feel, their tactics in pursuit of their goals are generally moderate. When they are concentrated in particular areas so that they constitute a significant proportion of the electorate, they may exercise political influence.

It should be observed that the number of people does not determine the use of a given mode. How acceptable that mode is to the possibile utilizers is also important. Spilerman (1970) studied racial disorders which occurred when riots are not widespread and when the rioters are usually white. Under those circumstances, the absolute number of blacks is not likely to explain the incidence or the severity of racial riots, and this is the finding of studies of riots from 1913 to 1963 (Lieberson and Silverman 1965).

In general, the particular resources available to a group channels the mode selected for its pursuit of its goals. Groups with resources that can be traded with an adversary can try that method. A dominant class, for example, may offer a concession to prevent a revolt; Skocpol (1979) describes how the Japanese rulers during the Meiji restoration of 1868–1873 used this mode. Groups skilled in manipulating symbols are likely to try persuasion. The degree and form of organization similarly help determine which form of coercion will be attempted. Social categories without well-developed organization are likely to resort to or utilize riots, uprisings, and other somewhat spontaneous outpourings of pressure and grievance. People who are deprived and have few resources for use in nonviolent means, who have little to be held hostage to attacks by the adversary, who have few alternative courses and are finally moved to protest will be likely to do so violently.

The many studies of participants in the American ghetto riots of the 1960s provide pertinent information. Involvement in collective behavior depends partly on being on the scene and becoming caught up in events, but there is some self-selection in who actively participates, particularly in large-scale rioting which persists for more than several hours. On the whole, comparisons of either those who are arrested in or self-admitted participants in riots with a sample of persons in the same residential areas reveal considerable similarity in socioeconomic characteristics, such as education, income, and occupation; but there are some differences even in these regards. Black rioters tend to have experienced more unemployment, have lower occupational status, and have lower education (if age is controlled) than nonrioters (Geschwender and Singer 1970; National Advisory Commission on Civil Disorders 1968, pp. 173–177; Flaming 1971).

A further specification of the reasons for differential participation in riots can be found by bringing together three disparate reports. First, the Los Angeles County Probation Department reported that only 27 percent of the juveniles arrested during the Watts riot came from intact families (*The New York Times,* November 24, 1965, p. 22). Second, between 1960 and 1965 the real income of female-headed black families declined as did that of blacks who lived in the ghettoes of Cleveland and Los Angeles; but at the same time real income of male-headed black families and those living elsewhere increased (Williams 1970). The poor blacks suffered an actual fall in real income, and the gap between them and better-off blacks increased. Finally, as Caplan and Paige (1968, p. 20) note on the basis of survey responses, "Rioters are particularly sensitive to where they stand in relation to other Negroes, not to whites."

In summary, the nature and magnitude of the grievance does not in itself determine the mode of pursuing goals. Violence is not simply an expression of grievance. As we noted previously, deprivation in many ways inhibits awareness of grievance and open pursuit of desired goals. The deprived have limited resources for making demands and seeking their fulfillment. Some data from a study by Gurr of civil strife throughout the world in the early 1960s is revealing in this regard (Gurr 1969, Table 17.11). Among nations with low levels of economic development there was little or no correlation between short-term or long-term deprivation and either turmoil or conspiracy. Among societies that have high or medium levels of development there are moderate correlations between each kind of deprivation and each kind of civil strife. Presumably a minimal level of resources is needed to react to deprivation with coercive efforts. Furthermore, the correlations, if anything, are higher for short-term than for long-term deprivation. Long-term deprivation, although more cause for grievance, very likely weakens the possibilities for protest.

Two concluding observations about how a unit's social organization affects the conflict modes it employs will be stated briefly. A conflict unit has a limited repertoire of conflict techniques. These are the methods that its members have used before and have not found utterly unsatisfactory; they generally emerge from their routine conduct (Tilly 1978, p. 156; 1979). Workers in factories can stop working as a coercive inducement: It is a readily and naturally available method.

Conflict parties are not unitary actors. Each collectivity is made up of many groups, differing in ideology, power, and traditional preferences. These many groups inevitably negotiate among themselves in order to shape a collective policy and a course of action against an enemy (George and Smoke 1974, p. 283).

We have examined several partisan characteristics: preferences, ideology, social organization, and particular resources. Some of these characteristics affect or at least limit the mixture of inducements that a conflict group chooses in waging a struggle. But the modes adopted in a fight are not solely determined by each party's own internal characteristics. How a conflict unit prepares for a fight or intends to wage it may be strongly affected by its internal attributes. Actual conduct, however, involves other parties, as is certainly the case when we consider indicators of coercive and violent events such as riots and wars. It may in fact be that an adversary initiates and imposes a means that the other side does not want to use.

This is why the search for national characteristics that predict proneness to war have been so disappointing. Zinnes (1980) has reviewed such studies and concludes that characteristics such as power, regime, type, size, and development are not related to proneness to war. Some combinations of factors, for example, internal revolutionary acts or turmoil in conjunction with particular kinds of regimes, show moderate relationships (Wilkenfeld 1969; Collins 1973). Military expenditures have also been found to be related to the likelihood of going to war (Weede 1970; Choucri and North 1975; Sylvan 1976). But evidence about the role of military expenditures bears on an important aspect of relations between adversaries. We next consider how those relations affect the choice of conflict mode.

Relations between Adversaries

The degree and kind of integration between the contenders, the feelings of people in the conflicting groups toward one another, and their relative power, all affect the mode selected by conflict groups in pursuit of their aims.

Integration. As defined earlier, integration is the degree of interaction between the members of different groups and the extent to which they have common and complementary relations relative to conflicting ones. The latter itself has many possible bases. One which is of special pertinence here is that of cross-cutting ties, whether these be of cross-cutting conflicts or of positive bonds. In social systems with many lines of cleavage, which are not superimposed, groups that are adversaries along one conflict line may be allies or have constituents who are allies on another issue (Dahrendorf 1959; Berelson, Lazarsfeld, and McPhee 1954, pp. 305–323).

In the preceding chapter we discussed how cross-cutting ties affect the likelihood of conflicts' becoming manifest and the form of their manifestation. The extent to which persons in conflict groups share common and complementary interests also has important consequences for the mode chosen. On the whole, the greater the overlap of statuses between groups, the less likely is either one to utilize coercion against the other, and if it does, the coercion is more likely to be nonviolent. For example, compare societies with patrilocal and matrilocal residence patterns (LeVine 1965). If the people do not marry within their own village and follow the patrilocal residence pattern, the bride would come to her husband's village to live. The husband and all his brothers would remain in the same village. If they follow matrilocal residence, the groom would move to his wife's village. The wife and her sisters remain in the same village with husbands from several villages. Consequently, if there is an intervillage conflict, under the matrilocal system the men in each village would be faced with the possibility of fighting their brothers in the other village. But under the patrilocal system, they would be allies with all their brothers, and their in-laws might be in the other village. In conjunction with other factors, matrilocal societies tend to have a sense of solidarity and lack intervillage warfare, while patrilocal societies are plagued by more dissension, fights, and feuds (Murdock 1949, pp. 204–206).

This idea of cross-cutting ties is broader than, but includes, the concept of status inconsistency, nonranked as well as ranked statuses. As discussed in the preceding chapter, status inconsistency might be expected to be a source of intensified grievance and hence of more coercive and violent modes of seeking redress. We are arguing that, on the whole, cross-cutting ties, even when associated with or arising from status inconsistency, inhibit violence and may even provide the basis for noncoercive pursuit of goals (Ross 1920, pp. 164ff; Coser 1956, pp. 72ff; Galtung 1966).

Illustrative evidence can be seen in studies of industrial conflict. Let us consider strikes as more coercive than collective bargaining conducted without recourse to strikes. Kerr and Siegel (1954) studied the rate of strikes in different industries in eleven industrial countries and found that certain industries generally had higher strike rates than did others. For example, the propensity to strike was generally high in mining and the maritime and longshore industries; medium-high in lumber and textiles; medium in the chemical and printing industries; medium-low in clothing and services; and low in railroad, agriculture, and trade.

Kerr and Siegel concluded that one important determinant of the interindustry differences in the propensity to strike was the location of the worker in society. Workers who form "isolated masses" are particularly prone to strike. For example, miners, sailors, and longshoremen tend to have separate communities, have their own codes, and have few neutrals to mediate the conflicts. The workers are relatively homogeneous in work roles and mobility out of the occupation is difficult.

Later studies, however, did not find the same pattern in France or Italy (Shorter and Tilly 1974; Snyder and Kelly 1976). It may be that sentiments about striking are related to the kinds of conditions stressed by Kerr and Siegel, but whether or not workers actually strike is determined by other factors. Organizational resources, the ability to mobilize for strikes, and the relative opportunity to strike as affected by employers and governments strongly affect conduct, as will be noted in later sections of this chapter.

Another test of these ideas can be found in studies of community conflicts. A systematic analysis of eighteen New England communities revealed that low interaction between opponents was related to rancorous conflicts (Gamson 1966). The fluoridation of water and two other issues were studied in each community. The use of illegitimate tactics, as volunteered by informants, identifies rancorous conflicts. Acquaintanceship between opponents was substantially lower in rancorous than in conventional communities. Furthermore, communities in which there was high cross-cutting on the issues were more likely to have conventional conflicts than communities with high cleavage. Cross-cutting ties were measured by the degree to which people of the same background shared the same position on the issues. Background was measured in terms of length of residence, nationality background, education, and religion.

In international relations, too, the nature and degree of interaction between adversary countries affect the mode chosen to pursue conflicting goals. Interdependence provides the basis for applying negative sanctions short of violence, by disrupting the interaction, as well as for providing reasons for not pursuing an issue coercively in order to prevent further disruption of the relationship. For example, after the Korean War, the American and North Korean governments had few relations, and the peoples of each country did not engage in significant exchange transactions. When the North Koreans seized the *U.S.S. Pueblo* and its crew in January 1968, the U.S. government lacked an array of sanctions that could be used to cajole, exchange, or coerce the return of the vessel and its crew. The option of a large-scale military venture to release them seemed out of proportion and might punish the adversary and yet fail to safely retrieve the ship and crew. There even was speculation about seizing a North Korean vessel so that the U.S. government would have something to exchange for the release of the *Pueblo*. The release of the *Pueblo* crew was finally accomplished in December 1968 after protracted negotiations. The United States agreed to acknowledge that the *Pueblo* had intruded into North Korean waters and apologized for the intrusion, but the chief U.S. negotiator also read into the record, before signing the written agreement, a statement disavowing the confession. Even when there seems to be little that one side can offer another, some concessions can be discovered.

An interesting set of data relates the level and nature of integration between societies and the occurrence of war between them. Naroll, Bullough, and Naroll (1974) selected major civilizations from the second century B.C. through the eighteenth century A.D. They selected for each civilization in each century the most conspicuous state and its major rival and then randomly selected one decade from each century. This process yielded twenty pairs of rivals. They examined the relationship of war frequency to many characteristics of the rivals and found that general cultural exchanges were negatively related to war frequency (−.44) as was trade (−.35).

Deutsch and others (1957) studied the emergence of "security communities," that is, groups of people within a territory who have a sense of community and have institutions and practices that assure, for a "long" time, that social problems will be resolved without recourse to large-scale physical force. Examples of such security communities include "amalgamated" cases, such as the United States since 1877, England-Scotland since 1707, Italy since 1859, and Switzerland since 1848, and "pluralistic" cases, such as Norway-Sweden since 1907, United States-

Canada since the 1870s, and England-Scotland between the late 1560s and 1707. Their analysis and findings are too complex to be summarized here, but the major findings that pertain to our concerns can be cited. Three conditions seem essential for the success of both amalgamated and pluralistic security communities: the compatibility of major values relative to political decision making; the capacity of the participating units to respond to each other; and mutual predictability of behavior. Of special interest to us is that the mobility of persons, at least among the politically relevant strata, was also found in successful cases. Furthermore, in amalgamated security communities they found that there were unbroken links of social communication both geographically between territories and socially between different strata, and there was a wide range of communication and transaction between the peoples.

Hopkins (1973) analyzed the relations between pairs of contiguous countries in the contemporary world. He found that countries with high levels of transactions were less likely than others to resort to violence. He also found that high levels of transactions were associated with subsequent relatively high levels of shared international organizational memberships.

Integration has consequences for other aspects of the relationship between parties, and these consequences in turn affect the mode selected for handling conflicts. High levels of integration tend to increase the levels of mutual trust, understanding, and legitimacy. Such feelings and beliefs tend to reduce the intensity of any given conflict and make the pursuit of goals by means of persuasion or reward seem more likely to be successful and intrinsically attractive.

Blumenthal, Kahn, Andrews, and Head (1972, pp. 135–178) studied opinions about violence and identifications with white student demonstrators, black protesters, and police. They found that identification with a group is positively associated with justifying its use of violence, and identification with the opponents or victims was negatively associated with justifying violence used against it. Furthermore, their analysis suggests that identification with the victims of violent actions is more important than identification with its performer in accounting for justifications of violence.

There is a variety of experimental and field evidence that belief in the legitimacy of leaders or their directives inhibits aggression and violence directed against them (Gurr 1970, pp. 189–191; Rothaus and Worchel 1960; Tanter and Midlarsky 1967). For example, Bwy (1968) found that in Latin American countries legitimacy was negatively correlated (−.71) with organized violence but insignificantly (−.14) with turmoil. Gurr (1969, pp. 605–606) gave high legitimacy scores to countries whose political system was developed indigenously and had survived for a long time. He found that legitimacy was negatively correlated with civil strife (−.38). He also found the relationship varied in different kinds of countries:

Legitimacy most strongly inhibits civil strife in the developing nations; in the democratic and the personalist nations; in the non-Communist Western nations; and in Latin, Islamic, and Asian nations. He has relatively weak effects in the most- and least-developed nations; the nations governed by modernizing elites; and in African and Communist nations. (p. 606)

Although integration generally reduces the likelihood that violence will be employed in the handling of any given social conflict, this should not be interpreted to mean that integration is a safeguard against all violence or even that the intensity of violence will be minimized within the social system. Issues in contention may come to be so formulated that among the alternatives available to the parties concerned, violence may be attempted by one or the other party even with relatively high levels of integration. Indeed, once a conflict becomes manifest and coercion is attempted, the violence may be particularly intense because of the added resentments, sense of betrayal, and pains suffered in the course of the conflict emergence. In a sense, integration means mutual dependence and vulnerability. The extensive brutalities of civil wars testify to these dangers.

Relative Resources. Undoubtedly, the differences in resources between adversaries affect the means of conflict each uses. Thus, parties that control resources desired by their opponent can promise rewards. For example, dominant groups can even co-opt or bribe leaders of challenging groups (Piven and Cloward 1979). In discussing the effects of resource differences, we will consider only the implication of differences in coercive resources for the adversaries' employment of coercion.

Large power differences do not necessarily make use of coercion unlikely. If large power differences deter the weaker from using coercion against the stronger, then they invite the stronger to use coercion for further aggrandizement against the weaker. We need to consider each possibility before trying to reconcile them.

In general, one would expect that when a government has overwhelming power over any segment of the population under its administrative authority even extreme deprivations will be endured with only occasional outbursts of violent protest. Thus, soldiers, sailors, and prisoners mutiny or riot relatively infrequently, if one considers only the poor conditions which they generally have endured (Lammers 1969).

On the whole, only when the weaker party believes it is gaining power and is about equal to the stronger adversary will it venture to use coercion. This can be illustrated in several contexts. We would expect strikes to be employed by trade unions when their chance of success is greatest. Strikes would be used, then, during upturns in the economy and, therefore, when labor is in shorter supply; this seems to be the case (Knowles 1954; Rees 1954; Christman, Kelly, and Galle 1981). Note, that in such cases, it is not increased grievances that explain the pursuit of conflicting goals, but the opportunity to impose one's conditions. It is true that business upturns may also be accompanied by price increases and a fall or slowing down of real income, but the relative power interpretation seems particularly compelling in that strikes to organize the unorganized show the same pattern as do strikes to secure wage increases and other benefits.

These considerations throw additional light upon the findings that revolutions and uprisings often occur when previously improving conditions show a downturn (Feierabend, Feierabend, and Nesvold 1969; Davies 1962; Gurr 1970). This is usually interpreted as an expression of increased dissatisfaction resulting from an increased gap between attainments and expectations. In the preceding chapter we discussed how a decrease in the rate of improvement could be the basis for increased dissatisfaction. But dissatisfaction is not always directly expressed in an effort to redress grievances. It can be accepted as an unfortunate but natural calamity. When another group, like the ruling government, is held responsible, coercive action or violence in the forms of revolutionary uprisings may occur. In that case, the downturn is attributable to the incompetence of the leaders. Such incompetence not only reduces their legitimacy but makes them weak and vulnerable. Assuming that there are always grounds for dissatisfaction, the weakness of the formerly stronger party invites rebellion. The deteriorated conditions and lack of authority also mean that the superordinates have fewer resources available to be traded off for continued obedience. Thus, Skocpol's (1979) analysis of the French, Russian, and Chinese revolutions shows how they broke out when the ruling governments had been weakened by international developments.

Even a government that brings about an improvement in the sense that it reduces repression of its own citizens may invite rebellion. The loosening of restrictions may facilitate communication among and mobilization of the previously oppressed groups; in this way the emergence of awareness of the many remaining grievances would be facilitated. The government may, however, also appear weak in allowing these liberties; it seems an admission of error that would give new credence and validity to the arguments of the dissidents. Sometimes concessions may be made as if to forestall violence, and these seem to admit that the utilization of violence would be successful.

The antigovernment uprisings and rebellions after the death of Stalin and the moderating of totalitarian controls in the Soviet Union and in East Germany, Poland, and Hungary testify to the risks to leaders of totalitarian regimes of giving a little liberty (Kecskemeti 1961; Gurr 1970, pp. 118–119; Crozier 1960). In many times and places evidence of an "inadequate police and military control apparatus" is followed by periods of hostile outbursts (Smelser 1963, p. 233).

Even within an authoritarian organization, when superiors appear weak and frightened of coercion from subordinates, the chances that subordinates will attempt to use force increases. Thus dissension among superordinates may appear and actually be an indication of the inability to act cohesively (as well as effectively) in using established ways of handling conflicts. If the subordinates believe that they will not suffer severe negative sanctions, they are more likely to risk collective protest and coercion outside of established channels. Lammers (1969), in his study of mutinies and strikes, found:

> In several of the mutinies in the sample . . . the mutineers knew that more or less successful promotion of interests' movements had taken place recently on other

ships of war. The factors here may not only be doubt that authorities would apply coercive sanctions but also awareness that authorities could neither quickly nor easily crush the uprising by force. This may be the reason why army units are so underrepresented in the sample and why air force units are completely absent. A ship, particularly a ship at sea, is not easily boarded or taken if its crew offers resistance, and the arrival of opposing ships may take days or weeks. In the case of army or air force units, military police or loyal troops can usually be rushed to the spot at short notice. (p. 565)

The argument is not that substantive concessions invite violence but that responsiveness to that mode or its threatened use makes that mode more attractive to its users. The same would be true of each other mode.

On the other hand, refusing to make substantive responses to noncoercive or nonviolent modes and trying to insist upon maintaining current power differences can provoke more coercive actions by the subordinates. For that reason prison riots are generally preceded by attempts of prison authorities to tighten security (Ohlin 1956, pp. 24–25). (The way in which a flaccid, permissive reaction by the supposed stronger party or the harsh imposition of severe sanctions by the stronger party may escalate the use of coercion will be discussed in the next chapter.)

The analysis thus far may seem to indicate that the greater the power differences and the greater the certainty that the stronger party will use its coercive force, the less likely is there to be violence. That is not the whole truth. The weaker side may often be intimidated and deterred, and its use of violence suppressed. But that does not mean that the stronger will not be tempted to use its superior force for further aggrandizement. Consequently, coercion and violence may be frequently employed because the weaker party does not deter the stronger.

Evidence for this possibility is readily available. When the blacks in the United States were even weaker in comparison to the whites than they are today, they were subject to a variety of violent and terroristic acts by the dominant whites. Race riots meant whites rioting and attacking blacks; the police often did little or nothing to suppress the violence (Lee and Humphrey 1943; Meier and Rudwick 1969). Group violence against individual blacks occurred in such acts as lynchings and was not subjected to governmental intervention. The very law and its enforcement could be implemented in a repressive manner.

Not only is the stronger party freer to indulge in coercion and violence than the weaker in seeking its aims, but it may formulate goals that result in the exchange of violent acts even if that were unintended. The powerful unit may act more imperiously and impetuously, more boldly and more aggressively; the consequence is violence. The evidence in support of these arguments can be found particularly in studies pertaining to international wars (Zinnes 1980).

One kind of evidence may be seen in the result of a series of "inter-nation simulations" (Raser and Crow 1968). In "inter-nation simulations" persons assume particular roles in a nation's government, each nation may have two or three roles, and there are several nations in the system. The actions of the persons in the simulation are unstructured, but they are given information about the other nations and their own population's response to their decisions in accord with processes that are programmed and carried out on a computer. In this study there were two blocs, and the leader of each had nuclear weapons. For some of the games in the series one of these powers had the capacity to delay its nuclear response. That is, its nuclear weapons system was secure from enemy attack and could survive any attack. According to many students of such matters, such a capacity would obviate preemptive strikes and reduce the chances for a nuclear exchange. In the simulations there was confirmation of some of the reasonings about deterrence, but the capacity to delay response actually increased the chance of war. What was not foreseen was the tendency for the nation with the capacity to delay response to be seen and to act more powerfully; its consequent aggressive posture precipitated nuclear war. Blechman and Kaplan (1978, pp. 48–49) examined instances of coercive threats between the U.S. and Soviet governments. They found that the U.S. government used nuclear threats more often when it was clearly dominant than when it was not.

There are a few studies using historical and cross-sectional data that examine the relationship between deterrence or power and the incidence of war. Naroll (1969) studied twenty periods selected from two thousand years of history in which one state, while in a defensive stance, was militarily stronger than its conspicuous rival. He then compared the same pair of states for periods when the same state was not militarily stronger than its conspicuous rival. Four different ways of assessing military strength were used. He found wars were not "less frequent during the periods when the conspicuous state, while in a defensive stance, enjoyed the specified military advantages than during other periods. . . . If anything, armament tends to make war more likely" (p. 152). In a study of primitive societies, Naroll (1966) also found no support to the deterrence idea; rather, military orientation was positively correlated with war frequency. Weede (1970) studied fifty-nine nations from 1955 to 1960 and found that militarization was correlated with violent foreign conflict. He also found that total national power was somewhat related to violent conflict behavior, but holding verbal foreign conflict constant, the powerful states were less likely to engage in violent foreign conflict.

Russett (1963) analyzed seventeen instances between 1935 and 1962 in which a potential attacker threatened a smaller country that was, to some degree, under the protection of another state. He found that military superiority by the defender was not a sufficient condition to deter attack. If the protector was highly integrated with the pawn, then successful deterrence did occur. Such integration presumably increased the probability, in the mind of the potential attacker, that the protector would indeed use force against the other state if it attacked the pawn country.

The analyses of arms races and the way in which one side's military preparations are matched by the other in escalating movement toward war will be examined in the next chapter. It is sufficient here to note that evidence of arms races' ending in war is evidence against the idea of deterrence.

The evidence we have reviewed about power differences and the utilization of coercion in the pursuit of goals does not seem consistent. We argued that in many spheres the rising strength of a previously subordinate group would tend to be associated with the use of coercion, but very great differences in power tempt the stronger party to use coercion; yet, we then saw that superior power did not generally deter attack—rather preparing for war was associated with waging war. Clearly, power differences per se do not determine the use of coercion; we must consider other simultaneous factors.

One of the crucial additional considerations is the issue at stake. Deterrence is likely to be successful not only if the threatened force is powerful and certain but also if what is being demanded is not too severe a deprivation. For example, during the Six-Day War of June 1967, while Israel was engaged in military actions against Egypt, Jordan, and Syria, the premier of Lebanon, Rashid Karami, ordered the army to attack Israel. The commanding general, Emile Bustani, refused, reportedly saying, "When you wear this uniform you can condemn the army to destruction. But while I wear it, you cannot" (*The New York Times,* June 21, 1967). Lebanon did not attack; it was deterred and suffered no losses. Compare this incident with Japanese leaders' not being deterred by the military might of the United States and launching their attack on Pearl Harbor in 1941. Russett (1967) had concluded that at the time Japan was deeply involved in a war with China and was faced with a severe shortage of war materials, particularly after the United States stopped shipping oil and scrap iron to Japan. The needed resources were available in the British and Dutch Pacific colonies. Believing the U.S. government would defend those colonies against attack and convinced that the United States would not retract its demands for the Japanese withdrawal from China and Indochina, the Japanese leaders perceived only unsatisfactory alternatives. The status quo was not long endurable; withdrawing from China would be a defeat, attacking the colonies without attacking the United States would make it subject to powerful American military intervention, and attacking the United States in addition to the colonies was a dangerous escalation, particularly if the United States waged a prolonged war. The Japanese leaders chose the risky alternative at least partly because the other alternatives, given the system within which they were operating, domestic and international, were at least as bad.

The Soviet-American cold war can also be considered in this context. Did the United States deter the Soviet Union from aggression? Or has the Soviet Union deterred the United States? Or has each deterred the other? Perhaps the threat of a nuclear holocaust has frozen both sides in terror. The avoidance of full-scale war between the United States and the Soviet Union may well owe something to this terror, but it also owes something to the limited claims each side has made upon the other. Neither side has sought to destroy the other side's government. If each side were basically defensive and sought only to consolidate its gains, then deterrence of expansionism could be easily attained (Gamson and Modigliani 1971).

In general, the effectiveness of deterrence depends upon the goals sought as well as the differences in power. The more that the stronger power demands of the weaker, the less deterred is the weaker. An oppressed and exploited group, feeling that there is some increase in its relative power, may well risk strong negative sanctions by using coercion to redress long-standing grievances.

In addition, other aspects of the relationship between the conflicting parties and the general context of the parties, affect the meaning and significance of the power difference. Approximate power between parties within a large integrated and highly organized social system tends to produce more equitable procedures for handling conflicts and mutual tolerance between the parties. Under those conditions noncoercive and nonviolent means are likely to be used. In the international system, with its relative absence of institutionalized conflict regulation, power is less likely to be a safeguard against others' coercion and violence (Singer and Wallace 1970). Indeed, Garnham (cited in Zinnes 1980) found that war was more likely between neighboring countries with about equal power than between ones with unequal power.

Responsiveness of the Adversary. In addition to the level of integration and the degree of power differences, conflict parties have particular relations with each other that affect the way each pursues its goal vis-à-vis the other. The basic matter here is the alternative conflict modes that are available to each party. What is available greatly depends on the adversary. An opponent may allow or be responsive to some modes and not others. Moreover, all adversaries may share understandings about how to struggle against one another. If conflict parties agree about the procedures, conflicting goals may be pursued with little violence or even with little coercion. What is also crucial is the extent to which an opponent is responsive to the demands made through legitimate channels and in accord with understandings (Smelser 1963, pp. 236–241).

The content of the understandings and the joint expectations, then, affect which mode each party will attempt to use. For example, American employer hostility to trade unions helps account for the violent and often bloody history of trade union organization in the United States (Taft and Ross 1969). It also helps account for the relatively high proportion of nonorganized workers in the United States (Bok and Dunlop 1970, p. 50). Collective bargaining is less well established in the United States than in other industrial and democratic societies. American union members are more likely to be involved in strikes and for longer periods than in other pluralistic industrial societies (Ross and Irwin 1951). Another indication of the importance of institutionalization of the relationship is the finding that over the decades, the average length of strikes has been reduced.

There are, finally, idiosyncratic qualities to the relationship between conflict parties that affect the choice of mode. How each party defines the other affects the way each responds to the other and limits the ways each can pursue its goals.

For example, Nazi ideology held that the Slavs were inferior to the Germans. Even when anti-Soviet Russians wished to aid the German invaders in World War II, they received little encouragement from the Nazis (Fischer 1952). The Nazis were hardly in a position to persuade Russians of the desirability of the ends they sought. Their extraordinary violence against the Russian people was a basis for Russian support of the Soviet government.

The Environment

In addition to the issue, the nature of the units in the conflict, and the character of the relationship between the conflicting parties, the context in which they exist affects the way in which the parties pursue their aims. Any parties in a social conflict are within a larger social system. That system includes other groups, encompassing understandings and patterns of interaction, and alternative means by which parties can pursue their objectives. As we have noted in other contexts, every fight is embedded within a large set of interlocking conflicts.

Other Parties. Adversaries in a focal conflict do not stand alone. There are possible allies, expanded constituencies and more encompassing organizations and groups. In the preceding chapter we discussed how the very aims of a conflict group are shaped in part by other parties as well as adversaries and internal factors. Similarly, the choice of the way to pursue conflicting goals is affected by parties who are not actors in the focal conflict.

First consider how the pursuit of a conflict group's goals is affected by parties who are possible allies of the primary conflict groups. Each conflict group tends to shape its pursuit of goals in persuasive as well as coercive terms because an audience and potential allies exist. In the civil rights movement of the 1950s and early 1960s nonviolent direct action and large demonstrations appeared to be appropriate means because carrying them out was educational and persuasive to large sections of the population and to governmental leaders who, on the whole, were not hostile to the demands for equality and integration in the South. Police attempts at repression in 1963 in Birmingham and elsewhere vividly revealed the prevailing oppression, which brought support for the blacks' demands and aided in the 1964 passage of civil rights legislation by the U.S. Congress. The effects of demonstrations upon others throughout the nation were not forgotten in planning, conducting, and interpreting nonviolent direct action (King 1963).

We should also seek to explain why the segregationists of the South did not choose means of pursuit that would avoid bringing allies to the blacks. As Kenneth Clark observed:

> . . . it would probably be all too easy to abort and to make impotent the whole King-SCLC approach, if white society could control the flagrant idiocy of some of its own leaders, suppress the more vulgar, atavistic tyrants like Sheriff Jim Clark, and created instead a quiet, if not genteel, intrasingence. . . . When love meets either indifference or passive refusal to change, it does not seem to have the power to mobilize the reactions of potential allies. (1966, pp. 256–257)

Indeed, in cities where such quiet intransigence was followed, the program was less successful. It may be that Sheriff Jim Clark of Selma and Commissioner of Public Safety Eugene "Bull" Conner of Birmingham were particularly and personally prone to use extreme violence against demonstrators. But the explanation must go deeper; they were public officials and part of another conflict group. Perhaps these groups did not understand the role and likely response of other parties in their own city, state, and nation. They were also committed, in part by past success, to the use of intimidation; it was consistent with their view of blacks. And fundamentally, the issue was not negotiable for them. They understood that what the blacks were ultimately asking for meant the ending of a kind of tyranny; holding on to that tyranny could not be compromised. Violent coercion was an appropriate means for the maintenance of their position.

Nonfocal parties affect the choice of means to pursue conflicting ends in another, quite different, way. The modes used by one comparable party can serve as a model to others; there can be a fashion quality in the techniques used to advance a party's cause. Demonstrations, strikes, riots, even revolutions seem to spread as if by contagion. For example, Skolnick (1969) writes:

> Despite the differences among student movements in developed and underdeveloped countries, however, it is clear that a process of mutual influence is at work among them. For example, the white student movement in America received inspiration in its early stages from dramatic student uprisings in Japan, Turkey, and South Korea. More recently, American activists have been influenced by street tactics learned from Japanese students and by ideological expressions emanating from France and West Germany. The French students were certainly inspired by the West Germans, and the Italians by the French. (p. 86)

The Kerner Commission also argued that geographic contagion was observable in the riots in 1967, particularly for the disorders centering around Newark and Detroit (National Advisory Commission on Civil Disorders 1968, p. 114).

Groups also follow historical precedents. The experience and techniques used in the Abolitionist movement were applied in the beginning of the women's movement (Flexner 1959, p. 41). The techniques of the women's suffrage movement provided examples to Gandhi and were taken back from there by the civil rights movement in the United States (Millett 1970, p. 82).

Because like-appearing events appear to be closely related in time and space does not in itself mean that there is a causal connection. Demonstrations, sit-ins, riots, or other ways of pursuing conflicting goals may be employed in one place for the same reasons they were employed elsewhere; that is, there is convergence of means. This point is made by Knowles (1954, p. 223) in regard to trade union strikes. The theoretical and empirical links of workers in one place being influenced by another must be demonstrated to argue that groups follow models of others' conduct in pursuit of their goals. There are several ways in which the use of a particular technique in a conflict relationship can induce imitation or adaptation of the technique by others. Its success will tend to make it attractive. If a group sees that others have attained at least something of what they wanted, it is likely to use the same tactic. Even the demonstration that people could have dared to try a certain act, like a strike or slowdown, makes it conceivable as an alternative to other groups. Sometimes, the tactic appears to be a social invention, a way to do something that had not been utilized before and which seems appropriate to others, for example, sit-ins.

Social Patterns and Understanding The general system of which the adversaries are parts also affects the selection of conflict modes. Included here are the general understandings shared by all or many of the units in the social system about what means are appropriate for what purposes by which kinds of actors. Also included here are the social structural patterns that characterize the system and how collective decisions are reached by its members. Illustrative evidence about how these aspects of the social system affect the way groups pursue their goals will be briefly reviewed.

The opponents, as well as the other units, may share cultural traditions or general understandings, for example, about the propriety of using violence of different kinds and the justifications for it (Smelser 1963, pp. 79–130). Governments at the national level are generally considered, by other governments, to have the prerogative of using force. This understanding means that war is generally regarded as a legitimate means of pursuing foreign policy. The public also tends to view support for government arms spending as conventional and, perhaps, indicative of patriotism (Kriesberg and Klein 1980).

Within the territory under a government's jurisdiction, its use of violence to put down rebellion is not a matter that other governments feel they have an obligation to limit. On the whole, nonintervention in the internal affairs of other states is the principle that governments assert. Intervention, then, is based more upon expedient calculations of which side is likely to win and which side's victory is desired than upon the enforcement of shared norms. Nevertheless, intervention in internal wars is more common than not (Kende 1971, Table 7).

The course of action pursued by a conflict group depends upon the range of alternatives available for the issue at stake. Those alternatives depend upon the whole set of interrelated structures within the social system. Consider the variety of settings within which trade union-management relations may operate. The trade unions may be more or less closely tied to political parties, in a two-party, multiparty, or one-party political system. There may be one or more trade unions representing workers within an enterprise. Management may be more or less closely tied to political parties and more or less autonomous of government. The ways in which workers seek redress of their grievances depends upon the way such variable conditions are combined. Efforts at reform or restructuring of labor-management relations could be channeled through political action and legislation, through lobbying within governmental agencies, or by strike action. Even struggles about wages and working conditions may be carried out through political pressure and demonstrations or by collective bargaining and strikes. That is why characteristics of workers in different industries, as identified, for example by Kerr and Siegel (1954) do not always predict strike activity (Tilly 1978, pp. 165–166). Christman, Kelly, and Galle (1981) reviewed historical and comparative analyses of strike activity. They found that strikes occur in countries where market, and not political, processes decide the allocation of resources.

Similarly, how universities are related to other institutions in a society affect, for example, the means that students use to pursue their goals (Weinberg and Walker 1969). Societies differ in the extent to which the government controls university finances and structure, and societies vary in the degree to which political parties sponsor student groups and recruit students into political careers. In the United States government control is relatively weak, and there is little political party recruitment through university groups. Consequently the political activity is local, as in student governments, but, students, relatively isolated from the main political system in the society, may resort to noninstitutionalized channels when they do become involved in society-wide issues. Where there is strong government control and low political recruitment, as in France, for example, powerful unions of students are more likely.

One of the fundamental aspects of the social patterns that affect the mode used in conflicts is the degree to which the system as a whole has cross-cutting ties, a sense of common identity, and institutionalized means of collective decision making. We discussed cross-cutting ties previously, but from the perspective of a conflict unit or from the perspective of the relations between units in conflict. Now we consider how cross-cutting ties at the social system affect the mode of pursuing conflicting goals.

Conflict parties also share adherence in larger entities, and such adherence might shape the means of struggle through many processes. If the shared membership is with a legitimate and strong superordinate, the conflict modes are likely to be regulated and institutionalized. The parties to a conflict tend to follow the procedures for conflict resolution. This may include legal and political procedures in which persuasive means would be important; persuasion would be directed at the superiors in terms of the values and standards they maintain. Within stable societies or organizations, these procedures may operate so readily that little coercion and no violence occurs. Such highly institutionalized means of conflict might not even be regarded as conflict behavior by the partisans and are not of central importance here. If one of the conflict parties claims to be the superordinate and all encompassing entity, but this standing is not recognized by the other party, the institutionalized and regulated means of conflict resolution will be followed under duress of the conflict will be waged outside the established procedures. This kind of issue arises, for example, when management claims to speak for the whole enterprise, but the workers believe they have interests that are in opposition to the management.

Shared membership is also a forum in which integrative transactions can transpire. Participating in common enterprises may be the basis for common interests and the development of shared understandings, perspectives, and values (Alger 1963). Shared memberships may also provide the basis for cross-cutting bonds. All this should make persuasion and bargaining more possible, more likely to be successful, and, therefore, more likely to be utilized. Coercion will be mitigated.

Even aside from shared memberships, the general level of integration in the social system in which the conflict parties are contending may constrain the conflict parties. The more integrated the entire social system is, the more implicated are nonfocal parties in the conflict between primary adversaries; and yet not being as involved in the issue in contention, the other parties would tend to limit the disruptiveness and coercion of the means used by the adversaries.

Plausible as these ideas may seem, the evidence supporting them is not unequivocal. We will consider evidence from the study of international relations. Smoker (1967) studied the relationship between arms races and international integration. International integration was measured by the growth in the number of international nongovernmental organizations (INGO's). Three arms races were studied: the one preceding and terminating in World War I, the one preceding and terminating in World War II, and the one between the United States and the Soviet Union after World War II. Smoker argues that the level of integration before the two world wars was not sufficient to prevent the arms race from escalating to the point at which war broke out; the growth of INGO's stopped and fell back as the arms race grew in intensity. After World War II, however, there was a very large increase in the rate of establishment of INGO's, and the level of integration apparently was sufficiently high to absorb and halt the arms race, which did fall off after 1951–1952.

Singer and Wallace (1970) used a different approach to the same issue and reached different conclusions. They related international governmental organizations (IGO's) with wars between 1816 and 1964. They correlated the number and the growth of IGO's in each five-year period during those years with the onset of war, number of battle dead, and number of months of war in the next five-year period. They found no relationship between the two and conclude that "war is basically inherent in the continued coexistence of the nation-state and the international system as we know it" (p. 545). In other words, the level of integration and the strengths of international organizations cannot overcome the forces that bring nation-states into conflicts that are pursued by means of organized violence.

The findings of Smoker and of Singer and Wallace might not be inconsistent. The measures of each study are necessarily gross, and, more important, they cover different periods. Smoker is arguing that the post–World War II increase in INGO's indicates a significantly greater level of integration than the past, which constrains current war making. But that should hold for conflicts among all countries and not just between the United States and the Soviet Union. Yet, the number of wars has been large and, if anything, has increased since 1945 (Kende 1971).

Another approach is to examine specific conflicts or potential conflicts. Hopkins (1973) analyzed pairs of neighboring countries and found that those who were members of INGO's were somewhat less likely to be in wars with each other than other dyads. Holsti (1966) examined the ways in which major conflicts were handled in two time periods: 1919–1939 and 1945–1965. He found that in 31 percent of the thirty-eight conflicts during the earlier period, settlements by international organizations were attempted, compared to 41 percent of the thirty-nine conflicts in the later period; but they were no more likely to be successful in the second period than the first. Furthermore, military force was employed in 71 percent of the conflicts during the first period and was hardly less frequent in the second period when 64 percent involved the employment of military force.

The international system, made up of nation-states with claims of sovereignty and with control over the means of mass destruction, has such low levels of overall integration that the variations in system integration have only a small effect upon the overall probability of armed conflict. The integration between pairs of adversary nations has more pertinence for the modes of settling conflicts between them. There is some evidence, however, that system characteristics in terms of the entire set of power relations, alliances, and resulting cross-cutting ties and cross-pressures also affect the incidence and severity of war. Thus, when countries are generally not committed to alliances, all are subject to pressure from more countries, and war is not as likely as when countries are tied into nonoverlapping alliances (Zinnes 1967). Haas (1968), focusing on patterns of relative power, studied twenty-one international subsystems and compared unipolar, bipolar, and multipolar systems. He found that systems with one dominant power were most pacific. International systems with several major powers have shorter wars, but more of them, than do systems with only two major powers. Other studies, using different measures of alliance structure, of wars have yielded other findings; we cannot draw definitive conclusions (Zinnes 1980).

Evidence from community studies is also pertinent to the issues raised here. Research indicates that in cities with more direct representation of the citizens in the government, where presumably there are more channels for expressing grievances, riots by blacks and by whites are somewhat less likely (Lieberson and Silverman 1965).

At the societal level there is also evidence that the amount of civil strife is related to the nature of the political structure, although we should keep in mind that nearly all such strife has a political purpose and hence is directed at the government (Gurr 1969). In many studies, four major types of political systems are distinguished: polyarchic—nations with Western democratic political structures; centrist—authoritarian regimes (includes Communist); elitist—small, modernizing elites, predominantly African; and personalist—characterized by unstable personal leadership, predominantly Latin American. The total magnitude of strife is lowest in the polyarchic system, particularly strife in the form of conspiracies and internal wars; centrist systems also tend to have low magnitudes of strife, partly because of higher coercion. Elitist systems have high magnitudes of strife, especially in the form of internal wars; and personalist systems have particularly high levels of strife in the form of turmoil (strikes, demonstrations, and riots). The strength of institutions is also variously related to civil strife. The strength of institutions was measured by "the proportion of gross national product utilized by the central government; the number and and stability of political parties; and the relative size of trade unions" (Gurr 1969, p. 614). So measured, the strength of institutions is positively related to civil strife in personalist systems. Apparently, in such systems trade union activity and some political parties are strongly opposed to the government and its policies; in the other systems strength of institutions is inversely related to civil strife or unrelated.

Governmental repression can suppress strife. Conversely, in countries with representative political systems and relative openness of expression, turmoil tends to occur (Cooper 1974). Political nonviolent and violent behavior vary together (Tilly and Snyder 1972; Dugan, 1979). Consequently, demonstrations may lead to violent confrontations, and this relatively minor-scale violence is relatively likely to occur in democratic societies.

We must conclude that the level of integration of the system, its degree of shared understandings, and the extent to which there are strong encompassing organizations do not have simple, direct, and unilinear effects upon the conflict modes used. The absolute level and nature of the integration, the content of the understandings, and the character of the encompassing organizations have their own significance, even if we consider only the variations in the use of violence.

Technology and Ecology. We have been discussing the social aspects of the system within which conflicting parties contend. There are also nonsocial aspects of the environment. The distinction is a matter of degree. Thus, physical distances between units have significance only as they are mediated through the technology of the time. Who is next to whom depends partly on the means of communication available to the people involved.

In any case, what one party can do to another, by way of persuasion, coercion, or reward, depends partly on the technology available. In general, countries have fought wars by marching armies against each other. In historical perspective, then, we expect that countries tend to fight with their neighbors. The more neighbors to fight with, the more frequent the wars. This is indeed what Richardson (1960, p. 176) found in his study of wars between 1820 and 1945. The number of borders was one of the few characteristics he found to be correlated with the incidence of war. Using the same data, Wesley (1962) calculated the geographical opportunity for warfare by combining the length of the frontier and the number of people along the frontier and found that that matched the number of battle deaths. Weede (1970) studied international conflicts from 1955 to 1960 and found that contiguity was moderately correlated with foreign conflict. Later studies confirm these findings, but with further specification (Starr and Most cited in Zinnes 1980).

We should keep in mind, however, that countries that are close together probably also have more objective and manifest conflicts simply because they have more to do with each other. We should examine the proportion of social conflicts that result in war and the proportion that are handled in other ways. It may be that the proportion does not vary with propinquity. It is also possible, particularly in the past, that wars could be waged against nonneighbors only with great difficulty, but more recent means of conflict are not so geographically constrained.

The geographic distribution and concentration of people of different social categories within a nation or a city also affect how its members can pursue their goals at a given technological level. This is pertinent for the organization and tactics of industrial workers and of managers, of blacks and whites, of students, faculty and administrators, and of women and of men.

One final aspect of the system within which the contending parties exist must be considered. The entire system may be changing in a way that channels the modes of struggling between conflict groups. For example, if a group of nations, like those of Europe, can expand overseas by building empires, they might find war among themselves not to be a useful way of pursuing their aims against each other. Each would seek to advance its interests vis-à-vis the other by actions directed at other parties outside the system. Indeed, during this period of expanding empires, wars were less frequent in Europe (Rosecrance 1963).

The possibility of an expanding pie so that each group could have more and more is an alluring prospect for finding noncoercive modes of conflict or for using regulated or nonviolent coercion. This might be a factor in labor-management relations in an expanding economy or an imperialist one, or in an expanding industry or company. At the same time, such expansion raises expectations and often increases the power of the relatively weaker party. Consequently, there may be more demands being made and, therefore, more conflict behavior, some of which will be coercive. Thus, there may be an absolute increase in the number of cases in which intense coercion is used, but it may still be a smaller proportion of the cases of manifest conflicts.

We should not be mechanical in interpreting data about the incidence of any particular mode of conflict. Increases in the incidence of illegitimate coercion or of violence can indicate that more is being demanded than before. It may be the dominants as well as the subdominants who are making these new demands. In any case, a higher incidence of violence need not mean that a larger proportion of conflicts are being pursued in more extreme fashion. More issues, or more profound ones, may be being raised, that is all.

SUMMARY AND CONCLUSIONS

Four sets of factors affect the mode chosen in pursuit of a goal: the issue, the characteristics of the conflict party, the relationship between the contending parties, and the environment of the parties in contention. It is important to keep in mind that these factors are interrelated, in the sense that they affect one another. Moreover, they all jointly affect the mode. Certain modes are especially attractive to particular kinds of people; some, all would agree, are especially appropriate to a particular end and with a given adversary.

Sometimes one or another factor is predominantly determining of the mode. For example, the relationship between opponents may be such, in terms of integration, power, and responsiveness, that certain modes are precluded and only a few options are really viable. Or, the characteristics of a unit are so overwhelming that certain modes are adhered to regardless of other considerations. If this were completely the case, we would consider the mode chosen as expressive rather than instrumental.

A major mode, like a war, revolution, or strike, is an emergent blend of coercive, rewarding, and persuasive inducements. No one party can completely determine a conflict mode. The primary adversaries shape each other's choices, and even the other parties influence the means used in waging a struggle.

We have also noted that the end shapes the means. Partisans choose a blend of inducements that they think will be effective for what they want. But we have also seen that each group also chooses modes that are attractive for internal reasons. Leaders of primary adversary groups take into account the preferences of their constituencies and are significantly constrained by the expectations and demands of their constituencies, or they cease to be leaders. When the adversary groups are clearly bounded and relatively autonomous, domestic considerations are particularly powerful and the adversaries have limited leverage on each other. Thus, in international conflicts the leaders who have emerged from domestic political struggles may underestimate the independent base that foreign leaders have. Halberstam (1973, p. 533) notes that President Johnson misunderstood Ho Chi Minh, neglecting the extent to which Ho Chi Minh was beholden to political groups and people in North Vietnam and overemphasizing the resources which a president of the United States could control.

The Norwegian sports strike against the Quisling government during the German-Nazi occupation of Norway illustrates some of the ways that goals, internal characteristics, relations between adversaries, and the environment affect a choice of mode (Gregg 1966; Sharp 1973; Wehr 1979). The ability of people to wage a nonviolent resistance effort, even against the Nazi-backed Quisling government, is clearly an impressive achievement. But note how the many factors we have considered in this chapter intertwine to explain the phenomenon. The German occupation did not offer many alternative modes of expressing grievances about the occupation. The power difference, measured in military strength, was very great. Open warfare against the Nazis had been defeated. By not participating in organized sports events, masses of people could indicate their refusal to cooperate with the Quisling government. This kind of noncooperation might seem relatively limited, but it was one of the few methods available, given the adversary. The issue was also one which could take on high significance to those conducting it and not become fundamentally significant to all the opponents. For many Norwegians this refusal expressed their opposition to the Nazis and the Quisling government. The aim was to demonstrate defiance of them and support the other forms of resistance. It was a difficult tactic for the Quisling government to overcome, and, as they tried and failed, the significance of the defiance, even in this area, took on greater importance to the Norwegians. The legitimacy and authority of the Quisling government was undermined. If the resistance expanded or was directed at other objects, other government policies could be thwarted. Thus, among the Nazi-occupied countries of Europe, the survival of Jews varied greatly, depending on the extent of popular solidarity with Jews as citizens or of collusion with the Nazis (Fein 1979).

Not only are many factors interrelated to determine the mode, but the mode itself also affects the unit, the relations between the adversaries, and the goal itself. This is part of the subject of Chapter 8. It is important to observe here that means and ends affect each other. If people choose a way of pursuing their goal because it seems appropriate for what they are trying to get, then, if they are using a particular mode, it must signify that there is an end that justifies the means.

There is an important implication of these arguments. If one kind of factor affects the selection of a mode and the mode affects the other factors, every conflict unit can influence what its adversary seeks and how the adversary goes about getting it. Hence, we help shape our own enemies.

In this chapter we have generally considered a means of pursuing a conflicting goal as a single choice. Actually, choices are constantly being made. As the means change in sequence, we think of the struggle as escalating or deescalating. That is the subject of the next chapter.

BIBLIOGRAPHY

ALGER, CHADWICK, F., "United Nations Participation as a Learning Experience," *Public Opionion Quarterly,* 27 (Fall 1963), 411–426.

ALLARD, SVEN, *Russia and the Austrian State Treaty* (University Park, Penn.: University of Pennsylvania State Press, 1970).

ARENDT, HANNAH, *The Origins of Totalitarianism* (New York: Harcourt, Brace & Co., 1951).

BALDWIN, DAVID A., "The Power of Positive Sanctions," *World Politics,* 24 (October 1971), 19–38.

————, "Power Analysis and World Politics," *World Politics,* 31 (January 1979), 161–194.

BECKER, W. C., "Consequences of Different Kinds of Parental Discipline," pp. 169–208 in M. L. Hoffman and L. W. Hoffman (eds.), *Review of Child Development Research,* Vol. 1 (New York: Russell Sage Foundation, 1964).

BELL, INGE POWELL, *CORE and the Strategy of Non-Violence* (New York: Random House, 1968).

BERELSON, BERNARD R., PAUL F. LAZARSFELD, AND WILLIAM N. McPHEE, *Voting* (Chicago: University of Chicago Press, 1954).

BLAU, PETER M., *Exchange and Power in Social Life* (New York: John Wiley, 1964).

BLECHMAN, BARRY M., "The Quantitative Evaluation of Foreign Policy Alternatives: Sinai, 1956," *Journal of Conflict Resolution,* 10 (March 1966), 408–426.

BLECHMAN, BARRY M. AND STEPHEN S. KAPLAN WITH DAVID K. HALL, WILLIAM B. QUANDT, JEROME N. SLATER, ROBERT M. SLUSSER, AND PHILIP WINDSOR, *Force Without War* (Washington, D.C.: The Brookings Institution, 1978).

BLUMENTHAL, MONICA D., ROBERT L. KAHN, FRANK M. ANDREWS, AND KENDRA B. HEAD, *Justifying Violence* (Ann Arbor: University of Michigan Press, 1972).

BOK, DEREK C. AND JOHN T. DUNLOP, *Labor and the American Community* (New York: Simon & Schuster, 1970).

BONDURANT, JOAN V., *Conquest of Violence: The Gandhian Philosophy of Conflict,* rev. ed. (Berkeley and Los Angeles: University of California Press, 1965).

BRINK, WILLIAM AND LOUIS HARRIS, *Black and White* (New York: Simon & Schuster, 1969).

BWY, DOUGLAS P., "Political Instability in Latin America: The Cross-Cultural Test of a Causal Model," *Latin American Research Review,* 3 (Spring 1968), 17–66.

CANTRIL, HADLEY, *The Pattern of Human Concerns* (New Brunswick, N.J.: Rutgers University Press, 1965).

CANTRIL, HADLEY AND MILDRED STRUNK, *Public Opinion, 1935–1946* (Princeton, N.J.: Princeton University Press, 1951).

CAPLAN, NATHAN S. AND JEFFERY M. PAIGE, "A Study of Ghetto Rioters," *Scientific American,* 219 (August 1968), 15–21.

CHOUCRI, NAZLI AND ROBERT C. NORTH, *Nations in Conflict: National Growth and International Violence* (San Francisco: W. H. Freeman & Co. Publishers, 1975).

CHRISTMAN, LILLIAN, WILLIAM R. KELLY, AND OMER R. GALLE, "Comparative Perspectives on Industrial Conflict," in Louis Kriesberg (ed.), *Research in Social Movements, Conflicts and Change,* Vol. 4 (Greenwich, Conn.: JAI Press, 1981).

CLARK, KENNETH B., "The Civil Rights Movement: Momentum and Organization," *Daedalus,* 95 (Winter 1966), 239–267.

COBB, STEPHEN, "The United States Senate and the Impact of Defense Spending Concentrations," pp. 197–223 in Steven Rosen (ed.), *Testing the Theory of the Military-Industrial Complex* (Lexington, Mass.: D. C. Heath, 1973).

COLLINS, J. N., "Foreign Conflict Behavior and Domestic Disorders in Africa," pp. 251–293 in J. Wilkenfeld (ed.), *Conflict and Linkage Politics* (New York: D. McKay, 1973).

COOPER, MARK N., "A Reinterpretation of the Causes of Turmoil: The Effects of Culture and Modernity," *Comparative Political Studies,* 7 (October 1974), 267–291.

COSER, LEWIS A., *The Functions of Social Conflict* (New York: Free Press, 1956).

———, *Continuities in the Study of Social Conflict* (New York: Free Press, 1967).

CROZIER, BRIAN, *The Rebels: A Study of Post-War Insurrections* (London: Chatto & Windus Ltd., 1960).

DAHRENDORF, RALF, *Class and Class Conflict in Industrial Society* (Stanford, Calif.: Stanford University Press, 1959).

DAVIES, JAMES C., "Toward a Theory of Revolution," *American Sociological Review,* 27 (February 1962), 5–19.

DEUTSCH, KARL W., SIDNEY A. BURRELL, ROBERT A. KANN, MAURICE LEE, JR., MARTIN LICHTERMAN, RAYMOND LINDGREN, FRANCIS L. LOEWENHEIM, AND RICHARD W. VAN WAGENEN, *Political Community and the North Atlantic Area* (Princeton, N.J.: Princeton University Press, 1957).

DEUTSCH, MORTON, *The Resolution of Conflict: Constructive and Destructive Processes,* (New Haven, Conn.: Yale University Press, 1973).

DUGAN, MAIRE AINE, "The Relationship Between Pre-Independence Internal Violence and Non-Violence and Post-Independence Internal Violence, External Belligerency, and Internal Governmental Repressiveness," unpublished Ph.D. dissertation, Social Sciences, Syracuse University, 1979.

ERLANGER, HOWARD, "The Empirical Status of the Subculture of Violence Thesis," *Social Problems,* 22 (December 1974), 280–292.

ERSKINE, HAZEL, "The Polls: Speed of Racial Integration," *Public Opinion Quarterly,* 32 (Fall 1968), 513–524.

ETZIONI, AMITAI, *A Comparative Analysis of Complex Organizations* (New York: Free Press, 1961).

FANON, FRANTZ, *The Wretched of the Earth* (New York: Grove Press, 1966).

FEAGIN, JOE R. AND PAUL B. SHEATSLEY, "Ghetto Resident Appraisals of a Riot," *Public Opinion Quarterly,* 32 (Fall 1968), 352–362.

FEIERABEND, IVO K., ROSALIND L. FEIERABEND, AND BETTY A. NESVOLD, "Social Change and Political Violence: Cross-National Patterns," pp. 632–687 in Hugh Davis Graham and Ted Robert Gurr (eds.), *Violence in America* (New York: Bantam, 1969).

FEIN, HELEN, *Accounting for Genocide* (New York: Free Press, 1979).

FISCHER, GEORGE, *Soviet Opposition to Stalin: A Case Study in World War II* (Cambridge, Mass.: Harvard University Press, 1952).

FLAMING, KARL H., "The 1967 Milwaukee Riot: An Historical and Comparative Analysis," unpublished Ph.D. dissertation, Department of Sociology, Syracuse University, 1971.

FLEXNER, ELEANOR, *Century of Struggle* (Cambridge, Mass., Harvard University Press, 1959).

GALTUNG, JOHAN, "International Relations and International Conflicts: A Sociological Approach," pp. 121–161 in *International Sociological Association, Transactions of the Sixth World Congress of Sociology* (1966).

————, "Violence, Peace, and Peace Research," *Journal of Peace Research,* 3 (1969), 167–191.

GAMSON, WILLIAM A., "Rancorous Conflict in Community Politics," *American Sociological Review,* 31 (February 1966), 71–81.

————, *Power and Discontent* (Homewood, Ill.: Dorsey Press, 1968).

GAMSON, WILLIAM A. AND ANDRE MODIGLIANI, "Knowledge and Foreign Policy Opinions: Some Models for Consideration," *Public Opinion Quarterly,* 30 (Summer 1966), 187–199.

————, *Untangling the Cold War* (Boston: Little, Brown, 1971).

GANDHI, MOHANDAS KARAMCHAND, *An Autobiography or The Story of My Experiments with Truth,* translated by Mahadev Desai, 2nd ed. (Almedabad, India: Nevajivan, 1940).

GEORGE, ALEXANDER L. AND RICHARD SMOKE, *Deterrence in American Foreign Policy* (New York: Columbia University Press, 1974).

GESCHWENDER, JAMES A. AND BENJAMIN D. SINGER, "Deprivation and the Detroit Riot," *Social Problems,* 17 (Spring, 1970), 457–463.

GREGG, RICHARD B., *The Power of Nonviolence* (New York: Schoken Books, 1966).

GREY, CHARLES AND GLEN GREGORY, "Military Spending and Senate Voting," *Journal of Peace Research* 5, no. 1 (1968), 44–54.

GURR, TED ROBERT, "A Comparative Study of Civil Strife," in Hugh Davis Graham and Ted Robert Gurr (eds.), *Violence in America: Historical and Comparative Perspectives* (New York: Bantam, 1969).

————, *Why Men Rebel* (Princeton, N.J.: Princeton University Press, 1970).

HAAS, MICHAEL, "Social Change and National Aggressiveness, 1900–1960," pp. 215–244 in J. David Singer (ed.), *Quantitative International Politics* (New York: Free Press, 1968).

HALBERSTAM, DAVID, *The Best and the Brightest* (New York: Fawcet Books Group/CBS Publications, 1973).

HAMILTON, RICHARD, "A Research Note on the Mass Support for Tough Military Initiatives," *American Sociological Review*, 33, no. 3 (1968), 439–445.

HILGARD, E. R. AND G. H. BOWER, *Theories of Learning*, 3rd ed. (New York: Appleton-Century-Crofts, 1966).

HITLER, ADOLF, *Mein Kampf* (New York: Reynal and Hitchcock, 1941). Originally published in 1925.

HOLSTI, K. J., "Resolving International Conflicts: A Taxonomy of Behavior and Some Figures," *Journal of Conflict Resolution*, 10 (September 1966), 272–296.

HOPKINS, DAVID MORSE, "Conflict and Contiguity: An Empirical Analysis of Institutionalization and Conflict in Contiguous Dyads," unpublished Ph.D. dissertation, International Relations, Syracuse University, 1973.

ISSAC, LARRY, ELIZABETH MUTRAN, AND SHELDON STRYKER, "Political Protest Orientations Among Black and White Adults," *American Sociological Review*, 45 (April 1980), 191–213.

KANTOR, ARNOLD AND STUART J. THORSEN, "The Weapons Procurement Process: Choosing Among Competing Theories," pp. 157–196, in Steven Rosen (ed.), *Testing the Theory of the Military-Industrial Complex* (Lexington, Mass.: D. C. Heath, 1973).

KECSKEMETI, PAUL, *The Unexpected Revolution: Social Forces in the Hungarian Uprising* (Stanford, Calif.: Stanford University Press, 1961).

KENDE, ISTVAN, "Twenty-Five Years of Local Wars," *Journal of Peace Research*, 1 (1971), 5–22.

KENNAN, GEORGE F., *Russia and the West Under Lenin and Stalin* (Boston: Little, Brown, 1961).

KERR, CLARK AND ABRAHAM SIEGEL, "The Interindustry Propensity to Strike: An International Comparison," pp. 189–212 in A. Kornhauser, R. Dubin, and A. M. Ross (eds.), *Industrial Conflict* (New York: McGraw-Hill, 1954).

KING, MARTIN LUTHER, JR., *Why We Can't Wait* (New York: Harper & Row, Pub., 1963).

KNOWLES, K. G. J. C., " 'Strike-Proneness' and Its Determinants," *American Journal of Sociology*, 60 (November 1954), 213–229.

KRIESBERG, LOUIS, *Mothers in Poverty* (Chicago: Aldine, 1970).

KRIESBERG, LOUIS AND ROSS KLEIN, "Changes in Public Support for U. S. Military Spending," *Journal of Conflict Resolution*, 24 (March 1980), 79–111.

KURTH, JAMES R., "A Widening Gyre," *Social Policy*, 19 (September 1971), 373–404.

LAMMERS, CORNELIS J., "Strikes and Mutinies: A Comparative Study of Organizational Conflicts Between Rulers and Ruled," *Administrative Science Quarterly,* 14 (December 1969), 558–572.

LEE, ALFRED MCCLUNG AND NORMAN D. HUMPHREY, *Race Riot: Detroit, 1943* (New York: Dryden Press, 1943).

LEEK, JOHN H., *Government and Labor in the United States* (New York: Rinehart & Company, 1952).

LEVINE, ROBERT A., "Socialization, Social Structure, and Intersocietal Images," pp. 45–69 in Herbert C. Kelman (ed.), *International Behavior* (New York: Holt, Rinehart & Winston, 1965).

LIEBERSON, STANLEY AND ARNOLD R. SILVERMAN, "The Precipitants and Underlying Conditions of Race Riots," *American Sociological Review,* 30 (December 1965), 887–889.

MARX, GARY T., *Protest and Prejudice* (New York: Harper & Row, Pub., 1969).

MARX, GARY T. AND JAMES L. WOOD, "Strands of Theory and Research in Collective Behavior," pp. 363–428 in A. Inkeles, J. Coleman, and N. Smelser (eds.), *Annual Review of Sociology,* Vol. 1 (Palo Alto, Calif.: Annual Reviews, 1975).

MCCORD, W. J. HOWARD, B. FRIEDBERG, AND E. HARWOOD, *Life Styles in the Black Ghetto* (New York: W. W. Norton & Company, Inc., 1969).

MCKINLEY, DONALD GILBERT, *Social Class and Family Life* (New York: Free Press, 1964).

MEIER, AUGUST AND ELLIOTT RUDWICK, "Black Violence in the 20th Century: A Study in Rhetoric and Retaliation," pp. 399–412 in Hugh Davis Graham and Ted Robert Gurr (eds.), *Violence in America,* (New York: Bantam, 1969).

MELMAN, SEYMOUR, *Pentagon Capitalism* (New York: McGraw-Hill, 1970).

MILLETT, KATE, *Sexual Politics* (New York: Doubleday, 1970).

MILLS, C. WRIGHT, *The New Men of Power* (New York: Harcourt, Brace & Co., 1948).

————, *The Power Elite* (New York: Oxford University Press, 1956).

MORRIS, CHANDLER (ed.), *Modernization by Design* (Ithaca, N.Y.: Cornell University Press, 1969).

MURDOCK, GEORGE PETER, *Social Structure* (New York: Macmillan, 1949).

NAROLL, RAOUL, "Does Military Deterrence Deter?" *Transaction,* 3 (January/February 1966), 14–20.

————, "Deterrence in History," pp. 150–164 in Dean G. Pruitt and Richard C. Snyder (eds.), *Theory and Research on the Causes of War* (Englewood Cliffs, N.J.: Prentice-Hall, 1969).

NAROLL, RAOUL, VERN L. BULLOUGH, AND FRADA NAROLL, *Military Deterrence in History: A Pilot Cross-Historical Survey* (Albany, N.Y.: State University of New York Press, 1974).

NATIONAL ADVISORY COMMISSION ON CIVIL DISORDERS (KERNER COMMISSION), *Report of the National Commission on Civil Disorders* (New York: Bantam, 1968).

NEF, JOHN V., *War and Human Progress* (Cambridge, Mass.: Harvard University Press, 1950).

OHLIN, LLOYD E., *Sociology and the Field of Corrections* (New York: Russell Sage Foundation, 1956).

PIVEN, FRANCES F. AND RICHARD A. CLOWARD, *Poor People's Movements: Why They Succeed, How They Fail* (New York: Vintage, 1979).

PORTES, ALEJANDRO, "Political Primitivism, Differential Socialization and Lower-Class Leftist Radicalism," *American Sociological Review,* 36 (October 1971), 820–835.

RASER, JOHN R. AND WAYMAN J. CROW, "A Simulation Study of Deterrence Theories," pp. 372–389 in Louis Kriesberg (ed.), *Social Processes in International Relations* (New York: John Wiley, 1968).

REES, ALBERT, "Industrial Conflict and Business Fluctuations," in A. Kornhauser, R. Dubin, and A. M. Ross (eds.), *Industrial Conflict* (New York: McGraw-Hill, 1954).

RICHARDSON, LEWIS, F., *Statistics of Deadly Quarrels* (Pittsburgh: Boxwood Press, 1960).

RINGER, BENJAMIN B. AND DAVID L. SILLS, "Political Extremists in Iran," *Public Opinion Quarterly,* 16 (Winter 1952–1953), 689–701.

ROSE, ARNOLD M., *The Power Structure* (New York: Oxford University Press, 1967).

ROSECRANCE, RICHARD N., *Action and Reaction in World Politics* (Boston: Little, Brown, 1963).

ROSI, EUGENE J., "Mass and Attentive Opinion on Nuclear Weapons Tests and Fallout, 1954–1963," *Public Opinion Quarterly,* 29 (Summer 1965), 280–297.

ROSS, ARTHUR M. AND DONALD IRWIN, "Strike Experience in Five Countries, 1927–1947: An Interpretation," *Industrial and Labor Relations Review,* 4 (April 1951), 323–342.

ROSS, EDWARD A., *The Principles of Sociology* (New York: Century Co., 1920).

ROTHAUS, PAUL AND PHILIP WORCHEL, "The Inhibition of Aggression Under Non-Arbitrary Frustration," *Journal of Personality,* 28 (March 1960), 108–117.

RUSSETT, BRUCE M., "The Calculus of Deterrence," *Journal of Conflict Resolution,* 7 (June 1963), 97–109.

———, "Refining Deterrence Theory: The Japanese Attack on Pearl Harbor," *Journal of Peace Research,* 2 (1967), 89–106.

SAYLES, LEONARD R. AND GEORGE STRAUSS, *The Local Union: Its Place in the Industrial Plant* (New York: Harper & Brothers, 1953).

SCHLESINGER, ARTHUR M., JR., *A Thousand Days* (Boston: Houghton Mifflin, 1965).

———, *What Price Vigilance?* (New Haven, Conn.: Yale University Press, 1970).

SEARS, DAVID O. AND JOHN B. MCCONAHAY, "Participation in the Los Angeles Riot," *Social Problems,* 17 (Summer 1969), 2–20.

SEARS, DAVID O. AND T. M. TOMLINSON, "Riot Ideology in Los Angeles: A Study in Negro Attitudes," *Social Science Quarterly,* 49 (December 1968), 485–503.

SHARP, GENE, "The Meanings of Non-Violence: A Typology," *Journal of Conflict Resolution,* 3 (March 1959), 41–66.

———, *The Politics of Nonviolent Action* (Boston: Porter Sargent, 1973).

SHORTER, EDWARD AND CHARLES TILLY, *Strikes in France, 1830–1968* (Cambridge, Eng.: Cambridge University Press, 1974).

SINGER, J. DAVID, "Inter-Nation Influence: A Formal Model," *American Political Science Review,* 57 (June 1963), 420–430.

SINGER, J. DAVID AND MICHAEL WALLACE, "Intergovernmental Organization and the Preservation of Peace, 1816–1964: Some Bivariate Relationships," *International Organization,* 24 (Summer 1970), 520–547.

SKOCPOL, THEDA, *States and Social Revolutions: A Comparative Analysis of France, Russia, and China* (Cambridge, Eng.: Cambridge University Press, 1979).

SKOLNICK, JEROME H., *The Politics of Protest* (New York: Simon & Schuster, 1969).

SMELSER, NEIL J., *Theory of Collective Behavior* (New York: Free Press, 1963).

SMOKER, PAUL, "Fear in the Arms Race: A Mathematical Study," *Journal of Peace Research,* 1 (1966), 55–64.

———, "Nation State Escalation and International Integration," *Journal of Peace Research,* 1 (1967), 60–74.

SNYDER, DAVID AND WILLIAM R. KELLY, "Industrial Violence in Italy, 1878–1903," *American Journal of Sociology,* 82 (July 1976), 131–162.

SOREL, GEORGES, *Reflections on Violence,* translated by T. E. Hulme and J. Roth (New York: Free Press, 1950). Originally published in 1906–1919.

SPILERMAN, SEYMOUR, "The Causes of Racial Disturbances: A Comparison of Alternative Explanations," *American Sociological Review,* 35 (August 1970), 627–649.

SUMNER, WILLIAM GRAHAM, *Folkways* (Lexington, Mass.: Ginn, 1906).

SYLVAN, DAVID A., "Consequences of Sharp Military Assistance Increases for International Conflict and Cooperation," *Journal of Conflict Resolution,* 20 (December 1976), 609–636.

TAFT, PHILIP, *Organized Labor in American History* (New York: Harper & Row, Pub., 1964).

TAFT, PHILIP AND PHILIP ROSS, "American Labor Violence: Its Causes, Character, and Outcome," pp. 281–395 in Hugh Davis Graham and Ted Robert Gurr (eds.), *Violence in America* (New York: Bantam, 1969).

TANTER, RAYMOND AND MANUS MIDLARSKY, "A Theory of Revolution," *Journal of Conflict Resolution,* 11 (September 1967), 264–280.

TILLY, CHARLES, *From Mobilization to Revolution* (Reading, Mass.: Addison-Wesley, 1978).

———, "Repertoires of Contention in America and Britain, 1750–1830," in M. N. Zald and J. D. McCarthy (eds.), *The Dynamics of Social Movements* (Cambridge, Mass.: Winthrop Publishers, 1979).

TILLY, CHARLES AND DAVID SNYDER, "Hardship and Collective Violence in France 1830–1960," *American Sociological Review,* 37 (October 1972), 520–532.

TURNER, RALPH H., "Determinants of Social Movement Strategies," in Tamotsu Shibutani (ed.), *Human Nature and Collective Behavior: Papers in Honor of Herbert Blumer* (Englewood Cliffs, N.J.: Prentice-Hall, 1970).

WANDERER, JULES J., "An Index of Riot Severity and Some Correlates," *American Journal of Sociology,* 74 (March 1969), 500–505.

WEEDE, ERICH, "Conflict Behavior of Nation-States," *Journal of Peace Research,* 3 (1970), 229–235.

WEHR, PAUL, *Conflict Regulation* (Boulder, Colo.: Westview Press, 1979).

WEINBERG, IAN AND KENNETH N. WALKER, "Student Politics and Political Systems: Toward a Typology," *American Journal of Sociology,* 75 (July 1969), 77–96.

WESLEY, JAMES PAUL, "Frequency of Wars and Geographical Opportunity," *Journal of Conflict Resolution,* 6 (December 1962), 387–389.

WILKENFELD, JONATHAN, "Some Further Findings regarding the Domestic and Foreign Conflict Behavior of Nations," *Journal of Peace Research,* 2 (1969), 147–156.

WILLIAMS, WALTER, "Cleveland's Crisis Ghetto," pp. 13–29 in Peter H. Rossi (ed.), *Ghetto Revolts* (Chicago: Aldine, 1970). Originally published in 1967.

WOLFE, ALAN, *The Rise and Fall of the "Soviet Threat": Domestic Sources of the Cold War Consensus* (Washington, D.C.: Institute for Policy Studies, 1979).

WOOD, JAMES L. AND WING-CHEUNG NG, "Socialization and Student Activism: Examination of a Relationship," pp. 21–43 in Louis Kriesberg (ed.), *Research in Social Movements, Conflicts and Change,* Vol. 3 (Greenwich, Conn.: JAI Press, 1980).

WRIGHT, CHRISTOPHER, "The Self-Government of Commercial Communities," A Report for the Arbitration Project, University of Chicago Law School, 1957.

WRONG, DENNIS H., *Power: Its Forms, Bases and Uses* (New York: Harper & Row, Pub., 1979).

ZINNES, DINA A., "An Analytical Study of the Balance of Power Theories," *Journal of Peace Research,* 3 (1967), 270–288.

———, "Empirical Evidence on the Outbreak of International Violence," in Ted Robert Gurr (ed.), *Handbook of Political Conflict: Theory and Research* (New York: Free Press, 1980).

5

Escalation
and
Deescalation

Any high level of conflict behavior will have been preceded by conflict behavior of a lesser magnitude, but not all conflict behavior inevitably escalates. Struggles terminate, and ways of conducting them may deescalate or remain frozen. A good predictor of high levels of coercion and violence is earlier conflict behavior of a lesser magnitude. Tanter (1966) studied various kinds of conflict in eighty-three countries in 1955–1957 and related them to other conflicts in 1958–1960. He found that antigovernment demonstrations, guerrilla warfare, and revolutions in 1955–1957 had a multiple correlation of .60 with revolutions in 1958–1960. Similarly, expulsion of foreign diplomats, severance of diplomatic relations, and the number killed in foreign conflicts in 1955–1957 had a multiple correlation of .66 with war in 1958–1960.

In this chapter we seek to understand how conflict behavior waxes and wanes. We examine the several processes that make for conflict escalation and those that make for deescalation. Then we examine the conditions that determine which processes are operative and to what extent. What we discussed in the previous chapter regarding the selection of conflict modes will help in our present quest. We can now examine the conditions and processes during a struggle that alter the issue, the conflict parties, the relationship between them, and their social environment in ways that lead to selecting modes that constitute escalation or deescalation.

Escalation means movement toward greater magnitudes of conflict behavior; deescalation means movement toward lesser magnitudes. Several dimensions of magnitudes must be distinguished. The conflicting parties' feelings toward each other is one dimension. We might consider that conflict behavior is of a higher magnitude if it is accompanied by greater feelings of animosity, hostility, or hatred toward an adversary. But feelings do not always match behavior. It will be best to restrict the magnitudes of conflict behavior to overt conduct; feelings may be helpful in explaining changes in conduct.

Two dimensions of conduct can be usefully distinguished—how conflicting goals are pursued and the scope or extent to which there is participation in the conflict behavior. In the first dimension, insofar as the parties increase coercion rather than persuasion or rewards, the magnitude of conflict behavior has risen. Similarly, insofar as violence is used rather than other forms of coercion, the magnitude of conflict behavior is greater. In the case of persuasion or rewards, it is not possible to calibrate increases in the magnitude of a conflict. The amount of resources devoted to each method is one indicator, but the quality of the appeals in persuasion or the significance of the resources offered for exchange are also relevant.

In addition to changes in conflicting modes, the scope of the conflict behavior may increase. This increase may involve more widespread participation by the members of each contending social category. It may also involve an increase in the number of conflicting relations between adversary parties. Finally, the scope of a conflict may increase in the number of other parties involved as partisans.

These several ways in which conflict behavior varies in magnitude are not necessarily related to one another. Thus, participation in conflict behavior may become more restricted within a social category as its reliance upon violence becomes greater. Therefore, references to escalation or deescalation should specify the sense in which it is used. In this work, our concern is largely with changes in the mode of pursuing conflicting goals, especially the use of coercion and particularly violence. When other meanings of escalation or deescalation are discussed, they will be explicitly stated.

Escalation occurs as people in a struggle believe that the gains if they triumph and the losses if they are defeated are greater than the costs of raising the magnitude of their own conflict behavior and absorbing the increased burdens that the adversary places upon them. This should not be seen as a simple calculation that each side regularly and carefully undertakes, but it may prove helpful to keep such a formula in mind as we consider what makes people willing to expend more resources to put pressure on an adversary and what makes them able to absorb increased pressure from their adversary. We will also discuss what factors increase the hopes and expectations of victory and the fears and expectations of defeat in the course of a social conflict. Such changes underlie the movement toward escalation or deescalation.

PROCESSES OF ESCALATION

In examining the processes of escalation, we will consider changes within a conflict unit and changes in the relations between the adversaries.

Changes within a Conflict Unit

Once a struggle has begun, each party to the conflict tends to undergo changes that engender escalation. Both social-psychological and organizational changes have this effect.

Social-Psychological Mechanisms. In many ways, once conflict behavior has started, mechanisms are triggered that tend to increase its magnitude. Having expressed hostility and coercive action against another party, the alleged reason for it assumes importance commensurate with the action taken. The cause is endowed with additional significance, and there is an increased commitment to it. In addition, as the other side reciprocates with coercion, the threats and injuries suffered also induce feelings of loyalty and commitment to the cause pursued (Lewin 1948, p. 199; Deutsch and Krauss 1960). Increased commitment to the goals pursued justifies increased effort toward their attainment and the willingness to absorb, without yielding, the coercive efforts of adversaries; hence these mechanisms are sources of escalation.

Finally, engagement in conflict behavior is often accompanied by a sense of crisis. There is a feeling of anxiety, surprise, and of having a limited time in which to act. Under such circumstances, fewer alternative courses of action are considered than in periods that are not viewed as a time of crisis (Hermann 1969; Holsti 1971). Constricted in the range of alternatives considered, each side tends to persist in the course of action already undertaken. In addition, crisis decision making tends to rely on stereotyped images of adversaries and on historical analogies and to view possible outcomes in terms of absolute victory and defeat. Levi and Tetlock's (1980) analysis of the Japanese leaders' decision to attack the United States in 1941, however, does not clearly support these ideas, but the situation did not include all elements of a crisis. Although the Japanese leaders felt national values were at stake and felt pressured by time, they thought they were in control of events and were not in a state of surprise.

Organizational Developments. Engaging in conflict behavior in itself tends to alter the group in ways that promote persistence and even escalation of the behavior. These alterations involve changes in the leadership and their relations with their constituencies, changes in the partisan supporters as they are mobilized, changes in the ideology about the struggle, and changes in the organizational goals. Each of these changes warrants separate discussion.

Leaders are particularly prominent in organizational relations with nonmembers. An entire organization can act as a single entity in relation to another organization only through representatives or leaders. Collectivities with any organization at all are differentiated to include roles for dealing with the social environment. Such differentiation is a basis for escalation.

First, there is a tendency for leaders who have made oppositional goals and means visible to their constituency to be particularly committed to those goals and the means used to attain them. In effect, they have made a public assertion that in their judgment the purpose and the ways used to serve that purpose are sound and beneficial. Consequently, once a course of action is entered, there is a tendency to persist upon the course. If coercion is begun, persistence in it, without success, leads to escalation. These tendencies exist in any public acts of leaders, but they are exaggerated in coercive external relations. "Mistakes" in foreign policy are, for several reasons, rarely admitted. Acts against an adversary will be condemned and opposed by the adversary; to reverse the course of action seems to be catering to the enemy. Furthermore, in taking actions against an adversary, the leaders have acted as representatives of the entire collectivity, and this tends to bind the internal constituency. Mistakes are also denied in external relations because it is easier to do so than in regard to internal issues. Since a course of action is directed against another party, the effects of that policy are more difficult for its partisans to assess than when the course of action is domestically oriented. The leaders can argue that the adversary is beginning to yield or has changed in ways that require even more of the same pressure. The step-by-step escalation of the U.S. involvement in the Vietnam War during the 1960s is illustrative (Halberstam 1973).

This discussion presumes that the leaders are conscious of the possibility of being replaced by another group of leaders. Competition and rivalry with alternative leaders can be a factor that contributes to escalation. For example, McWorter and Crain (1967) studied civil rights leaders in fifteen American cities in 1964–1965. On the basis of interviews with them and others in each city, they assessed the extent of organized and individual competition for civil rights leadership in each city. Organized competition refers to rivalry between groups or organizations committed more or less permanently to different programs or ideological stances. Individual competition refers to the competition among individuals for leadership in such a way that the leaders are not permanently committed to one side. McWorter and Crain found that militancy, as measured by responses to four agree-disagree questions, was lower among leaders in cities with minimal competition and higher in cities with either individual or group competition. Demonstrations, although short-lived, were also more frequent where there was competition; organized competition weakened the ability to sustain the demonstrations.

The threat of being outflanked by more militant rivals for leadership puts pressure on the leaders of both sides to escalate the means of struggle. Leaders may also face the threat of being outflanked by rivals who argue for moderation, admission of defeat, or less intensive efforts in pursuit of the goal. Competition is likely to promote escalation rather than deescalation under several circumstances. Notably, if the conflict is emerging, then the leaders of the challenging party are likely to have a constituency that would support more intense action to get quicker results. Another circumstance in which competition may promote escalation is when the conflict relationship between adversary parties has become institutionalized. Even if only informal, the understandings, mutual respect, and interdependence that leaders of parties in recurrent conflicts develop makes them vulnerable to more radical rivals. Thus the constituency may be suspicious of its representatives who regularly traffic with the enemy and may even become suspicious that the leaders are being co-opted by the opposition, are getting "soft," or are "selling out." Under such circumstances the threatening rivals are likely to be those who argued for more forceful means, and competition is likely to result in escalation of conflict behavior once a struggle has begun. Competition also tends to escalate fights when the conflict party is homogeneous and is treated like a united antagonist by the adversary.

Another process explains why competition for leadership is a source of conflict escalation. Specialists in the use of coercion come to the fore. In international relations, the military assume predominance once armed forces are engaged (Iklé 1971). This assumption of superiority was dramatically evident in Vietnam when regular U.S. military forces became engaged in the struggle (Halberstam 1973). Even in less organized adversaries as a conflict moves toward more coercive action, additional persons are likely to become actively involved in the struggle. These new partisans are a source of competition for leadership and may try to assume leadership positions. They are less likely to have had nonconflicting relations with the adversary and they are less likely to have some stake in the status quo. For example, in community conflicts the new leaders who tend to take over the dispute are rarely former community leaders, do not have the constraints of maintaining a previous community position, and are not subject to the cross-pressures felt by members of community organizations (Coleman 1957, p. 12).

The McWorter and Crain (1967) study should remind us, however, that even if competition is an inducement for more intense and coercive conflict behavior, it may be divisive to the extent that the ability to conduct sustained forceful action would be reduced. This seems to be the case, at least in part, among the various Arab states and organizations in their conflict with Israel.

Under some circumstances, competition may be the source of pressures for deescalating a conflict. This kind of pressure is most likely to occur in later stages of a struggle, in particularly heterogeneous conflict units, with an adversary who is divisively conciliatory, and in conflict relationships that are regulated but not institutionalized to the point of rigidity.

Changes in the rank and file also may induce escalation. As the confrontation between adversary groups occurs, the partisans and potential partisans of both sides become more involved in the struggle and more "radicalized." The adversary groups tend to become more committed to the goals pursued, and, therefore, the means used to pursue them can be escalated. This occurs wittingly and unwittingly.

At the early stages of conflict, when awareness is first emerging within a social category, the members begin to share their grievances, and, by identification, the sense of deprivation resulting from membership in the social category increases. These shared sentiments may be expressed by leaders who articulate the deprivations or by the members themselves, sharing their experiences and mutually interpreting them. For example, an important component of the women's liberation movement is "consciousness-raising" groups. In these small groups, women meet to share their experiences as women in the society. Together they learn that difficulties that had seemed personal are general and societal and, therefore, require societal solutions, not simply personal accommodation.

The membership composition of the partisan groups changes as the conflict proceeds, and this can also make for escalation. The development of a struggle may expand participation in the conflict behavior, and this expansion will bring in not only less moderate potential leaders but also a constituency that is more prone to use intense means. This change occurs for a number of reasons. First, in the case of oppressed categories, the segments that are most oppressed tend to become involved only when there are visible signs of possible gains. But their sense of grievance, once aroused, is likely to be greater than for persons who had the resources to initiate the struggle (Fanon 1966). The newly aroused are less moderate, not only because their grievances are greater but also because they are less constrained by understandings arrived at with the adversaries and are less likely to have experienced finding compromises with organized opponents. For example, a national study of opinions regarding civil liberties for Communists, atheists, and others expressing minority sentiments was conducted during the Joseph McCarthy period in the United States (Stouffer 1955). A cross section of the population and of community leaders was interviewed. On the whole, the community leaders were more tolerant of the rights of nonconformists than was the public at large. A national survey of blacks and of black civil rights leaders conducted in 1966 also is illustrative of the same point (Brink and Harris 1969, Appendix D). When compared to blacks in general, the leaders, although less satisfied about the progress being made by blacks and more militant about the goals to be pursued, were less likely to say they would engage in violent conduct.

The composition of a group also changes by some people's leaving it, insofar as membership is voluntary. Consequently, if the conflict behavior escalates, the members who are unwilling to engage in more intense conflict behavior withdraw, and those who are willing to engage in it become a larger and larger component of the conflict group. Such intensification of the means may be accompanied by a restriction in membership. Broad coalitions dissolve, and the scope of the conflict, in the sense of the numbers involved, deescalates at the same time that the intensity of the coercion increases.

Related to the changes in the leaders and the rank and file, but significant enough to warrant separate discussion, are the changes in the beliefs and expectations of the partisan groups. At the initial stages of a social conflict, each side rallies its forces. Before any test of strength is made against an adversary, the forces may seem powerful indeed. A group's conviction of victory may increase at the sight of their massed forces. Within the insularity of the partisan group, reassuring rumors may reinforce the conviction of strength and success in pursuing the course of conduct entered. If, in addition, there is some initial gain, the support for escalation may grow rapidly. This conviction is particularly true for people who are in a state of collective excitement and contagion. Such swellings of feelings may be short-lived, but they can escalate rapidly in such forms as riots or nonregulated strikes. In the American student strikes of May 1970, almost continuous rallies were maintained at which announcements of "shut downs" at other colleges were proclaimed. The élan and conviction of an ever-grander victory could sustain relatively extreme action, at least for a few days. Some students voiced the expectation that the strike would expand and go beyond the 1968 events in France in which students and workers joined together in a widespread strike.

Once a conflict group has emerged and assumed a differentiated form, the persons committed to the purpose of the organization also become committed to the maintenance of the organization per se. In itself this is not escalating and, indeed, as we discuss later, it can be deescalating. But the maintenance of an organization may require finding continuing activites to sustain participation. This is a reason why leaders of an organization must search out new activities; membership will wane and involvement lessen if it is not sustained by activities. If an organization fails in this regard, it will wither away or, if part of a larger social movement, lose out in competition to a more active rival organization. In itself, then, concern with maintaining the viability of an organization may help perpetuate at least a moderate level of conflicting activity.

Finally, conflict units with specialized substructures for waging conflicts may escalate conflict behavior rapidly once the specialized agencies begin operations. The agencies, following their own standard operating procedures, can produce outcomes that are not appropriate to the circumstances and trigger escalations (Allison 1971). There is, therefore, widespread recognition of the dangers of "unleashing the dogs of war"; once agencies are let loose, escalation seems uncontrolled. The outbreak of World War I is prototypical example of this process (Tuchman 1962). The German general staff had prepared plans for mobilization and for an overall major military campaign. Once mobilization had been ordered, the German kaiser himself felt he was no longer able to halt or even modify the next steps.

Changes in Relations between Adversaries

Once a conflict emerges, the changes in the relations between the conflicting parties are fundamental for escalation. We consider three such changes: the expansion of the issues in contention, the polarization of relations, and intervention.

Expansion of the Issues. Once a struggle has begun about a particular issue in contention, it often brings more general and additional issues into awareness.

Often more fundamental disputes are discovered. As Coleman (1957) writes of community conflicts:

> It seems that movement from specific to general issues occurs whenever there are deep cleavages of values or interests in the community which require a spark to set them off—usually a specific incident representing only a small part of the underlying difference. (p. 10)

For example, a community controversy over the kinds of books in the school library is generalized to the whole educational philosophy (Shaplen 1950).

The deterioration of relations between groups in conflict is self-escalating because as they deteriorate, contentious issues that had previously been ignored or denied are brought out. There is less need to deny them and indeed the overt conflict may seem a good time to "settle accounts" (Iklé 1971).

Additional issues also arise because as each side pursues its major aim, subgoals or preliminary ones emerge and soon take on independent importance as issues in contention. In international relations this is clear; a military base, for example, becomes important not in itself but as a protection of another position. A specific example is Sharm el Sheik. It was long a matter of contention between Israel and Egypt, not for its intrinsic attractiveness, but because it controls access to the Gulf of Aqabah and, hence, the port of Eilat (see the map on page 59). Similar developments occur within societies. Often it is difficult to say which goal is a means to which other goal since all the issues are so inextricably tied together. Thus, blacks in the United States may be struggling for integrated housing in order to get integrated schools, strive for income equality in order to increase housing desegregation, and seek integrated schools to get better jobs and more income equality.

In addition, as one side imposes sanctions upon the other, those sanctions become issues. For example, when women were struggling for suffrage in the United States, they picketed the White House, they were harassed by the police, many were arrested and when maltreated in prison, they went on hunger strikes that resulted in forced feeding (Flexner 1959, p. 251). As far as the women's movement was concerned, such behavior by the opposition created new issues of contention. Allies were drawn to the women's cause by the repressive police conduct.

Escalation often, then, is inadvertent. One party misperceives how the opponents will respond and commits acts that result in greater escalation than was intended by either party (Snyder and Diesing 1977, pp. 96–97). This may occur when one party tries to intimidate the adversary and instead provokes a harsh counterreaction. Sometimes the intimidation is a threat intended as a bluff; that is, the threatener expects the threat will suffice to bring about the desired action by the adversary. The adversary may, however, disregard the threat; the threatener may then feel it is necessary to act on the threat simply to maintain credibility, although acting on it was not what the threatener wanted to do or even regarded as appropriate for the issue at stake.

Finally, once conflict behavior proceeds to the point that severe coercive threats and actions are employed, there is an interactive dynamic that expands the issues in contention. Threats and coercion reverberate between adversaries. If one party is threatened, it tends to respond with hostility and aggression toward its adversary (Gurr 1970, p. 35; Berkowitz 1969, pp. 42–46). Then the adversary reciprocates, and harming the other party may become an end in itself. Once inflicting harm or indulging in revenge becomes a goal, runaway escalation may ensue, or, in any case, deescalation would become extremely difficult, viz., Northern Ireland and Lebanon.

It is also possible that the other side's responding with a lower magnitude of conflict behavior would result in escalating behavior. Underreaction may invite expansion of goals. After all, what a conflict party seeks as a goal, what it perceives as an aim, depends at least partly on what it believes it can get. Hence, if the other side responds less vigorously and less coercively than anticipated, its reaction may be viewed as an indication of weakness and embolden the conflict party to seek more. This then means an expansion of the issues at stake and often a prolongation of the conflict. Whether underresponse leads to escalation or deescalation depends upon many attributes of the response, as we discuss later in this chapter.

Polarization. As a conflict emerges and develops, the adversaries tend to become increasingly isolated from each other. For example, before war erupts between governments, they tend to withdraw from joint membership in international organizations (Skjelsbaek and Singer 1971). As conflict parties reduce the number of nonconflicting relations, they are less and less constrained by cross pressures and cross-cutting ties and are freer to indulge in more intensive coercive means.

Polarization also takes the form of reducing the neutrals and potential mediators. Parties to a conflict generally try to induce others to join them. Insofar as a party feels morally superior and confident that most of the audience are likely to be allies, it will urge everyone to choose sides. As the coal miners in Harlan County, Kentucky, sang in the thirties, "You either are a union man or a thug for J. H. Blair. Which side are you on, man, which side are you on?" Or as Eldridge Cleaver said, "If you're not part of the solution, you are part of the problem." Or, as the German Nazis put it, "If you are not for us, you are against us."

The polarization of relations between antagonists means that there are fewer opportunities to communicate about noncontentious issues and even about issues in contention. In addition, as the magnitude of conflict behavior increases, the fear and hostility between adversaries create suspicion and communication barriers increase; it is, therefore, difficult to signal any deescalation efforts. Tentative efforts to reduce the magnitude of conflict behavior may be viewed as a trap or as weakness and an invitation for applying more pressure. In any case, lack of responsiveness to tentative efforts at decreasing the magnitude of a conflict is likely to be viewed with resentment and increased anger and to be taken as an indication that deescalation is not possible. Whereupon the other side can feel it was correct in rebuffing the gestures that were alleged to be conciliatory.

As coercion increases, the perceptions of the opponents and the reality upon which those perceptions are based makes them seem more and more inhuman. In extreme cases, the enemy is degraded and brutalized and then held in contempt and regarded as subhuman. The relations between prisoners and guards in concentration camps is an extreme case, but, to some extent, the same is true of many conflict relations. In these circumstances the pain and suffering of the adversary does not arouse sympathy and compassion. The very suffering of adversaries can make them seem despicable; their pain can be an invitation for further violence. In battle, pleas for pity may make the weaker seem contemptible (Near 1971).

Similarly, the brutality of the other side makes brutality in return, not only a matter of retribution or vengeance, but also perfectly reasonable because the other side is a brute and presumably understands only brutal acts. The imagery of nonhuman animals used in conflict relations is revealing for it allows treating the enemy in an inhuman fashion, viz., the use of words like pigs, dogs, and cattle.

Polarization may not take such an extreme form, but the commission of a certain kind of action precipitates breaks in relations that inevitably lead to more extreme actions. For example, once elements in a revolutionary group seize buildings of the government or even of an opposition party, a revolutionary act will be viewed as having been taken; this action therefore commits all supporters of the elements who seized the buildings to a full-scale revolutionary effort and the opponents to full-scale repression. Moore (1978, p. 307) describes the failed Spartacist uprising in Germany in 1918–1919 as being prematurely undertaken when initiated.

Intervention. The social context of conflicting parties can be the basis of escalation by the involvement of other parties in the struggle. Intervention could cause deescalation, as we examine later, but it tends to promote escalation. Thus, Gurr (1970, pp. 270–271) in his study of civil strife in 114 nations, found that external support for dissidents was correlated .37 with the length of the civil strife and .22 with its pervasiveness. Similarly, external support for regimes was correlated .30 with duration and .28 with pervasiveness. External support results in escalation through several mechanisms. External support makes it possible for an adversary with limited resources to persevere and even expand its conflict behavior (Gross 1966, pp. 162–186). Moreover, if one side is aided by an outside party, its enemy will tend to be aided by a different outsider. Thus, Gurr found that external support for dissidents was very highly correlated with external support for the regime (.83). Finally, the very intervention of outside parties as partisans, in itself, means an escalation in the scope of the conflict.

Parties are drawn into conflicts by a variety of circumstances. For example, if adversaries A and B are in a fight and C is helping A, then the opponents of C will have reason to assist B; this is illustrated by the shifting of involvement with and support of the Pol Pot led government in Kampuchea (Cambodia). It is consistent with the maxim: My enemy's enemy is my friend. Furthermore, each party appeals in terms of values and standards that make claims for others to intervene on its side. More fundamentally, other parties are likely to see some advantage accruing to them by the victory of one adversary rather than the other and, unless constrained by other considerations, will try to aid the preferred victor (Eckstein 1966).

Involvement may also expand because, as the partisans pursue their goals, they infringe upon the interests of other parties. If one primary group more than others does this, the offended nonprimary party will have increasingly conflicting relations with the more offending group. In World War I, for example, Germany's use of submarines to attack shipping to Great Britain aggravated the emerging conflict with the United States. Partisans in a struggle may be more or less conscious of the possible effects of their actions upon other parties. Depending upon their expectations of the likely responses of other parties, consideration of those reactions may set limits to escalation. If other parties hold normative standards about what they regard as intolerable kinds of conflict behavior, the antagonists may limit their own behavior to avoid outraging other parties that might intervene.

As a fight escalates, the means of waging the struggle tend to become more and more removed from the underlying conflict. In this sense, the conflict may be considered to have increasingly "unrealistic" components. One could also argue, as the partisans are likely to do, that the objective conflict has shifted, that the adversaries have more at stake in the fight as the way of waging it has escalated.

PROCESSES OF DEESCALATION

Conflict behavior does not increase in magnitude indefinitely. It must deescalate, stagnate, or stop. We now consider the processes of deescalation, and we will note their similarity with the processes of escalation. Our understanding of each will help our understanding of the other. Analysts of social conflicts have concentrated on escalating processes to the neglect of deescalating ones, and, therefore, we have relatively fewer research findings to draw from for the ideas presented in this section. After reviewing the processes of deescalation, we will examine the conditions that affect whether the processes act to escalate or deescalate the fight. As in the discussion of escalating processes, we will consider deescalating processes within individual conflict units and between them.

Changes within a Conflict Unit

As conflict behavior continues, it triggers mechanisms within a conflict party that can limit its escalation or produce deescalation.

Social-Psychological Mechanisms. Earlier, we noted how engaging in conflict behavior may produce a greater commitment to the goals pursued and, hence, a willingness to persist and even escalate conflict behavior. But expending resources in pursuit of a goal becomes increasingly costly as it is maintained without gaining the end sought. The cost for each additional increment of coercive effort may increase at a higher and higher rate as alternative expenditures are foregone. For example, a few hours at the picket lines or at the barricades may be a diversion; days or weeks so engaged threaten other interests.

Increased commitment to an aim resulting from sacrifices trying to attain it makes subjective sense—one's self-esteem is sustained by believing the goal is worth the effort so long as the effort is being expended. It is also soothing to one's self-esteem to decide that something that appears very difficult to attain is not desired. Following Aesop's fable about the fox and the grapes it could not reach, making this decision may be called the "sour grapes" mechanism. When the costs for attaining a goal become too great, the goal may be devalued. When such turning points are reached depends upon a number of other circumstances, which we will consider in this and the next chapter.

Organizational Developments. We noted in the discussion of escalation processes that competition for leadership may induce increased magnitudes of conflict behavior. Under certain conditions, however, leadership competition hastens deescalation of conflict behavior. The basic condition is that a segment of a conflict party prefers to reduce the efforts being exercised in pursuit of the conflicting goal; that is, there is a constituency for more moderate action.

A constituency for more moderation is likely to develop after conflict behavior has been pursued at an increasing cost without giving signs of successfully attaining the proclaimed ends. Leaders who can offer a plausible way of attaining the goal by deescalating the means used provide a source of deescalation. Deescalation, however, increases the probability of not attaining the goal and is, therefore, facilitated by a decreasing commitment to the aim being pursued. Even without abandoning the goal, downgrading its importance makes more intense coercive action seem inappropriate and wasteful. Potential leaders who can articulate such changes and the new alternatives pose a threat to the established leaders. Divisions among the leadership give legitimacy to popular disavowal of support for a fight, as happened in the United States about the Vietnam War.

Another condition that increases the likelihood of deescalating leadership competition is the heterogeneity of the conflict group in regard to the goal. That is, if the segments of a conflict party differ about the goal's importance, potential leaders have the basis for a constituency to support a more moderate means toward the end.

Some of the ways in which leaders pursue group aims may promote the very differences that are the basis for deescalation. Thus, as coercive action is intensified, leaders often increase pressure for greater rank-and-file support of the policies being pursued. Tolerance for dissent declines, and criticism of leaders is made to appear treasonous. Consequently, leaders create more division and dissent than would otherwise be the case. This is done by defining those who disagree as traitors and treating them as such; in that case, they tend to reciprocate and indeed expand their dissent to more general opposition. In times of intense conflict behavior, it may not even be necessary for people in some segment to express disagreement. They may be viewed as potential or likely dissenters and closely watched, preventively intimidated, or even physically isolated or punished. For example, in the United States in World War II Americans of Japanese descent were removed from their homes and placed in "relocation centers." "Disloyalty" was created (Grodzins 1956). Would-be loyal followers can be made into traitors and dissension can be fostered in any conflict group. The creation of such dissent provides the basis for a constituency that would support a more moderate course of action. The rank and file, rather than becoming uniformly mobilized for more intense action, may have segments that become increasingly disenchanted. The coalition mobilized to wage the struggle may begin to dissolve, and we can speak of demobilization of a conflict group (Tilly 1978).

Finally, concern with maintaining the organization is often deescalating. Once a conflict organization has developed, many persons, especially those in leadership positions, feel a commitment to the survival of the organization. This commitment is in addition to any other purpose which the leaders proclaim for the organization. Concern with survival limits the tendencies toward escalation, since continued escalation can threaten the continued existence of the organization. (Of course, this limitation is true insofar as the adversary is not seen as threatening the very life of the organization.)

Changes in Relations between Adversaries

Conflict behavior does not only increase polarization between conflict units, expand the issues in contention, and draw in other parties; but it may also develop new ties between adversaries, devalue goals, and introduce other parties who deescalate the conflict.

Emerging Ties. As a social conflict continues, opponents can develop new bonds even while they are struggling against each other. This change, of course, is more likely for recurring conflicts that have ended with some degree of compromise. As noted in Chapter 4, this is one of the bases of institutionalization of conflict regulation. Even in the course of a single, specific conflict, however, the adversaries may develop mutual respect and understanding. This is especially likely when the conflict behavior being followed is at least somewhat regulated and the issues in contention are not considered vital. Under these circumstances, it is possible for adversaries to respect the skill with which the other side has pursued its goal. Such mutual respect may even develop in international wars. When there is mutual respect, some limits on escalation exist.

Such mutual understanding and respect are particularly likely between those persons on both sides occupying similar statuses, for example, soldiers, generals, and leaders. Leaders in every conflict situation are in positions that bring them into interaction with their opposing counterparts. The leaders can recognize that they share many problems with each other; they seek to maintain themselves in leadership positions, make some progress toward their proclaimed goals, and not require too much sacrifice of their followers.

Under these circumstances, leaders can reach understandings to deescalate a fight. Such arrangements usually entail reaching an agreement about the outcome of a conflict as well, as in the 1962 Kennedy-Khrushchev agreement about the missile bases in Cuba (Holsti, Brody, and North 1964). Agreements may sometimes, however, be only about the means of pursuing goals. In any case, this distinction is never absolute: An agreement about ends includes understandings about means, and an agreement about means has implications about ends.

Mutual understandings about deescalating a struggle (without making an agreement about the outcome) may be reached in open negotiations, but they may also be reached surreptitiously. Peace initiatives are often ventured only after some covert communications indicate they will be welcomed (Kriesberg 1981a).

When conflict behavior has reached high levels and a major escalating change seems about to occur, leaders may covertly seek an understanding to avoid that escalation. Presumably both sides see too great a risk in engaging in the higher level of conflict behavior but do not want to give any appearance to their own followers of "backing down." Intermediaries can be helpful at such times.

These points may be illustrated by the events of March 1963 in Selma, Alabama (Hinckle and Welsh 1969). The SCLC, under Dr. Martin Luther King, Jr.'s, leadership, and SNCC were cooperating in organizing activities in Selma. Their members, in conjunction with those efforts, attempted a mass march to Montgomery, Alabama, on Sunday, March 7. They were stopped by the state troopers, under Colonel Al Lingo, and the police, under Sheriff Jim Clark. They were beaten and gassed. A second march was planned for Tuesday. Former Florida Governor LeRoy Collins, head of the Federal Community Service and unofficial ambassador of President Johnson, flew in to try to avoid a repetition of Sunday's bloodshed.

A federal judge had issued a temporary restraining order against the march and Dr. King was in a quandary. His organization prided itself on never violating the law —or a court order; yet, he had pledged to lead this march (King was absent Sunday), and civil rights workers and ministers from all over the South were gathering. . . . They all wanted to march. Collins offered a typically Johnson compromise; he had conferred with Colonel Lingo and obtained a pledge that the marchers would be unharmed if they turned back a small distance down Highway 80. Lingo had even drawn a rough map, showing where the Union [civil-rights] forces must halt. Collins handed the . . . map to King: this way, he said, both sides would save face—and King would have a dramatic moment. King hesitated, then took the map. . . . The plan worked. The marchers were halted, knelt, said a prayer and turned back. The deal became obvious to SNCC people when Colonel Lingo, in a mild Southern double-cross, pulled his troopers back, leaving the highway to Montgomery open as King rose to lead his followers in retreat to Selma. The move was meant to embarrass King and it did. King's fall from favor was only momentary. The diverse elements . . . were united later that week by the death of the Rev. James J. Reeb, a white Unitarian minister from Boston, who died of wounds from a nighttime beating at the hands of some Selma white citizens. . . . (Hinckle and Welsh 1969, pp. 108–109)

Contraction of Goals. Each party in a conflict presumably believes that its actions will stop or prevent the escalation of conflict behavior by its enemies. For example, the U.S. bombing of North Vietnam was intended, according to some American leaders, to impede the movement of soldiers and supplies from North Vietnam to the war in the South. Whatever the intentions of one side may be, the other side may not deescalate. Indeed, violence and coercion are likely to be reciprocated. For the several reasons already discussed, threats and coercion resulted in further escalation. Bombing of cities has not led to the intimidation of the people and their withdrawal of support from their own leaders, not in North Vietnam and not in Japan, Germany, or Great Britain during World War II (U.S. Strategic Bombing Survey 1946–1947; Sheehan and others 1971, pp. 307–344).

Coercion by one party can lead to deescalation by its adversaries in two basic ways. One possibility is that the coercion is sufficient to prevent the other side from physically continuing in its conflict behavior. The adversary then loses its capacity to continue its conflict behavior at the same level and must deescalate. Thus, a conflict group may be repressed by its much stronger opposition; its leaders may be harassed and imprisoned. Similarly, the armed forces of one side may so decimate the ranks of the other that it cannot continue to field an effective army. The other possibility is that an adversary loses its will to persist; it doubts its ability and questions the desirability of continuing its conflict behavior. In actuality, the will to continue conflict behavior is highly related to the capacity to do so. Neither factor alone determines deescalation. Klingberg (1966) studied war casualties in relationship to the termination of war. He found some evidence that in modern times nations have tended to surrender before suffering population losses of 3 or 4 percent. There is variation, however; Paraguay may have lost 80 percent of its population in the Lopez War (1865–1870). Surrender is often preceded by unfavorable trends in four indices, when viewed as a whole: casualty percentage ratios between opposing belligerents, army-size ratios, proportion of battle defeats, the intensity of fighting. An abnormal increase in the proportion of soldiers who are taken prisoner or become sick sometimes preceded surrender by several months. These findings indicate that the losses in war are related to ending the fighting, but assessing what magnitude of loss will lead to termination is not easy. This is in large measure due to the importance of considering the goals of the opposing forces.

However it is brought about, if one party finds that the adversary's coercion has reduced its ability to pursue its goals, it is likely to contract the goals. At least within the confines of a particular conflict, the issues in contention are likely to become more limited. In that sense, deescalation has happened.

The loss of capacity and the will to continue conflict behavior is related to many conditions which will be analyzed in more detail later in this chapter and in the next two chapters. At this point it is necessary only to outline two of the ways in which the interaction between adversaries can affect a conflict party, through loss of will and the capacity to fight on.

The possibility of one party's physically preventing its adversary from engaging in conflict behavior depends on their relative resources. In a peculiar but fundamental sense, the opponents help determine the magnitude of each other's resources. That is, one conflict party can define and treat its adversary as a more or less isolated group. The more isolated it is, the more limited are its resources. So each adversary might be expected to try and isolate the "hard core" opposition and attack only it. But, as we discussed in the section on escalation, conflicts tend toward polarization and expansion of the partisans on each side. Now we must add the possibility that one or more adversaries may consciously try to avoid that expansion in order to keep the adversary isolated and small. This argues for each party's being careful to engage in conflict behavior that is not so large in scope as to expand its opposition. A government that tries to put down a small band of dissidents by widespread repression of potential supporters would create more opposition and conflict escalation. More on this later.

We also noted in discussing escalation that as a conflict persists, the issue in contention tends to expand and become more general. To deescalate a conflict, one or more parties may try to "fractionate" it (Fisher 1964). The general issues in contention may be broken up into more specific items and dealt with one at a time. One or more parties may come to believe that the expansion of the issues has gone too far and try to concentrate upon a more delimited matter of contention. This change in concentration may mean a shift in the focal conflict, as happens when leaders of one conflict group become fearful of losing to a moderate internal competing leadership group and seek a quick settlement with the adversary.

The extent to which a conflict party's actions divides rather than unifies the adversary lessens the adversary's capacity to sustain even the same level of conflict behavior. External pressure can be a source of unity; members of a threatened group may rally together against the enemy. But external pressures can also aggravate internal dissension, and large segments of the conflict group may withdraw support from their own leaders. It is easy to point to cases that exemplify each development. Whether external pressure is a unifier or not obviously depends on many conditions. The matter is important and complex enough that we will discuss it separately in Chapter 8. Here we need to point out only that external pressure may be divisive, and whether it is or not depends partly upon the character of the pressures and the context of their application. If a group can engage in conflict behavior that weakens the solidarity of its adversary, then the adversary may deescalate its conflict behavior.

A conflict group may aggravate the dissension within its adversary in many ways. One way is to be divisively conciliatory. It may phrase or rephrase its demands so that they require sacrifices from some segment of the enemy and not from the enemy as a single unit. Or, the limited nature of the demands may be stressed so that escalation seems increasingly inappropriate. On the other hand, the coercion may be applied divisively. It may be conducted selectively so that only a segment of the adversary party experiences it. The segment of the conflict group suffering a disproportionate burden of the fight may be especially likely to become disenchanted with the struggle.

Peace initiatives and other blends of reward and persuasion can be employed possibly to divide the opposition. When Khrushchev launched a peaceful coexistence campaign in the mid-1950s, he promised to limit escalation; his campaign was an inducement which might prevent, slow, or lessen the rearmament of West Germany (Kriesberg 1981b).

Intervention. The social context of a conflict can importantly contribute to its deescalation. If other parties do not become involved as partisans, this in itself limits the expansion of the conflict. The isolation of the conflict may be agreed upon by the other parties in order to prevent their own involvement. In some cases there are norms about neutrality to support such noninvolvement, namely, the norm in international relations against interference in the domestic affairs of other states. Needless to say, the norm is often violated.

Other parties also act as enforcers to correct breeches of understandings about conflict behavior. Violations of norms can bring about the interference of previously uninvolved parties. The recognition of this possibility serves to limit the tactics used in conflicts and to maintain the boundaries of appropriate action. This is true, for example, in community conflicts (Coleman 1957, p. 12). Even where all the parties are not members of a relatively integrated social system with institutionalized conflict regulation, other parties sometimes become similarly involved, as occurs in international relations when a civil war breaks out in one country. In these cases, however, additional considerations affecting interference and noninterference in the internal affairs of a country are so great that other parties are relatively unimportant in setting limits to the escalation of conflict behavior.

Finally, other parties can act as mediators. Aside from helping to reach a settlement of the issues in contention, mediators may help reach an understanding about the means used in the conflict. Mediation can be particularly helpful when both sides are fearful of further escalation. A mediator can convey the mutual interest in limiting escalation, which no conflict party would be willing to communicate to the other openly and unilaterally. A mediator can also help devise formulas that permit both sides to continue a conflict at a lower level and presumably without changing the relative positions of the two sides. This mediation may occur even in the midst of a rapidly escalating situation. For example, as described earlier, in the 1963 march on Montgomery from Selma, Collins was able to negotiate a compromise between Lingo and King that probably averted widespread violence against the marchers by the state troopers (Hinckle and Welsh 1969).

CONDITIONS OF ESCALATION
AND DEESCALATION

We have considered several processes that contribute to escalation and deescalation of conflict behavior. Since the same processes are involved in both courses of development, their outcome depends on a variety of specific conditions. It is to those conditions that we now turn. We will discuss the conflict modes, the characteristics of the partisans, the responses of the adversary, the issues in contention, and the social context.

Consideration of the interaction between conflict parties under varying conditions may be facilitated by using diagrammatic formulations as well as verbal ones. Before analyzing the specific conditions affecting escalation and deescalation, then, we will briefly discuss such formulations. We can best begin with the equations developed by Richardson in regard to arms races (Richardson 1960; Rapoport 1957). He reasoned that the amount of arms one side amassed was a function of how much the other side had, modified by the amount of hostility it had toward the other side and the costs of the arms. An arms race could, therefore, be described by two simultaneous equations:

$$\frac{dx}{dt} = ky = ax + g$$

and

$$\frac{dy}{dt} = lx - by + h$$

In these equations, defense expenditures of each side, x and y, over time, equal the other side's defense expenditures (k and l), minus the cost of the defense effort (a and b) plus the grievances against the other side (g and h).

These equations could fit any process in which a movement by one party changes the field so that the other party moves, and it thereby alters the situation so that the first party will change its position. This process underlies all social interaction and is particularly pertinent to analysis of escalation and deescalation. Following Boulding (1962), we can present these equations graphically and examine some properties of such interactive processes. Assume a single dimension of hostility and friendship along which two parties can move toward each other. In Figure 5.1 the origin, marked by an O, is the neutral point for both parties. Any movement upward or to the right is a movement of escalating hostility. Along OH_a, A's hostility to B is measured, and B's hostility toward A is measured along OH_b. Similarly, movement downward or leftward is deescalating; the other side of the origin is called friendliness. Now we postulate two curves that show

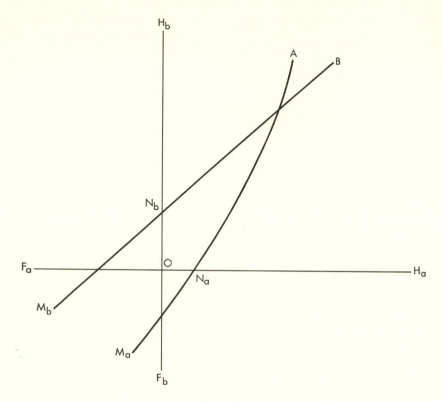

Figure 5.1

the amount of hostility each side has toward the other at each level of the other side's hostility. Thus, the A curve, M_aA, shows how much hostility A has at every level of B's hostility or friendliness. As the curves are drawn, each party has some hostility toward the other initially—even if the other side is neutral. Thus, when B is neutral, A has ON_a hostility. The lines are also drawn with positive slopes or positive reaction coefficients. That is, each party increases its hostility toward the other by more than one unit for each unit the other side increases its hostility. In other words, the higher the reaction coefficient, the touchier is the party.

Figure 5.2 is the same as Figure 5.1, except now we can see the dynamics of the system. The two curves intersect at E. Let us see if that is a stable equilibrium point. Suppose the parties were at point P_0. For A, this is OP_a amount of hostility; for B, it is OP_b hostility. For the amount of hostility A has, B has too much. B would reduce its hostility as indicated by the arrow's going down from P_0. A, however, has too little hostility for the amount B has and would increase its hostility, as indicated by the arrow's pointing to the right from P_0. The vector for those two directions is the arrow between them, pointing to E; this is the direction the two parties would move. Indeed, from each point in the graph, the vector lines would lead to the equilibrium, E, which is thus indicated to be a

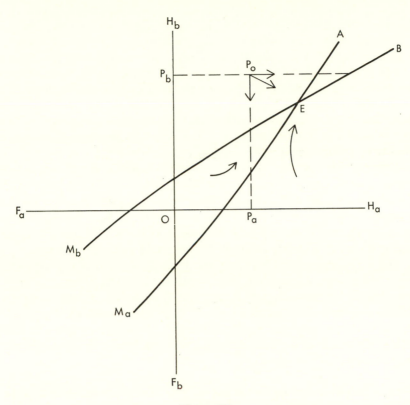

Figure 5.2

stable equilibrium point. Given these reaction coefficients, then, the two parties would remain hostile to each other. A more friendly equilibrium would require different reaction coefficients. With still other curves there may be no stable equilibrium; as in a run-away arms race, there may be ever-increasing hostility until the limits of the system are reached. Boulding discusses many properties of such graphs and a variety of reaction coefficients; the presentation here should be sufficient to assist us in describing and understanding escalating and deescalating movements.

Mode

How a conflicting goal is pursued has consequences for future escalation. One side's having initiated a certain kind of conflict behavior alters the probability of using the opponent's kind. This is true because engaging in any particular conflict behavior affects those conducting it, those against whom it is being directed, and often even outside parties. The mode employed has costs and may have gratifications to those using it. It imposes burdens upon the adversary, and, therefore, the choice of mode has implications for conflict escalation and deescalation.

Although attempting to coerce the other side is costly in many ways, we must also recognize that many persons derive gratification from certain aspects of coercion. Such gratification makes deescalating responses to overtures from the other side unlikely. Enjoying engagement in a particular kind of coercive action makes persistence in it relatively independent of the opponent's actions.

Gratifications from certain kinds of conflict behavior derive from several sources. One source is the pleasure of solidarity with one's own people. Conflict behavior that brings people together to share danger in facing an adversary can be exciting and pleasurable. Particularly at an early stage in a confrontation, the massing of persons can create a feeling of brotherhood or sisterhood, of brave comrades standing firmly together. At the barricades, in the streets, before storming the enemy's positions, the sense of collective solidarity and even love for those with whom these times are shared arises and is savored. Such feelings not only make for persistence in the behavior because it is pleasurable, but the sense of solidarity also gives a feeling of strength that enables people to continue even when they are suffering setbacks. The sense of solidarity is itself strengthened by seeing how well comrades are behaving. Their sacrifices and strength in the face of the adversary make each person feel proud to be allied with them; their sacrifices make them worth sacrificing for. Some of these points are illustrated by the account of one participant in the civil rights movement in the early 1960s. He tells of thousands of students marching to a southern city jail in support of a group that had been arrested.

> When we had all arrived we started singing "We Shall Overcome" and after we finished there was a peaceful quiet, like I've never heard before in my whole life. We stood there, the police stood there, and the white mob stood there—we all just stood there. And then, in the background, faintly we heard the students in the jail sing to us. We couldn't see them but they chanted, "Oh students don't you mourn." It brought tears to my eyes. . . .

Then the police charged.

> I saw one little girl—weighed about seventy pounds—and the policeman gave the command for a dog to leap at her. And one of the basketball players—a great big boy—put himself in front of her. The dog leaped and came back down with his suit and all his clothes torn off and the boy just smiled and walked off. I saw beauty that day.

He was blinded temporarily by the tear gas attack.

> When I was able to see again I saw some of the girls getting themselves together. Some went back to the campus in an ambulance; they had been hit in the legs with nightsticks. And all of them—their clothes were torn and they were many of them bleeding—they were all standing in line again. In that few minutes they had pulled themselves back together and they were singing as loud as they could, "I'm gonna sit at the welcoming table." And the police stood there and didn't say a word. (Bell 1968, p. 115)

Another source of gratification that certain kinds of conflict behavior provides is the feeling of being important and of being part of something that is momentous. Actions that disrupt the routine for significant proportions of a social system must be important. And it is gratifying to be doing something important. If it is momentous enough, "history" is being made and one is part of its creation. This feeling of excitement and importance can be experienced by persons who are merely cogs in the great machinery of war or revolution. But the feeling can animate the leaders too. Even the occupiers of the most powerful positions in a society feel an extra excitement and pleasure at directing vast enterprises. They certainly are making history and there is a thrill in it, as indicated in Harry Hopkins's papers about Franklin Roosevelt and leaders of the United States, Great Britain, and the Soviet Union during World War II (Sherwood 1948). People enjoy the excitement of crises and may even help create them or define some events as a crisis in order to increase their own feelings of importance and the significance of their coping with it (Argyris 1967, p. 42).

A third source of gratification that contributes to the persistence of some kinds of conflict behavior is the pleasure people find in "proving themselves." In confrontations with an adversary, courage, stamina, and quick judgment are all put to the test. Many people enjoy such challenges and look for them; once found they help sustain people in the conflict behavior. There is the joy of handling heavy and expensive equipment in international wars, of staying up nights at the barricades, or bravely enduring pain, of marshaling legions of men, and of conferring long hours to make grave decisions. These gratifications seem to be more readily associated with coercion (nonviolent and violent) than persuasion or reward.

Feelings of collective solidarity, excitement, making history, and proving oneself cannot be sustained for long and cannot in themselves maintain a group in continuing conflict. Even the extraordinary, if continuously performed, can become routine. But these emotions, aroused by collective action that faces coercion from an adversary, can overcome initial doubts and fears. Once engaged in an exchange of coercive acts, other processes may become operative to sustain the escalation. The feelings also promote escalation at the early stages of conflict behavior since many people may be drawn into the action by the initial excitement. Commitments thus made have an enduring quality.

Extreme coercive acts, once executed, tend to be justified by their perpetrators. People committing what they regard as terrible acts vindicate themselves. For example, if people riot and property is burned and if people are hurt and killed, then a cause worthy of such losses must be found. Sympathizers and participants in a riot are likely to feel even more than before that conditions were very bad to lead to such events.

Riots, however, also have a self-limiting character. Stolen or burned goods and property cannot be taken or destroyed again. Riots can be part of an escalating development only by spreading rapidly to encompass larger and larger segments of the society. Unless the conditions for this extension are present, however, riots burn themselves out. From the ashes more organized and radicalized groups may emerge to continue the conflict in other ways. How the riots are put down may also increase the sense of grievance and provide the basis for increased levels of conflict behavior at another time.

Modes vary widely in their possible effects upon opponents. The effect depends partly upon the adversary's understanding of the meaning of the actions. Modes vary in the clarity of the message. For example, terrorism is particularly unclear —the terrorist acts themselves do not reveal what is being demanded or of whom it is being demanded. They imply that the enemy should "drop dead," go away, or otherwise disappear. That is not a goal that the enemy is likely or even able to accede to easily. When the enemy is a foreign occupying force, however, there may be more possibility of doing so. Terrorism, because of its accompanying secrecy, is hard to be explained and interpreted by its perpetrators. Faced by unclear but vaguely total demands and no visible adversary with whom discussion is possible, terrorism is likely to provoke strong reactions from the other side. Riots, too, are unclear in meaning. There are no authoritative interpretators. Thus when a national sample of whites was asked in August 1967 what the two or three main reasons for the ghetto riots were, 45 percent said "outside agitators" (Erskine 1967–1968, p. 665).

The meaning of acts also depends on the conventions of the adversaries. In a period of inflation of rhetoric and actions, voices may become shriller and actions more extreme in order to be noticed and to be taken seriously. The adversary's conventions also serve as criteria to evaluate the appropriateness of coercive acts. If a conflict party acts in a manner that goes beyond the normative expectations of the opponent, for example, the reaction may be one of such outrage that the acts would be counterproductive—instead of intimidating, they would provoke further escalation. The police "bust" at Columbia University in 1968 served to make the university authorities illegitimate in the eyes of the students and faculty. Actually seeing the police clubbing students and dragging them from the seized buildings was much more likely to make student and faculty regard the police action as brutal than only hearing or reading about it had done. Among those who did not see the police action, 28 percent of the faculty and 41 percent of the students thought the police action was brutal, compared to 66 percent and 74 percent of the faculty and students who did see it (Barton 1968).

In general, the more severe the action of one side, the more likely is it that escalation occurs. Evidence for this is found in a study of colleges that had their first demonstrations against certain kinds of campus recruitment during October-December 1967 (Morgan 1970). The severity of the control measures against civil disobedience was assessed as well as the frequency of expansion of protest. The more severe the control measures, the more likely was it that the protest expanded. For example, in only 2 percent of the cases in which there was no confrontation did the protest expand; in 50 percent of the schools in which police were used, protest expanded; and in 73 percent of the cases in which some demonstrators were arrested by the police, there was expansion of the protest.

The earlier discussion of the effects upon the perpetrators of conflict behavior suggests that conduct which does not arouse great feelings of solidarity against an adversary permits responsiveness to deescalating efforts by the adversary. Modes that involve more attention to the ideas and feelings of the adversary also make responsiveness more likely and probably also inhibit rapid escalation. For example, this would be the case insofar as persuasion is used as the way of pursuing conflicting goals.

In general, violence is provocative. It hurts the opponent so that the newly created grievance cries for retribution, and increased violence may be used to suppress efforts at retribution. Nonviolent acts are not as likely to have the same effect. Escalation may occur as more people are drawn in as participants in the nonviolent actions, but increases in the magnitude of coercion are probably less likely than if violence had been used.

Each party to a conflict considers how the opponents will be affected by its choice of means, and this very anticipation then affects its choice and the likelihood of escalation. For example, a foreign minister threatens the use of a particular negative sanction with an assessment of the likelihood that the adversary will yield or counterthreat. Insofar as conflict is regulated and institutionalized, each side can anticipate with relative accuracy the response of the other. Such accuracy lessens the likelihood of rapid escalation. Acts that provoke escalating behavior from the other side are less likely to be taken mistakenly. This is one reason why stable conditions contribute to the moderation of conflict behavior—accurate expectations can develop.

In two circumstances, however, shared understandings about ways of pursuing conflicting goals may be the basis of escalation. First, one party to a conflict may try to provoke the other side into escalation in order to make the other side behave in a reprehensible manner. Second, boundaries of acceptable conduct are constraining, but once crossed there may be a sense of unlimited license.

Many illustrations of consciously provocative actions can be found, even in cases of governments' acting against other governments. For example, in May 1967 the Egyptian government requested the United Nations Emergency Force (UNEF) to withdraw from Egypt. This withdrawal meant that Egyptian military forces again controlled Sharm el Sheik and would not permit Israeli vessels to pass through to the Gulf of Aqabah and the port of Eilat in Israel (Nasser 1970). (See map on p. 59.) Hassanain Haykal (1970), the Egyptian spokesman, writing in *Al Ahram,* interpreted the action thus:

> The closure of the Gulf of Aqabah to Israeli navigation and the ban on the import of strategic goods, even when carried by non-Israeli ships, means first and last that the Arab nation represented by the UAR has succeeded for the first time, vis-à-vis Israel, in changing by force a *fait accompli* imposed on it by force. . . . Egypt has exercised its power and achieved the objectives of this stage without resorting to arms so far. But Israel has no alternative but to use arms if it wants to exercise power. This means that the logic of the fearful confrontation now taking place between Egypt . . . and Israel . . . dictates that Egypt . . . must wait, even though it has to wait for a blow. This is necessitated also by the sound conduct of the battle, *particularly from the international point of view.* Let Israel begin. Let our second blow be ready. Let it be a knockout. (Haykal 1970, pp. 180, 185; emphasis added)

Crossing a boundary of acceptable conduct has implications for escalation; it opens up new vistas of possible conflict modes. Once one side has broken a barrier, it feels relatively unrestrained and so does its adversary. In international conflicts, there may be agreed upon limits, for example, about the use of nuclear, bacteriological, or chemical weapons. Each side may be careful about using a "little bit" of such weapons because a barrier would be broken. The anticipation of rapid nuclear escalation once tactical nuclear weapons are used inhibits their employment. This understanding was part of the issue in the American utilization of chemical weapons in Vietnam. It was argued that their use in combat, even if only the kinds used in domestic riot control were employed, could easily evolve into the employment of more and more potent gases. Forces differ in the degree to which clear boundaries may be demarcated; for example, the distinction between having some military advisers in a country and then sending in special combat units is not as sharp a crossing of a boundary as the introduction of aerial bombing across national borders would be (Schelling 1960).

The existence of boundaries in conflict behavior may be shown graphically in irregularities in the curves of the reaction coefficients. That is, there would be step-wise progression in the level of conflict behavior, as shown in Figure 5.3. A number of equilibrium points would be reached and then passed if one or the

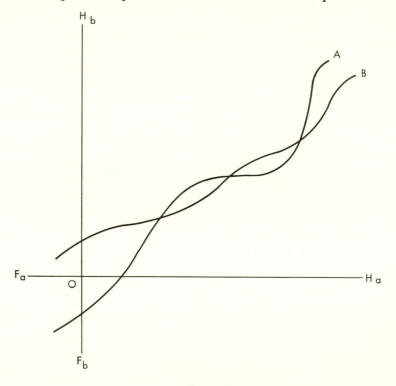

Figure 5.3

other side acts in an extreme fashion. A variety of understandings can serve as boundaries in conflict behavior. They may pertain to the weapons used, deception in their use, or their targets. Weapons vary from personal vilification, verbal manipulation, and armed violence to withdrawal of previously provided goods and services.

Finally, one other attribute of conflict modes with implications for escalation and deescalation should be mentioned. Modes differ in the secrecy with which they are pursued. Typically, secrecy means that the constituency of the conflicting parties' leaders are not allowed to know what the leaders are doing. This is most likely to be the case in an exchange and when a sudden shift is contemplated. Followers are then faced with a *fait accompli.* This subjects them to the claims of collective solidarity and loyalty to the leaders for support. Secrecy may facilitate deescalation because mobilization and arousal of the rank and file are less likely, and then rank-and-file pressure for continued firmness is lessened.

At an early stage of a conflict, however, secrecy may permit leaders to act and make commitments that are part of movement to escalate. Probing an adversary, using subversion, and conducting propaganda may be kept secret from the rank and file, while the adversary experiences the impact of the tactics, and polarization and hostility grow. The U.S. bombing of Cambodia in 1969 is illustrative (Szulc 1978; Shawcross 1979).

Partisan Characteristics

In addition to the conflict mode chosen, several characteristics of the partisans affect the likelihood of escalation or deescalation. We will discuss their degree of heterogeneity, the nature of their diversity, and the stability and nature of their organization.

Heterogeneity. The diversity of the conflict unit has implications for the escalation and deescalation of conflict behavior. Diversity in the unit provides the basis for deescalation insofar as support for the pursuit of any particular policy will not have the same priority for all segments of the conflict party (Landecker 1970). In that case, lack of success in the pursuit of the goal will more readily result in devaluating the objective—a "sour grapes" reaction. Those segments that did not give the goal high priority at the outset would then reduce even their moderate support. Diversity also makes it more likely that the conflict unit segments will not suffer the costs and burdens of the conflict behavior equitably. Furthermore, the unit is more subject to divisive efforts by the other side.

Finally, diversity facilitates responsiveness to the other side and consideration of more alternatives than would be the case in a more homogeneous unit. We noted in the discussion of escalation processes that as a conflict develops and particularly as coercion is applied, the sense of crisis and feelings of anger and fear would restrict the number of alternatives reviewed. People become increasingly rigid in the pursuit of their aims. Plunging forward with more of the same and insensitive to the witting and unwitting signals from the other side, opportunities for deescalation are missed and the conflict behavior escalates (Quester 1970). If the adversaries have some components that are not caught up in the same experiences, they may be able to consider new alternatives and be more responsive to overtures from the other side.

The extent to which this possible consequence of diversity is actualized depends on the organizational form it takes (Wilensky 1967). Insofar as diverse segments of the unit have their own information gathering, analyzing, and policy development capacities and a way of introducing their ideas into the decision-making processes at the highest level of the unit, then the diversity is likely to be effective and correct in matching the conduct of the other side. Such organizational forms for diverse segments are generally rare. For example, even in large units such as the nation-state, few groups have resources to develop alternative policies to the central government's. The agency that is most likely to have developed a number of detailed contingency plans is the military one. The defense establishment alternatives are then most likely to be drawn upon when changes in courses of action are considered.

Nature of Diversity. The critical aspect of a conflict unit's diversity is the range of positions regarding possible escalation among the unit's members relative to the unit's operating position. That is, at any given time in a struggle, a group is pursuing its goal with a particular mixture of means; the proportions of persons and their relative influence favoring escalation and deescalation obviously affect the direction of the unit's movement. This is phrased mechanically. It should be understood in conjunction with the previously discussed processes of escalation and deescalation. Thus, the consequences of competition for leadership significantly depend upon the relative size of constituencies for escalation and deescalation. For example, insofar as the bulk of active rank-and-file union members are dissatisfied with recent union gains and ready to exercise more militancy in pursuit of their demands, the union leaders will vigorously seek larger benefits and be willing to use more coercion for a longer time to reach a settlement. Otherwise, the leaders may find their leadership position challenged by more forceful and demanding competition and find their positions undercut by the rank-and-file's wildcat strikes.

The relative proportions of each unit's favoring different conflict modes also directly affect the means used. Thus, disaffection with the purpose and the means used in its pursuit may result in people's withdrawing support. They desert. In Lenin's memorable phrase, they "vote with their feet." This has happened in many wars when even large military units desert to the enemy or simply dissolve (Brooks 1969; Morison, Merk, and Freidel 1970).

If people favor deescalation strongly enough, they may actively intervene to bring it about. This can occur even in the midst of violent confrontations, as in a riot. In the urban U.S. ghetto riots of the 1960s, for instance, some people in the community tried to stop looting and burning. As we would expect from the analysis in the preceding chapter, counterrioters tend to be better educated and have higher income than the rioters or than the noninvolved (National Advisory Commission on Civil Disorders 1968, p. 132).

Finally, the diversity which is derived from the coalition character of the conflict party has additional possible consequences. If the coalition has been formed primarily as an alliance against a particular adversary, then pressure from that adversary tends to strengthen the coalition. Thus, Soviet-Chinese political friendship seems to have varied directly with hostility toward the United States; the North Atlantic Treaty Organization (NATO) solidarity has also varied directly with presumed threats from the Soviet Union (Holsti 1969; Hopmann 1967; Travis 1970). Coalition solidarity, then, is the basis for more intense and pervasive conflict behavior between adversary coalitions. The strengthening of coalition ties in the face of opposition then becomes the basis of stronger action against the adversary, and the reciprocal consequences for the adversary keeps the spiraling escalation going.

The diversity of interests within a coalition can be the basis for escalation to the extent that the group within the coalition that is committed to the highest magnitude of conflict behavior may engage in acts that bind other elements in the coalition to the same course. Often it is the smaller or weaker elements in the coalition that do this. They are more vulnerable to attacks from the adversary and, therefore, they are more likely to have issues of vital importance in contention compared to the stronger elements in the coalition. Moreover, they may believe that a large portion of the burden of pursuing the conflict will be borne by the stronger allies; this may be one of the mechanisms that explains the finding that alliance formation is associated with international wars (Singer and Small 1968). Illustrative cases abound. The Great Powers honored their alliance commitments and followed Serbia and the Austro-Hungarian empire into the conflagration that became World War I. But the United States and the Soviet Union, once the Cuban missile crisis emerged, ignored Cuba and its claims (Holsti, Brody, and North 1964). They reached an accommodation without escalating their conflict behavior to the use of violence. Coalitions then, that include segments that are willing to pursue more escalating actions can commit and bring along the rest of the coalition. For example, relatively small but extreme elements in a coalition may have disproportionate influence toward escalation because the issue in contention is more vital to them; the others in the coalition must be willing to go along with the more radical proposals in order to maintain the coalition. This is illustrated by the role of the Palestine Liberation Organization within the Arab coalition.

Differentiation and Stability. Units with clearly differentiated leaders who are relatively secure from constituency challenges are freer both to escalate and to deescalate than are units with vulnerable and relatively undifferentiated leadership positions. A tradition that supports the leader in pursuing unpopular courses may help the leader persist in actions with the conviction that history will vindicate her or him. With that assurance, the leader may persevere despite considerable dissension. The American presidency offers some illustrations of this phenomenon, most recently in regard to the Vietnam War. The findings from Naroll, Bullough, and Naroll's (1974) historical survey of wars suggest that older hereditary monarchs ruling centralized states are more likely to be involved in wars than are younger rulers, elective or self-appointed ones, or ones from less centralized states. Perhaps such rulers regard their positions in the state more possessively and, therefore, are likely to become involved in war.

The degree to which the conflict party is tightly organized and under hierarchical control of the highest decision-making authority also affects the chances of limiting escalation. In many struggles the persons in direct confrontation are not under effective control of their presumed superiors, which can readily lead to escalation of conflict behavior. Thus the Chicago police who acted against the demonstrators at the 1968 Democratic party convention used more violence than was probably intended (Walker and others 1968). This violence in itself was an escalation; in addition, it led to a further polarization of different segments of the society (Robinson 1970). When the police were called in to remove students from the Columbia University buildings they had occupied, the violence of the police was greater than had been expected by the university administrators (Rader and Anderson 1969). The shooting of students at Kent State in May 1970 was an unplanned act of escalation that led to further escalation; it exemplifies the loss of control or lack of control that occurs when violence is threatened (The President's Commission on Campus Unrest 1970; cf. Davies 1973). A final illustration will be cited: General Douglas MacArthur had enough autonomy to act in ways that expanded the war in Korea (Paige 1968; McCartney 1954; Friedman 1969).

Inability to control or coordinate action makes it difficult to deescalate. If the primary adversaries are seeking to reduce the level of conflict behavior without losing relative power, each party wants its message to the other to be clear and understood and each must correctly understand the other. The greater the hostility and the higher the level of conflict behavior, the more difficult it is to comprehend the adversary's overtures for deescalation. One source of difficulty is that actions inconsistent with the overtures may occur as subordinates pursue their regular conflict behavior, and those actions erupt into major events. In 1960, for example, the heads of government of the United States, Great Britain, France, and the Soviet Union were to meet in Paris as part of a nascent movement to deescalate the East-West tension. A high flying U.S. reconnaissance plane, the U-2, was shot down over Soviet territory (Wise and Ross 1962). The resulting tempest prevented the meeting and disrupted the movement.

The ability to be responsive to the opponents is another important characteristic affecting escalation. If a challenged conflict party can discern accurately what the adversary seeks and can make appropriate concessions, escalation is less likely; when the challenged party is divided, such concessions are more difficult. Skocpol (1979) found that such inability by dominant groups was an important component in the emergence of revolutions later.

Finally, the strength and solidarity of each adversary affect the ability to escalate or at least to persist at the same level of conflict behavior. The ability to withstand the pressures that the opponents bring to bear depends partly on the partisans' sense of identification with their own side in terms of time perspective and the significance of the issue in contention. As we will examine in more detail in Chapter 7, if there is considerable dissension within a conflict party, external conflict tends to aggravate the dissension (Coser 1956, pp. 92–95; Smith 1970). Such dissension decreases the possibility of pursuing a policy of escalation. Dissension within a conflict party may also encourage the other side, however, to raise its demands and may, therefore, reduce the likelihood of a general deescalation. This brings us to a consideration of the reciprocal actions of adversaries.

Response of Opponent

The basic condition that affects escalation and deescalation is the way the conflict parties interact (Milstein 1972). In discussions of social conflict, much attention is given to overreaction and underreaction. We have already noted how each can produce either escalation or deescalation. In short, a very strong reaction can either intimidate the adversary and result in conflict deescalation, or it may provoke the adversary and cause escalation. Conversely, a mild reaction can either placate opponents and produce deescalation, or it can invite further escalation by showing weakness. Clearly, we must specify many attributes of responses and conditions of the interaction between opponents if these plausible but contradictory possibilities are to be reconciled. We shall discuss the severity and consistency of the response, the accompanying interpretation, the recipient's expectations, and the reciprocity over time.

The first response attribute to be considered is its severity. Increasing severity of response does not produce deescalation. We saw, for example, in Morgan's (1970) study of colleges, that the more severe the administration's response to student demonstration was, the greater was the probability of expansion of the conflict. Part of the explanation is that the response of the other side becomes an issue in itself. If the other side reacts severely, the recipients have a new grievance, and an even more severe response would be necessary to suppress the reaction to the new grievance. There is a variety of evidence to support this interpretation (Gurr 1970, pp. 238–251). For example, the very large South Vietnamese army was ineffective in repressing insurgency partly because it was too massive for the task; it acted as an invader in its own country (Thompson 1966). Yet, at some point, force can and does suppress an adversary. Indeed, quantitative studies indicate a curvilinear relationship between the repressiveness of governments and political violence. For example, Walton (1965) rated eighty-four nations on the degree of coerciveness or permissiveness of their national political systems and on their degree of political stability in 1955–1961. She found that the most highly coercive countries were either stable or only moderately stable; those with intermediate levels of coercion had a disproportionate number of the most unstable countries; and those that were highly permissive tended to have stable regimes.

This curvilinear relationship may be portrayed in terms of the graphs presented earlier. We may posit two reaction coefficients and initial levels of hostility, as presented in Figure 5.4. Note that B (perhaps the burghers) had some initial hostility toward A (perhaps the authorities), but a little friendliness goes a

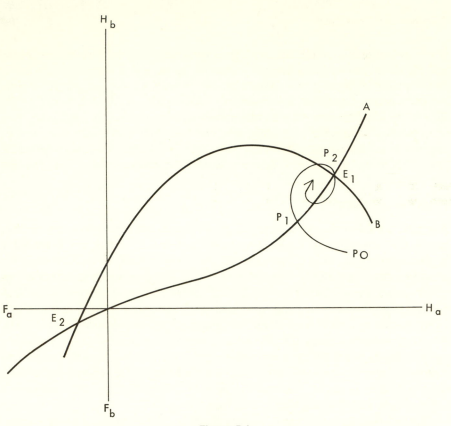

Figure 5.4

long way; also, B will be quite hostile to A at moderate levels of hostility or coercion by A, but, at higher levels of hostility, it submits and does not exhibit hostility to A. In such a system, there are two equilibrium points, E_1 and E_2. One point represents a coercive regime and a coerced populace, and the other point represents a responsive regime and a grateful populace. In between is a vast arena for a hostile population and confrontations that might lead to one or the other equilibrium point.

Boulding (1962, p. 32) has noted some peculiar features of an equilibrium point, such as E_1. Note that the vector lines circle around it like a spiral. This may be explained as follows: Suppose we start at P_O, where A is very hostile and B has been cowed into submission. A can afford to be a little more permissive, B becomes less cowed and increases hostility to P_1. Until P_2, both become more hostile toward the other—A because it fears B's rising hostility and B because A's level is not yet severe enough to suppress it. After P_2, B's hostility begins to decline under pressure. Thus, regimes may oscillate between harsh repression and moderation.

The consistency with which a way of pursuing conflicting goals is exercised helps determine the other side's response. We assumed this relationship in our earlier discussion of a conflict party's ability to coordinate its conflict behavior and, hence, pursue a convincing effort toward deescalation. A conflict party may include subgroups that make statements or commit acts so inconsistent with the major conflict mode that the adversary does not respond as intended. Persuasive efforts are not convincing if actions are taken at variance with the persuasive arguments. This is part of the reason, too, why contingency planning for escalation increases the likelihood of escalation—the adversary doubts the commitment to more moderate means. Thus, a government's peace initiative if coupled with readying military units would not be convincing.

Consistency is particularly pertinent in the use of coercion by a conflict party that is claiming jurisdiction over its adversary, for example a government that is responding to dissension (Gurr 1970, pp. 250–258). Consistency in this context means that coercion is always applied in proportion to the violation of proscriptions. That is, only those persons who commit undesired acts suffer negative sanctions, and the severity of the sanctions are clearly related to the magnitude of the acts (Schonborn 1975). Governments often do not so respond to dissension. For example, police and military units may respond to riots by seizing some participants and bystanders who are close and beat or arrest them, or both. Some are released, and the majority, those who get away, are ignored. Military forces may try to control insurgency by shooting a few dissidents and supposed sympathizers. Such actions are often ineffective or counterproductive. Persons who engage in the proscribed activity have not suffered any negative sanctions, and others who did no "wrong" have suffered greatly at the hands of the regime.

When massive force is threatened and applied precisely, it has a better chance of limiting escalation. For example, in the 1967 Detroit riot, heavy firing by fearful National Guardsmen was part of an escalating movement. Subsequently army troops, with strict orders not to fire unless they could see the specific person at whom they were aiming, quickly established order; they then helped residents clean up the streets (National Advisory Commission on Civil Disorders 1968, pp. 84–108).

Although words may belie actions, the interpretations accompanying actions can affect the other side's reactions, as is most often revealed in assertions regarding limited goals. But interpretations often also accompany a variety of actions that might otherwise be construed as coercive. For example, weapons are alleged to be built and stockpiled only for defensive purposes. Sometimes allies, sympathizers, or subgroups within a conflict organization "explain" the organization's action as being less hostile or coercive than it appears. They may explain that what seems like a threat is meant only for internal consumption or that the threat should not be taken literally, since it is really intended to forestall more severe actions by rival leaders or organizations. Sometimes, leaders themselves may severely threaten an adversary in public and secretly indicate that the threat should not be taken too seriously. Such understandings and comradeship between adversary leaders, of course, make them vulnerable to rank-and-file suspicion and challenge.

In addition to the interpretations made of their own actions, leaders of a conflict party try to interpret and define who the adversary is and what its characteristics are. Such attempts affect the opponents' reaction and the likelihood of escalation and deescalation. Thus, if the coercion is accompanied by assertions that the adversary is to be collectively destroyed or subjugated, that adversary is likely to be unified and ready to increase the magnitude of coercion in order to maintain its opposition. This is particularly likely when the adversary is defined in terms of an ascribed characteristic, such as race or ethnicity. For example, the Nazi definition of the Slavs as lesser beings increased the solidarity of the Russians with the regime and intensified the violence and the extensiveness of the conflict.

One reason that satyagraha, or nonviolent direct action (see Chapter 4), is likely to inhibit escalation, even when critical and profound issues are in contention, is that it implies and is usually accompanied by assertions that the opponent is recognized as equally human and worthy of consideration. This kind of regard inhibits the coerciveness of the opponent.

In a sense, interpretations and explanations of one's own action, directed at an adversary, are forms of persuasion. This is even true when a conflict party explains why it is doing what it is doing. For example, Mario Savio, a leader of the Free Speech Movement (FSM) at the University of California at Berkeley in 1964, said that the movement was directed against bureaucratization of life and against the idea that nothing new can happen and, therefore, unusual and even extraordinary means are needed to shake people up (Savio 1965). Such interpretations convey ideas and feelings that constitute appeals for understanding and also attempts at persuasion.

The mixture of ways used to reach an end affects escalation. Each way of pursuing a goal, in actuality, is exercised in conjunction with other ways. Coercion is accompanied by some persuasive efforts and often even by rewards or the promise of rewards. The extent to which a particular coercive tactic, then, may escalate or deescalate depends partly on the entire mixture of ways being used.

The recipients' expectations and feelings about an adversary and that adversary's actions affect the likelihood of the recipient's reacting in an escalating fashion. Suppose, for example, both parties have mutual ties and friendly feelings. As shown in Figure 5.5, each starts out with initial friendliness toward the other. In this relationship, a hostile action by one side, even if responded to with hostility, will tend to move both parties toward greater friendliness. For example, if side A acts as hostile as P_0, B will increase its hostility and A will decrease its, since A's is already at a higher level than is appropriate for the amount B has. The vector line shows that as a result they will move to P_1. After which they will *both* reduce their hostility. Some evidence consistent with this interpretation was cited in the preceding chapter. Naroll (1969) found that with higher levels of cultural exchange between rival nations, wars between them were less likely. Conversely, conflict parties who have high initial hostility, are sensitive to in-

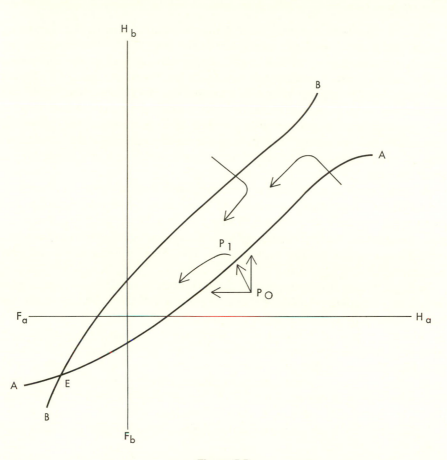

Figure 5.5

juries from the opponents, and enjoy seeing them suffer will tend to escalate conflict behavior (Valavanis 1958).

The specific expectations each party has about the other's goals and about the other's conflict behavior have particular implications for escalation. For example, if party A expects no serious challenges from party B, the first signs of challenge will tend to be ignored and not treated seriously. Party B is likely to then increase the magnitude of its conflict behavior to gain attention. Such conduct may then be dismissed by party A as just "attention getting" and still not be treated seriously, further infuriating B. There are many variations of this pattern. For example, in response to the women's liberation movement, men have often conveyed a sense of ridicule. They may assert or imply that the protestors are simply sexually unsatisfied and need a "good man." Such defenses make it unnecessary and even impossible to understand what the other party is saying. Those put-downs are infuriating to and help radicalize the protesting group.

Student objections, too, may be initially responded to with the dismissing notion that youth is idealistic, unrealistic, and a little wild. What students say, therefore, can be ignored because it will change when they grow up. Elders may believe and even say, "I thought that way, too, when I was your age. . . ." All such put-downs seem to require the protestor to raise the magnitude of conflict behavior. Persuasion as a mode of pursuing goals seems particularly ineffective until the other side takes the issue seriously. Not taking the protests seriously, however, does inhibit the escalation of conflict behavior by the recipient of the protests. At least initially, the behavior response may be benevolent and permissive, even if condescending.

Whether words and acts deter or invite escalation depends upon the interpretations made of those words and acts by the adversaries. Those interpretations rest partly upon expectations developed from past events. If one party has, for example, usually made concessions, the opponents may expect more concessions and not believe a refusal coupled with a threat. The threat is not credible and does not deter (Iklé 1971, p. 116).

Each party may also have specific expectations and standards about particular techniques of conflict behavior. We have already noted that some actions are not taken seriously by the adversary and, hence, a conflict party escalates its mode of pursuing its goal. In addition, if the adversary is outraged by an antagonist's conduct, a boundary may be crossed and the adversary will feel free to escalate its tactics. There are also implications for escalation for violations of more specific expectations. Thus, if a conflict party, A, commits what B regards as an atrocity, B may consider A to be subhuman and, hence, justifiably subject A to treatment that it in turn would regard as an atrocity. Soldiers who have witnessed enemy atrocities are more likely to be vindictive against the enemy (Stouffer and others 1949, Vol. 2, p. 163).

Expectations about how to wage a conflict may, of course, inhibit escalation, as long as all parties adhere to the rules. Coercive forces, rather than being actually employed, may be tallied by all sides and the results accepted. This seems to be the case in some coups. Thus, a dissident faction tries to assemble sufficient military commanders to its side to make the other side vulnerable; when superiority is gained, the dissident faction may inform the incumbents. After careful negotiations and bargaining, the incumbents may recognize that they have lost, quietly yield, and be allowed to depart (Gurr 1970, pp. 271–272; Lieuwen 1964).

The reciprocity in interaction over time certainly affects escalation and deescalation. At the early stages of conflict, mutual probing is important. Each party needs to discover how strongly the adversaries' positions are held. That information influences how strongly a goal will be pursued. A firm response to a probe, therefore, may inhibit escalation (Snyder and Diesing 1977, pp. 98–100). A vague or yielding response may lead to stronger probes, and then higher levels of conflict behavior may be necessary to indicate that major concessions will not be made.

It is interesting to note that as conflict behavior erupts and escalates, the prospects for an exchange relationship alter and in some ways are enhanced. The need for what the adversary can give may increase, and its ability to offer concessions or rewards may grow. For example, the very arousal and organization of a people in a previously neglected social category give them desired resources. They acquire some power and merit so that their loyalty and respect are now valued. Thus, in the United States, the growth of protest and liberation movements among blacks, students, women, and the poor has resulted in some courting of these groups by whites, faculty and administrators, men, and the wealthy.

Issues. Matters of contention vary in their susceptibility for escalation and deescalation. The more important is the issue in contention, the more likely is the conflict to escalate. Insofar as a party feels its vital interests are at stake, it will be willing to endure the other side's coercion and expend resources in trying to coerce the other side. For example, labor strikes about union recognition or about attempts to weaken the union are more likely to escalate to violence than are strikes about wages and hours (Oberschall 1969).

The depth of the grievance may help to sustain conflict behavior and increase its magnitude once violence has erupted. Although community variations in the condition of blacks has not been found to be related to the outbreak of riots, the severity of riots has been. For example, Wanderer (1969) found that the percentage of nonwhites living in ten-year or older housing was highly correlated (.86) with the severity of riots.

In the preceding chapter we argued that in dissensual conflicts persuasion was more likely to be tried initially than in consensual ones. Now we suggest that once a conflict is being handled coercively or especially violently, then dissensual struggles generally have more potential for escalation than do consensual conflicts. In dissensual conflicts, the opposition is less likely to be considered equally human than in consensual ones. Dissensual conflicts seem more indivisible and, therefore, less able to be fractionated. Dissensual fights in which partisans proclaim exclusiveness relative to the opponent and that are coupled with an expandable domain are peculiarly subject to escalation, as in ideological control of territory. As one side gains more, even a simple expansion of the domain sought, the magnitude of the issue at stake increases. For example, when the Communist North Korean military forces pushed the anti-Communist South Korean and U.S. forces, under U.N. authority, further and further south of the border at the 38th parallel, the U.S. goal became a return to that border. After the successful Inchon landing beyond enemy lines and the rapid movement northward, the 38th parallel was crossed and the troops continued to advance. Even suggestions of buffer zones below the Yalu River bordering China were ignored. "Appetites rose as the troops went forward" (Neustadt 1960, p. 127; Paige 1968).

The magnitude of the issue in contention underlies the evaluation of an adversary's "over-" or "under-" reacting. It underlies the interpretation each party makes of the other and of its conflict behavior. It underlies the mixture of modes each can utilize, what persuasive efforts, what exchanges, and what magnitudes of coercion each can offer and sustain.

Issues also differ in the degree to which the aims are collective or aggregate. Insofar as they are collective, escalation is more likely because resistance to group reallocations seems more threatening than individual accommodations, even if numerous. Furthermore, collective goals usually require acknowledgment of change by the opponent.

In addition to the issue of contention, the full range of possible issues underlies the chances of escalation and deescalation. Thus, the grievances that could arise between adversaries are the fuel for escalation. More generally, and more abstractly, the matrix of possible outcomes and the preferences of each party for every outcome help determine the struggle's course—this is the overall payoff matrix. This matrix underlies the shifting issues in contention and, therefore, the changes in conflict modes since the issue in contention strongly affects the choice of mode (Snyder and Diesing 1977).

For example, the central issue in a conflict between a student organization and the administration may be the setting of dormitory hours. In addition, there are underlying differences regarding such other dormitory rights as those concerning classroom attendance, curriculum, tuition, dining halls, university investments, and faculty consultations. Depending upon how strongly each side feels about various degrees and ways of student participation in the management of such areas, the chances for escalation or deescalation are different. The reactions help determine what concessions are promised and what exchanges are likely as well as how high each side is ready to go in raising the level of conflict behavior.

The nature and magnitude of the incompatibility of the goals pursued by adversaries profoundly affect the course of a struggle. But each party's perception of the other's goals also affects escalation and deescalation. The governments of the United States and the Soviet Union may each fear the expansionism of the other side and believe that the other must recognize its own nonexpansionist goals. Continuing hostility and mutual threats then would be likely. But if both governments really have goals that are limited and defensive and goals to consolidate—not expand—then the struggle between them may continue with lower chances of escalating the use of coercion and violence. Gamson and Modigliani's (1971) systematic analysis of how each country actually responded to the other's foreign actions indicates that on the whole American and Soviet government leaders pursued limited, consolidationist aims.

Social Context. We discussed in the last chapter how the environment affects the selection of the conflict modes: How other parties, as possible allies and as possible models, affect the means chosen; how the social patterns and understandings within which the conflict parties operate affect the choice of mode; and, finally, the possible effects of technology and ecology. The same factors and processes affect moving from one mode to another. For example, the characteristics of the parties that might become allies affect the likelihood of escalation as well as the initial choice of mode. At this point, then, we need add only a few additional specifications about the possible impact of the social context upon escalation or deescalation.

Parties that are not partisan in the focal conflict may be more or less attentive to primary adversaries and to the conflict behavior they are exhibiting. If other party inattention is sufficiently great, a conflict group may be successfully ignored even by the presumed opposition. For example, in 1948, when the World War II draft law was expiring, peacetime military conscription was about to be enacted for the first time in America's history. Protests were held, but ignored—even the burning of draft cards was ignored—and the protests deescalated. Inattentiveness can also mean allowing conflict parties to fight it out without intervention. Doing so limits the scope of conflict, but it may permit higher and higher levels of conflict behavior, as in civil wars or the suppression of rebellion. The inattention of other parties may be an incentive to escalate in order to involve them in the struggle. For example, protestors may escalate their means in order to ensure television coverage and public notice. Modes and antagonists differ in visibility. Some modes are conducted secretly, as in negotiated exchanges, and, in general, persuasion is a matter of relative disinterest to nonfocal parties. Some conflict parties are relatively ignored in the mass media; internationally some countries receive little attention and domestically the less powerful and less threatening are also the less noticed.

Visibility and attentiveness are dependent upon the means of communication available to the nonfocal parties. Television has become particularly important in conveying information about conflict events. The growth of the civil rights movement and its success in getting voting rights and public accommodations legislation through Congress is in part due to the support engendered by the spectacles on television of mass demonstrations and rallies and of the violence of the authorities in places like Birmingham, Alabama. This use of television even sets a model for possibly courting police violence (Walker and others 1968, pp. 287–331; Larsen 1968; Baker and Ball 1969). When the Chicago police charged repeatedly against the demonstrators during the 1968 Democratic party convention, the demonstrators chanted, "The whole world is watching."

The events in Chicago in the summer of 1968, however, demonstrate that the consequences of visibility and attentiveness depend upon the standards, interests, and expectations of the other parties. Maybe the world was watching, but not with disapproval of what the police were doing. As a matter of fact, the American public generally thought the police did not use excessive force (Robinson 1970; Gamson and McEvoy 1970). The media coverage also has an impact upon the conflict parties—affecting for example the relations between leaders and rank-and-file members (Gitlin 1980).

The mass media are also often credited with feeding the flames of riots by giving them a great deal of attention, which increases participation in a given riot and hastens their spread from place to place. The media sometimes have played down such events to keep them from spreading. Mass media may well have such effects, and we need to examine such possibilities carefully. We should keep in mind, however, that riots have spread quickly even before the era of mass media. Riots spread rapidly even in East Germany in 1953 and in Poland in 1956.

The consequences of other parties' noticing what a conflict party does depend upon the other parties' interests and expectations. In a rapidly escalating conflict, crossing a boundary of previously expected and acceptable behavior may provide the basis, or the excuse, for intervention and, hence, for escalation followed by deescalation under the weight of the new balance of forces. For example, in September 1970 Palestinian Arab groups were growing in international stature and vying for leadership in the struggle against Israel. Then the Popular Front for the Liberation of Palestine, one of the groups, hijacked four airplanes to Jordan, blew them up after the passengers had been removed, and held the passengers as hostages. There was considerable outrage expressed by many nations. The Jordanian government, under King Hussein, had felt threatened by the Palestinian Arab groups on Jordanian territory. There had been fighting between Jordanian troops and the Palestinian Arab groups. At this juncture, extensive open fighting broke out between the Jordanian army and the Palestinian Arab organizations. This incident was a major step in the suppression of these organizations in Jordan.

In Chapter 4 we discussed how other parties constitute models or potential allies for the parties in conflict. That discussion generally treated conflict groups as single entities, but in the course of a struggle subgroups within each party also look for support and models from elsewhere. The general social atmosphere may lend support to one faction or another within conflict organizations. This support helps determine the consequences of competition for leadership. For example, in the United States in the early cold war years and in the 1950s of McCarthyism, organization leaders were likely to be challenged internally by alternative leaders who were more "anti-Communist," and established leaders could successfully dismiss rivals for not being sufficiently "anti-Communist." These challenges could be reflected in struggles over a variety of issues, such as civil liberties or militancy of demands within trade unions, political parties, and other organizations. Consequently, protesting groups would tend to be more ready to deescalate than they would be if the temper of the times were different. On the other hand, conflict parties opposing protest groups might feel more able to escalate their demands and means of pursuing them. In the 1960s internal challenges were more likely to have moved organizations toward a more militant direction and thus tended toward escalations, at least by protesting groups.

SUMMARY AND CONCLUSIONS

The attributes of the conflict mode, the conflict units, the response of the other side, the issue in contention, and the social context all combine to determine the course of escalation or deescalation. Furthermore, all the attributes have significance in the context of the parties' interaction over time. We discuss this sequential reciprocation as illustrated by two kinds of cases: (1) efforts by dissidents to provoke the authorities' escalation of conflict behavior in order to mobilize support, and (2) efforts at deescalating the tension between the United States and the Soviet Union in 1963.

Independence and revolutionary movements have sometimes tried to create a revolutionary situation by provocation of the government. This strategy, for example, was used in the mid-1950s in Cyprus by Grivas (Purcell 1969, pp. 261 ff). In the 1960s, some of these efforts were modeled on what allegedly happened in Cuba (Debray 1967; de Gramont 1970). A small guerrilla band, under the leadership of Fidel Castro, operated from the rugged terrain of the Sierra Maestra mountains and raided small army units. The reprisals unleashed by Batista's government alienated more and more segments of Cuban society. Such defections strengthened the revolutionary movement as success seemed more likely and as the movement's claims and interpretations seemed to be confirmed by at least some segments of the opposition. Finally, even the army withdrew support, and Batista fled. But similar efforts in Venezuela failed, as they did in Bolivia, even under the leadership of Che Guevara. Such failures are illuminating. In Venezuela, President Betancourt used very specific and limited countermeasures, waiting until there was public pressure to increase the countermeasures (Gude 1969). The revolutionaries, instead of rallying support, found themselves isolated. The scope of the conflict behavior did not increase.

Clearly, making things worse for the people by provoking the government to harsh measures is an inadequate revolutionary program or course of action. Whether or not it even hastens the development of a revolutionary situation depends upon many other factors—the responsiveness of the government, the level of public discontent, and the degree of integration and mutual trust between the government and the masses. In the case of Bolivia, the conditions for a revolutionary movement, following the strategy attempted by Che Guevara, were not present. His small band remained isolated from popular support until they were destroyed by Bolivian military units.

In student uprisings, too, administrators may fail to be provoked. As the data from Morgan's (1970) study indicate, lower magnitude responses to demonstrations tend to prevent expansion of the conflict. We need to specify a variety of conditions in the extended interaction in order to explain why a low level of response is not interpreted as weakness and as an incitement for escalation in itself. The student sit-in at the University of Chicago is illustrative in this regard (Editors of the University of Chicago Magazine 1969). On December 15, 1968, Marlene Dixon, assistant professor in the department of sociology and in the Committee of Human Development, was notified that her contract would not be renewed after it expired on September 30, 1969. A group of students demanded that Dr. Dixon not be terminated and that students share equally in all future decisions in the hiring and firing of faculty. On January 19, 1969, the university vice-president and dean of faculties appointed a committee to review the case, including allegations that Dr. Dixon was not reappointed because she was a woman, a political radical, or approached sociology differently than others in the department. Edward Levi, president of the university, released a statement from the academic deans emphasizing the desirability of regularly obtaining student views and having institutionalized channels for doing so, in accord with a policy announced over a year earlier. The Council of the University Senate also warned on January 21 that students engaged in disruptive acts are subject to disciplinary action.

At a January 29 meeting 444 students voted for some form of militant action, 430 voted against it, and 85 abstained. On the same day, President Levi issued a statement that any decision about rehiring Dr. Dixon would await the results of the investigating committee and that he did not endorse the principle of equal student power in decisions about hiring and rehiring faculty. The next day the students began to occupy the administration building. The university administration did not indicate any change in its position and tried to continue with its procedures for investigation and disciplinary action.

The administration seemed to be responsive to the substance of some demands but also indicated an unyielding position on other matters. The students were not united in the goals or the means to be used. On the question of deciding upon reappointing Dr. Dixon, the faculty and administrators were probably more united than on other issues in university uprisings.

The sit-in lasted two weeks. On February 12 the investigating committee released its report recommending that Dr. Dixon's contract be extended for one year in the Committee of Human Development alone. At a press conference the same day, Marlene Dixon refused the contract extension. Meanwhile, students were being suspended for failing to appear before the Disciplinary Committee. On February 14 the students voted to open or not open the university files; the affirmative vote did not have the two-thirds majority needed. The students then voted to leave the building. Jeffrey Blum, one of the sit-in leaders, reportedly said, "We must admit to ourselves that we lost. There was no campus uproar over the failure to rehire Mrs. Dixon, nor was there any campus backing for our demand for amnesty for sit-inners" (*Chicago American,* February 15, 1969). They retained a platform urging the end to discrimination against women faculty, halting the displacement of residents from a largely black neighboring area, the addition of courses in the sociology of deprived groups, and the admission of more youth from working class origins. Individual hearings continued and by April 8, forty-two students had been expelled and eighty-one suspended; others were expelled in the course of the summer.

Now we turn to a brief review of mutual reciprocity in the deescalation of tension. We will consider the deescalating movement between the American and Soviet governments in 1963 (Etzioni 1967; Kriesberg 1981). On June 10 President Kennedy made a conciliatory speech that provided a context for particular gestures. He announced the unilateral cessation of all nuclear tests in the atmosphere and stated they would not be resumed unless another country did. The Soviets published the speech in full and did not jam the Voice of America broadcasting of the speech. On June 15 Premier Khrushchev spoke welcoming the Kennedy initiative and announced a halt to the production of strategic bombers. In the United Nations on June 11 the Soviet Union ceased objecting to a Western-backed proposal to send observers to Yemen and the United States reciprocated by removing its objection to restoring full status, for the first time since 1956, to the Hungarian delegation. The Soviet Union agreed on June 20 to establish a direct communications line with the United States, first proposed by the U.S. government in 1962.

It should be recognized that these unilateral gestures probably neither substantively effected the balance of power nor altered the underlying bases of conflict between the United States and the Soviet Union. But they could have reduced tensions, facilitating the recognition of common and complementary relations. Then, more formal negotiations regarding more substantive matters could be pursued. Indeed, multilateral negotiations on a test-ban agreement were renewed in July, and, on August 5, the agreement was signed.

Other symbolic gestures, expressions of hope for additional cooperative acts, and formal agreements followed. On October 9 President Kennedy approved the sale of $250 million worth of wheat to the Soviet Union. On September 19 the Soviet government suggested banning orbiting weapons of mass destruction; an agreement in principle was announced on October 3 and embodied in a U.N. resolution passed on October 19. Spies were also exchanged in October. The movement, however, did not continue indefinitely. After President Kennedy's assassination in November 1963, President Johnson was absorbed in domestic programs and then the Vietnam War. Khrushchev fell from the Soviet leadership in October 1964.

How shall we explain the sequence of deescalation? It may be that the Cuban missile crisis of October 1962 marked a point of hostility above the equilibrium point, and these events merely marked the movement from a very hostile point, P_0, as shown in Figure 5.6. But the movement seems to have carried the two parties toward a lower level of mutual hostility than they previously held. It may be that a new equilibrium was reached. The *joint* movement made it possible to reach a position that unilateral acts could not readily attain. Thus, let us return to the arms race dilemma discussed in Chapter 1 and illustrated in Table 1.4. In that case, it would be advantageous for A to increase its arms if B did *or* did not do so, and similarly for B. Consequently they would both continue to increase their arms, although if they *both did not* they would both be better off. That movement requires communication and mutual trust. Perhaps the series of gestures made possible such a joint movement, as indicated in the dotted line of Figure 5.7.

The reaching of a new equilibrium point would indicate that one or both curves have shifted. Perhaps with the new understanding reached, initial hostility would be less and the reaction coefficient not as sharp. Such a shift is illustrated in Figure 5.8.

If a new equilibrium is reached, however, it generally reflects substantive changes in the underlying bases of the conflict. In this case, several such changes may have occurred. The solidarity of the two blocs was weakening. This reduced the forces which might be available against the other side and raised the costs of threatening it. It also led to a shift in the focal conflict, for example, the rise in the salience of the struggle between the Soviet and Chinese governments and political parties. Also, the ideological fervor of the Soviet and U.S. govern-

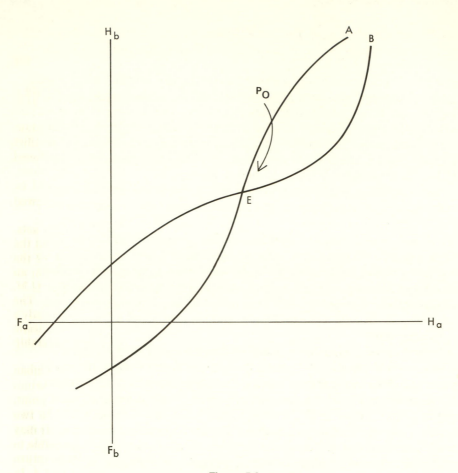

Figure 5.6

ments may have been reduced when the monolithic quality of communism and capitalism became patently absent. In addition, there were changes in the world system. The growth of organizations and the increased role of noncommitted nations may have tempered some of the cold war salience. Even the repeated handling of crises may have helped develop a nascent institutionalization of conflict regulation that reflected and became the basis for further acts of mutual confidence (Galtung 1966). Additional factors might be suggested as causing a shift in the underlying causes of the conflict. They are not needed to point out that a shift occurred. Partisan recognition of such shifts also is needed for deescalation, and that requires appropriate mutual response between the adversaries.

The Gamson and Modigliani (1971) analysis of the cold war suggests a somewhat different interpretation. For a short time prior to the Cuban missile crisis, the Soviets under Khrushchev pursued more expansionist aims than previously; it was a period of rash Soviet actions. After the Cuban missile crisis the Soviet Union returned to its prior goals of consolidation rather than expansion.

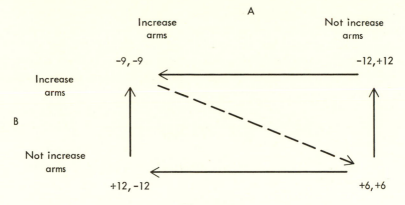

A

Increase arms   Not increase arms

B

Increase arms

Not increase arms

-9, -9   -12, +12

+12, -12   +6, +6

Figure 5.7

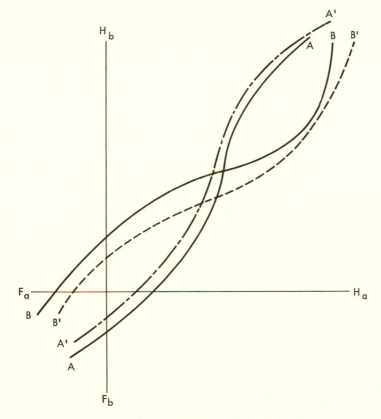

H_b

A'
B
B'
A

F_a H_a

B
B'
A'
A

F_b

Figure 5.8

In summary, once a conflict relationship erupts into coercive action, whether or not it escalates and how far it escalates, is dependent upon the underlying conditions as well as upon how the conflict parties perceive and respond to each other. The possible outcomes, that is, the payoff matrices, indicate what concessions are feasible and attractive. In the next chapter we discuss the actual outcomes of parties' pursuing conflicting goals.

BIBLIOGRAPHY

ALLISON, GRAHAM T., *Essence of Decision: Explaining the Cuban Missile Crisis* (Boston: Little, Brown, 1971.)

ARGYRIS, CHRIS, *Some Causes of Organizational Ineffectiveness within the Department of State* (Washington, D.C.: Center for International Systems Research, Department of State, 1967).

BAKER, ROBERT K. AND SANDRA J. BALL, *Mass Media and Violence* (Washington, D.C.: U.S. Government Printing Office, 1969).

BARTON, ALLEN H., "The Columbia Crisis: Campus, Vietnam, and the Ghetto," *Public Opinion Quarterly,* 32 (Fall 1968), 333–351.

BELL, INGE POWELL, *CORE and the Strategy of Non-Violence* (New York: Random House, 1968).

BERKOWITZ, LEONARD, "The Frustration-Aggression Hypothesis Revisited," pp. 1–28 in Leonard Berkowitz (ed.), *Roots of Aggression* (New York: Lieber-Atherton Inc., 1969).

BOULDING, KENNETH E., *Conflict and Defense* (New York: Harper & Row, Pub., 1962).

BRINK, WILLIAM AND LOUIS HARRIS, *Black and White* (New York: Simon & Schuster, 1969).

BROOKS, ROBIN, "Domestic Violence and America's Wars: An Historical Interpretation," pp. 529–550 in Hugh Davis Graham and Ted Robert Gurr (eds.), *Violence in America* (New York: Bantam, 1969).

BWY, DOUGLAS P., "Political Instability in Latin America: The Cross-Cultural Test of a Causal Model," *Latin American Research Review,* 3 (Spring 1968), 17–66.

Chicago American, February 15, 1969.

COLEMAN, JAMES, *Community Conflict* (New York: Free Press, 1957).

COSER, LEWIS A., *The Functions of Social Conflict* (New York: Free Press, 1956.)

DAVIES, PETER, "Another White House Horror Story," *The Village Voice,* 18 (November 8, 1973), 138–140.

DEBRAY, REGIS, *Revolution in the Revolution?* (New York: Grove Press, 1967).

DE GRAMONT, SANCHE, "How One Pleasant, Scholarly Young Man from Brazil Became a Kidnapping, Gun-Toting, Bombing Revolutionary," *The New York Times Magazine* (November 15, 1970), pp. 43–45, 136–153.

DEUTSCH, MORTON AND ROBERT M. KRAUSS, "The Effects of Threat upon Interpersonal Bargaining," *Journal of Abnormal and Social Psychology,* 61 (1960), 181–189.

ECKSTEIN, HARRY (ed.), *Internal War: Problems and Approaches* (New York: Free Press, 1966.)

EDITORS OF THE UNIVERSITY OF CHICAGO MAGAZINE, "The Sit-In: A Chronology," *The University of Chicago Magazine,* 61 (March/April 1969), 39–47.

ERSKINE, HAZEL, "The Polls: Demonstrations and Race Riots," *Public Opinion Quarterly,* 31 (Winter 1967–1968), 655–677.

ETZIONI, AMITAI, "The Kennedy Experiment," *Western Political Quarterly,* 20 (June 1967), 361–380.

FANON, FRANTZ, *The Wretched of the Earth* (New York: Grove Press, 1966).

FISHER, ROGER, "Fractionating Conflict," in R. Fisher (ed.), *International Conflict and Behavioral Science* (New York: Basic Books, 1964).

FLEXNER, ELEANOR, *Century of Struggle* (Cambridge, Mass.: Harvard University Press, 1959).

FRIEDMAN, EDWARD, "Problems in Dealing with an Irrational Power: America Declares War on China," pp. 207–252 in Edward Friedman and Mark Selden (eds.), *America's Asia: Dissenting Essays on Asian-American Relations* (New York: Random House, 1969).

GALTUNG, JOHAN, "East-West Interaction Patterns," *Journal of Peace Research,* 2 (1966), 146–176.

GAMSON, WILLIAM A. AND JAMES MCEVOY, "Police Violence and Its Public Support," *The Annals,* 391 (September 1970), 97–110.

GAMSON, WILLIAM A. AND ANDRE MODIGLIANI, *Untangling the Cold War* (Boston: Little, Brown, 1971).

GITLIN, TODD, *The Whole World is Watching: Mass Media in the Making and Unmaking of the New Left* (Berkeley: University of California Press, 1980).

GRODZINS, MORTON, *The Loyal and the Disloyal* (Chicago: The University of Chicago Press, 1956).

GROSS, FELIKS, *World Politics and Tension Areas* (New York: New York University Press, 1966).

GUDE, EDWARD W., "Batista and Betancourt: Alternative Responses to Violence," pp. 731–748 in Hugh Davis Graham and Ted Robert Gurr (eds.), *Violence in America* (New York: Bantam, 1969).

GURR, TED ROBERT, *Why Men Rebel* (Princeton, N.J.: Princeton University Press, 1970).

HALBERSTAM, DAVID, *The Best and the Brightest* (New York: Fawcet, 1973).

HAYKAL, HASSANAIN, "An Armed Clash with Israel is Inevitable—Why?" pp. 179–185 in Walter Laqueur (ed.), *The Israel-Arab Reader,* rev. ed. (New York: Bantam, 1970). Originally published in *Al Ahram,* May 26, 1967.

HERMANN, CHARLES F., *Crises in Foreign Policy* (Indianapolis, Ind.: Bobbs-Merrill, 1969).

HINCKLE, WARREN AND DAVID WELSH, "The Battles of Selma," pp. 100–109 in Walt Anderson (ed.), *The Age of Protest* (Santa Monica, Calif.: Goodyear, 1969).

HOLSTI, OLE R., "External Conflict and Internal Cohesion: The Sino-Soviet Case," pp. 337–352 in Jan F. Triska (ed.), *Communist Party-States* (Indianapolis, Ind.: Bobbs-Merrill 1969).

———, "Crises, Stress, and Decision-Making," *International Social Science Journal,* 23, no. 1 (1971), 53–67.

HOLSTI, OLE R., RICHARD A. BRODY, AND ROBERT C. NORTH, "Measuring Affect and Action in International Reaction Models: Empirical Materials from the 1962 Cuban Crisis," *Journal of Peace Research,* nos. 3–4 (1964), 170–189.

HOPMANN, P. T., "International Conflict and Cohesion in the Communist System," *International Studies Quarterly* 11 (September 1967), p. 212–236.

IKLÉ, FRED CHARLES, *Every War Must End* (New York: Columbia University Press, 1971).

KLINGBERG, FRANK L., "Predicting the Termination of War: Battle Casualties and Population Losses," *Journal of Conflict Resolution,* 10 (June 1966), 129–171.

KRIESBERG, LOUIS, "Noncoercive Inducements in International Conflicts," *Peace and Change: A Journal of Peace Research,* 7 (Fall 1981a).

———, "Peace Initiatives in the U.S.-Soviet Conflict," *Journal of Political and Military Sociology,* 9 (Spring 1981b).

LANDECKER, WERNER S., "Status Congruence, Class Crystallization, and Social Cleavage," *Sociology and Social Research,* 54 (April 1970), 343–355.

LARSEN, OTTO N. (ed.), *Violence and the Mass Media* (New York: Harper & Row, Pub., 1968).

LEVI, ARIEL AND PHILIP E. TETLOCK, "A Cognitive Analysis of Japan's 1941 Decision for War," *Journal of Conflict Resolution,* 24 (June 1980), 195–211.

LEWIN, KURT, *Resolving Social Conflicts* (New York: Harper & Brothers, 1948).

LIEUWEN, EDWIN, *Generals vs. Presidents: Neo-Militarism in Latin America* (New York: Frederick A. Praeger, Inc., 1964).

McCARTNEY, ROY, "How War Came to Korea," in Norman Bartlett (ed.), *With the Australians in Korea* (Canberra, Aust.: Australian War Memorial, 1954).

McWORTER, GERALD A. AND ROBERT L. CRAIN, "Subcommunity Gladitorial Competition: Civil Rights Leadership as a Competitve Process," *Social Forces,* 46 (September 1967), 8–21.

MILSTEIN, JEFFREY S., "American and Soviet Influence, Balance of Power, and Arab-Israeli Violence," pp. 139–166 in Bruce M. Russett (ed.), *Peace, War, and Numbers* (Beverly Hills, Calif.: Sage Publications, Inc., 1972).

MOORE, BARRINGTON, JR., *Injustice: The Social Bases of Obedience and Revolt* (White Plains, N.Y.: M. E. Sharpe, 1978).

MORGAN, WILLIAM R., "Faculty Mediation of Student War Protests," pp. 365–382 in Julian Foster and Durward Long (eds.), *Protest! Student Activism in America* (New York: Morrow, 1970).

MORISON, SAMUEL ELIOT, FREDERICK MERK, AND FRANK FREIDEL, *Dissent in Three American Wars* (Cambridge, Mass.: Harvard University Press, 1970).

NAROLL, RAOUL, "Deterrence in History," pp. 150–164 in Dean G. Pruitt and Richard C. Snyder (eds.), *Theory and Research on the Causes of War* (Englewood Cliffs, N.J.: Prentice-Hall, 1969).

NAROLL, RAOUL, VERN L. BULLOUGH, AND FRADA NAROLL, *Military Deterrence in History* (Albany, N.Y.: State University of New York Press, 1974).

NASSER, GAMAL ABDEL, "Speech at UAR Advanced Air Headquarters, May 25, 1967," pp. 169–174 in Walter Laqueur (ed.), *The Israel-Arab Reader,* rev. ed. (New York: Bantam, 1970).

NATIONAL ADVISORY COMMISSION ON CIVIL DISORDERS (KERNER COMMISSION), *Report of the National Commission on Civil Disorders* (New York: Bantam, 1968).

NEAR, HENRY (ed.), *The Seventh Day: Soldiers' Talk About the Six-Day War* (London: Penguin, 1971).

NEUSTADT, RICHARD, *Presidential Power* (New York: John Wiley, 1960), cited in Edward Friedman, "Problems in Dealing with an Irrational Power: America Declares War on China," p. 239 in Edward Friedman and Mark Selden (eds.), *America's Asia: Dissenting Essays on Asian-American Relations* (New York: Random House, 1969).

OBERSCHALL, ANTHONY, "Group Violence: Some Hypotheses and Empirical Uniformities," paper presented at the meeting of the American Sociological Association, 1969.

PAIGE, GLENN, *The Korean Decision* (New York: Free Press, 1968).

PRESIDENT'S COMMISSION ON CAMPUS UNREST, THE (SCRANTON COMMITTEE), *Campus Unrest* (Washington, D.C.: U.S. Government Printing Office, 1970).

PURCELL, HUGH D., *Cyprus* (New York: Frederick A. Praeger, Inc., 1969).

QUESTER, GEORGE H., "Wars Prolonged by Misunderstood Signals," *The Annals of the American Academy of Political and Social Science,* 392 (November 1970), 30–39.

RADER, DOTSON AND CRAIG ANDERSON, "Rebellion at Columbia," pp. 67–72 in Walt Anderson (ed.), *The Age of Protest* (Santa Monica, Calif.: Goodyear, 1969).

RAPOPORT, ANATOL, "Lewis F. Richardson's Mathematical Theory of War," *Journal of Conflict Resolution,* 1 (September 1957), 249–304.

RICHARDSON, LEWIS F., *Statistics of Deadly Quarrels* (Pittsburgh, Pa.: Boxwood Press, 1960).

ROBINSON, JOHN P., "Public Reaction to Political Protest: Chicago 1968," *Public Opinion Quarterly,* 34 (Spring 1970), 1–9.

SAVIO, MARIO, "An End to History," pp. 216–219 in Seymour Martin Lipset and Sheldon S. Wolin (eds.), *The Berkeley Student Revolt* (Garden City, N.Y.: Anchor, 1965).

SCHELLING, THOMAS, *The Strategy of Conflict* (Cambridge, Mass.: Harvard University Press, 1960).

SCHONBORN, KARL, *Dealing with Violence* (Springfield, Ill.: Chas. C Thomas, 1975).

SHAPLEN, ROBERT, "Scarsdale's Battle of the Books," *Commentary,* 10 (December 1950), 530–540.

SHAWCROSS, WILLIAM, *Sideshow: Kissinger, Nixon and the Destruction of Cambodia* (New York: Simon & Schuster, 1979).

SHEEHAN, NEIL, HEDRICK SMITH, E. W. KENWORTHY, AND FOX BUTTERFIELD, *The Pentagon Papers; As Published in The New York Times* (New York: Bantam, 1971).

SHERWOOD, ROBERT E., *Roosevelt and Hopkins: An Intimate History* (New York: Harper & Brothers, 1948).

SINGER, J. DAVID AND MELVIN SMALL, "Alliance Aggregation and the Onset of War, 1814–1945," in J. David Singer (ed.), *Quantitative International Politics* (New York: Free Press, 1968).

SKJELSBAEK, KJELL AND J. DAVID SINGER, "Shared IGO Memberships and Dyadic War, 1865–1964," paper presented to Conference on the United Nations, Center for International Studies, 1971.

SKOCPOL, THEDA, *States and Social Revolutions: A Comparative Analysis of France, Russia, and China* (Cambridge, Eng.: Cambridge University Press, 1979).

SMITH, ROBERT B., "Rebellion and Repression and the Vietnam War," *The Annals of the American Academy of Political and Social Science,* 391 (September 1970), 156–167.

SNYDER, GLENN H. AND PAUL DIESING, *Conflict among Nations: Bargaining, Decision Making, and System Structure in International Crises* (Princeton, N.J.: Princeton University Press, 1977).

STOUFFER, SAMUEL A., *Communism, Conformity, and Civil Liberties* (New York: Doubleday, 1955).

STOUFFER, SAMUEL A., ARTHUR A. LUMSDAINE, MARION HARPER LUMSDAINE, ROBIN M. WILLIAMS, JR., M. BREWSTER SMITH, IRVING L. JANIS, SHIRLEY A. STAR, AND LEONARD S. COTTRELL, JR., *The American Soldier: Combat and Its Aftermath,* Vol. 2 (Princeton, N. J.: Princeton University Press, 1949).

SZULC, TAD, *The Illusion of Peace: Foreign Policy in the Nixon Years* (New York: Viking, 1978).

TANTER, RAYMOND, "Dimensions of Conflict Behavior Within and Between Nations, 1958–1960," *Journal of Conflict Resolution,* 10 (March 1966), 41–64.

THOMPSON, SIR ROBERT, *Defeating Communist Insurgency* (New York: Frederick A. Praeger, Inc., 1966), cited on p. 248 in Ted Robert Gurr, *Why Men Rebel* (Princeton, N. J.: Princeton University Press, 1970).

TILLY, CHARLES, *From Mobilization to Revolution* (Reading, Mass.: Addison-Wesley, 1978).

TRAVIS, TOM ALLEN, "A Theoretical and Empirical Study of Communications Relations in the NATO and Warsaw Interbloc and Intrabloc International Sub-Systems," unpublished Ph.D. dissertation, Department of Political Science, Syracuse University, 1970.

TUCHMAN, BARBARA W., *The Guns of August* (New York: Macmillan, 1962).

U.S. STRATEGIC BOMBING SURVEY, *The Effects of Strategic Bombing on German Morale,* 2 vols. (Washington, D.C.: U.S. Government Printing Office, 1946), and *The Effects of Strategic Bombing on Japanese Morale* (Washington, D.C.: U.S. Government Printing Office, 1947).

VALAVANIS, STEFAN, "The Resolution of Conflict when Utilities Interact," *Journal of Conflict Resolution,* 2 (June 1958), 156–169.

WALKER, DANIEL AND OTHERS, *Rights in Conflict: A Report to the National Commission on the Causes and Prevention of Violence* (New York: Bantam, 1968).

WALTON, JENNIFER G., "Correlates of Coerciveness and Permissiveness of National Political Systems: A Cross-National Study," M. A. thesis, San Diego State College, June 1965, cited on p. 250 in Ted Robert Gurr, *Why Men Rebel* (Princeton, N.J.: Princeton University Press, 1970).

WANDERER, JULES J., "An Index of Riot Severity and Some Correlates," *American Journal of Sociology,* 74 (March 1969), 500–505.

WILENSKY, HAROLD L., *Organizational Intelligence: Knowledge and Policy in Government and Industry* (New York: Basic Books, 1967).

WISE, DAVID AND THOMAS B. ROSS, *The U-2 Affair* (New York: Random House, 1962).

6

Termination
and
Outcomes

Every struggle ends. Of course the end is usually the beginning of a new conflict and other struggles continue concurrently. But each specific conflict terminates and has an outcome. In this chapter we outline possible outcomes and how they are affected by termination processes. Then we analyze how various aspects of the struggle itself affect outcomes. We also point out how outcomes are affected by factors aside from the struggle. Finally, we examine a few specific outcomes and how they emerged.

Although obviously important, the analysis of conflict termination has been particularly neglected in the study of social conflicts (Fox 1970; Iklé 1971; Carroll 1970). Recently, analysts of social conflicts have begun to give attention to the results of riots and threats as well as of strikes and wars. This chapter focuses upon the termination and immediate outcome of particular struggles. In the next chapter we will examine intermediary activities, particularly mediation, and in Chapter 8, we will consider longer run issues such as the consequences of a conflict and its outcome for each party, for their relations with each other, and for the system of which they are a part.

The first matter that confronts us in this chapter is how to decide that a conflict has ended. One consideration is how general or how specific to regard the conflict. In a sense, the divisions we have been using between social categories, such as sex, race, and class, are permanent aspects of social life and objective conflicts between them are never ending. This discussion of termination is about specific fights. Even these, however, range broadly. The conflict between blacks and whites in America, for example, consists of innumerable struggles. They are in different social settings (neighborhoods, cities, states, or the nation), about various issues (school integration, housing, public accommodations, or jobs), and over different time periods (days, weeks, or years). There are no inherent boundaries to a conflict. The beginning and end of a conflict have arbitrary qualities. But who decides?

Terminating a conflict means that some people agree that it has ended. Either partisans or observers assert that it has ended. Partisan definitions of conflict termination may be explicit or implicit and may be asserted by only one adversary or agreed upon by all. There is usually a symbolically important event or an explicit agreement in order for the major opponents to agree that a conflict has ended (Coser 1961). For example, the U.S. Constitution may be amended (as with women's suffrage), or an agreement between the adversaries may be signed (as in a labor-management agreement), or a capital city may be seized by rebels or by a foreign invader. Lacking such events, or simply not accepting their significance, one adversary may refuse to agree that the struggle has ended. Obviously, this adversary is generally the "defeated" party. Its continuance, or renewal of conflict behavior, generally forces the other conflict groups to do so also.

Explicitness and mutuality of agreement are not always associated with each other. A conflict may wither away and, by mutual indifference, be implicitly ended. On the other hand, even an explicit agreement between two adversaries terminating a dispute may be regarded by one as an act committed under duress and not binding, or segments of one group may not accept what their leaders have done in their name and they, therefore, will not regard the struggle as ended. They continue the fight.

Observers or analysts of social conflicts should take such partisan acts, definitions, and assertions into account in making their own decision about when a conflict has terminated. Nevertheless, a student of social conflict must choose criteria to define a conflict as terminated. When there are clear partisan definitions, it is useful and sensible to use them. Even when there are not, partisan cues may be significant. Thus we have seen how goals change in the course of a dispute. When the goals have changed very greatly, it may be useful to consider that a conflict has ended and a new one begun. For example, the emergence of significant groups with black separatist goals in the United States helps mark an end to the previous civil rights struggle.

Sometimes students of social conflict use arbitrary time periods to demarcate beginnings and endings. For example, we talk about the 1930s or the 1960s as being periods of particular social conflicts, being guided by numerical conventions. Fixed time periods are also used because of the availability of data that aid assessment of changes induced by conflict behavior. This use of time periods may seem utterly arbitrary, but most general struggles are continuous and demarcations must be somewhat arbitrary and boundaries are needed in order to assess conflict outcomes.

History does not end. But that does not, and should not, stop us from writing histories. We must accept the often arbitrary demarcations of conflict terminations, but we should be explicit about the criteria used to mark the end of a conflict.

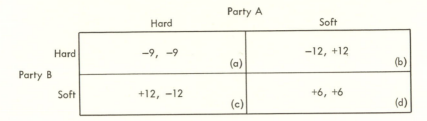

Figure 6.1

POSSIBLE OUTCOMES

People generally refer to outcomes as victories for one side and defeats for the other. Whether members of an adversary group consider themselves to be defeated or victorious has important consequences. These terms are not, however, the most useful for analyzing outcomes. They are too laden with connotations and they obscure variations. We cannot characterize the immediate outcomes of a fight independently of the adversaries' goals. One aspect of the outcome we will consider then, is the relative distribution of gains each part makes at the expense of the other. However, this is not enough to characterize outcomes because conflicts are not purely zero sum. Even enemies have common and complementary interests. The other aspect of conflict outcomes we will examine is the extent to which they entail shared benefits and damages for the adversaries. It is possible that all the adversaries gain in the outcome (perhaps at the expense of some other parties) because new solutions have been discovered. On the other hand, the adversaries may so injure one another that none gains anything approaching what it sought, and, instead, they all are losers. Such outcomes are illustrated in the payoff matrix depicted in Figure 6.1. The outcomes are similar to those shown in Figure 1.3 (see p. 8). If both antagonists impose harsh sanctions on each other, they both suffer (cell a); but if one is strong and the other is soft, the opponent that follows a soft strategy will lose (cells c and b); if both are restrained and do not impose hard sanctions, they both benefit (cell d) in what is called a win/win outcome.

We will first examine the distributive character of outcomes—the extent to which each adversary attained what it sought from the others. Such outcomes are most clearly evident in consensual conflicts, for example in conflicts over the division of money or land that is desired by all the adversaries. Coercive means are particularly significant for those outcomes. After discussing the separate gains and losses, we will examine the extent to which adversaries mutually benefit and lose from the outcome; we call this the joint aspect of the conflict outcome. Mutual benefit outcomes are also called integrative (Deutsch 1973; Walton and McKersie 1965). In dissensual conflicts integrative outcomes are especially pertinent in that they make possible the advancement of each party's interests in a mutually beneficial fashion. These aspects of an outcome are diagrammed in Figure 6.2.

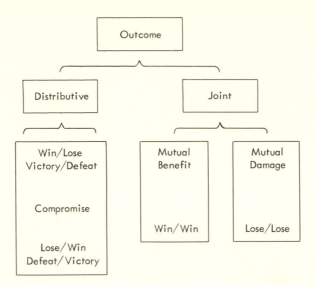

Figure 6.2

Distributive

Presumably each adversary desires to impose its aims upon its opponents. One party wins, the other loses; there is a victory and a defeat. Such outcomes occur but they are never pure. Some elements of compromise nearly always enter into an outcome. Even the demand for unconditional surrender by the Allies against Japan in World War II was tempered at the very end by agreeing to allow the emperor of Japan to retain his throne.

There is a more fundamental difficulty in assessing to what degree a given outcome represents a victory for one party and a defeat for another. Victory and defeat have meaning only relative to the goals that adversaries have. But goals change in the course of a conflict. They expand with wins and contract with losses. Enemies may claim victories in terms of what they "really" wanted. We consider outcomes in terms of the original aims of each participant, but even this is ambiguous. Aims are often amorphous, gradually take specific shape, and are not shared equally by all segments of a conflict group. This vagueness indicates an additional difficulty. The leadership of one party may change, and with that change new goals may be asserted. For our purposes this would mark the end of one conflict and the beginning of a new one. For example, when the Bolsheviks seized power in Russia, that marked the end of one fight between Germany and Russia and the beginning of a different one. Again, any resolution of all these difficulties has an arbitrary quality. What is important is to be explicit about the meaning of the terms and to use concepts that are most useful for the widest range of cases.

We note three forms of distributive outcomes: (1) The party seeking a change in the situation succeeds in obtaining most of what it wanted from its opponents; (2) the outcome is a kind of compromise between the goals of the adversaries; and (3) the party seeking to change the status quo does not, and the outcome is similar to the situation before the conflict erupted.

The outcome in which one party largely wins by imposing its demands on the other seems to be the model most people carry with them in their minds. Indeed, in many fights this is an important aspect of the outcome. For example, one state wins control of a particular piece of territory after a war, or a union wins recognition as the collective bargaining agent for the workers in the company.

Nearly all outcomes, however, entail compromises. Compromise may refer to mutual concessions explicitly made by adversaries to terminate a conflict. Adversaries may also trade-off gains in one area for gains in another. A compromise outcome need not be the result of an explicit agreement. It may also be an outcome that an analyst judges to be a mutual accommodation. In any case, neither party obtains all that it wants. Pervasive as compromise may be in outcomes, delimiting its terms in a specific termination is difficult. The matter is further complicated by the emergence of new demands and conflicts as previous ones lose salience.

One party often initiates a fight by making demands and beginning to pursue its goals. A possible outcome is that the initiator simply withdraws its demands, and the situation returns to the status quo ante. Of course, the situation cannot return to the identical one prior to the attempt to alter it; the attempt has effects upon each participant and their relationship. The matter in contention may not, however, be substantially altered. For example, university students may make demands and demonstrate in support of them. After a short time, with no progress toward the satisfaction of the demands, the attempt to attain them dissipates. Similarly, the status of West Berlin has been threatened several times only to return to the uneasy situation that prevailed before the threat.

Joint

In addition to separate wins and losses, outcomes also differ in joint benefits and damages. We will discuss two kinds of mutually beneficial or integrative outcomes: the mutually beneficial solution and collusion against others. Then we will comment on a neglected aspect of conflict outcomes: the joint damages.

Adversaries begin a conflict with what appear to be mutually incompatible demands, but which, when pursued, may turn out to be compatible. The opponents may discover that there are ways to attain what each wants without losing anything of significance to the other. They have found a solution to a shared problem. Walton and McKersie (1965) describe a union-management *dispute* around the issue of promotion that was tranformed into a *problem* and then solved. Few senior employees were being promoted because management said they lacked the requisite skills; the union wanted to improve the promotional chances of employees with most years of service. Initially, the employees said they wanted more weight to be given to seniority. "After considerable discussion, it was agreed that the company would inaugurate a 'self-help' program for employees. It would pay for outside education and do everything possible to help the employees improve their skills in advance of promotion opportunities" (Walton and McKersie 1965, p. 132).

Another way in which an outcome may have joint benefits is that the adversaries gain at the expense of bystanders. Given the interlocking character of conflicts, adversaries may shift their view of which conflict is the focal one. They may come to consider themselves to be allied against a threat from a common enemy and may together benefit by joining forces. Or they may agree to pass on the costs of a mutually satisfactory agreement to other parties. A union-management agreement that includes a high wage increase may be accepted by the union and management negotiators when the management representatives are confident that their company can pass on the costs of the wage increase in the form of increased prices. Negotiators can reach a mutually satisfactory agreement at the expense of nonfocal parties in still another way. The negotiators can conspire with each other so that the constituency of one set of negotiators fails to attain what it had sought. For example, trade union negotiators may gain personal benefits from the management negotiators and, in exchange, agree to accept relatively small gains for the union members they are supposed to be representing.

In addition to joint benefits, an outcome may entail joint damages. Most obviously, a struggle between adversaries may weaken them so that a third party becomes relatively stronger than the adversaries. Thus, when the West European powers fought one another in World War II, they all lost in relative global power and the United States and the Soviet Union become relatively much more powerful. Thus, too, the ruling dynasties of imperial Germany and imperial Russia both were destroyed at the end of World War I, partly as a result of fighting each other.

Both distributive and integrative components are aspects of every actual outcome. There are always some joint costs and joint benefits from the perspective of an observer. Nevertheless, some outcomes are largely integrative and others largely distributive.

One matter that greatly complicates the extent to which a given conflict is integrative and distributive is the shifting nature of conflict goals. Adversaries alter their goals in the course of a struggle. One party may come to agree with its enemy about what it seeks and be persuaded that their dissensual disagreement was in error. In other words, it may be converted to the other side's faith, or the consensual conflict may be terminated as one side comes to agree that, indeed, what they both want ought properly belong to the other side. Conversion may also take the form of one or more adversaries' acquiring values or beliefs that supersede the contentious goals. Thus, antagonists may come to devalue the ends sought and believe that other values that they now hold, and which are not in conflict, are more important. For example, after an extended struggle about religious differences, conflict parties may develop a norm of religious tolerance. In effect, both sides agree to disagree. They may even come to feel that pluralism is a desirable state. The expansion of fringe benefits instead of wage increases in industrial relations is another example.

Conversion is often a part of compromise outcomes, and even of ones that are predominately imposition. For some contentious issues, conflict termination, short of destroying one side, requires some conversion, at least to the right of the other side to disagree. Conversion varies in degree and especially in its extent within each conflict party. The different modes of pursuing conflict all have some effect upon the convictions of each party; persuasion is not the only way to bring about conversion. In the course of a struggle the contending parties perceive, if only dimly, the reality of what is happening. The resistance of an adversary, how members of the antagonistic collectivity talk and work with one another, or the way they present themselves to third parties, all convey important information.

TERMINATION PROCESSES

The outcome of a specific conflict may be reached through a variety of courses. How the outcome is reached helps form it. In order to understand the ending of a conflict and its outcome, we must consider the implicit and explicit processes that bring it about. As already indicated, a dispute may be implicitly terminated by participants or by observers. For purposes of analysis, observers may simply regard a conflict as terminated and examine what the outcome is at that time. The considerations they use in deciding about terminations are relevant to the interpretation of their findings regarding conflicts but do not tell us anything about the termination processes.

Implicit

Participants themselves may implicitly terminate a struggle. What occurs is basically a continuing deescalation of conflict behavior. At a low enough level both sides may acknowledge that the status quo is the outcome of the conflict, or one side may claim that the outcome has been attained, and, if the other side does not actively try to alter it, an implicit outcome has been reached. Even if the adversaries do not interpret the situation in the same way, if they have ceased trying to change it or to alter the other's views of it, then an implicit outcome has been reached. An implicit outcome, finally, may be reached without open acknowledgment from any conflict party. The adversaries may simply cease conflict behavior in pursuit of their contrary goals.

Some kinds of outcomes can be attained by implicit acknowledgment and indeed may be more likely to be attained implicitly than explicitly. Thus a withdrawal to the status quo ante can be done more easily if not openly admitted. The contentious demand is simply dropped. The adversary, too, may facilitate this arrangement by allowing whatever face saving is accomplished by silence. For example, in the recurrent crises about West Berlin during the 1950s, Khrushchev's efforts to change the status of Berlin were resisted and, when they lessened, U.S. leaders did not triumphantly announce victories.

Conversion is also more likely to be attained implicitly than explicitly. If one side has changed its mind under the efforts of the other side, it may deny this to itself or in any case no open announcement is needed. The same is true for mutual conversions when a new shared value or norm that covers the previous conflict arises.

Implicit withdrawals to the status quo ante are most likely when one side seeks to attain a goal that is strongly countered by the adversary without fundamental escalation. That is, the adversary firmly and with enough power refuses to yield, and its counterpressure and demands are contingent only upon the withdrawal of the initial conflicting goal. Implicit withdrawal is also possible if, after conflicting behavior has been pursued, the conflict party that is seeking a change is so overwhelmed that it dissolves as an effective conflict group. Thus, revolutionary movements have spawned parties and groups that may even have mustered armed units and waged guerrilla warfare only, finally, to be dissolved. For example, the Hukbalahap movement in the Philippines was defeated by social-political reforms, in part conducted by the army. The secretary of defense, Ramón Magsaysay, so effectively pursued a course of pressure and opportunities for the peasantry that the Hukbalahap movement began to split up, and the leader himself surrendered to work with the government (Gross 1966, pp. 162–86; Starner 1961).

Explicit

Conflict outcomes are often preceded by explicit negotiations. The negotiations are explicit insofar as the parties communicate symbolically with each other in seeking an agreement about an outcome that will be mutually acceptable. Explicit negotiations may also, however, ratify an implicitly achieved outcome, even an imposed one. In the course of negotiations, some conversion is likely to occur, but the basic form of outcome is compromise if an agreement is reached. All negotiations need not and do not end in agreement. Coercive efforts to attain conflicting goals may be continued, renewed, initiated, or escalated if no agreement is reached. In such cases, negotiations are an episode in the course of a struggle. We now consider how the negotiating process itself affects the distributive and the integrative character of the agreement reached and whether or not any agreement is reached.

Relative Gains

Many elements in negotiations affect the distribution of what is sought by the adversaries (Sawyer and Guetzkow 1965). This discussion will concentrate on consenual conflicts, emphasizing parties' wanting more, or no less, of the same goal. As we have observed, no aim is unidimensional. There are almost certainly differing priorities regarding aspects of what might appear to be a single goal; consequently, trading is possible. Nevertheless, for the sake of simplicity, we will sometimes discuss negotiating as if there were a single dimension in dispute.

As Schelling (1960, pp. 21–52) has pointed out, although it might seem that the stronger and more skillful must win in negotiation, this is not necessarily so unless strength and skill are retroactively attributed to the winner. Power and many other factors are certainly important in producing the situation within which the parties are negotiating. They are also relevant to making an agreement, any agreement, desirable. Under certain conditions, however, weakness and even stupidity can help a party in the negotiating process. If a distributive agreement is to be reached, one side must concede and the other side accept, the concession. To induce the other side to accept, a negotiating party must convince it that the adversary will not alter its position or make further concessions. If the other side is convinced, it believes that it must accept the terms or no agreement will be reached. A negotiating party that seems to be too ignorant or irresponsible to worry about longer run interests may thus have a bargaining advantage over the party that considers longer run interests and is responsible to the other side.

There are many ways in which negotiating parties try to influence the bargaining partners' perception of the probability of getting what they seek. One set of techniques pertains to lowering the probability of making concessions. Negotiators may try to commit themselves so that they induce the adversary to believe it must accept their terms or fail to reach any agreement. One such technique is by a public announcement that binds the party's reputation to a particular stand. Loudly proclaimed "nonnegotiable" demands are one form this method may take. Such public announcements may be discounted by the other side; to what extent depends upon the conventional understandings about such pronouncements. When both sides have taken fixed positions in public, reaching an agreement is made more difficult, but it is in each side's interest to stake out its position first. This way of making commitments is possible insofar as one side recognizes that the other negotiating party has a reputation to maintain with its constituency or third parties.

A negotiating party may also assume an unalterable position by entering the negotiations with binding instructions. The negotiating party then forces the other side either to accept the profferred terms or risk breaking up the negotiations without an agreement. In negotiations between the Soviet Union and the United States, Soviet negotiating intransigence is often attributed to the inability of the negotiators to deviate from strict instructions (Dennett and Johnson 1951). Mosley (1951, p. 288) reports how he used the same technique in 1944 in negotiating with the Russians about the armistice terms for Bulgaria. The issue pertained to the payment of reparations; the Soviet Union opposed this payment for Bulgaria. Mosley reports that he informally explained to the Soviet representatives that if it was not included, a review by Congress might lead to an investigation, and he might be punished. The next day the Russians agreed to the inclusion of the disputed provision.

The initial bargaining position also affects the relative gains or losses in the final outcome. If a negotiating party asks initially for much more than it would minimally accept, it will generally do better than if the initial demands are modest (Siegel and Fouraker 1960). There is the risk, however, that if the opening bids are so unrealistically high, no agreement will be reached (Bartos 1970). Assuming that negotiations continue, high demands are advantageous for a few reasons. Suppose two parties, A and B, have minimal positions Am and Bm, as shown in Figure 6.3. An agreement would be possible anywhere between Am and Bm. Now suppose A opens the negotiations by asking for Ai. B is likely to believe that A's minimal position is Apb, and, therefore, agreement is possible only very close to its own minimal position, Bm. That is, B makes some judgment about what A will finally accept on the basis of A's initial demands. Furthermore, if there is pressure to reach an agreement, the more A has asked, the longer it would take to bargain it down to an acceptable position, and, therefore, the more likely is B to settle for an agreement closer to Bm than Am (Cross 1969). This brings us to another factor.

How far and in what way each side makes concessions also depends on possible "focal" points (Schelling 1960). That is, some positions seem like natural stopping points or dividing lines, and negotiating parties may move toward such positions as "natural" even if they might favor one side over the other. In international negotiations, natural borders such as rivers and mountains are examples of these points. In many bargaining situations, a fifty-fifty division, or "splitting the differ-ence," seems like a naturally fair and equitable position. Therefore, it is a focal point. That is why the side that initially makes a high demand has an advantage.

The cohesion of one or both adversaries also affects the terms offered for settlement and, hence, the outcome. If one side lacks cohesion, reaching a com-promise is difficult; the outcome is more likely to be a victory or a defeat than if both sides are unified. In World War II the anti-Fascist alliance held out for the unconditional surrender of the Axis, partly in order to avoid allied recrimina-tions about a separate peace or allied dissension regarding peace terms. In the more recent case of the Arab governments and Arab Palestinian organizations, disunity among them contributed to their insistence upon total Israeli defeat; they could all agree upon that as desirable. Of course, the disarray that underlay that goal also hampered achieving it. The goal and the disarray made it difficult to agree to any partial or general termination of the conflict. President Sadat's break

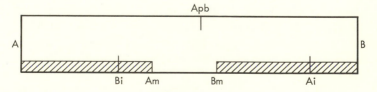

Figure 6.3

from this goal is all the more remarkable in this light, but other Arab governments and groups remained mutually inhibiting in making a comprehensive settlement.

Finally, the outcome may be more favorable to one side than another because one side may be able to use common values or standards to support its position more readily than can another. This is obviously true of dissensual conflicts where persuasion is particularly important. But even in consensual conflicts, the closeness of one side's goals to a shared value is helpful in negotiation. Presumably the aim of integration and equality between blacks and whites could be pursued in each specific case by calls to the basic American standards of equality (Myrdal 1944). In conflicts between superordinates and subordintes, the subordinates often find that those in authority are armed with values and standards that support the basic relationship of the parties. Thus, in many disputes those with authority or who have had power longer are likely to find legal justifications for their positions while the protestors argue in terms of general moral precepts or in terms of raw power. For example, the dominance of whites, of males, of colonial powers, or of university administrators is embedded in law and regulations. Consequently, people who are dominated are likely to argue in terms of fundamental human rights.

In any distributive outcome compromises between the negotiating parties are involved. We have been discussing compromises largely in terms of bridging the gap between the adversaries by splitting the difference. The parties each give something; in monetary bargaining the simple fifty-fifty split has salience and is likely to seem fair (Schelling 1960). The other major kind of compromise is logrolling. Each party gives something to the other side and receives some things that it wants in return. In other words, there is a trade-off in which each party foregoes something it wants and yet attains some of what it seeks.

Joint Benefits

Research has been relatively neglected on the aspects of negotiations that affect the likelihood that an outcome will be integrative; much of the research that does exist pertains to the role of mediators and other intermediaries, discussed in the next chapter. A few writers suggest negotiating techniques for reaching integrative outcomes and cite instances that illustrate such techniques. We will draw on these materials as well as relevant research to examine the aspects of the negotiating process affecting the probability of an intregrative outcome.

Two elements in negotiation are fundamental for successfully reaching an integrative outcome (Walton and McKersie 1965; Fisher 1978). The negotiators must consider themselves to be facing a problem, rather than simply being divided by an issue, and they must discover a solution to their problem. The first element entails, then, a mutual recognition that they have a problem to be solved. Each conflict party has a problem in the sense that it must find an acceptable solution; in addition, all the parties regard themselves as having a common problem in trying to find a solution acceptable to all parties. The second element entails considering new alternatives, going beyond each adversary's positions.

Facing a Problem. Negotiators will consider and perhaps agree to an integrative outcome if they come to think of themselves as sharing a problem. This state is facilitated when adversaries shift their view of which conflict is the focal one. The adversaries may come to regard their conflict with each other as subordinate to another conflict in which they share a common enemy or danger. They may also shift the time period within which they view their conflict; they may come to regard the divisive conflict as a dispute within the context of longer run mutual dependence and need.

Negotiators are also likely to think they have a problem to be solved when there is a perceived decline in conflicting interests relative to common and complementary ones. That is, every relationship has conflicting, complementary, and common interests, but when a fight is waged, the conflicting interests are considered predominate. As a fight escalates, the attention to those conflicting aspects of the relationship increases. In order to deescalate the fight and to turn to face a problem together, increased attention to the possible bases of mutually benefiting exchange, to the possible joint gains, or to the avoidance of joint damage is important.

Such shifts in perspective largely depend upon the variety of interlocking conflicts in which the adversaries are engaged. Actors outside of the focal conflict may threaten and so increase the salience of conflicts with them and thus lead the negotiators in the focal conflict to shift their views. But in this discussion, we are interested in how one or more of the negotiators can do or say something that facilitates or even produces shifts in perspective.

Positive inducements are especially important in generating such shifts in perspective. Persuasion and reward are especially significant when peace initiatives are undertaken between struggling parties in the midst of contracted negotiations. A well-timed concession may help an adversary recognize the existence of a common problem. For example, we noted in Chapter 5 that President Kennedy made a conciliatory speech at American University, in June 1963, that preceded the Partial Nuclear Test Ban Agreement among the U.S., Soviet, and British governments. The speech included rewards, such as recognizing that the United States may have borne some responsibility for the cold war. The speech was a response to informal indications from Khrushchev that he wanted a signal from the U.S. government that would enable him to move toward an agreement on nuclear weapons testing (Schlesinger 1965; Gromyko 1973; Kriesberg 1981a).

The speech and the associated statements and actions of the U.S. and Soviet government leaders enabled them to discover and accept a solution to the problem dealing with their testing nuclear weapons in the atmosphere. They had failed to agree to a comprehensive ban on nuclear arms testing, including underground testing, because of differences about the means of inspection and overseeing compliance. But many people in the United States and throughout the world were worried and angry about the radiation released by atmospheric nuclear tests and the resulting dangers of food contamination. Furthermore, France and the People's Republic of China were testing weapons in the atmosphere in order to develop their own nuclear capability. In the summer of 1963 the split between the Soviet and the Chinese Communist parties intensified immediately prior to the arrival in Moscow of the American and British delegations to negotiate the Partial Nuclear Test Ban Agreement. For the Soviet, American, and British leaders, then, a convergence of common interests could be recognized. The American University speech by President Kennedy helped the adversary parties perceive it.

Consider another example. The Arab-Israeli conflicts have been particularly intense and long-standing. It has therefore been particularly difficult to make deescalatory moves credible (Kriesberg 1980, 1981b; Sadat 1978; Khouri 1976). In 1977 President Carter and the U.S. government urged a Geneva conference to seek a comprehensive peace agreement in the Middle East. The conference would be cochaired by the U.S. and the Soviet governments. These developments, among others, made it possible to recognize important common and complementary interests for the Egyptian and Israeli governments. They both wanted to minimize Soviet involvement in the area and to maintain as much autonomy in foreign policy as possible by minimizing the role of radical movements and governments' exercising a veto power on any agreement. The Egyptian and Israeli governments each controlled resources that the other greatly wanted: recognition and real peace by Egypt and the return of the Sinai by Israel. To make such an exchange possible, President Sadat had to make credible his assurance of Israeli national security. He developed and executed a bold and creative series of statements and actions, most notably associated with his visit to Jerusalem in November 1977 (Sadat 1978). That action dramatically affected the perceptions of the focal conflict for the Israelis and for people throughout the region, as well as in the United States and the Soviet Union.

Negotiators routinely make efforts to build bonds of common interest, at least on the personal level. They may exchange information about their children or grandchildren as a way of demonstrating their common humanity and shared experience in parental or grandparental roles. Dinners and cocktail parties similarly are occasions for engaging in shared activities that cross-cut the divisive issues in dispute.

Discovering a Solution. Recognizing that the parties in conflict have problems to be solved, the negotiators must discover or invent possible solutions. Often in negotiations each side presents its position, and the negotiation process consists of the adversary's making concessions by yielding ground from its position in exchange for the other side's doing the same. This exchange is the normal way of reaching a distributive agreement. In order to reach an integrative solution, it is useful to distinguish between the underlying interests of each party and the positions each asserts (Fisher 1978). For example, a government may assert that it wants a particular piece of territory, but its interests have largely to do with security. Once attention is given to the interests at stake, it is possible to think about a variety of ways they may be served. One or more of those ways may also satisfy the interests of the adversary groups.

Understanding what interests may underlie stated positions can be facilitated by several methods. Each side, in explaining why it takes a particular position, is often providing information about its interests. An integrative solution is facilitated if the negotiators make clear what problem they are seeking to solve by asserting their position. Furthermore, an integrative solution is facilitated insofar as each side listens to the other, trying to learn what the underlying interest may be.

Pruitt and others have conducted a variety of experiments involving pairs of subjects taking the roles of buyer and seller. They must negotiate an agreement on the price of three commodities, which have differing importance for the two bargainers. Integrative agreements require trade-offs in which each negotiator makes concessions on those items of least personal importance. Pruitt and his colleagues analyzed the kinds of strategies the negotiators have followed that have resulted in more integrative solutions. They concluded that integrative solutions are facilitated when the negotiators are firm about the ends they seek but flexible about the means of attaining them (Pruitt and Lewis 1977). Large, early, or frequent concessions do not engender a mutually satisfactory and, hence, integrative solution.

Snyder and Diesing (1977) examined the bargaining that occurred in sixteen international crises between 1898 and 1973. They concluded that "An initial period of mutual firmness is necessary to clarify the balance of bargaining power and the structure of the crisis and only then are the parties in a position to estimate whether and how much they must reduce their initial claims" (p. 489).

Many techniques facilitate the flexibility and inventiveness needed to discover or create new proposals. The adversary negotiating teams may be broken into joint subgroups with instructions to work on different aspects of the issues in contention and develop several alternative solutions—even if they clearly would not appear to be acceptable to anyone. Each negotiating team might engage in role playing in which some members take the role of the other side and try to articulate the concerns that underlie their positions. The negotiating teams also may alter their physical setting or engage in an absorbing and diverting joint activity, simply to break out of rigidities that have developed in the reiteration of established positions. Finally, the negotiators may seek outside assistance in the form of intermediaries, such as mediators. As we will examine in the next chapter, mediators can help in many ways to generate new options.

Reaching Agreement

Now we consider what variations in the negotiating process affect the chances of reaching any settlement. We will consider the degree of institutionalization, timing, and secrecy. Intermediaries are so important that the next chapter is set aside to analyze their roles.

Institutionalization. Insofar as a conflict is conducted within institutionalized procedures, its termination will be explicit. One of the ways in which institutionalization significantly affects outcomes is by specifying who is involved in terminating the dispute. In highly institutionalized conflicts with highly organized conflict parties, there usually are special roles to be followed by the adversaries in their interaction. The occupants of those roles are the persons who usually engage in the direct negotiations to terminate a conflict. Sometimes the roles make possible a wide latitude in the negotiation of an outcome. The existence of such roles increases the likelihood that a termination will be explicitly reached.

In relatively undifferentiated conflict parties or in broad social movements there may be no clear role for negotiating with an adversary. A self-appointed or adversary-appointed spokesperson may try to negotiate a settlement, but such settlements may not bind the conflict parties. The actual outcome may be implicit rather than explicit. Sometimes conflict parties try to avoid any designation of leaders or representatives. In this way the rank and file believe they can participate more fully in the negotiations. This arrangement has sometimes occurred in student insurrections. In cases like riots there may not be enough of an organization even to refuse to designate leaders. In such circumstances the adversary may proffer some terms, and these may be implicitly accepted.

Each side would like to choose the representative of the other side for negotiation. Indeed, sometimes the designation of the negotiating representative by a conflict party is contested by the other side. Even in institutionalized conflict relations and with highly organized conflict parties, one party may refuse to negotiate with a particular person from the antagonist group. This has occurred in collective bargaining between trade unions and management and between governments.

Institutionalization may also give legitimacy to intervention in the form of mediation. Insofar as the partisans feel that the mediator is legitimate and they have in effect selected the mediator, his or her suggestions will be more readily accepted, and, therefore, the chances of reaching an agreement will be enhanced.

Generally, insofar as the negotiations are institutionalized, the parties will have more information about each other and better understanding of the meaning of each other's assertions and demands. Consequently, promises of future actions are more likely to be correctly understood by the other side. Similarly, the proper discounting of the other side's demands are more likely to be made. Therefore the negotiations are more likely to be concluded in agreement.

Timing. Negotiations to terminate a conflict explicitly may occur at a wide range of times in the course of a struggle. At one extreme, negotiations may simply formalize what has already happened; the parties recognize an implicit outcome. At the other extreme, it is within the context of a negotiating process that an outcome is arrived at with little conflict behavior prior to or aside from those efforts. In that case, both sides' coercive forces may be assessed and threatened and possible rewards in exchange for concessions tentatively proffered, but they may not actually be exercised until a termination has been reached. Meanwhile, however, persuasive efforts may be conducted vigorously. Negotiations at such an early stage in the course of a struggle are typical in institutionalized conflicts.

Efforts to work out an explicit mutual recognition of a conflict termination may be unsuccessful. That is, parties try to agree about the nature of the outcome of a struggle, but they cannot. In that case, the direct efforts may be ended and the conflict behavior continued, renewed, or escalated. Later, new efforts at reaching an explicit agreement may be made, or an implicit ending finally occurs. The failure of direct efforts may not be followed by any new conflict behavior, but by an implicit termination. Both parties may be willing, at least for a time, to accept a given situation, if they do not have to admit openly that they recognize and, therefore, acknowledge it. For example, the status of Germany and its borders were not officially recognized by the many governments that defeated Germany for many years after World War II ended.

Efforts to reach an explicit termination are often initiated after conflict behavior has begun and prior to a large anticipated escalation. Such negotiations are conducted with a threat hanging over the negotiators and sometimes with tremendous time pressures. The sense of tension has been recounted in reports of the Cuban missile crisis negotiations. The mobilization of coercive forces takes on a dynamic of its own; it cannot be sustained for long without being let loose. All of these pressures burden negotiators at the same time that the demands of some kind of agreement may be high. At such times there is the spectacle of round-the-clock negotiations before a strike deadline or before the expiration of a military ultimatum.

Lacking well-developed conflict regulation, direct efforts to negotiate a settlement without considerable agreement about what a mutually acceptable settlement would be are likely to fail. Insofar as conflict regulation is not institutionalized, the parties must be closed to an implicit termination in order to have an explicit one successfully achieved.

Of course, the discovery of an integrative solution or a minimally acceptable distributive outcome underlies reaching an agreement. Even the appearance of such a solution or outcome is helpful. Negotiators may decide to act *as if* that has happened. One party may offer a "face-saving" concession to the other side that enables the "losing" side to accept unfavorable terms (Snyder and Diesing 1977, p. 491). Avoiding a humiliation of the other side also fosters a longer lasting agreement.

Secrecy. Explicit agreements about the termination of a conflict may be reached more or less openly. It is possible for only a few representatives from each side to negotiate an agreement. Their constituencies may be kept ignorant of the negotiations and even of the terms. It was against such practices that President

Wilson raised the banner of open covenants openly arrived at. At the other extreme, the entire negotiating process may be conducted in public with widespread participation of the constituencies of both sides. In between are various degrees of openness and secrecy. The delegations involved in the negotiations vary in size and representativeness; the constituencies are more or less informed about the negotiations; and the constituencies have varying opportunities to ratify the agreements.

Secrecy in many ways makes it possible to reach agreements about terminations that openness would preclude. Particularly noteworthy is the flexibility in considering alternative outcomes that secrecy permits. Social-psychological experiments indicate that if negotiators are subject to attention and evaluation by their constituencies, they will be more intransigent in their bargaining (Rubin and Brown 1975).

In real-life situations, this tendency is further aggravated by special circumstances. In the heat of battle, for example, the constituencies have been mobilized to the point that concessions would seem traitorous, and discussion of compromise would seem to be an admission of weakness that, if acknowledged, would hasten the collapse of will to persevere in the struggle.

Confidential negotiations have another set of advantages for reaching agreements. Spokespersons for each side can conduct negotiations until a package of mutual concessions is constructed and present it as an entity that is acceptable to the opposing sides. This may be accepted by the rank and file, who would have refused support if the plan had been suggested only in part and only as a possibility for bargaining. Furthermore, negotiators with many items in dispute often settle one at a time but regard none as completely and finally settled until all are agreed upon.

The secrecy of negotiations, nevertheless, leaves the leaders open to the suspicion of betrayal. In the extreme form of secrecy, when even the terms are not made public, implementation of the terms is difficult indeed, unless they simply reflect an implicit accommodation. Consider the alleged agreement between the student leaders and the administrators of Columbia University in the 1968 rebellion (Rader and Anderson 1969). President Kirk agreed not to build the gymnasium planned for Harlem's Morningside Park, to sever university ties with the Institute for Defense Analysis, to resign within a year for reasons of health, and, although refusing a general amnesty, he promised only reprimands. The student Steering Committee agreed not to seize additional buildings and, if a police raid became necessary, not to resist it. In this arrangement the Steering Committee would have held out to the bitter end for amnesty and the administration would not have yielded openly on this fundamental issue although agreeing on other issues. When the police made their raid, however, they violently removed persons in buildings held by whites. This action led to the closing down of classes and widespread support for the rebellious students. A termination was not reached;

rather, the conflict escalated. The police had not participated in any agreements. The agreement was not valid after the escalating, and a new accommodation had to be reached.

Conflict Structure and Skills. Whether or not an agreement is reached depends largely on the structure of the conflict: How incompatible the objectives of the contending parties are and what is the relative balance of forces the adversaries can apply to the conflict. If no agreement is reached, the conflict may escalate into a test of strength and resolve, or it may remain frozen at the status quo. Major conflicts abound with failed efforts to negotiate a termination. Peace feelers and overtures by one party to a dispute frequently go unnoticed, and, even when negotiations are begun, they may persist for a long time without the parties' reaching any agreement. The Arab-Israeli conflicts have included many such efforts, for example, the 1949–1950 peace negotiations of Israeli, Jordanian, Syrian, Lebanese, and U.S. leaders about the establishment of a Jordan Valley Authority (Khouri 1976).

In addition to underlying conflict structure, the skills of the negotiators contribute to the success or failure of reaching an agreement. This contribution, however, generally lies within the constraints set by the structure of the focal conflict. Negotiators can contribute to reaching an agreement by the skillful exercise of those same techniques and strategies that were previously discussed in terms of relative gains and, particularly, joint benefits.

Snyder and Diesing (1977) examined sixteen major international crises from 1898 to 1973. Two of the crises eventuated in full-scale wars: the European crisis of 1914 and the United States–Japan crisis of 1940–1941. In the first case, misperceptions about other states' intentions were not corrected in time to stop the initiation of military plans that seemed to compel the next steps toward war. In the U.S.-Japanese crisis, the negotiators did not perceive the gravity of the conflict of interests, and, when they did, war seemed the only option. In both cases, the adversaries underestimated the costs of failing to reach an agreement. If either side in 1914 had foreseen the ultimate costs of war, almost any compromise would have seemed preferable. If the Japanese in 1941 had more accurately estimated the costs of the war with the United States, some compromise would probably have been reached.

ASPECTS OF CONFLICT AFFECTING OUTCOME

The outcome of a conflict also depends upon many aspects of the conflict process prior to and underlying the termination processes. We shall consider particularly the goals of the contending parties, the way they pursue their aims, their relative power, and the role of third parties in terms of how these attributes help determine what the conflict's outcome is. The outcome is not determined by the struggle alone. Many other events and developments, quite independent of the efforts of the contending parties, may largely decide the outcome. These influences will be considered in the next section of this chapter.

Goals

The nature and the magnitude of the goals in contention very significantly effect a conflict's outcome. The relationship, however, is not a simple one. For example, it is not always true that the more a conflict party seeks, the more it gets of what it wants.

Nature of the Goals. In general, when the conflicting goals, are consensual, the outcomes tend to be distributive, with some degree of compromise most likely. When the aims entail large components of dissensual conflict, the outcome may result in integrative outcomes as well as distributive ones. If the outcome is largely distributive, it may take the form of withdrawal in the sense of breaking relations, as in secession. Integrative outcomes are likely to involve conversion in values and beliefs. Conversion may take the form of tolerance of the differences rather than one side's accepting the abhorrent views of its erstwhile adversary. For example, consider universities where students have won rights to have liquor and visitors in the dormitories. The increased freedom of university students in their living arrangements in part represents an outcome in which administrators are more tolerant of the variations in the way students may live. To some extent they were converted to believe that students should have considerable control over their own lives.

Goals also differ in regard to the collective or aggregate nature of the benefits sought. When the aim is a collective one, that is, when the members of the conflict party as an entity seek a particular benefit, the outcome is likely to be either imposition or withdrawal, but conversion and compromise are also possible. When the goals pertain more to the aggregate of individuals, compromise is likely either as conversion in the form of tolerance or withdrawal to the status quo ante. Furthermore, aggregate goals are generally more readily attained then collective ones, since the adversary need not as openly acknowledge what has happened and need not make as comprehensive concessions. For example, an improvement in opportunities for many blacks in the United States may be attained without immediately improving the collective status of blacks. As we noted in Chapter 2, Paige (1975) analyzed the agricultural class relations that underlie agrarian revolutions. He argued and found that when noncultivators earned their livelihood from the land, they had difficulty in yielding a little and compromising. When the noncultivators earned their income from capital, reform measures were easier since the cultivators could be given a larger share of the proceeds without overthrowing the entire system.

Another variation in goals is the degree to which a conflict party seeks autonomy or domination, that is, freedom *from* or control *over* the other side. In general, autonomy is easier to attain than control over others. This partly follows from two aspects of the relativity of power: First, the effectiveness of power diminishes the more extended it is (Boulding 1962, pp. 58–79), and second, the willingness to expand resources in exercising power and absorbing the pressure from the other side decreases as the goals diminishes in centrality. A group wishing to be free from control by an adversary generally would be exercising power closer to itself than to the other side. Seeking autonomy also generally means defending something that is more important to its seekers than is control by the other side to its opponent. The centrality and importance of autonomy are sources of advantage that smaller countries have relative to powerful but distant adversaries. Even within a society, a group, particularly if it is relatively weak, has a better chance of attaining some autonomy than in gaining dominance over an adversary. Workers in a factory may gain some control over their own work activities through trade union power; acquiring effective worker control over the factory as an entity would be more difficult.

Magnitude of the Goals. The last observations suggest that the very magnitude of the aims affects the chances of attaining them—the more a conflict party seeks to get, the more likely it is to fail to get it. The more it seeks, the more opposition it arouses from the other side. This line of reasoning can easily be reduced to absurdity: If you don't ask anything from the other side, the other side will give you what you ask for—nothing. The relationship between how much is sought and how much is actually gained, then, is complex.

One complicating matter is that the magnitude of an aim is largely defined by the response of the other side. Some issues may be regarded as terribly significant, they take on symbolic importance, representing many other issues. For example, the termination of conflicts within organizations may be prolonged when the dissident faction demands amnesty for its protest actions. For those in authority granting amnesty seems like an abdication of their authority. The insistence upon punishing the leaders of a rebellion may be the basis for a new grievance and for the continuation of the conflict behavior and even its escalation, as in the Columbia University rebellion of 1968 (Cox Commission 1968, pp. 182–183). On the other hand, the claim for amnesty may be insisted upon as an admission of error by the other side. As a leader of the Columbia students, Mark Rudd said, "We demanded an amnesty to all who participated in the demonstration. This would have forced the administration of Columbia to say we were right" (Rudd 1968, p. 321).

When an issue takes on such symbolic significance, its final resolution does signal much about the outcome. Weighted with significance, the way it falls means victory for one side and defeat for the other. The point is, this need not be the case. An issue may not be regarded as important, and then compromises are more likely and a certain amount of conversion may also occur. Even as crucial an issue as amnesty may be so treated. On the one hand, the authorities may regard the demonstrations, even if illegal activity was included, as simple protest, with illegal action resulting from contagion and collective behavior for which no individuals could be held responsible. On the other hand, the demonstrators may regard punishments as appropriate and their willingness to endure them a further form of demonstrating the strength of their convictions (although a termination of the conflict usually includes ending the leaders' punishment).

The magnitude of the issue in contention is not entirely a subject matter that is dependent only upon the perspectives of the partisans. In general, goals that pertain to changing the rules under which conflicts are pursued are of greater magnitude than goals that seek to modify apportionments within the previous understandings (Baumgartner, Burns, and DeVille 1978). In labor-management relations a conflict over wages is more limited and of lesser magnitude than is one about union recognition or worker control of investment and marketing policies. In order to bring about changes of large magnitude, changing the rules governing the relationship, for example, third party involvement is necessary to assist the conflict party seeking such changes. This was true in industrial relations when fundamental changes in labor-management regulations were made with the aid of the government, viz., the New Deal in the United States, the introduction of codetermination in Germany (Kerr 1954; McPherson 1951), and the establishment of worker councils in Yugoslavia (Ward 1957; Meier 1956).

Revolutionary changes, such as in Russia in 1917 and in China in 1949, involve fundamental changes in social order. The changes occur over a long period of time before and after control of the state has changed. But the weakening of the old order and its partial dissolution are greatly affected by pressures from external third parties, as manifest, for example, in wars (Skocpol 1979).

Another aspect of the magnitude of conflict goals is the degree to which the basic relations between the contending parties is to be altered. In some struggles a conflict party may be seeking a fundamental or radical restructuring of the relationship, in others only a small modification or reform. Since the structure of the relationship is part of a larger social system, any major restructuring also depends upon the involvement of third parties. Basic changes in the relations between students and administrators, between the American and Soviet governments, or between white American segregationists and black American integrationists have depended in part upon the positions taken by other parties.

A different dimension of magnitude pertains to either the alteration of personnel in or removal of personnel from the other side. That is, a conflict party may seek to make the other side's members more attentive and responsive, or it may seek to displace and replace them. The "other side" may refer to an entire social unit or to its leaders. In the event that the other side is an entire unit, its removal means either genocide or withdrawal in the form of cessation of relations. A genocidal outcome requires extraordinary power differences and widespread and intense hostile feelings (Fein 1979). A cessation outcome requires the ability to move or to secede, or sufficient indifference by the other side for it to accept the termination of relations; such outcomes are rare in social conflicts. The displacement of the other side usually refers to a leadership segment of the opposing unit, not to the entire social unit which the leaders purport to represent. In a displacement the outcome may entail a simple exchange of incumbents and no alteration even in the basic relations between the conflict parties. That is, the "ins" may change places with the "outs" and not alter the meaning of being "in" and "out." The success in such exchanges depends upon the rules by which the turnover is accomplished and the relative capacities and skills of each side according to those rules.

At the other end of this dimension, a conflict party may seek more attentiveness and responsiveness to its claims; this is generally more easily attained than the removal of the opposition. Gaining more responsiveness means an outcome that includes compromises or conversions, and the outcome may well have mutually beneficial qualities for all adversaries. Withdrawal, in the sense that the conflict party drops its demands for change and returns to the status quo ante, is, of course, another possible outcome. Responsiveness, entailing as it does conversion or compromise, is appropriately sought by persuasion or reward, offering the other side something that it wants in addition to coercion. Poor capacities in these ways lessen the chances of such outcomes.

Gamson (1975) studied a sample of fifty-three challenging groups, drawn from the several hundred groups that arose in the United States between 1800 and 1945. These groups sought to mobilize an unmobilized constituency and ranged from narrow reform groups to revolutionary groups. Gamson examined many characteristics of the groups and their protest strategy and related those characteristics to the groups successes: Did they gain the advantages they sought and did they win minimal acceptance? For our purposes here, his analysis of the varying success of different magnitudes of goals is particularly relevant.

He compared the success of groups that did and did not seek to displace their antagonists, single-issue and multiple-issue groups, and groups that had limited or more-than-limited goals. Gamson found that the goal variation that was most clearly related to success or failure was whether or not the challenging group sought to displace its antagonists. Nondisplacing groups were much more likely than others to gain acceptance (62 percent compared to 12 percent) and more likely to gain new advantages (68 percent compared to 6 percent).

A final aspect of the magnitude of the goal being sought warrants notice. It is generally easier to prevent an adversary from doing something it has not yet done than to make it stop doing something it has started. Blechman and Kaplan (1978) examined many cases in which the U.S. military force was more likely to be effective in preventing another government from doing something than in making it change policy by stopping what it was already doing. In general, it is easier to induce an adversary to continue current conduct than to modify its behavior.

Modes

Coercive, rewarding, and persuasive inducements are blended together in a variety of ways as each partisan group struggles to attain its objectives. The interaction of these blendings constitute the conflict mode. How effective a particular package of inducements and conflict mode is for each group trying to attain its objectives varies with the goals and resources as well as with other circumstances of the adversaries.

In this section we concentrate on comparing the effectiveness of coercive and noncoercive inducements for relative gains in distributive outcomes. This comparison requires giving some attention to many important aspects of social conflicts: the multiplicity of goals, the joint as well as distributive aspects of conflict outcomes, the persuasive and reward inducements that are blended with coercion, and, the interaction of the adversaries' conflict means. In specific fights, a variety of partisans within each adversary group use a blend of inducements for diverse purposes (Katz and Hunt 1979). The outcome may not be the one sought by any of the antagonists, or it may combine disparate gains and losses and joint effects for the adversaries. Thus, in the late 1960s university student demonstrations and nonviolent coercive actions were conducted to end military recruitment on campuses. The persuasive elements in the protests were often attended to, as well as the coercive. The outcome was often a compromise in the form of ending special privileges to military recruiters; they would have to share the same relatively inconspicuous locations as private recruiters using the student placement centers (Morgan 1970). The ghetto riots of the 1960s, while bringing some governmental attention to the plight and dissatisfactions of American blacks, probably did not increase the general social status of blacks as a category in the United States. For several decades a growing proportion of whites in America acknowledged that Negroes had as much native intelligence as whites (Schwartz 1967; Sheatsley 1966), but this movement showed some signs of possible disruption in the 1960s. In a series of surveys conducted in 1963, 1966, and 1967, whites were asked if they tended to agree or disagree with a variety of statements about Negroes. The proportion agreeing with derogatory statements about Negroes decreased slightly from 1963 to 1966 but then increased to above the 1963 level in 1967 (Erskine 1967–1968, p. 666). (See Table 6.1.)

Violent and nonviolent coercion can be effective by raising the costs for the adversary of not yielding what is being demanded. The use of certain kinds of violence and nonviolence may also demonstrate intensity of feeling, commitment, and readiness to suffer losses oneself in order to win. But, as our discussion of escalation indicated, violence may also stiffen resistance by the adversary. Coercion and especially violence have significant implications for distributive out-

TABLE 6.1   Proportion of American Whites Agreeing with Various Statements about American Negroes, 1963, 1966, 1967

Statement about Negroes Compared to Whites	1963	1966	1967
Negroes have less native intelligence	39	36	47
Negroes have less ambition	66	65	70
Negroes have looser morals	55	50	58

Source: Louis Harris and Associates national surveys as reported in Erskine, 1967–1968, p. 666.

comes because of their impact on nonfocal parties. Some kinds of coercive actions tend to expand the coalition of adversaries as well as to loosen it. If coercive action or violence appears to violate law or social conventions, the target of those violations may gather support from bystanders. This situation is more obviously the case when a target group can induce the state and its organized means of violence to suppress the party's resorting to nonviolent or violent coercion.

Conflict parties that can most readily call upon the state's organized means of violence generally will have greater coercive and violent sanctions to employ. Thus, groups challenging state authorities or groups representing important established interests will be overwhelmed if they resort to violence. Violent uprisings against authorities often result in many deaths among those conducting the uprisings, and their demands are effectively withdrawn. In civil strife those in authority are generally much more powerful and have access to much more violent and nonviolent means of coercion than are those who rise against them domestically. Coercive action, even in the form of strikes, can be met with overwhelming force and set back the organizational efforts of the protesting groups. This type of action and reaction has been the history of trade union efforts in the United States during the nineteenth century and even the beginning of the twentieth century (Taft and Ross 1969). In this sense, violence is counterproductive—especially for the weaker party. In the longer run, however, the revelation of the other side's brutality and the creation of martyrs may help solidify the weaker party. Furthermore, for relatively excluded groups, coercive unruliness is often necessary to win attention and responsiveness from powerful antagonists.

Under certain conditions, moreover, highly repressive action by government forces outrage bystanders and nonfocal parties and prove counterproductive for the ostensible purposes. The conflict party that uses coercion to triumph over the adversary may then find that other parties effectively prevent it from attaining the desired outcome, although the adversary has been defeated in the struggle. Thus, in universities, when police force was ultimately used to suppress student protest, very substantial concessions were made to the students. In those universities at which as high magnitudes of coercion were not reached, the concessions often were less. Thus, too, the widespread popular outrage at the use of violent means in suppressing nonviolent civil rights demonstrations in Selma, Alabama, in 1965 contributed greatly to passing the Voting Rights Act of 1965. Sharp (1973) uses the term *political jiu-jitsu* to refer to the use of such processes by practitioners of nonviolent action. He writes, "By combining nonviolent discipline with solidarity and persistence in struggle, the nonviolent actionists cause the violence of the opponent's repression to be exposed in the worst possible light. This in turn may lead to shifts in opinion and then to shifts in power relationships favorable to the nonviolent group" (p. 657).

Several studies have tried to assess the role of coercion and of violent and nonviolent coercion by challenging groups. Piven and Cloward (1978) examined movements of the unemployed and of unorganized workers in the United States in the 1930s and the civil rights and the national welfare rights movements of the

1960s. They argue that the disruptions and threat of greater disorder were effective means to gain the small and immediate advantages the people in the movements won. But others have argued that the gains in welfare programs are better explained by increases in the capability of providing welfare programs, by changes in the norms about social welfare obligations, and by variations in the need for social welfare provisions (Gronbjerg 1977). Probably the large-scale forces set the guidelines within which disruptive actions can have impact (Wilensky 1975).

Some systematic comparative analyses have been made of the effectiveness of different means of seeking gains by subordinated groups. Gamson's (1975) previously cited analysis of challenging groups found that groups using violent or nonviolent coercive tactics were more likely to gain acceptance than groups that did neither to gain new advantages. However, weak groups that threatened violence suffered repression from those they sought to displace. Furthermore, an examination of Gamson's findings reveals that nonviolent coercive tactics are as successful as violent ones.

Other studies have been made of the use of violence in industrial strikes. Shorter and Tilly (cited in Snyder and Kelly 1976) found evidence that in France strikes in which workers engaged in violence were more likely to be successful than were nonviolent strikes. Snyder and Kelly (1976) examined over six thousand strikes in Italy between 1878 and 1903. They were able to examine the degree to which many different factors contributed to the success of strikes and test the possibility that the success due to violence was really the consequence of other factors that themselves were associated with strike violence and victories. Thus, they found that "strikes were more likely to end favorably for workers when they were large in size, involved offensive demands which were not union related, and occurred over multiple issues" (p. 159). Taking these variables into account, they found that violent strikes, especially ones involving violence by workers against police, were much more likely to *fail* than were work stoppages without violence.

Obviously, one cannot say that violence is or is not effective. After all, violence is often mutual, and, in the nature of distributive outcomes, one party will appear to lose and another to gain by the recourse to violence. Furthermore, this discussion has not dealt with joint gains and losses in the conflict outcomes nor with long-term indirect consequences. We will consider the latter in Chapter 8.

The extent to which conflicts are regulated also tends to affect conflict outcomes. The more regulated the means of conflict employed, the more likely is the outcome to encompass compromise. Holsti (1966) analyzed seventy-seven major international conflicts between 1919 and 1939 and between 1945 and 1965. Using his categorizations of settlement attempts and outcomes, it is possible to analyze the differences in outcomes associated with different attempts (see Table 6.2). In fourteen of the seventy-seven conflicts, there were no settlement attempts—the two sides battled it out; not surprisingly, the outcomes were conquest or annexation (64 percent of the conflicts) or forced submission, withdrawal, or deterrence (36 percent of the conflicts). In the fourteen conflicts in which there were only bilateral talks or an effort at a settlement limited to the adversaries themselves, forced submission, withdrawal, or deterrence were particularly likely (36 percent of the cases); conquest or annexation was another relatively frequent outcome (29 percent of the cases). Equally frequent were outcomes that entailed withdrawals, but relatively voluntary ones, passive settlements in which both sides begin to accept the new situation as legitimate, or frozen ones in which both sides still had their incompatible goals but did not pursue them. In forty-nine of the seventy-seven conflicts there was third party intervention in the form of mediation, adjudication, involvement of international organizations, or multilateral conferences. In these cases, forced submission, withdrawal, or deterrence was relatively rare; conquest or annexation was also not very frequent. In 20 percent there were voluntary withdrawals, passive understandings, or frozen outcomes. Compromise and awards were relatively common, as shown by 23 percent each.

Power Differences

The major determinant of the outcome of a social conflict might seem to be the differences in power between the two parties. But several considerations limit the significance of this obviously important factor. First, in any concrete pursuit of conflicting goals, coercion is mixed with persuasion and rewards. Power differences are particularly relevant to coercion; in the case of persuasion and rewards, other resources determine their effectiveness. Thus, parties may differ in persuasive skills, and these differences affect the outcome. Depending on the mode used in pursuing conflicting aims, such skills may help compensate for weaker power positions.

Second, power is always relative to the point of its application. Nearly all kinds of power dissipate as they are extended. A group defending itself against a distant antagonist need not have equal total forces to sustain itself against the antagonist.

TABLE 6.2   Outcomes   of   International   Conflicts,   1919 – 1965,   by
Settlement Attempts

| | Settlement Attempts | | |
| | | Bilateral | Third |
Outcomes	None	Only	Party
Conquest, annexation	64	29	20
Forced submission,			
withdrawal, deterrence	36	36	14
Passive settlement	—	14	—
"Frozen" conflicts	—	—	6
Withdrawal-avoidance	—	7	14
Awards	—	—	23
Compromise	—	14	23
Totals, percent	100	100	100
(N)	(14)	(14)	(49)

Source: Based upon data from Holsti 1966.

The nature of the forces, the intervening space, and the technologies involved all affect the rate at which power is dissipated. Guerrilla bands may be able to hold a small territory if the terrain is inhospitable to the adversary's superior forces (Gurr 1970, pp. 262–263). In a small country that is covered by extensive means of ground transportation, a contemporary army can suppress dissident bands more readily than in an economically underdeveloped nation with rugged terrain, viz., the success of the Israeli armed forces against Arab Palestinian armed units trying to operate in Israeli-occupied territory (O'Neill 1978).

Power is also relative to the issue in contention; this is true in a few senses. Power and coercion may be appropriate for some goals and not for others, and if one side is seeking to convert another, power differences may be irrelevant. It should be obvious that love is not to be forced and hence a conflict party usually says it is not seeking love, perhaps because that is unattainable by the methods it restricts itself to use.

Issues differ in significance to each party in a conflict. The more important a goal is to one side compared to another, the more it is ready to absorb coercion from the adversary and to expend its resources to coerce the enemy; this nullifies, to some extent, the adversary's superior power. Very often one party's goal of autonomy is more vital to it than is the other party's desire for dominance over it. A group may be willing to make a proportionately greater sacrifice to sustain itself as a collective entity or to maintain self-control over its members' lives than would another group to impose upon them. This relative willingness to sacrifice is one reason why groups struggling for autonomy may be able to attain much of their goal even against what seem to be stronger forces.

This ability is related to the phenomenon of the "strength of weakness" (Schelling 1960, p. 22). A weak party may have few alternatives, and this not only gives it the strength of desperation but also has a compelling quality to its adversary when the terminating efforts are made. The stronger party may well recognize that the weaker has no retreat open to it, and that makes its aims seem more invulnerable. A weaker party may ultimately defy the stronger to use its forces and inhibit it from doing so because of the unfairness of such conduct. This does presume normative constraints; but these constraints may be held by the stronger parties' constituency and may deter the leaders even if their own norms were not constraining. U.S. leaders found such limits in waging war in Vietnam and French leaders in fighting in Algeria.

The significance of power differences in determining the outcome of a conflict, finally, is mitigated by the effectiveness with which each side organizes and applies its force. Herein lies the importance of strategy for applying coercion against a particular adversary as well as the importance of ideology in mobilizing one's own side and disorganizing the adversary. Analysis can develop measures of power difference that incorporate some indicators of effective application of force. Lammers (1969) studied strikes and mutinies; he rated the relative strength of the adversaries by assessing each side's degree of participation, degree of agreement among the leaders, and degree of clarity of strategy. He found that the greater the relative strength of the strikers, the speedier and more completely did they attain their goals; the correlation was .51 for strikers and somewhat smaller, .43, for mutineers. Presumably in the case of mutinies other aspects of relative power were more important but unmeasured by the indicators used.

Despite these limitations and qualifications, power differences very significantly determine the outcome of conflicts. From their analysis of major international crises between 1898 and 1973, Snyder and Diesing (1977) concluded that "the outcome of a crisis reflects pretty closely the 'inherent bargaining power' of the parties that derives essentially from the relative valuation of their interests and their relative disutility for war or the risk of war" (p. 498).

In general, we expect that the greater the power differences, the more likely is the outcome to be (1) withdrawal in the sense that relations are terminated, or (2) domination, even to the point that the defeated party dissolves as an orgainized partisan. Neither of these may be the sought-for goal of the stronger party. The totality of victory can alter the defeated in ways unforeseen by the victor. Thus, overwhelmingly powerful groups may so repress the defeated that they turn to religious or drug-aided ideologies that are overtly accommodating but covertly hostile (Smelser 1963, pp. 327ff). For example, Slotkin (1956) describes American Indian responses to the whites in the form of the peyote religion.

Extreme power differences almost invite domination and repression as an outcome once conflict behavior has escalated to intense forms. The victor may impose retributions and punishments that are not checked by the defeated and go beyond the initial aims of the victor.

Presumably, when the power differences are not extreme, the outcome is more likely to be a compromise than an imposition. Conversion is also likely in the form of new common values and rules. The new norms tend to reflect the interests and concerns of both sides and to be shared. When the power differences are great, the imposed outcome may also yield conversions, but they are likely to be either one sided or unshared. The defeated may come to accept the victor's values and norms, or the defeated may develop their own values and norms that are not shared with the victor.

Jensen (1965) studied disarmament negotiations of the United States and the Soviet Union between 1947 and 1960. He related the concessions and retractions of concessions each side made to confidence in military capabilities and to popular confidence that war would be avoided. He concluded that concessions were most likely when one side had a slight lack of confidence and there was almost parity between them.

The importance of power differences in determining a conflict outcome depends on other aspects of the conflict, particularly the rules that govern its conduct. Institutionalization often tends to equalize adversaries' strength, but the formality of institutionalized negotiations may inhibit the interpersonal bonds that would lessen the impact of unequal power. There is experimental evidence that the stronger party is more likely to win bargaining sessions in relatively formal settings than in less formal ones (Morley and Stephenson 1969), indicating that interpersonal factors can mitigate the full effects of having a stronger case.

Allies

The fourth set of factors that help determine the outcome of a conflict is the involvement of bystander parties as allies. Insofar as one party can garner support from previously uncommitted groups, it has a better chance of gaining the outcome it seeks. Allies increase its strength, persuasive resources, and even capacity to reward adversaries. Before considering the ways in which allies help determine the outcome of a conflict, we must acknowledge some of the ambiguities about the distinction between active partisans and allies.

As our discussions of the interlocking character of all social conflicts reveal, the boundaries of partisan groups are not sharp and the groups may disagree about where the boundaries are. Even in international conflicts, ethnic or ideological ties cross political borders and are the basis of cleavege. Furthermore, the degree of involvement is multidimensional and infinitely graduated.

To illustrate, consider the many partisans in the conflicts pertaining to the Vietnam War between 1964 and 1974: the U.S. government, the North Vietnamese government, the South Vietnamese government, the National Liberation Front, and the U.S. "peace movement," to cite a few. In a sense the U.S. government in the form of the Johnson administration was "defeated"; but who was the adversary and who was the ally of the adversary? Did the peace movement defeat the Johnson administration with the assistance of the North Vietnamese government and the National Liberation Front? Or, did the peace movement aid the North Vietnamese government and the National Liberation Front? These could well seem to be merely choices in perspective. A more substantive matter is raised by asking whether the peace movement contributed at all to the defeat of the Johnson administration or actually helped sustain it by provoking countermovements to its demands. The defeat of the Johnson administration, in that case, would be attributed to events in the international sphere and particularly in South Vietnam, events which the leaders of the peace movement accurately assessed but did not affect.

Such questions can hardly be answered in any particular conflict. We consider them here to sensitize us to the complexities of the possible role of allies in a conflict. Rather than seek to assess the role of different factors in determining a particular outcome, we wish to understand the major processes and tendencies in terminating conflicts and shaping outcomes. We now turn to those general tendencies.

The involvement of allies is necessary to attain certain kinds of outcomes. Leaving aside the relativity of power to the issue in contention, if power differences are great, the weaker can impose its aims or attain a compromise only if strong parties become allies. For example, Lammers (1969), in his study of strikes and mutinies, found that intervention was correlated with outcome; outcome was measured by the speed and degree to which the aided party, whether mutineers or strikers, attained its ends. In the case of mutinies, the correlation between intervention and realization of goals was high, .67; it was much lower in the case of strikes, .18. Without outside intervention, mutineers have little chance of winning. For most of the issues about which workers strike, outside intervention is not necessary for the union to attain its aims. Workers cannot, however, attain goals of large magnitude without alliances. Thus, the major shifts in worker-management relations, as occurred in general union recognition or worker participation in management, needed outside assistance. This was the case in the United States with the New Deal of the 1930s and with the Communist party in Yugoslavia in the establishment of worker control in Yugoslav factories after World War II.

The importance of outside intervention in determining the outcome of a conflict makes it desirable to understand what affects the choices of possible allies. Each tries to win others to its own side. Outside parties make their choices in terms of their own assessments of their relations with the primary adversaries and their own preferences for possible outcomes that would occur with or without their intervention.

Answers to questions about the choices of allies can draw from the burgeoning theoretical and empirical studies of coalitions and alliances (Groennings, Kelley, and Leiserson 1970; Riker 1962; Friedman, Bladen, and Rosen 1970). It is impossible to summarize here all the ideas and findings from these studies. We mention those that are particularly relevant to our present concerns. Coalition theory usually begins with parties that could form any possible coalition. In the present context, there are contending adversaries who are not potential coalition partners. Nevertheless, three major sets of considerations affect the parties' choices in forming a coalition at the beginning or at the end of a conflict: (1) the distribution of power resources among the contending parties and possible allies, (2) the preferences of each party for alternative outcomes, and (3) the particular ties connecting the parties and the context of the outcome.

A primary focus of attention in coalition theory and studies is the distribution of power among the parties. How much does each party have and how much is needed to win? Let us consider three parties, A, B, and C; suppose A is stronger than B, B is equal to C, but B and C together are stronger than A. The theories of Caplow (1968) and Gamson (1961) predict that BC would be the most likely coalition. Hence, if A and B were adversaries, C would join B; if A and C were adversaries, then B would join C; and if B and C were adversaries, it is indeterminate whether A would join B or C. The reasoning is as follows: Weaker parties would ally themselves if they could win because each would then benefit more than each would if allied with a much stronger party. This possible advantage makes the weaker party attractive as an ally if its contribution is sufficient to help form a winning coalition. Experimental evidence is consistent with this reasoning (Chertkoff 1970). To illustrate, a strong university administration and a weak faculty group make a faculty-student alliance more likely than if the faculty were at least as strong as the administration. For example, the weakness of the faculty group at Columbia University contributed to the isolation of administrators and an outcome that lessened adminstration authority (Cox Commission 1968).

The second set of considerations pertains to the substance of the issue in contention and the preferences of each party for possible outcomes. This may be conceptualized as the payoffs in coalition theory, wherein the winning coalition divides the spoils of victory. We may presume that the value of the spoils is the same for all parties, and in simple consensual conflicts it may be the same for power or material benefits. In actual conflicts, however, possible outcomes have different and changing values to the parties. For example, the women's suffrage movement was able to obtain more allies among males after World War I by arguing in terms of fairness and justice and pointing to the contribution women made to the war effort (Flexner 1959). For those males who allied themselves with the cause, many supported women's right to vote at least partly because they believed it was right and not merely expedient in terms of political power calculations. Or, consider support for increasing the right for legal abortions. Feminist groups have urged the legalization of abortion under specified conditions. Although until the mid-1960s there was almost universal opposition to extending the grounds for legal abortions, support for such extensions was slightly greater among men than women, according to national surveys (Blake 1971). Moreover, the segment of the population most likely to support legalized abortion was college-educated non-Catholic men. As Blake points out, upper-class men had little to lose and much to gain by easing legal restrictions against abortion. They were satisfied with small families, their sexual freedom was not curtailed, and they suffered no risks; on the other hand, women (and less-advantaged persons generally) derived their greatest rewards from their families, and, therefore, norms that seem to uphold the institution would be supported.

Third, particular ties linking each party and its possible allies and the general context of the conflict strongly affect which side an outsider would choose. All else being equal, an outside party would ally itself with the partisan group with which it is already most friendly or least hostile. This is analogous, then, to "balance theory" (Taylor 1970, pp. 288–93). In specific conflicts, according to this theory, ideological commonalities, interpersonal friendships, general cooperative relations in other contexts, all may help determine alliances. For example, the various liberation groups of the 1960s tended to ally themselves with one another and constitute a movement (Leahy and Mazur 1978).

The ties may be indirect and arise from the preferences that bring outside parties closer to one of the adversaries. Thus, Wences and Abramson (1970) found that University of Connecticut faculty members, by means of longer residence and common interests with the local community, tended to oppose the promotion of dissent and not oppose on-campus military recruiting, compared to newly arrived faculty. Presumably, newly arrived faculty would tend to ally themselves with student dissidents more than would faculty with longer local residence.

The context within which the parties view the conflict also affects the coalitions formed. This is true in part because the context indicates other possible ties. Thus if the conflict is among parties with common interest against an external power, an alliance of a weak and a strong partner is likely, but if the conflict is among the parties themselves, the two weaker groups will join together (Chertkoff 1966; 1970). We may refer back to the earlier illustration. If A is stronger than B, B equals C, and B and C together are stronger than A, then the coalition of BC is most likely. If there is an external threat, however, then in a conflict between A and C, B might well join A rather than C in order to form a stronger front against the external adversary. This last alliance may help explain a faculty's siding with its administration against students when a university is threatened externally.

Outside parties are not merely potential and then actual partisans. Their intervention and active involvement is much more complex than making a simple choice of sides. Their intervention changes the dimensions of the conflict and the possible payoffs for all parties. As the previous discussion indicated, outside parties have their own interest and these affect their conduct in any given conflict. If the outside party is sufficiently powerful relative to the contestants, it may be able to impose its terms upon the contending parties. The outcome of the 1956 war between Egypt and Israel illustrates this. The withdrawal of Israeli forces from the Sinai and Gaza and the stationing of U.N. forces along the cease-fire line and at Sharm el Sheikh were the results largely of U.S. and U.N. pressure and persuasion (Campbell 1960, pp. 108–120).

NONCONFLICT DETERMINANTS OF OUTCOMES

It might seem reasonable to suppose that the outcome of a conflict is determined by the struggle itself. But the relations between adversaries are affected by many factors and processes that have existed before and during and will exist after any specific conflict. The outcome of a conflict is affected by other factors than those we have analyzed in accounting for a social conflict's trajectory. We shall review only a few here: the general level of resources, the alternatives available, and the social context.

Resources

Many particular outcomes depend upon the availability of resources for their implementation. Without needed preconditions certain outcomes cannot be attained or maintained. Once those preconditions exist, goals that might otherwise be conflicting may be attained with little controversy and by institutionalized conflict behavior, including regular political processes. For example, Cutright (1965) studied the introduction of social security programs in seventy-six nations. He found that the level of social security programs was very highly correlated with the level of economic development. Wilensky (1975) found similar results in a later study. Numerous studies have been made of income equality in different countries, and here too a strong relationship has been found between a country's level of economic development and income equality (Kriesberg 1979). Of course, many different linkages connect the level of ecomonic development with these outcomes, and many factors in addition to the level of development affect them particularly among the relatively economically advanced countries. But struggles for welfare programs or for increased economic equality seem to be more success-ful when the resources are less constraining for their attainment.

Alternatives

The outcome of any specific struggle is affected by the alternatives each party has and by each party's efforts to change the other, particulary when the conflicting goals pertain to the members of the conflict parties as aggregates. Their bearing on the outcome can be seen in the profound effects that changes in the general employment rate, occupational distribution, or technology have had upon the relative income, status, and power of American workers and managers, of blacks and whites, and of women and men. For example, the growing participation of women in the labor force is in part due to changes in occupational distribution, namely, the increased proportion of white collar jobs. Large short-term variations have been due to such major shifts in the availability of men for employment as during World War II when women's participation rose rapidly, only to fall precipitously at the end of the war. Similarly, the proportion of women making up the college classes increased rapidly during the war, as men left and as the colleges' need for paying students also grew (Millett 1970, p. 76).

Social Context

Any specific conflict between parties is embedded in a larger set of social relations, which may have the effect of interfering with the attainment of particular goals. Within a given social context, certain sets of goals are inconsistent. For example, there are incompatible components in the aims of racial integration and black separatism, and it is difficult for most women to play all the same occupational roles as men, while the nuclear family and the division of labor within it is structured so differently for men and women (Millett 1970, p. 158). Similarly, there are contradictory implications in workers' being subordinate employees and a constituency's electing or otherwise directing higher management (Strauss and Rosenstein 1970; Kolaja 1966).

All this means that there are limits to reaching any particular goal. It may not be attainable without reordering other aspects of the social context. In some cases such reordering must be massive and fundamental. Unless such changes are made, the specific goal will not be achieved regardless of efforts. Of course, there may be a variety of partial attainments and successes among some segments of a population for certain periods of time. The point is that the outcome of any specific struggle is constrained by a variety of interrelations between roles and social patterns. It is not determined by the contending parties within the confines of their struggle as they define it.

ILLUSTRATIVE OUTCOMES

The actual outcome of a conflict is the result of many forces outside of the struggle itself and of the interaction among all aspects of the conflict process—the goals, modes of conflict behavior, power differences, and allies. We will consider the combined effect of all these factors when we examine the outcomes of the major conflicts we have been considering throughout the book—those between workers and managers, blacks and whites, men and women, governments and revolutionaries, the United States and the Soviet Union, and Israel and the neighboring Arab countries. We will not focus upon the outcomes of limited specific struggles; rather, we will look at information about changes in the relative position of contending groups and discuss the variety of forces that resulted in those outcomes.

Workers–Managers

Changes in the position of workers relative to managers as aggregates and as collectivities warrant attention. Evidence pertaining to the possibility of labor militancy and trade union activity as a factor in the changes is especially noted.

Workers as an Aggregate. One aspect of changes in the position of workers as an aggregate is the extent to which they leave the category and enter the superordinate group. Mobility into the managerial stratum is not an avowed major goal of trade unions or of labor groups generally. Such social aims for the society as a whole seem to presume more ideological goals than the American workers have shown. Nevertheless, the wish for equality of opportunity, generally voiced in American society, does exist among workers and their leaders. Improvements in the relative position of workers presumably should ease their mobility out of the stratum, even if the improvements might reduce the pressure to seek movement out of the stratum. In any case, there is evidence that over the last three generations before 1950, the business elite drawn from the worker stratum has increased slightly; although even in 1950, only 15 percent of the business elite had fathers who were manual workers (Warner and Abegglen 1955, p. 66; Keller 1963, p. 307). Presumably the general increase in the standards of life of workers makes more of their children available for recruitment into the managerial stratum. Whether or not the trade union efforts contributed to that general increase of the workers' conditions is less clear (Kriesberg 1979, pp. 393–398).

Do trade union efforts redound to the benefit of all workers or only union members? It might be argued that this is a false question; whatever helps one helps the other. Undoubtedly there is a positive relationship between the two, but the relationship is not always perfect. Part of the issue here is the extent of unionization. Given the degree of unionization in different industries, trade unions have had little impact upon the relative inequality of wages among all workers—about 6 percent. This is the net effect of increased inequality among industries and decreased inequality within industries (Lewis 1963, pp. 292–295).

Workers as a Collectivity. The primary goals of trade unions have been to improve their members' working conditions and to raise their wages. Undoubtedly, unions have led to improved working conditions in several ways. First, security against arbitrary firing and protection against harassment by supervisory personnel have been gained. Through the union, workers have some group control over the pace of work and the organization of work activities, although the extent of such control varies by industry and trade union. The union effort has played an important role in introducing such worker autonomy and promoting its extension, so that it now exists to some extent even in factories that are not unionized.

The impact of unions upon the wages of union members has been extensively studied by economists. Studies of particular industries and of the American economy as a whole indicate that unionized workers earn higher wages than nonunionized workers, but the differences vary considerably, depending upon a number of conditions. As Lewis (1963, p. 194) concludes, in the early 1930s unionism may have raised the relative wages of union workers by more than 23 percent. Unionism had little effect during the inflation following World War II, however, and later it may have raised the relative wages of union labor by about 7 to 11 percent. Ashenfelter and Johnson (1972) reviewed recent data, and, controlling for differences in personal quality, they estimated the impact of unionism to range generally between 16 to over 30 percent. Market forces as well as conflict behavior cause the differences.

Although manual workers as a whole are not organized in conflict groups in the form of trade unions, there has been a general increase in the material well being of workers in an absolute sense. Trade union activity has helped the development of worker autonomy within the work place. Such changes in the condition of workers might be reflected in a raised status of manual workers in general. There is evidence of a small change of this sort. Hodge, Siegel, and Rossi (1966) compared the prestige of many occupation's assessed in 1947 and 1963. They found that blue collar work in general and particularly dead-end jobs had increased in general prestige more than had white-collar work.

Given the modest goals of most trade unions, they have made some progress toward their realization, if assessed over a period of a few decades. More fundamental changes in the structure of the economy, the role of workers in it, and income differentials between workers and managers were not sought by most trade unions and did not occur.

College and university-based student conflicts of the 1960s were largely directed at collective goals. Although students have been engaged in conflicts about community, national, and international issues, we restrict this discussion to outcomes of struggles within colleges and universities. Some conflicts were about the role of the university in national and neighborhood affairs. For example, university investment policies and research activities were disputed as was university expansion displacing poor people in the surrounding area. Some issues pertained to academic matters, such as the relevance or irrelevance of courses and study programs and the mode of teaching and grading. Another set of issues pertained to living conditions on college and university campuses, for example, regarding dormitory rules.

By the end of the 1960s significant changes in these areas had occurred on campuses throughout the country. In dormitories rules regarding hours for checking in, the right to have visitors of the opposite sex in the room, and the drinking of alcohol were broadened or eliminated. Informal permissiveness of rule violations became widespread (Young 1972). There were also significant changes in the curriculum and even grading procedures; special programs in black studies and new courses on women in society and on environmental pollution were added to the curriculum on many campuses. Flexibility in the requirements for graduation also increased, allowing students more course alternatives. In addition, in many schools work done outside of the classroom in an intern capacity was accorded academic credit, and courses given in whole or in part under student leadership were accepted for academic credit. Overall, too, there was an inflation of grades; "A" and "B" were awarded more frequently. Finally, schools increasingly found alternatives to the simple grading of each student in each course. One alternative allowed students to choose to take a course on a pass or fail basis. By the end of the 1970–1971 academic year, about three-fourths of the institutions of higher learning utilized to some degree the pass-fail grade as an option (*The New York Times,* June 7, 1971).

Student claims about the direction of institutional policies in the neighborhood and nationally were not as clearly incorporated in outcomes. Yet, the general direction of change was that urged by student protestors. Several institutions of higher learning had research-affiliated organizations that engaged in research under contract with the armed services; some of these affiliations were terminated. The recruitment activities of the armed services were often made to conform to the same procedures as recruitment by private companies.

Fundamentally, students gained a more direct voice in the management of college and university affairs, particularly as it pertained to internal affairs. Thus, responses to a questionnaire mailed in September 1969 indicated that students participated on the board of trustees of 20 percent of the institutions, 3 percent on a voting basis; in 58 percent of the institutions students participated in faculty curriculum committees, 46 percent as voting members (McGrath 1970, p. 170). In only 5 percent of the schools, however, did students have any participation on committees pertaining to faculty selection, promotion, and tenure.

These changes were certainly partly a result of the student protests of the 1960s. In many institutions student demonstrations sought to coerce a few of these changes. In many other institutions changes were introduced without widespread coercive action, indeed without much student demand, but in anticipation of possible demands. Perhaps administrative and faculty fears of student coercive actions hastened concessions not yet demanded or even widely considered by the bulk of students.

It would be an error, however, to regard all these changes as the product of a simple conflict between students and administrators and faculty in which coercion was the sole or even dominant way of changing the other side's position. First of all, to some degree the changes reflect ideas widely shared by the society; these are ideas that the students helped to formulate and are, at the same time, ideas from which they derived their thinking. Changed social conventions about prescribing and proscribing personal conduct, then, would encourage students to think they should have more autonomy in their private lives and would encourage faculty and administrators to believe so also. Undoubtedly, too, considerable mutual persuasion was attempted, and some of it succeeded. Heightened interaction may have reduced dissensus. The outcome, hence, had significant integrative, and not simply distributive, aspects. From the perspective of some students, however, the outcomes involved considerable co-optation (Oberschall 1978).

Some of these changes also reflect nonconflicting forces. Shifts in the general level of the economy and in the population of students have fostered changes in the curriculum in a kind of market response. That is, faculty and administrators, taking into account student interests, changed course offerings and ways of teaching and grading to maintain enrollment. In the later 1970s some practices have reverted to earlier patterns, more in curricular than extracurricular areas. This reflects both the lessening of pressure from students in struggles against faculty and administrators and the enduring changes from the conflict.

It is useful to compare, even briefly, these outcomes with those in European universities. In many universities in European countries, even more radical transformations occurred than in the United States so that students gained more power relative to faculty. In part, these changes may have been the consequence of more radical demands arising from previously more oppressive faculty-student relations. The power of the professor over students and junior faculty was great. In addition, the greater pervasiveness of Marxist thought among university students may have fostered more radical student goals. Furthermore, the professors had power over academic affairs, which in America often are in the control of administrators. The extracurricular supervision of American college students has fostered a large administrative component. When American students sought changes, they more directly confronted the administrators; the faculty at times could mediate and gain power at the expense of the administration. In European universities, clearer separation of responsibilities and a reduced administrative component meant that students could and would make direct claims against the faculty or senior professors. A gain in student autonomy and academic power would then come at the expense of the professors. Nevertheless, many universities and some institutes within the universities have changed little.

Since American blacks, in the 1960s, sought aggregate and collective goals, we will examine both kinds of outcomes. Demands by blacks for economic gains were generally for blacks in the aggregate. They were to have the same opportunities as whites in schools and in work settings, which would result in similar occupational distribution and income.

Educational attainment generally did increase during the 1960s and 1970s. The increase was at a higher rate among blacks than among whites, particularly at the precollege level, so that the gap closes somewhat (U.S. Bureau of the Census 1979). This was true during the 1970s as well as the 1960s. Occupational distribution also became somewhat more similar for whites and nonwhites, but the shift was most marked during the 1960s and was not as great during the 1970s. For example, the proportion of whites in professional and technical occupations was 10.8 in 1957, 12.1 in 1960, 14.8 in 1970, and 15.5 in 1975 and 1978; for blacks and others, the comparable percentages are: 3.7, 4.8, 9.1, 11.4, and 11.7.

Income differences between whites and nonwhites were little changed between 1950 and 1965; they became somewhat more equal in the later 1960s but then remained little changed. For example, the median income of nonwhite families as a percentage of the median income of white families was 54 percent in 1950, 55 percent in 1955, and 55 percent in both 1960 and 1965; it rose to 64 percent in 1970, was 65 percent in 1975, and fell to 61 percent in 1977.

The proportion of blacks below the poverty level, as defined by the Social Security Administration, fell from 56 percent in 1959 to 40 percent in 1966 and 31 percent in 1969, but then changed little. It was 29 percent in 1975 and in 1977. The poverty rate for whites was much less, but the pattern of change was similar. The proportion of whites below the poverty line was 18 percent in 1959; it fell to 11 percent in 1966, to 10 percent in 1969, remained at 10 percent in 1975, and was 9 percent in 1977.

These changes certainly reflect many social forces unrelated to the struggle waged by blacks, other minorities, and their white allies. Changes in technology, migration, and the level of economic activity had considerable impact on these outcomes. The outcomes also were partly a result of the conflicts waged, particularly in the latter 1960s, as is indicated by the sharpest changes in the indicators having occurred during that period. More specifically, Piven and Cloward (1978) argue that the expansion of the welfare rolls in the latter part of the 1960s was in response to the protests of blacks, the poor, and groups such as the National Welfare Rights Organization. Betz (1974) compared the financial support for welfare programs at the local level between cities that had riots during the 1960s with those that did not. He found that cities in which riots occurred had larger budgetary increases in welfare in the year after the riot than did cities in which there had been no riots. Durman (1974), however, found no relationship between riots and increased Families with Dependent Children (AFDC) cases and argued that increases in the number of eligible families explains the increased welfare rolls. Yet there is other evidence that expanded public assistance programs were at least partly a response to the disorders of the later 1960s (Piven and Cloward 1974; Rossi, Berk, and Edison 1974).

The passage of civil rights legislation and the establishment of programs for affirmative action in reponse to the coercive and persuasive efforts of the civil rights movement and organizations also have contributed to the outcomes (Williams 1977). The lack of continuing change in the 1970s, in some areas, indicates the strength of resistance, especially when conflict behavior is not sustained. It also reflects the limitations upon changes that the prevailing structures and past experiences impose. All the changes and failures to change interact with the collective aspects of the outcomes. Changes in status and power of blacks pertain more to collective than to aggregate goals. One indicator of the status of blacks is the opinion of whites. A minimal status is that whites accord the same rights to blacks as to whites. For example, they think it is proper for blacks to have equal civil rights, as answers to questions in national surveys conducted in 1964, 1968, and 1970 show (Campbell 1971). The percentage of whites saying Negroes have a right to live wherever they can afford to rose from 53 percent in 1964 to 65 percent in 1968 and 67 percent in 1970.

Increasing acknowledgment of the rights of blacks is not simply a response to the civil rights movement and the protests by blacks. There has been a constantly growing recognition of the legitimacy of the claims of blacks from as early as survey data on this point are available (Schwartz 1967). Furthermore, there is evidence that the support for governmental intervention to gain equal rights for blacks may have declined in the face of the most coercive actions. For example, the percentage of whites who said the government in Washington should see to it that white and Negro children are allowed to go to the same schools declined from 38 percent in 1964 to 33 percent in 1968 and rose to 41 percent in 1970 (Campbell 1971, p. 130). In the 1970s and 1980s opposition to particular programs to further integration and equality of opportunity arose. Groups opposed to busing in order to integrate public schools and groups opposed to affirmative action programs exemplify the emergence of new issues and social conflicts from the outcome of previous social conflicts.

The political power of blacks as a collectivity in American society is still minor considering their proportion in the population. Nevertheless, the last decades have seen important gains in the collective power of blacks, particularly at the community and city level. The changes are especially noteworthy in the South, where they reflect the changes in voting rights after the passage of the federal voting rights bill and the registration efforts of many organizations.

Growing numbers of blacks in urban centers and no easing of residential segregation (Farley and Taeuber 1968) provide one base for dissensus. The polarization of society between blacks and whites foreseen by the Kerner Commission could be the consequence of black efforts toward equality and the failure to realize those aims. Actually, there is no clear evidence that this polarization is occurring. Rather, there has been a growing acceptance of the rights of blacks. There seems to have been no dramatic change in feelings between the races even during the most intense periods of conflict behavior. It is discernible, however, that general feelings of approval of whites by blacks and of blacks by whites decreased slightly between 1968 and 1970 (Campbell 1971, Table 7.12). Nevertheless direct personal interaction between the races has not decreased, and personal friendships have even increased. This mixture of evidence is what one should expect about the results of many interlocking struggles in large-scale categories and organizations. All aspects of a struggle do not affect outcomes in the same direction.

We should also consider the effects of different modes of pursuing conflicting goals. Some of the changes in the 1960s seem to have involved conversion of whites, resulting from effective persuasion. There is evidence, for example, that between 1968 and 1971 the importance of equality as a value increased among whites (Rokeach 1974). Pluralist values that acknowledge the propriety of ethnic groups' exhibiting more autonomy may also have increased in salience. The emergence of such views is one way in which differences can be accepted without dissensual conflict and yet can reduce consensual conflicts. This is similar to norms of tolerance in religious conflicts and represents integrative solutions.

Females–Males

The conflict between men and women has involved only a small percentage of each group in overt partisan activities. But the struggle has also been conducted at a more individual level within places of work and study and in the home. The aims, from the perspective of the challenging group, women, have been largely consensual and perhaps more for aggregate goals than collective ones. We shall begin then, with a consideration of aggregate outcomes and review the evidence regarding occupational, educational, and income distribution of women compared to men.

As we noted in Chapter 2, women in the United States were less likely than men to have completed college and postcollege training, to occupy high-prestige occupations, or to earn as much as men, and these differences generally persisted from 1940 to the mid-1960s (Knudsen 1969). Since the mid-1960s, when women's rights organizations became active, some changes have been observable, but notable constants also exist.

Female participation in the labor force has risen markedly since the mid-1960s. In 1960, 35 percent of the female population was in the civilian labor force; in 1965, 37 percent were; in 1970, 43 percent; and in 1978, 49 percent (U.S. Bureau of the Census 1971; 1979). But, as can be seen in Table 6.3, the occupational distribution of women has not significantly changed. Women have remained particularly in clerical and service occupations, where men are much less likely to be employed. There has been a slight increase in the proportion of women in professional and technical occupations, but the increase was even greater among men. Women's earnings relative to men's also have not changed. In 1970 the

TABLE 6.3 Proportion of Women and Men in Selected Occupations, 1960–1978

Occupations	1960		1965		1970		1975		1978	
	Women	Men	Women	Men	Women	Men	Women	Men	Women	Men
Professional and technical	12.3	10.9	13.2	12.1	14.5	14.0	15.7	14.6	15.6	14.2
Managers and administrators	5.0	13.4	4.5	13.4	4.4	14.2	5.1	14.0	6.1	13.5
Clerical workers	30.2	7.2	31.8	7.1	34.5	7.1	35.1	6.9	34.6	6.2
Service workers	23.7	6.5	23.2	6.9	21.7	6.7	21.6	8.6	20.1	8.7

Source: U.S. Bureau of the Census 1979, p. 415.

median weekly earnings of full-time employed women was 62.2 percent of the median earnings of men; in 1975 it was 62.0 percent and in 1978, 61.0 percent.

As can be seen in Table 6.4, women have gradually been increasing their share of higher educational degrees. It was only in the 1970s, however, that the proportion exceeded that reached before World War II.

The collective status of women also has changed since the 1950s. The general acceptance of the propriety of women's holding public office and of working for pay outside the home has risen. For example, one similarly worded question has been asked in national surveys several times: "If your party nominated a woman for president, would you vote for her if she were qualified for the job?" As shown in Table 6.5, the percentage of men who said they would was very small in the 1930s and mid-1940s; it rose during the 1950s; and then rose substantially in the 1970s. Interestingly, women were less likely than men to say they would vote for a woman as president until the late 1950s but then led the men in their readiness to do so. In the late 1970s men and women were about equally likely to say they would. Attitudes about sex role segregation within the home also have changed. For example, a study of women interviewed in 1962, 1963, 1966, and 1977 found a tremendous shift toward more egalitarian attitudes (Thornton and Freedman 1979).

A dramatic shift seems to have occurred in another sphere. One issue that has been pursued by several groups within the women's movement has been the reduction or removal of restrictions regarding abortion. This cause has been

TABLE 6.4 Percentage of Bachelor's or First Professional Degree Awarded to Women by Year

1900	1930	1940	1950	1960	1965	1970	1975	1977
19.1	39.9	41.3	23.9	35.3	40.7	41.5	43.5	44.4

Sources: 1900–1965 adapted from Epstein 1970, pp. 57–58; 1970–1977, U.S. Bureau of the Census 1979, p. 168.

TABLE 6.5 Percentage of Men and Women Who Would Vote
for a Woman for President by Year

	Women	Men
1937	27	40
1945	29	37
1949	45	51
1955	47	57
1963	58	51
1967	61	53
1969	58	49
1975	75	71
1978	76	77

Sources: 1937–1969, Erskine 1971; 1975–1978, Gallup, 1978.

phrased in terms of a woman's right to control her own body. Until the mid-1960s there had been almost total popular opposition to liberalization of abortion policies (Blake 1971). But, the proportion of the population opposed to more liberal abortion policies has declined from 91 percent in 1965 to 85 percent in 1968, 79 percent in 1969, and to less than 50 percent in 1971 (*The New York Times,* October 28, 1971). Despite vigorous "right-to-life" campaigns against abortion, public opinion in support of legalizing abortion in the first three months of pregnancy continued to increase during the 1970s (de Boer 1977–1978).

Certainly, such changes cannot be attributed solely to the conflict behavior of groups within the women's movement. A variety of other forces are affecting the relative position of women and men and even the degree of dissensus between them. Nevertheless, it is also probable that the persuasive and coercive efforts of women's groups have affected the views many men have of women and reduced the degree of outright discrimination in public accommodations, employment, and legal rights (Rossi 1970). For example, the Civil Rights Act of 1964 prohibits discrimination based upon sex by employers of 25 or more employees. The proportion of men and women who favor "most of the efforts to strengthen and change women's status in society" increased in the 1970s from 42 percent in 1970 to 63 percent in 1975 (de Boer 1977).

In the 1970s and 1980s groups opposed to further extension of women's rights or even to the continuation of the changes already introduced became active. Countermovements to the enactment of the Equal Rights Amendment to the U.S. Constitution and to legalized abortion under nearly all circumstances emerged. Such reactions to the changes resulting from earlier conflicts are typical of the sequence of many struggles. As one movement and the organized groups that constitute it make gains against opposition, they arouse resistance from groups whose values or interests are seen to be attacked. New issues emerge and new conflicts arise from the outcome of the previous ones, in a continuing cycle of conflicts. Very often, nevertheless, there is a "ratchet effect" so that the gains by a social movement, even when under attack, do not slip back to where they started. The fights are renewed from a different starting ground.

Governments–Revolutionaries

Massive changes are the hallmark of revolutions. But we must ask why some revolutionary efforts have succeeded and others have failed. We can ask, more specifically, is the degree of revolutionary change dependent on the radical nature of the revolutionaries' goals and the extent of violence used? There is undoubtedly at least a moderate relationship among these variables. Some cases seem to fit well: The Russian Revolution of October 1917 did result in massive changes, and it was led by revolutionaries with radical objectives and was sustained through a civil war and extensive violence. The revolution in China, culminating in the Communist party's establishment of a new state and government in 1949, is another case that seems to fit. The steps toward revolutionary change that Salvador Allende began to introduce after he became president of Chile in 1970 might also be viewed as fitting the same pattern of relationship. The changes were to be carried out without violence, and they failed; the government of Allende was overthrown in 1974 by a military junta, led by General Pinochet. Considerable violent repression then followed. Other cases fit less well: The Mexican Revolution of 1910 led to major changes in the 1930s after years of turmoil, but the leadership was less radical and ideological than in Russia or China. Still other cases do not fit well for additional reasons. Sometimes massive changes have been introduced after a small radical revolutionary group has seized power through a coup, through imposition by a foreign power, or through limited fighting. Revolutionary change after World War II in countries such as Poland, Czechoslovakia, Vietnam, the German Democratic Republic (East Germany), Iran, Ethiopia, and Cuba illustrate variations in these regards. Fundamental change often occurs when alternative agencies begin functioning and people shift their loyalty and obedience to the new authorities undermining the legitimacy of the established state. This may happen concurrently with large-scale violence, but it can occur with little violence as well, as in national liberation struggles: Consider the nonviolent movement toward independence of India.

We focus here on social revolutions from below, considering both "successful" and "unsuccessful" revolutions. We first discuss some aspects of the outcomes and then examine how the elements discussed in this chapter help explicate why the outcomes took the shape they did.

It is worth considering the extent to which revolutionary struggles have integrative and distributive outcomes. Presumably, in a revolution the adversaries are locked in a struggle in which one side risks losing all to a challenging group. Yet, the contending parties are numerous and, depending on the outcome, different sets may gain at the expense of others. If a revolution is successful, one conflict party, or at least a segment of it, may cease to exist whether as persons or as a social category. For example, the large landowners may be abolished as a class, but many of them and their families may (or may not) survive and even join in the leadership or managerial elite of the new society.

In addition, possible joint losses and gains should not be overlooked. Revolutions involving large-scale violence are costly to all parties in the conflict. Such violence not only causes deaths and casualties to the persons in combat and others caught up in the fighting, but also disruption of the political, social, and economic order, which typically interferes with the provision of services and the production of goods so that the general well being of nearly everyone in the society suffers (Huntington 1968, pp. 309–312). For example, Skocpol (1979, p. 176), in her analysis of the 1789 French Revolution noted that French industries had been nourished by expanding foreign trade but that the trade collapsed as a result of the revolution and ensuing wars so that it did not regain its prerevolutionary levels until after 1815. A revolution often also produces a sense of pride and euphoria, which is likely to be shared by some groups that had not been initially active in the revolution, but would not include the disposed classes. We will consider the longer run consequences of revolutions for different groups and for the polity as a whole in Chapter 8.

We must also consider the distributive aspects of revolutionary outcomes: To what extent do the revolutionary parties overthrow the previously dominating groups and what determines that outcome? Once a revolutionary struggle has been entered, the relative coercive strength of adversary parties is critical. In the case of seizing state power, the military forces are crucial components of that coercive strength. One might think that since the state controls the military forces, the existing government can use the forces to repress revolutions. Obviously, this does not always occur. Sometimes the armed forces join the revolutionaries against the old government, and sometimes the armies dissolve as the government's authority wanes. Russell (1974) compared fourteen revolutions that began between 1911 and 1958. He found that armed force disloyalty was necessary for a successful outcome of rebellion. It is not, however, sufficient: In three cases, the revolutions were unsuccessful although the armed forces were disloyal to the regime (for example, Burma in 1954).

The armed forces are not simply an instrument of coercion. They constitute an organization that can replace the government organization. The internal cohesion and solidarity of the adversary parties are important elements in determining which conflict party will be able to capture and hold state power. The Bolsheviks in 1917 Russia were a relatively well organized party; adversary and competing parties were not as well organized and they lost.

The interlocking nature of conflicts is critical in effecting their outcome. Revolutionary groups with external bases of support are difficult to defeat and when external bases do not exist or are cut off, the revolutionary groups are likely to be defeated (Gross 1966). For example, Greek Communist rebels were defeated by the government when their base in Yugoslavia was lost following the Yugoslavian government's break with the Soviet government in 1948. Concurrent or external fighting significantly weakens the government forces and thus makes them vulnerable; we already noted that as a reason for the emergence of a revolutionary struggle (Skocpol 1979), and it is also a reason for its victory.

International

No comprehensive termination of the conflicts between the Soviet and American governments or among the Arabs and Israelis has occurred since 1948. But many particular fights in the series of interlocked fights have ended, some after armed conflict and some after protracted negotiations. In Chapter 5 we examined the 1962–1963 period of conflict deescalation and the conditions related to reaching an agreement about issues in contention between the Soviet and American governments. Here we will examine one deescalating movement and the negotiation of a peace treaty between two primary adversaries in the Middle East conflicts: the Egyptian and Israeli governments.

The visit of President Sadat to Jerusalem in November 1977 and the subsequent negotiations resulting in the Egyptian-Israeli Peace Treaty in 1979 mark a clear outcome (Kriesberg 1980). Several factors underlie President Sadat's decision to attempt a break with the past. The Egyptian military effort in 1973, although not an unqualified victory, demonstrated military prowess and the ability to inflict heavy damage and gain political fruits from war. Hence, a concession could appear to be coming from strength and equality and not from weakness and dishonor (Sadat 1978). The earlier Egyptian government's move away from reliance on the Soviet Union limited future military strength, and the U.S. government would not replace the Soviet Union as a military supplier without a demonstration of Egyptian willingness to make peace with Israel. Economic conditions in Egypt were extremely poor and even aid from the oil-rich Arab countries seemed inadequate, especially when tied to military preparedness to wage war against Israel. The U.S. government seemed more and more an essential source for assistance in developing the economy.

The underlying conditions for Israel had also changed since 1971. The costs of the 1973 war and the demonstration of the oil-producing Arab countries' power raised the specter of further costly wars and isolation, even from the United States. Consequently, Israeli dependence on the United States increased as did the importance of seeming reasonable and flexible to the U.S. government and public. The new Israeli government was led by a party and a leader who had always seemed particularly intransigent about making concessions. But that legacy gave the government some freedom of movement since the opposition was not likely to decry concessions that would make peace attainable (Avishai 1979). Moreover, the Likud and its coalition partners were particularly concerned with the West Bank for ideological and religious reasons, which were less significant for the Sinai.

The efforts of President Carter and his new administration to bring about a comprehensive settlement to the Middle East conflicts posed problems both for President Sadat and for the new Israeli government led by Prime Minister Begin.

The proposed Geneva conference would bring the Soviet government more actively into the conflict, which both disliked. In addition, for President Sadat, participation even indirectly by the PLO, by Syria, and by other hard-line Arab groups would put them in a veto position, restricting Egypt's freedom of movement. For the Israeli government, the participation of these groups at a Geneva conference would isolate it and might be a step toward recognition of the PLO and the creation of an Arab Palestinian State.

Preliminary indirect soundings between Egyptian and Israeli leaders indicated a common interest in a direct bilateral effort to reach an agreement (Zion and Dan 1979). For Sadat a dramatic concession, such as going to Jerusalem, promised to bring the U.S. government and public sufficiently to his side to bring pressure on Israel to make the concessions he sought. For Begin and the Israeli government, welcoming Sadat and making concessions to him promised to divide the Arab alliance and ensure Israeli security from a major war. Both leaders viewed the focal conflict as one between Egypt and Israel rather than between Arabs and Zionists or between communism and the West.

Once a mutual commitment to conduct negotiations had been made, the representatives of Egypt and Israel could view their conflict as a series of disputes that were amenable to trade-offs. Integrative bargaining was more likely if concessions on one dispute could be compensated for by gains in another and, more fundamentally, when a problem was seen as shared. The representatives of each side then had an interest in discovering solutions that were at least acceptable to both primary parties and their domestic constituencies.

The negotiations leading to the peace treaty were difficult and intermediary actions by the U.S. government played a critical role several times. This is illustrated in the discussion of mediator activities in the next chapter. The peace treaty did not settle all issues between the focal adversaries, and the conflict between them was not isolated from the larger interlocking set of conflicts in the Middle East. Nevertheless, the peace treaty clearly marked one outcome within that vortex of conflicts, and we should note a few of its aspects.

The outcome of the Egyptian and Israeli governments' conflict, as embodied in their peace treaty, contained integrative qualities and an exchange of concessions signifying a compromise along distributive dimensions. The chance of preventing further wars opened the way for the leaders in both countries to devote their countries' resources and energy to productive domestic purposes. The mutual concessions incorporated in the treaty were carefully linked to each other over time, balanced, and responsive to vital concerns of each party. For example, the Egyptian government won sovereignty over the entire Sinai. A detailed set of provisions limited military forces in the Sinai: Limits are greater in areas closer to Israel. These provisions met many of the Israeli security concerns. (Israel also agreed to demilitarization of zones on its side of the new border with Egypt.) The outcome reflected relative power, negotiating and mediating dynamics, and the context of multiple conflicts.

SUMMARY AND CONCLUSIONS

Even this brief review of changes and outcomes reveals a few important conclusions. First, no one party determines the outcome of any conflict. As any group pursues its aims, they are modified in interaction. In unforeseen ways, pursuing one goal modifies the adversary and the group itself. The outcome embodies new elements unanticipated by any side. In ongoing social relations, these new elements often entail mutual recognition of the other side's claims.

Second, within any struggle, coercion is only one of the ways that are used to accomplish any changes. Persuasion and reward are inevitably intertwined and hence help shape the outcome. Coercion is particularly relevant to the power component of outcomes and especially to collective goals regarding power. There is another implication, related to these two: Collective autonomy is more readily attained than a change in relative domination between major social categories.

Finally, it is important to keep in mind that the efforts of contending parties in pursuit of their goals do not themselves determine outcomes. Many other social forces and processes help shape them, including nonconflicting aspects of the relations. Furthermore, contending parties are part of a larger social environment of other units and relations. Those, too, are important in shaping all outcomes.

In this chapter we have focused our attention upon the termination and immediate outcome of social conflicts. We have been concerned especially with the outcomes relative to the goals of the contending parties. In Chapter 8 we consider the longer run consequences of struggles. This will require consideration, too, of unintended consequences.

BIBLIOGRAPHY

ASHENFELTER, O. AND G. E. JOHNSON, "Unionism, Relative Wages, and Labor Quality in U.S. Manufacturing Industries," *International Economic Review,* 13 (October 1972), 488–508.

AVISHAI, BERNARD, "Begin vs. Begin," *New York Review of Books,* May 31, 1979.

BARTOS, OTOMAR J., "Determinants and Consequences of Toughness," pp. 45–68 in Paul G. Swingle (ed.), *The Structure and Conflict* (New York: Academic Press, 1970).

BAUMGARTNER, TOM, TOM R. BURNS, AND PHILIPE DEVILLE, "Conflict Resolution and Conflict Development," pp. 105–142 in Louis Kriesberg (ed.), *Research in Social Movements, Conflicts, and Change,* Vol. 1 (Greenwich, Conn.: JAI Press, 1978).

BETZ, MICHAEL, "Riots and Welfare: Are They Related?" *Social Problems,* 21, no. 3 (1974), 345–355.

BLAKE, JUDITH, "Abortion and Public Opinion: The 1960–1970 Decade," *Science,* 171 (February 1971), 540–549.

BLECHMAN, BARRY M. AND STEPHEN S. KAPLAN WITH DAVID K. HALL, WILLIAM B. QUANDT, JEROME N. SLATER, ROBERT M. SLUSSER, AND PHILIP WINDSOR, *Force without War* (Washington, D.C.: The Brookings Institution, 1978).

BOULDING, KENNETH E., *Conflict and Defense* (New York: Harper & Row, Pub., 1962).

CAMPBELL, ANGUS, *White Attitudes toward Black People* (Ann Arbor, Mich.: Institute for Social Research, University of Michigan, 1971).

CAMPBELL, JOHN C., *Defense of the Middle East,* rev. ed. (New York: Frederick A. Praeger, Inc., 1960).

CAPLOW, THEODORE, *Two Against One: Coalitions in Triads* (Englewood Cliffs, N.J.: Prentice-Hall, 1968).

CARROLL, BERENICE A., "War Termination and Conflict Theory: Value Premises Theories and Policies," *The Annals of the American Academy of Political and Social Science,* 392 (November 1970), 14–29.

CHERTKOFF, JEROME M., "The Effects of Probability of Future Success on Coalition Formation," *Journal of Experimental Social Psychology,* 2 (1966), 265–277.

———, "Sociopsychological Theories and Research on Coalition Formation," pp. 297–322 in S. Groennings, E. W. Kelley, and M. Leiserson (eds.), *The Study of Coalition Behavior* (New York: Holt, Rinehart & Winston, 1970).

COSER, LEWIS A., "The Termination of Conflict," *Journal of Conflict Resolution,* 5 (December 1961), 347–353.

COX COMMISSION, THE, *Crisis at Columbia: Report of the Fact-Finding Commission Appointed to Investigate the Disturbances at Columbia University in April and May 1968* (New York: Vintage, 1968).

CROSS, JOHN G., *The Economics of Bargaining* (New York: Basic Books, 1969).

CUTRIGHT, PHILLIPS, "Political Structure, Economic Development, and National Security Programs," *American Journal of Sociology,* 70 (March 1965), 537–550.

DE BOER, CONNIE, "The Polls: Women at Work," *Public Opinion Quarterly,* 41 (Summer 1977), 268–277.

———, "The Polls: Abortion," *Public Opinion Quarterly,* 41 (Winter 1977–1978), 553–564.

DENNETT, RAYMOND AND JOSEPH E. JOHNSON (eds.), *Negotiating with the Russians* (Boston: World Peace Foundation, 1951).

DEUTSCH, MORTON, *The Resolution of Conflict* (New Haven, Conn.: Yale University Press, 1973).

DURMAN, EUGENE, "Have the Poor Been Regulated? Toward a Multivariate Understanding of Welfare Growth," *Social Service Review,* 47 (September 1974), 339–359.

EPSTEIN, CYNTHIA FUCHS, *Woman's Place: Options and Limits in Professional Careers* (Berkeley: University of California Press, 1970).

ERSKINE, HAZEL, "The Polls: Demonstrations and Race Riots," *Public Opinion Quarterly,* 31 (Winter 1967–1968), 655–677.

———, "Polls: Women's Role," *Public Opinion Quarterly,* 35 (Summer 1971), 275–290.

FARLEY, REYNOLDS AND KARL E. TAEUBER, "Population Trends and Residential Segregation since 1960," *Science,* 159 (March 1968), 953–956.

FEIN, HELEN, *Accounting for Genocide* (New York: Free Press, 1979).

FISHER, ROGER WITH THE HELP OF WILLIAM URY, *International Mediation: A Working Guide* (New York: International Peace Academy, 1978).

FLEXNER, ELEANOR, *Century of Struggle* (Cambridge, Mass.: Harvard University Press, 1959).

FOX, WILLIAM T. R., "The Causes of Peace and Conditions of War," *The Annals of the American Academy of Political and Social Science,* 392 (November 1970), 1–13.

FRIEDMAN, JULIAN R., CHRISTOPHER BLADEN, AND STEVEN ROSEN (eds.), *Alliance in International Politics* (Boston: Allyn & Bacon, 1970).

GALLUP, GEORGE H., *The Gallup Poll:* Vol. 1 and Vol. 2 (Wilmington, Del.: Scholarly Resources, Inc., 1978).

GAMSON, WILLIAM A., "Experimental Test of a Theory of Coalition Formation," *American Sociological Review,* 26 (August 1961), 565–573.

————, *The Strategy of Social Protest* (Homewood, Ill.: Dorsey Press, 1975).

GROENNINGS, SVEN, E. W. KELLEY, AND MICHAEL LEISERSON (eds.), *The Study of Coalition Behavior: Theoretical Perspectives and Cases from Four Continents* (New York: Holt, Rinehart & Winston, 1970).

GROMYKO, ANATOLII ANDREIEVICH, *Through Russian Eyes: President Kennedy's 1036 Days* (Washington, D.C.: International Library, 1973).

GRONBJERG, KIRSTEN, *Mass Society and the Extension of Welfare* (Chicago: University of Chicago Press, 1977).

GROSS, FELIKS, *World Politics and Tension Areas* (New York: New York University Press, 1966).

GURR, TED ROBERT, *Why Men Rebel* (Princeton, N.J.: Princeton University Press, 1970).

HINCKLE, WARREN AND DAVID WELSH, "The Battles of Selma," pp. 100–109 in Walt Anderson (ed.), *The Age of Protest* (Santa Monica, Calif.: Goodyear, 1969).

HODGE, ROBERT W., PAUL M. SIEGEL, AND PETER H. ROSSI, "Occupational Prestige in the United States: 1925–1963," pp. 322–334 in R. Bendix and S. M. Lipset (eds.), *Class Status and Power* (New York: Free Press, 1966).

HOLSTI, K. J., "Resolving International Conflicts: A Taxonomy of Behavior and Some Figures," *Journal of Conflict Resolution,* 10 (September 1966), 272–296.

HUNTINGTON, SAMUEL P., *Political Order in Changing Societies* (New Haven, Conn.: Yale University Press, 1968).

IKLÉ, FRED CHARLES, *Every War Must End* (New York: Columbia University Press, 1971).

JACKSON, ELMORE, *Meeting of Minds: A Way of Peace through Mediation* (New York: McGraw-Hill, 1952).

JENSEN, LLOYD, "Military Capabilities and Bargaining Behavior," *Journal of Conflict Resolution,* 9 (June 1965), 155–163.

KATZ, NEIL H. AND JOHN P. HUNT, "Nonviolent Struggle in Albany, Georgia," pp. 128–146 in Severyn T. Bruyn and Paula M. Rayman (eds.), *Nonviolent Action and Social Change* (New York: Irvington Publishers, 1979).

KELLER, SUZANNE, *Beyond the Ruling Class* (New York: Random House, 1963).

KELLOR, FRANCES, *American Arbitration: Its History, Functions and Achievements* (New York: Harper & Brothers, 1948).

KERR, CLARK, "The Trade Union Movement and the Redistribution of Power in Postwar Germany," *Quarterly Journal of Economics,* 68 (November 1954), 535–564.

KHOURI, FRED J., *The Arab Israeli Dilemma,* 2nd ed. (Syracuse, N.Y.: Syracuse University Press, 1976).

KNUDSEN, DEAN D., "The Declining Status of Women: Popular Myths and the Failure of Functionalist Thought," *Social Forces,* 48 (December 1969), 183–193.

KOLAJA, JIRI, *Workers' Councils: The Yugoslav Experience* (New York: Frederick A. Praeger, Inc., 1966).

KRIESBERG, LOUIS, *Social Inequality* (Englewood Cliffs, N.J.: Prentice-Hall, 1979).

———, "Interlocking Conflicts in the Middle East," pp. 99–118 in Louis Kriesberg (ed.), *Research in Social Movements, Conflicts and Change,* Vol. 3 (Greenwich, Conn.: JAI Press, 1980a).

———, "Changes in Public Support for U.S. Military Spending," *Journal Conflict Resolution,* 24 (March 1980b), 79–111.

———, "Noncoercive Inducements in U.S.–Soviet Conflicts: Ending the Occupation of Austria and Nuclear Weapons Tests," *Journal of Political and Military Sociology* 9 (Spring 1981a).

———, "Noncoercive Inducements in International Conflicts," *Peace and Change: A Journal of Peace Research,* 7 (Fall 1981b).

LAMMERS, CORNELIS J. "Strikes and Mutinies: A Comparative Study of Organizational Conflicts between Rulers and Ruled," *Administrative Science Quarterly,* 14 (December 1969), 558–572.

LEAHY, PETER AND ALLAN MAZUR, "A Comparison of Movements Opposed to Nuclear Power, Fluoridation and Abortion," pp. 143–154 in Louis Kriesberg (ed.), *Research in Social Movements, Conflicts and Change,* Vol. 1 (Greenwich, Conn.: JAI Press, 1978).

LEWIS, H. GREGG, *Unionism and Relative Wages in the United States* (Chicago: University of Chicago Press, 1963).

McGRATH, EARL J., *Should Students Share the Power?* (Philadelphia: Temple University Press, 1970).

McPHERSON, WILLIAM H., "Codetermination: Germany's Move toward a New Economy," *Industrial and Labor Relations Review,* 5 (October 1951), 20–32.

MEIER, VIKTOR, *Das Neue Jugoslawische Wirtschafts-system* (Zurich: Polygraphischer Verlag, 1956).

MILLETT, KATE, *Sexual Politics* (New York: Doubleday, 1970).

MORGAN, WILLIAM R., "Faculty Mediation of Student War Protests," pp. 365–382 in Julian Foster and Durward Long (eds), *Protest! Student Activism in America* (New York: Morrow, 1970).

MORLEY, IAN E. AND GEOFFREY M. STEPHENSON, "International and Inter-Party Exchange: A Laboratory Simulation of an Industrial Negotiation at the Plant Level," *British Journal of Psychology,* 60, no. 4 (1969), 543–545.

MOSLEY, PHILIP E., "Some Soviet Techniques of Negotiation," pp. 271–303 in Raymond Dennett and Joseph E. Johnson (eds.), *Negotiating with the Russians* (Boston: World Peace Foundation, 1951).

MYRDAL, GUNNAR, *An American Dilemma* (New York: Harper & Brothers, 1944).

OBERSCHALL, ANTHONY, "The Decline of the 1960s Social Movements," pp. 257–290 in Louis Kriesberg (ed.), *Research in Social Movements, Conflicts and Change,* Vol. 1 (Greenwich, Conn.: JAI Press, 1978).

O'NEILL, BARD E., *Armed Struggle in Palestine: A Political-Military Analysis* (Boulder, Colo.: Westview Press, 1978).

PAIGE, JEFFREY M., *Agrarian Revolution* (New York: Free Press, 1975).

PIVEN, FRANCES FOX AND RICHARD A. CLOWARD, "Reaffirming the Regulation of the Poor," *Social Science Review,* 48 (June 1974), 147–169.

————, *Poor People's Movements: Why They Succeed, How They Fail* (New York: Vintage, 1978).

PRUITT, DEAN G. AND STEVEN A. LEWIS, "The Psychology of Integrative Bargaining," pp. 161–192 in Daniel Druckman (ed.), *Negotiations* (Beverly Hills, Calif.: Sage Publications, 1977).

RADER, DOTSON AND CRAIG ANDERSON, "Rebellion at Columbia," in Walt Anderson (ed.), *The Age of Protest* (Santa Monica, Calif.: Goodyear, 1969).

RIKER, WILLIAM H., *The Theory of Political Coalitions* (New Haven, Conn.: Yale University Press, 1962).

ROKEACH, MILTON, "Change and Stability in American Value Systems, 1968–1971," *Public Opinion Quarterly,* 38 (Summer 1974), 222–238.

ROSSI, ALICE S., "Women—Terms of Liberation," *Dissent* (November-December 1970), 531–541.

ROSSI, PETER H., RICHARD A. BERK, AND BETTYE K. EDISON, *The Roots of Urban Discontent* (New York: John Wiley, 1974).

RUBIN, JEFFREY Z. AND BERT R. BROWN, *The Social Psychology of Bargaining and Negotiation* (New York: Academic Press, 1975).

RUDD, MARK, "We Want Revolution," *Saturday Evening Post,* pp. 319–322 as reprinted in William Lutz and Harry Brent (eds.), *On Revolution* (Cambridge, Mass.: Winthrop, 1968).

RUSSELL, E. E. H., *Rebellion, Revolution, and Armed Forces: A Comparative Study of Fifteen Countries with Special Emphases on Cuba and South Africa* (New York: Academic Press, 1974).

SADAT, ANWAR EL, *In Search of Identity: An Autobiography* (New York: Harper & Row, Pub., 1978).

SAWYER, JACK AND HAROLD GUETZKOW, "Bargaining and Negotiation in International Relations," pp. 466–520 in Herbert C. Kelman (ed.), *International Behavior* (New York: Holt, Rinehart & Winston, 1965).

SCHELLING, THOMAS C., *The Strategy of Conflict* (Cambridge, Mass.: Harvard University Press, 1960).

SCHLESINGER, ARTHUR M., JR., *A Thousand Days: John F. Kennedy in the White House* (Boston: Houghton Mifflin, 1965).

SCHWARTZ, MILDRED, *Trends in White Attitudes toward Negroes* (Chicago: National Opion Research Center, 1967).

SHARP, GENE, *The Politics of Nonviolent Action* (Boston: Porter Sargent Publisher, 1973).

SHEATSLEY, PAUL B., "White Attitudes Toward the Negro," *Daedalus,* 95 (Winter 1966), 217–238.

SIEGEL, BARNARD J., "Defensive Cultural Adaptation," pp. 764–787 in Hugh Davis Graham and Ted Robert Gurr (eds.), *Violence in America* (New York: Bantam, 1969).

SIEGEL, SIDNEY AND LAWRENCE FOURAKER, *Bargaining and Group Decision-Making* (New York: McGraw-Hill, 1960).

SKOCPOL, THEDA, *States and Social Revolutions: A Comparative Analysis of France, Russia, and China* (Cambridge, Eng.: Cambridge University Press, 1979).

SLOTKIN, JAMES S., *The Peyote Religion: A Study in Indian-White Relations* (New York: Free Press, 1956).

SMELSER, NEIL J., *Theory of Collective Behavior* (New York: Free Press, 1963).

SNYDER, DAVID AND WILLIAM R. KELLY, "Industrial Violence in Italy, 1978–1903," *American Journal of Sociology*, 82 (July 1976), 131–162.

SNYDER, GLENN H. AND PAUL DIESING, *Conflict among Nations: Bargaining, Decision Making, and System Structure in International Crises* (Princeton, N.J.: Princeton University Press, 1977).

STARNER, FRANCES LUCILLE, *Magsaysay and the Philippine Peasantry* (Berkeley: University of California Press, 1961).

STRAUSS, GEORGE AND ELIEZER ROSENSTEIN, "Workers' Participation: A Critical View," *Industrial Relations*, 9 (February 1970), 197–214.

TAFT, PHILIP AND PHILIP ROSS, "American Labor Violence: Its Causes, Character, and Outcome," pp. 281–395 in Hugh Davis Graham and Ted Robert Gurr (eds.), *Violence in America* (New York: Bantam, 1969).

TAYLOR, HOWARD F., *Balance in Small Groups* (New York: Van Nostrand Reinhold, 1970).

THORNTON, ARLAND AND DEBORAH FREEDMAN, "Changes in Sex Roles Attitudes of Women, 1962–1977: Evidence from a Panel Study," *American Sociological Review*, 44 (October 1979), 831–842.

U.S. BUREAU OF THE CENSUS, *Current Population Reports*, Series p-60, No. 80, "Income in 1970 of Families and Persons in the United States" (Washington, D.C.: U.S. Government Printing Office, 1971).

————, *Statistical Abstract of the United States: 1979* (100th ed.) (Washington, D.C.: U.S. Government Printing Office, 1979).

WALTON, RICHARD E. AND ROBERT B. McKERSIE, *A Behavioral Theory of Labor Negotiations: An Analysis of a Social Interaction System* (New York: McGraw-Hill, 1965).

WARD, BENJAMIN, "Worker's Management in Yugoslavia," *Journal of Political Economy*, 65 (October 1957), 373–386.

WARNER, W. LLOYD AND JAMES C. ABEGGLEN, *Occupational Mobility in American Business and Industry, 1928–1952* (Minneapolis, Minn.: University of Minnesota Press, 1955).

WENCES, ROSALIO AND HAROLD J. ABRAMSON, "Faculty Opinion on the Issues of Job Placement and Dissent in the University," *Social Problems*, 18 (Summer 1970), 27–38.

WILENSKY, HAROLD L., *The Welfare State and Equality: Structural and Ideological Roots of Public Expenditures* (Berkeley: University of California Press, 1975).

WILLIAMS, ROBIN M., JR., *Mutual Accommodation: Ethnic Conflict and Cooperation* (Minneapolis, Minn.: University of Minnesota Press, 1977).

YOUNG, ESTHER, N., "Sources of Campus Control Agents' Orientations toward Drug Use," unpublished Ph.D. dissertation, Department of Sociology, Syracuse University, 1972.

ZION, SIDNEY AND URI DAN, "Untold Story of the Mideast Talks," *The New York Times Magazine*, January 21, 1979.

7

Intermediaries
and
Mediation

In this chapter we turn our attention to how intermediaries intercede in a conflict to prevent its emergence, limit its escalation, minimize its violence, hasten its conclusion, or enhance its durability. We examine the many possible roles that intermediaries can and do play in conflicts. This kind of intervention is a major component in conflict mitigation and we discuss that context before examining the specific methods used by intermediaries.

Since conflicts often impose heavy burdens, sometimes much greater than the intended benefits, many people have sought ways to reduce the costs by managing or controlling the conflicts. Many terms have been used to refer to such efforts or processes—*resolution, conciliation, regulation, facilitation, management,* or *control* (Wehr 1979a), and there is no general agreement on precise definitions of each. Different connotations are associated with each term. They vary in their emphasis on mitigation of specific disputes or conflicts generally; they differ in the stage of the struggle in which efforts to minimize the unwanted burdens are made, and they also vary in who is acting to moderate the conflict, the adversaries in the struggle or outside intermediaries. Despite different connotations, some people use the terms interchangeably, and others use one term to encompass the others. For purposes of this book, we use the term *conflict mitigation,* or moderation, to incorporate control, management, resolution, conciliation, facilitation, or regulation of conflicts. We will briefly note the usual connotations of each specific term and use them in this book in the sense given by those connotations.

Controlling conflict usually refers to limiting the emergence or escalation of specific conflicts or hastening their conclusion; sometimes it is used to refer to efforts to prevent the emergence of a specific conflict. It often refers to methods used by the adversaries themselves, as well as by intermediaries, to moderate the conflict. Conflict *management* typically has a broader meaning: It refers to mitigating specific conflicts or conflicts generally. It may involve actions by the adversaries themselves and by intermediaries. It usually refers to mitigating conflict escalation and hastening settlements, but not to preventing the emergence of conflicts. Conflict *resolution* is generally focused on speeding the settlement of conflicts, either specific ones or conflicts generally. It may involve actions of intermediaries or the adversaries themselves. *Conciliation* and *facilitation* also usually refer to efforts to speed the settlement of a dispute, typically by a mediator or other intermediary. Finally, conflict *regulation* generally refers to established procedures for conducting recurrent conflicts. It entails practices adhered to by the adversaries but often also involves intermediaries who participate in the procedures and also help to maintain them.

None of these terms usually pertains to the possibility of mitigating the costs of social conflicts by reducing the conditions that underlie the emergence of conflicts. Conflicts may be prevented by reducing the grievances or the expectation of being able to redress them by contending with an adversary. We will consider, if only briefly, the role intermediaries play in preventing conflicts in these ways.

Even if the premise of conflict management is to minimize the disruption or escalation of a struggle, evaluations of the merits of the issues in the struggle should not be ignored. Indeed, any consideration of controlling conflicts must recognize the different values that are involved. As discussed in Chapter 1, many people may regard a particular fight as correct and the use of violence as proper in order to attain greater justice. In this discussion of conflict management we do not suggest that trying to prevent the escalation of a conflict is an absolute value. We will examine ways in which intermediaries can stop conflicts from escalating and ways in which conflicts may be prevented from erupting, taking into account how those very efforts can also enhance justice. But readers must keep in mind their own perferences and balance their different values in choosing a policy of conflict intercession.

The costs and burdens of social conflicts can be limited by actions of the partisans themselves, who may pursue modes of conflict that are likely to minimize escalation. In this chapter, however, we focus our attention on the ways in which *intermediaries* can act to mitigate the least desired aspects of social conflicts in general and especially of specific fights. We review the possible roles of intermediaries and then consider how those roles are played in different stages of a conflict's course. We devote particular attention to how intermediaries play a mediator role in deescalating and helping to terminate a fight. We also review the consequences of intermediaries' activities.

INTERMEDIARY ROLES

In this analysis of intermediary roles, we do not include parties who enter a conflict as allies of an adversary. We have discussed such intervention at various points in this book. Such intervention, in which more and more parties are drawn into a struggle, is an important element in conflict escalation. The intervention of additional partisans, of course, can also serve to bring about the termination of a fight. The additional force brought to bear by the interveners can help one party impose a settlement on another. In this chapter, however, we focus on intermediary roles in which a person or group does not enter primarily as a partisan in the fight.

This criterion suggests that intermediaries are neutral, but this is rarely the case. In fact, some analysts argue that it never is possible to intervene and act impartially (Laue and Cormick 1978). Even if the intermediary intends to be neutral, feels unbiased, and tries to act in an even-handed manner, the consequences of the intermediary's activities are to strengthen one party more than another. Other observers stress the importance of intermediaries' being neutral (Burton 1969). Striving to be neutral and balanced, or at least appearing to be so in the eyes of the adversaries, may be essential for certain intermediary roles. Neutrality, then, may refer to intentions, consequences, or appearances. The feasibility and relevance of each vary with the kind of intervener role being played. Interestingly, in an experimental study of mediation, Brookmire and Sistrunk (1980) found that mediators who appeared to be acting impartially produced no different effects than those who appeared to be acting partially. In this experiment 140 male undergraduate students participated in a simulated labor-management negotiation.

POSSIBLE ROLES

Although in this chapter we focus on the mediator role, it is useful to discuss the many other possible roles intermediaries play in mitigating conflict (Fisher 1972; Walton 1969; Laue 1979). We consider the ways intermediaries work with some or all of the conflicting parties as enforcers, fact finders, and trainers as well as mediators. We are omitting the intervener roles in which persons or groups join one of the adversary parties as combatants in the struggle, even if that may ultimately result in hastening the end of the struggle. In discussing possible intermediary roles, we may refer to roles being played by individuals, groups within larger collectivities, or large-scale organizations or other collectivities. These roles are combined in various blends by actual intermediaries.

One important role is that of the enforcer, that is, an intermediary who imposes a settlement or a cessation to hostilities (Schonborn 1975). This role may be played by a police officer in a family dispute, a U.N. peace-keeping force made up of military units from several countries, an arbitrator in a labor dispute, or a national government when it intervenes in another country to support one faction in its struggle against an opponent. In all of these cases, the enforcer is using coercion or the threat of coercion to stop the fighting between other parties and to impose cessation of the hostilities or even to impose a settlement of the conflict. The ability to impose a settlement may derive from the enforcer's own strength and power relative to the combatants; or it may be due to previous understandings among the adversaries to abide by the decisions of the arbitrator. In the former instances, the enforcer generally intervenes without the invitation or perhaps even without the consent of one or more of the adversaries; in the latter instances, the adversaries invite the intervention or acknowledge the right of the party playing an enforcer role to intervene.

In cases where the enforcer is viewed as legitimate by the adversaries, they are acknowledging that they are part of a larger system with a moral and political order. One or more of the adversaries may nevertheless try to prevent an intermediary from entering the fray to impose a cease fire or a settlement. A police officer trying to stop a family fight faces a strong risk of being attacked by one or more of the family members who are fighting. Peace-keeping forces sent by the United Nations, similarly, may be accepted by some parties to a struggle, but not by others. Consequently, the peace-keeping forces may become involved in combat themselves, as was the case most dramatically when the United Nations intervened in the fighting in the former Belgian Congo in the early 1960s.

Enforcer intercession can be conducted with various blends of other intermediary roles, and it can be performed more or less coercively. Schonborn (1975) has analyzed over two thousand cases of peace-keeping interventions at the interpersonal, intergroup, interorganizational, intercommunal, and international levels. He classified the interventions as humanitarian (a flexible, nonjudgmental approach relying primarily on words, moral power, and social science expertise) or as authoritarian (a rigid, judgmental approach relying primarily on weapons, physical power, and sharp-shooter expertise). He found that humanitarian peace-keeping interventions were more likely than authoritarian interventions to result in compromise and integration outcomes and less likely to result in domination outcomes. These results were not the case at the international peace-keeping level, but were most clearly evident in interorganizational (campus) peace-keeping and in intercommunal (racial) peace-keeping. Compared to authoritarian interventions, humanitarian peace-keeping interventions also tended to result in fewer casualties, but the outcomes were less likely to be permanent in the sense that interventions were more likely to be repeated.

In some cases, the role of an arbitrator is highly institutionalized (Kellor 1948). Adversaries have reached formal agreements specifying the circumstances under which they will call in an arbitrator to make a settlement that is binding on the adversaries. Such agreements may be enforced by legal means and, hence, have the power of a government to uphold them. In many countries trade unions and management have contractual agreements that include clauses specifying that disputes that are not settled through negotiation and mediation must be arbitrated. Panels of arbitrators are available for this purpose, and procedures for choosing persons from the panels are also agreed upon in the contract.

In an important sense, the legal system is a way of resolving conflicts by imposition by intermediaries. Judges and juries, in accordance with existing laws, decide on the terms of settlement between adversaries. Thus, in the United States many of the disputes between groups regarding discrimination against women and minority members have been resolved in a series of court actions.

A second kind of role that intermediaries may play is that of fact finder. This is at the opposite extreme from enforcer in terms of the amount of influence the intermediary has on the way the conflict is settled. When parties in conflict feel that an intermediary may infringe on their sovereignty or interfere with their ability to reach an agreement for themselves, they may be willing to allow only fact finding as an intermediary activity. This process may entail conducting research about the issues in contention. Disputants may, for example, agree to an investigation into the actual conditions affecting the lives of a segment of the community, and the results of the investigation may settle some factual matters in question. An investigation may also be a way of delaying a confrontation, or even an agreement. Fact finding may be part of a monitoring activity to help implement policies enforced by another intermediary, as happens when a judge orders a particular method to achieve school integration and a variety of different organizations monitor compliance (Laue and Monti 1980).

Fact-finding activities can also play a role in limiting the escalation of a struggle after it has begun or to prevent its eruption into violence. For example, in cities in which the fear of interracial violence has developed, a central and authoritative place for people to check out rumors can inhibit the spreading of allegations that incite attacks and riots.

Fact finders may also help to discover what each side believes and wants from a conflict. Such clarification is often useful to the adversaries themselves (Wehr 1979b). If the adversaries are clear about their objectives, they may be able to negotiate more effectively than if the objectives are vague and undifferentiated. The fact finders may also draw information from each side and present their findings to the disputants. This can be a useful form of communication between enemies. Each adversary can better hear what the other says when the information is conveyed in the dispassionate language of an intermediary. This technique has been used by unofficial intermediaries in the Middle East, for example, by the American Friends Service Committee following the June 1967 War (Bolling 1977). Such fact finding is often part of conciliatory efforts involving mediating or other activities.

Some adversaries, like national governments, are reluctant to agree to mediation, but they will accede to intervention by a fact-finding mission, which seems to be less threatening. It also does not entail mutual recognition by the adversaries and, hence, is more palatable to a government in dispute with an organization whose legitimacy it would deny.

A third intermediary role, that of trainer, is relatively new. Intermediaries may assist persons engaged in conflict to learn how to fight and negotiate more skillfully. Such training, or educational interventions, may be held in workshops, seminars, or special courses and is usually undertaken in anticipation of specific conflicts. Diplomats, trade union officials, or community workers may practice —through role playing—a variety of negotiating skills. The training is done with the understanding that these skills will be used in many conflict situations. Training activities are conducted by many organizations focusing on community, industrial, and international conflicts. For example, the International Peace Academy conducts workshops and seminars about peace-keeping operations and negotiations for military officers and diplomats from many countries (International Peace Academy 1978). Specialized workshops have been held to provide persons from adversary collectivities with sensitivity training and an opportunity to discuss substantive issues. These methods were used to seek innovative solutions to border disputes involving Somalia, Ethiopia, and Kenya (Doob 1970).

Sometimes, as in community disputes, the training workshops include persons who are actively involved in a specific fight. The training session may include persons from only one side and provide them with the techniques they can use in conducting their fight in a more disciplined and problem-solving fashion. Sometimes, however, the training may involve persons from more than one adversary (Goldaber and Porter 1974). The training session becomes a place where the disputants can speak out and where it is more likely that a disputant can hear what an adversary is saying. Such training becomes, in effect, mediation; we will discuss such mediation activity in more detail later.

The final intermediary role we distinguish is that of mediator. As we will discuss later, mediators use a wide variety of methods to intercede. Typically, a mediator does not impose a settlement but assists the adversaries to reach an agreement themselves. The mediator is not based within any of the adversary parties but is situated outside of them, providing a conciliatory service to them.

Variations

These intermediary roles and their practitioners vary in three significant ways. The roles are more or less institutionalized, the intermediaries are more or less neutral, and the resources they bring to a conflict differ.

The intermediary role will be highly institutionalized or will be loosely structured and relatively spontaneously conducted. In settings in which conflicts recur and are within a well-established moral and political order, the intermediary roles tend to be institutionalized. Even if the intermediary essentially mediates and conciliates rather than enforces decisions, how that is to be done is well understood and accepted by all parties. In less institutionalized situations, the intermediaries tend to vary greatly in their performance of the role. Even where there is institutionalization, it exists for a definite set of issues. When disputes arise over issues that are not within the agreed-upon range, the procedures are found wanting. In industiral relations, some issues are considered subject to collective bargaining and other issues are not. Contracts reached through collective bargaining usually include procedures for handling grievances of workers; if there is a dispute about the suitability of a new matter to be processed through the grievance procedure, however, then an unregulated conflict will emerge (Gouldner 1954).

Intermediaries vary in the degree to which they are expected to be neutral in sentiment and conduct. In some cases, the intermediary role is performed by a group that includes persons understood to be sympathetic to the adversaries, who, in varying degrees, serve as advocates and conduits for information from the disputants. In addition, impartial persons are included in such groups. When the role is highly institutionalized, it is easier for a person with feelings of sympathy for one side to act in an impartial manner. It is unlikely that a person knowledgeable enough to play an intermediary role would not have some sentiments about the adversaries and the rights and wrongs of the positions they have taken on the issues in contention. But it is also possible for effective intermediaries to put those sentiments aside when it is necessary.

Intermediaries have their own interests, and these are an important, but different, potential source of bias and interference in conciliation between adversaries. When the intermediary represents a major actor in the setting within which the focal adversaries are contending, the possibilities for exploitation are obviously great. If a major power in the world intervenes to enforce a settlement or even mediate a conflict between two other governments, the interests of that major power may be advanced to the detriment of both adversaries. The intermediaries' interests may, however, coincide with both adversaries', so that they reach an agreement that all find satisfactory. For intermediaries whose careers are based on mediation or arbitration, the reputation of being fair and seeking to assist the adversaries rather than advance their own interests turns out to be the best way of advancing their careers.

The complexity of these matters is illustrated by considering the role of President Carter in mediating the Egyptian and Israeli governmental negotiations at Camp David. In terms of his own political career, Mr. Carter had an interest in having the adversaries reach an agreement and one that the opponents would agree met their own major concerns. President Carter wanted, as a representative of a major world power with concerns in the Middle East, to reach an agreement between the Egyptian and Israeli governments that would not harm and might even advance U.S. interests in the Middle East.

Finally, intermediaries vary greatly in the resources they bring into the negotiations. Intermediaries, as individual persons, vary in many ways. They differ in their skills as mediators, fact finders, arbitrators, and trainers. They are more or less creative in introducing ideas to advance the negotiations. They also vary in their interpersonal ties with the adversaries; those with closer bonds can make greater claims for cooperative conduct and risk taking. Intermediaries differ in their reputations and public stature; greater reputations give them coercive resources when deadlocks or breakdowns in the negotiations threaten. Dilemmas exist even here. Unofficial intermediaries in international negotiations, unlike official ones, can meet with certain emissaries, but their authority in interceding is correspondingly less (Berman and Johnson 1977).

Intermediaries are often not only individual, but they also represent other collectivities and can draw on their resources. This means that they can add money or promises of security to sweeten aspects of a settlement that otherwise would be bitter. For example, President Carter contributed to the Egyptian and Israeli governmental negotiations leading to a peace treaty by promising aid to compensate for the losses to be expected as a result of fulfilling the terms of the treaty. In addition, the power of the United States was pledged to help enforce the terms of the treaty.

Adding resources to the negotiations enlarges the pie that the adversaries are seeking to divide. If the pie is enlarged, the dispute is less likely to be perceived as zero sum. For example, in a community dispute about the use of a local high school for sports events, an intermediary may be able to assist the adversaries in making a claim on city or state funds to expand the school's facilities.

INTERCESSION IN DIFFERENT CONFLICT STAGES

Intermediaries may intervene to mitigate a conflict at each stage. We will discuss ways of mitigation in relation to three stages in the course of conflicts. Intermediaries may try to prevent a conflict from emerging, they may try to limit its escalation and hasten its conclusion, or they may try to develop and sustain a lasting settlement. Since conflicts are interlocked in so many ways, actions to serve one purpose necessarily contribute to the others. Nevertheless, it will prove useful to examine each of them separately.

Intermediaries may try to prevent the emergence of a conflict by altering the underlying conditions or by inhibiting the awareness of the conflict. Many organizations and persons strive to prevent conflicts by reducing the injustices that they believe could generate them. The United Nations and agencies such as the Food and Agricultural Organization, the World Health Organization, and the World Bank purport to be aiding less-developed countries and regions within countries so that disparities in economic well-being are less immense. Many U.S. governmental policies are pursued in order to be responsive to the claims of collectivities that might come to feel aggrieved. Of course, such policies are often advanced in response to explicit demands and even coercive conflict behavior, but the programs then are to forestall further fights. For example, Piven and Cloward (1971) have studied the growth of social welfare programs in the United States as responses to protests by the unemployed and the poor.

Many private charitable and social action groups strive to improve conditions of ethnic minorities, women, residents in low-income neighborhoods, and other relatively low-ranking groups of persons. Such efforts have many purposes, one of which may be to reduce the likelihood of social conflicts.

In addition to trying to alter the conditions underlying the emergence of a conflict, intermediaries may strive to prevent social conflicts by preventing awareness of the conflict from emerging. Intermediaries may try, for example, to increase the salience of common interests among potential antagonists. Thus, church leaders or community organizations may encourage union members and factory managers in a local plant to consider their shared interest in keeping the factory in the locality; or potentially antagonistic ethnic groups may be encouraged to note their common desire of maintaining a peaceful community. Such efforts help to submerge the incompatible interests within larger common ones and, thus, prevent the emergence of coercively conducted struggles.

Intermediaries may also serve as transmitters of information between potential adversaries so that mutual responsiveness can occur before a fight erupts. Rumors and misunderstandings can be more easily dispelled before a fight has broken out than afterward. In tense situations such intermediary activities can even be introduced to inhibit the escalation of a conflict.

Intermediaries may also help prevent conflicts from erupting by training potential adversaries and other intermediaries in conflict management. Adversaries who are skilled in negotiating may be able to resolve their disputes more successfully and with less mutual coercion than are those who lack such skills. They may be able to transform issues in dispute to problems for mutual solution. One of the difficulties in many negotiations is their great complexity; intermediaries can facilitate a successful resolution of such negotiations by providing techniques to manage the complexity (Straus 1979). In addition, training in conflict management of persons who routinely intervene in disputes may contribute to successful intervention and even to the prevention of conflict emergence. This brings us to intermediary activity in the next stage of social conflicts: escalation.

Intermediaries can and do perform a variety of activities that help limit conflict escalation and speed conflict settlement. In general, intermediaries are more likely to intervene in a conflict once hostilities have broken out rather than before (Bloomfield and Leiss 1969). This is true particularly for intermediaries who are filling mediator roles. In the next section of this chapter we examine the variety of ways mediators facilitate adversaries in reaching an agreement. At this point we will consider characteristics of the conflict and of the intermediary that affect intermediary intervention in an ongoing dispute.

Several characteristics of social conflicts and of available intermediaries affect the likelihood of intervention by intermediaries to limit escalation. These characteristics themselves have great relevance for the escalation of conflicts, the amount of coercion involved, and how long the fight persists. Knowing the conditions that affect when intermediaries intervene, therefore, is essential to assess the intermediaries' contribution to the settlement of a conflict. For example, if intermediaries generally intervene when the adversaries are deadlocked and seek a face-saving way to end the fight, intermediaries are likely to be successful in quickly settling the fights. We will have to bear that in mind when we try to assess the effectiveness of intermediaries in mitigating social conflicts.

Four characteristics of conflicts are particularly relevant to an intermediary's intervention to limit escalation: the degree of institutionalization of conflicts, the degree of integration between the adversaries, their degree of organization, and the relative balance among the adversaries in the means at their disposal. Insofar as the dispute is an example of conflicts that are regulated and the regulation includes a role for intervention by intermediaries, intervention will tend to occur in accordance with the regulatory rules. In labor disputes in some industries, for example, U.S. laws specify when federal mediation should be used.

Insofar as the adversaries are highly integrated, they may have institutionalized means for negotiating directly with each other without recourse to intermediaries. When and if such negotiations fail, they are likely to invite intermediaries' assistance in order to prevent the dispute from escalating and damaging their relations. Indeed, each adversary with extensive cooperative ties with other parties may tend to avoid escalation and seek to mitigate a conflict that might endanger their mutual ties. This kind of caution may be engendered by having something to lose. Some consistent evidence can be seen in Wolf's (1978) analyses of major international conflicts between 1920 and 1965. He examined characteristics of the adversaries possibly related to intervention by international organizations or other intermediaries. He found that adversaries with relatively greater cooperative ties, such as trade or membership in international organizations, were more likely than others to have their conflicts resolved with intermediaries rather than bilaterally.

When integration between adversaries is in the form of their being constituent parts of a larger collectivity, intercession is very likely and the role of enforcer is especially likely. Thus, disputes with a university, city, or a factory can be readily entered by an agent's acting in the name of the transcending collectivity.

Intercession, particularly by mediators, is relatively likely between clearly bounded and well-organized collectivities, for example, between conflict groups such as governments and agents in collective bargaining. In conflicts where the antagonists are not highly organized, as in social movements based on class, race, or gender conflicts, mediation is not likely. Only when specialized organizations within the movement have emerged and begun to engage in specific fights is mediation likely.

The fourth characteristic of the conflict related to the intervention of intermediaries is the relative balance in the means available to the adversaries. Contenders who are relatively equally balanced in strength are more likely to utilize intermediaries to settle a dispute than are adversaries who differ greatly in strength (Wolf 1978). In addition, the means available to the parties affect their recourse to intermediaries. Thus, countries that are less militarized are more likely to resort to international intermediaries than are countries that are more militarized (Wolf 1978). Many conflicts are self-limiting given the resources available to one or more adversaries. They may exhaust the war-making material or other resources necessary to pursue the conflict; such a limitation gives intermediaries relative strength in intervening to deescalate the conflict, as happened in the brief war between El Salvador and Honduras in the summer of 1969.

In general, intermediaries are most likely to intervene after the conflict has clearly erupted and even after hostilities and the exchange of coercive actions have occurred (Bloomfield and Leiss 1969). Sometimes, then, intervention occurs as the conflict begins to escalate, which may be at a stage where successful intervention is unlikely. Intervention may then occur later when the adversaries have expended considerable resources but are not able to foresee a clear triumph.

Whether or not an intermediary enters a conflict situation in order to deescalate the conflict is also affected by characteristics of the available intermediaries. The fundamental issue here is the purposes that intermediaries have for intervening. They may be moved by the spectacle of enemies' carrying out terrible acts of mutual destruction. They may intervene, then, from a sense of moral concern and may seek to hasten the termination of a destructive and harmful fight. They may also calculate the possible benefits of intervention for the advancement of personal career interests or the advancement of the prestige, influence, or power of the collectivity in whose name an intermediary is acting. In these cases, it is likely that the intermediaries will try to intervene even when the adversaries do not invite them to do so.

Noncontending observers, either persons or groups, may also try to intervene as intermediaries because of their sense of role obligation. Doing so is related to the idea that a dispute may be within the realm of conflict regulation, even though the role obligations may not be mandatory. Thus, a political leader may enter a dispute to hasten its settlement, even if there is no clearly established regulatory role for such intervention. During the newspaper strike in New York City for example, in the winter of 1962–1963, the mayor invited himself into the dispute as an intermediary (Raskin 1963).

Intermediaries, finally, may intervene at the end of the conflict. They enter to help solemnize an agreement to stop the fighting. By entering to witness and concur in terminating a conflict, intermediaries also may serve to guarantee the agreement that has been reached. In some cases, the intermediaries act to preserve the agreement by establishing agencies or procedures for enforcing it. For example, in the Middle East, U.N. military units have served as peace-keeping forces, separating the adversary armies. In disputes relating to school desegregation, judges have sometimes acted as supervisors of agreements or court decisions after they have been reached. Such intermediary activity is intended to prevent the renewal of a conflict after it has been terminated. Sometimes, as in the case of U.N. actions, peace-keeping efforts freeze a conflict without bringing it to the stage at which the primary adversaries accept the resolution.

MEDIATOR ACTIVITIES

Having discussed intermediaries as enforcers, researchers, trainers, and mediators, we now focus on mediator activities. The central objective of mediation is to facilitate the adversaries themselves in reaching a mutually acceptable agreement terminating a conflict. Mediators, like other intermediaries, may be pursuing their own interests, which, in some degree, may be incompatible with the needs of the adversaries; they may also be enhanced by doing so. In this discussion we will concentrate on the ways mediators can and do encourage adversaries to construct their own resolutions. We will leave aside how mediators lead, manipulate, or otherwise direct the adversaries to an agreement that serves the interests of the mediator rather than of the antagonists. When we examine the effectiveness and consequences of the interventions by mediators, we will return to this matter.

In this section we examine the specific methods mediators can and do use in mitigating conflicts: They provide a neutral setting for communication, provide information, reduce interpersonal barriers, improve procedures, invent options, add resources, and build support for an agreement (Kerr 1954; Rubin and Brown 1975). When mediators enter a conflict, they must first analyze what problems are interfering with the adversaries' reaching a mutually acceptable agreement (Fisher and Ury 1978). After diagnosing the problems, the mediator can more wisely and effectively select the appropriate methods to reduce the problems and facilitate the adversaries' reaching an agreement. The mediator's various activities are blended in different combinations as mediation proceeds.

Provide a Neutral Setting

The minimal kind of mediator activity is providing a neutral and safe place for the adversaries' representatives to meet. A mediator may be needed for this minimal activity when the hostilities are so great that neither adversary will meet in places which seem to be in the other's territory. Sometimes, the very existence of the neutral meeting place and of the negotiations themselves are kept secret. This may be done at an early stage of negotiations between enemies who are exploring the value of direct negotiations. Such privacy was, for example, accorded the meetings in Morocco by Israeli and Egyptian government representatives immediately prior to President Sadat's statement that he would be willing to go to Jerusalem (Zion and Dan 1979).

Provide Information

As a conflict escalates, the protaganists are increasingly likely to distort what each other is saying and trying to do. It is hard to hear accurately what your enemy is saying while that adversary is hurting you. Adversaries may also lack information about the likely consequences of their actions on their relations with nonadversary parties or even the future relations among themselves. Mediators, then, can facilitate conflict resolution by transmitting relevant, accurate information. Such information may be conveyed by many channels in addition to mediators —by journalists, business travelers, or scientists attending professional meetings.

The provision of information by mediators may be seen as one of the techniques in the repertoire of a mediator or the basic and even exclusive mediation mode. Burton (1969), for example, argues that a mediator should restrict himself or herself to giving information about the nature of conflicts and not offer any suggestions about possible agreements. In this view, the mediator draws on theoretical knowledge about conflicts and helps the adversaries see the conflict as a problem to be solved rather than as one to win or lose. The mediator controls the communication to focus on analyzing the conflict.

In addition to providing information about social conflicts in general or about the likely course of the dispute in which the mediator is interceding, a mediator can be a significant transmitter of information between the antagonists. In some conflicts, when, for example, one party refuses to recognize another as legitimate, adversaries will not meet directly and, consequently, negotiations between the antagonists may be conducted through intermediaries. The soundings between Prime Minister Begin of Israel and President Sadat of Egypt prior to President Sadat's visit to Jerusalem in November of 1977 were conducted through separate meetings with President Ceasescu of Romania. Earlier, extensive indirect negotiations had been conducted that had not led to any agreements—Gunnar Jarring, the special U.N. representative to the Middle East, acted as an intermediary between the Egyptian and Israeli governments, and the U.S. secretary of state and other officials also conducted indirect negotiations.

Intermediaries also serve as transmitters of information even when the adversaries are engaged in their own direct negotiations. The mediator can convey what each party is saying in a way that facilitates an adversary's hearing it. The mediator may omit particularly provocative elements of a message, or introduce the message with an explanation that accounts for it in terms of constituency concerns; or the message may simply be taken at face value when not transmitted by an enemy. In any case, the mediator, to function effectively, must listen carefully to the essential message being given for transmission. Some mediators use the information they gain in conversations with each party to develop information about the possiblility of a settlement and the timing for it. A labor mediator may find out what the bottom line is for each side—discovering that although the sides seem to be very far apart, a deal could be struck. The mediator cannot reveal what either side is willing to settle for without losing credibility and destroying his or her future utility as a labor mediator. The mediator may also encourage one party to make an offer it is contemplating presenting. If the union representative is holding out for a 10 percent increase but would settle for 6 percent, and management is holding out for 4 percent but would settle for 8 percent, a mediator might encourage management to make the 7 percent offer it was considering. The offer would be accepted, both sides would be satisfied, and the mediator would look good to all parties.

Reduce Interpersonal Barriers

Antagonists in a fight feel anger and fear, and these emotions interfere with communication. Negotiators may not speak clearly or in a manner most likely to be heard by the antagonist, and they may not accurately hear what the other party is saying when they are fearful and angry. In addition to the barriers caused by such emotions, communication may be blocked by stereotypes and distorted views based on past experiences that resulted in rigid and no longer valid expectations. The training and workshop experiences noted earlier are important ways in which mutual understanding can be enhanced. Mediators can more directly help to reduce the damaging effects of emotional and cognitive barriers to clear communication.

Mediators may provide a private audience to which antagonists can express their feelings without causing any reaction from the adversary. Allowing negotiators to express their feelings, to "let off steam," can reduce the tension and help them think more rationally. Mediators can allow each side to let feelings out in safety and confidence; this release can allow the negotiators to be more circumspect in their direct negotiations with each other. When emotions are hot, a "cooling-off" period is sometimes suggested and sometimes even mandated by law for a certain period. A cooling-off period in which nothing is done to advance the negotiations, however, is not likely to be helpful and can even help freeze positions (Jackson 1952, p. 163).

Breaking through others' barriers of misconceptions can also occur when antagonists share some common goals. A variety of evidence has shown that adversaries who can be brought together to work on a common task on an egalitarian basis will reduce their feelings of hostility toward each other and perceive each other in a less derogatory fashion (Sherif 1966). Mediators can help devise tasks and situations that bring adversaries together (Wedge 1971). Social activities, such as meals and parties, especially if they are planned by a committee made up of representatives from the adversary negotiating teams, can serve this function in a minor way.

Mediators can also suggest particular devices to break through communication barriers. A mediator may encourage one side to make a symbolic gift or a unilateral action that would be difficult for the adversary to ignore or misinterpret. Such gestures, if effective, can get the adversary's attention and facilitate a fresh look at the side making the gesture. In order to be effective, the gesture must be as unambiguous as possible and attuned to the adversary's own ways of thinking. A gesture as simple as an acknowledgment of the bravery of the adversary's people and their past sacrifices for the ends they sought may be moving and effective.

A mediator may also suggest techniques such as asking adversaries to write down what each thinks the other says it wants. This activity encourages each side to listen carefully. The written statement is commented upon by the adversary whose views are being summarized, and the writer revises the statement in the light of the comments. Such exchanges are a kind of exercise that can improve the accuracy of each party's perception of what the others are actually saying (Fisher and Ury 1978).

Improve Procedures

Negotiators sometimes become frozen in unproductive procedures. A mediator may help invent or support practices that will improve communication and the discovery of an acceptable agreement. One way this happens is to give salience to norms of equity. More balanced presentations and rules of procedure are likely to emerge with the participation of a mediator.

Mediators can provide specific ways of breaking out of situations where the adversaries are stating their positions over and over again. The mediator may suggest that the negotiators leave aside the specific demands they have been making (and which the other side has found unacceptable) and discuss the principles about which they agree and the interests they seek to maintain (Fisher and Ury 1978).

The mediator may also seek to restructure the negotiation process, by for example, changing the degree of formality, altering seating arrangements, or moving to secret meetings if they had been public. The level of the negotiators may also be changed. For example, it may be advisable to shift to negotiation between higher ranking representatives of the adversaries. Sometimes only higher ranking persons have the authority to make the necessary concessions to reach an agreement. It may, however, be advisable to shift downward in the bureaucratic hierarchy, which would, for example, allow technical experts to discuss the issues in contention and with less passion and role commitment than the higher ranking negotiators could do. The set of roles in the negotiations may be restructured such that one person would chair the meeting while another acts as a facilitator (Doyle and Straus 1976). The facilitator would moderate a discussion of each proposal that members put forward. Clarifying questions only may be asked and then concerns expressed. The facilitator would summarize what has been agreed to and what has not, setting the stage for new proposals to deal with matters not yet in agreement.

The mediator also may resturcture the negotiations by breaking up the negotiation into two or more subnegotiations. The working parties or committees may be assigned particular issues to negotiate. When each working group has reached an agreement about its set of issues, the full negotiating teams can reassemble to complete the overall negotiations. This is another way to fractionate the conflict.

In improving the procedures, as in inventing new options, a major task of the mediator is to help the adversaries analyze what the problems are that they have in their negotiations and help them discover new procedural arrangements to minimize the problems.

Invent Options

The problem in many negotiations that have gone on for a long time is that the adversaries have developed a few fixed positions. They have asserted their demands and have very limited ideas about possible settlements. They can see only one side's or the other's getting its way and no integrative solutions, as discussed in the previous chapter. The perceived options for a settlement may all appear worse than having no agreement. Mediators, then, will try to increase the options that the adversaries consider. They can do this by suggesting options or by helping the negotiators themselves be creative and inventive.

Mediators can sometimes be more inventive than the immediate antagonists because they can recognize the real interests that the negotiators are trying to advance. Furthermore, they have less commitment to previous terms of settlement offered by the adversaries and are, therefore, more likely to think of ways in which the adversaries' interests might be enhanced by a newly invented option. Even if the mediator's solution is not the best one imaginable, it can provide a useful basis for renewed adversary negotiation. The mediator's suggested agreement becomes salient and the focus for discussion in a way that one of the adversary's solution could not be (Schelling 1960). The contending parties may then regard that agreement as having a particularly compelling quality. As Cross (1969, pp. 92–97) also points out, if an adversary offers a terminating compromise, an antagonist is likely to regard it as a negotiating bid and try to bargain further. Only an intermediary can present a compromise that adversaries can regard as nonnegotiable.

A mediator's suggestion can also allow a negotiator to make a concession in a face-saving fashion. Rather than meekly giving in to the opponent's demands, agreement is given to a fair-minded mediator (Rubin and Brown 1975). For example, in the negotiations between the Israeli government and the Egyptian government, mediated by Kissinger in 1973, the Israelis wanted a commitment from Egypt to reopen the Suez Canal and allow Israeli shipping to use the canal. President Sadat was not willing to make such commitments to the Israelis, which would appear to be putting limits on Egyptian sovereignty. The commitments were made to the U.S. government, which conveyed them to the Israeli government (Golan 1976, pp. 168–169).

Sometimes a mediator can combine transmitting information with developing a mediator-formulated solution. An intermediary may, for example, suggest possible formulations that none of the adversaries would have offered, viz., the compromise suggested by Collins to King and Lingo in Selma, Alabama (Hinckle and Welsh 1969), discussed in the preceding chapter. In the Camp David negotiations between the Egyptian and Israeli governmental representatives, U.S. officials conducted elaborate mediations in this fashion. At the outset of the meetings, Egyptian and Israeli draft treaties were presented, but it quickly became apparent that neither side would work from the other's draft proposal and direct negotiations were difficlut. The U.S. officials, in an intermediary role, presented a draft proposal and asked each side to suggest improvements. This process went on through twenty-three revisions of the draft proposal. Finally, a proposal was presented as the best that could be reached, and the adversaries had to accept it as a whole or reject it as a whole. President Sadat for Egypt and Prime Minister Begin for Israel accepted the proposal and the Camp David accords were made.

There are, of course, risks when a mediator makes substantive suggestions. The mediator may grossly misinterpret what one or more of the adversaries regard as their fundamental interests and lose credibility as an impartial or balanced intermediary. The mediators may even in effect impose a settlement reflecting the mediator's interests. Suggestions are best made on the basis of very good information about the interests and preferences of the adversaries. A method that includes repeated opportunities for the primary adversaries to respond to the mediator proposal also helps minimize the risks of a poor proposal.

A mediator can also help the adversaries to invent more options themselves. One step in this may be to discuss the range of present options under negotiation, recognizing that they seem to be vague and partisan. This may make the need for new options clearer and even induce suggestions of some. Brainstorming sessions can also be used to stimulate new options. In such sessions, participants are encouraged to present options that they might think wild and not likely to be acceptable. During the session, critical comments are not to be made. This allows people to think imaginatively and not abort an idea out of fear that others will ridicule it or demonstrate its futility. Once many fresh ideas have been presented, the critical assessment of the new ideas can begin. New options can also be stimulated by encouraging negotiators to look at the issues in contention from new perspectives—from another role (within or outside their delegation), from different disciplines or professional identities, or from different time perspectives.

Add Resources

A basic problem in negotiating a termination of a conflict is that the adversaries perceive a long-enduring conflict as one in which each concession by them is a victory for the other side and a gain by them means a loss to the other side. A mediator who alters that view (and the reality behind it) will facilitate the adversaries' reaching a satisfactory agreement.

The mediator may reduce the zero-sum quality of a conflict by expanding the resources to be divided by the adversaries. Specifically, mediators may offer side payments of compensations to each side so that a deal can be reached. In domestic disputes a mediator may be able to suggest sources for additional resources, and, hence, all the primary adversaries can obtain much of what they would like. In a neighborhood dispute over use of school facilities, additional funds from the city or state might allow an expansion of hours and facilities at the school so that programs that had been competitive could become noncompetitive. Or, a mediator may point out that if the adversaries join together they can benefit jointly at the expense of third parties.

In addition to enlarging the pie to be divided, mediators may aid one party in the dispute so that a satisfactory agreement is more likely to be reached. Such assistance may take the form of training in important negotiating skills. Parties with little experience in conflicts may be unskilled in formulating negotiable positions and conducting negotiations. This is true of those in community disputes and of many groups that are seeking entrance into the decision-making process from which they had been excluded. Introducing a mediator into a struggle may, in itself, tend to equalize the adversaries and hasten an agreement, particularly when one party does not recognize the legitimacy of the other. The intervention of a mediator confers a kind of legitimacy on each of the adversaries. Obviously, an agreement is more likely to be reached by parties who recognize each other as legitimate bargaining partners than by parties who do not. Such intervention by a mediator means strengthening one of the parties in the struggle. This is one reason that mediators often do not try to intervene in a dispute: They do not wish to give added strength to the party seeking legitimacy.

Build Support for Agreement

One of the important obstacles to reaching an agreement is that the negotiators for one or more parties fear that their constituency will reject the agreement. The negotiators may come to an understanding that seems reasonable but fear disapproval not only of the solution but even of themselves. Another obstacle to reaching an agreement is that the negotiators feel no urgency in doing so. One or more set of negotiators may feel that the status quo and the ongoing negotiations are satisfactory and are in no hurry to end them. Mediators can act to reduce these obstacles.

Mediators can help negotiators think of ways to present an agreement that makes it appealing to their constituents. For example, a labor mediator may suggest to the trade union representatives that a settlement of 50 cents more an hour in the first year and 25 cents more in the second year of the contract could be presented as 75 cents an hour in two years. Or, if an increase is given in percentages, the importance of compounding the increase on a higher base can be explained. The mediators themselves may try to influence public opinion and the constituencies of the negotiators. The mediator may priase the skill, perserverance, and toughness of the negotiators.

Mediators can also seek to influence the negotiators' constituencies to build support for reaching an agreement. One way of doing so is to create an illusion that movement toward an agreement is progressing rapidly. This sense of movement builds pressure to reach a settlement; it also supposedly puts pressure on each party to make concessions to make an agreement or else appear to be blocking a resolution that is almost reached. Such efforts are risky as is any deception by a mediator; one or another party may lose confidence in the mediator or repudiate the mediator's assertions. U.S. Secretary of State Kissinger, in the shuttle diplomacy in which he arranged a partial withdrawal of Israeli military forces from the Sinai after the 1973 war, was sometimes viewed with suspicion because of his manipulation of news media (Golan 1976, p. 235).

Mediators can also build support for an agreement by making salient the common interests of the adversaries. Their ties of mutuality are stressed as are possible gains from an agreement; this would appear to raise the costs of failing to reach a settlement, and it makes an integrative solution more likely. Mediators can apply pressure to one or more sides in order to raise the costs of failing to make an agreement. Some analysts of industrial conflict regard the essence of mediation to be channeling pressure on the negotiating parties to make the necessary concessions (Warren 1954).

Finally, since time pressure tends to produce settlements (Brookmire and Sistrunk 1980), mediators may enhance the chances of an agreement by setting deadlines. They may fix a deadline in terms of their own participation in the negotiations and if their involvement is crucial, their withdrawal would mean the end of negotiations and no agreement. Clearly, the timing of such deadlines requires a good sense of the stage of the negotiations. President Carter, at the Camp David negotiations between the Israeli and Egyptian governments, set a deadline when he felt there was little room for further agreement and wanted to ensure agreement to the last elements of the accords. Giving a deadline helped move the negotiators to make the final concessions needed to reach an agreement. Critics might still argue that waiting another day would have permitted working out the few remaining details that otherwise resulted in acrimony and much more prolonged negotiations, but trying to settle all the details may have prevented reaching any agreement.

In summary, mediators pursue a wide variety of actions in trying to facilitate an agreement between adversaries. Many of these courses of action are compatible and even complementary, but some of them are not. A mediator must often choose which strategy to employ. The selection should suit the issues in dispute and the contending parties, but it should also reflect the character of the mediator. Even a good strategy, if it is not personally fitting, may turn out to be unsuccessful. Mediators are more or less assertive, creative, and affable, and such personality variations make the use of certain techniques more or less likely to be effective. Of course, the strategies that a mediator will follow are generally within the constraints set by the nature of the adversaries, their conflict, and the role of the mediator. We turn next to consider the effects of mediator efforts on conflict mitigation.

CONSEQUENCES OF MEDIATION

It is certainly difficult to assess the consequences of mediators' efforts to mitigate conflict behavior. On the one hand, efforts often fail to resolve a fight (Berman and Johnson 1977; Young 1967; Wehr 1979a). But even in clear failures, a sympathetic observer might argue that the groundwork was laid for future successes or that the conflict escalation would have been even worse without the intercession. Many conflicts are so intense and apparently intractable that mediation cannot resolve them, but intercession may prevent escalation until circumstances sufficiently alter so that an agreement among the primary adversaries would be possible. On the other hand, what appears to be speedy and effective mediation may be the result of opportune timing: The adversaries were ready to reach an agreement and would have done so with or without the presence of a mediator. Wise mediators may refuse to intercede until they are certain the parties are willing to make an agreement. Nevertheless, it is also undoubtedly the case that mediators do sometimes play a critical role in settling a fight. They may speed the resolution of a conflict, lessen or reduce violence, and help produce a more just and lasting resolution. We examine those possibilities in this section.

Difficult as it is to assess consequences of intercession by mediators, it is even more difficult to assess the relative effectiveness of different techniques and strategies of mediation. Moreover, there have been hardly any systematic assessments of different forms of mediation. We will refer to the available evidence about different kinds of mediation efforts in conjunction with the discussion of possible contributions to conflict mitigation.

Limiting Escalation

A major possible contribution of intermediaries, and particularly of mediators, is to limit the escalation of a conflict. Mediators may be able to draw on the range of activities previously described and prevent a conflict from becoming more intense and more extensive. There is experimental evidence, for example, that creating a sense of superordinate goals can reduce feelings and expressions of hostility and replace them with cooperative relations. Thus, Sherif (1966) reduced conflict among different groups in a boys' camp by producing common goals for the groups.

Other experiments demonstrate that the mere presence of an observer who monitored the bargaining behavior seemed to generate cooperative behavior between bargainers. Apparently without the presence of the third party, the bargainers were less likely to act ethically (Rubin and Brown 1975).

Analyses of the course of international conflicts also indicate that conflicts in which intermediaries are involved in attempts at a settlement are less likely to escalate to involve violence. Thus, Wolf (1978) examined seventy-two major international conflicts between 1920 and 1965 (as summarized by Holsti 1966). He found that international conflicts that were handled through procedures involving intermediaries were much less likely to have outcomes determined by violence than were conflicts in which the parties did not make use of such procedures (28 percent compared to 76 percent).

Speeding Resolutions

Mediators may also tend to hasten the reaching of an agreement that the adversaries would otherwise be slow to attain. Indeed, they may be crucial in reaching any agreement at all in some cases. There is a variety of experimental evidence about the ways in which mediators help to speed up the negotiating process.

Rubin and Brown (1975) summarize many experimental studies. They note that in experimental games where a mediator intervened to make suggestions, the subjects made larger and more frequent concessions. Apparently, the intervention enabled negotiators to make concessions without considering themselves weak for doing so.

Observations and analyses of industrial disputes indicate that mediators are able to make suggestions and generate pressures that tend to result in concessions that hasten reaching an agreement (Douglas 1962). Kochan and Jick (1978) conducted an analysis of labor mediation in a sample of actual negotiations involving municipal governments and police and fire-fighter unions in the state of New York. They compared the effectiveness of mediators' using a relatively passive and a relatively aggressive strategy. They found that the use of aggressive tactics was associated with narrowing the differences between the bargainers particularly about nonsalary issues and was less clearly associated with reaching an agreement and movement on salary issues.

Increasing Equity

Perhaps the intervention of mediators into negotiations helps produce agreements that are more just and equitable than agreements reached without mediation. Mediators may encourage innovative and integrative outcomes. There is experimental evidence that third party observers or mediators making even small interventions increase the pressures toward adhering to norms of fairness and equity (Rubin and Brown 1975, pp. 58–59). Another experimental study found that mediators who are perceived as high in ability are especially likely to help produce outcomes that yield high gains for the negotiators, perhaps because suggestions by mediators can be more readily accepted without loss of face (Brookmire and Sistrunk 1980).

Observations and interviews with persons involved in negotiations indicate other ways in which mediators may help produce agreements and outcomes that are considered fair. The presence of a mediator who is trusted and who is viewed as skillful in mediation facilitates a fuller discussion of the issues in contention (Walton 1968). The bargainers often feel that a more open expression of their preferences is possible with mediation than alone with one another; the mediator may be viewed as welcoming such expressions, capable of handling adverse consequences of the openness, and of using the expressions for the common benefit of the bargainers. With more information available to all parties about what they want, an agreement is more likely to reflect all the interests. The presence of a mediator may particularly help the weaker party to feel able to express its views and preferences. It is possible, however, that such open and full discussions will prolong the negotiations. To promote this openness, the mediator is likely to set aside his or her own suggestions. By emphasizing the process of seeking understanding in order to reach an agreement, the mediator would not try to pressure the bargainers to make concessions or to accept any particular agreement.

Another indication that intercession contributes to an equitable solution is that the outcome is less likely to be imposed when intermediaries participate in reaching an agreement between the adversaries. This was noted in the previous chapter and supportive evidence was found in the reanalysis of Holsti's data about international conflicts between 1919 and 1965. Settlement attempts that involved intermediaries were less likely than those without intermediaries to result in conquest or forced submission and more likely to have outcomes that were compromises or awards.

Finally, it may be that the participation of intermediaries in reaching an agreement reduced the chances that the outcome will be at the expense of parties not involved in the focal conflict. In reaching an agreement, it is always possible for the primary adversaries to advance their common interests at the expense of third parties. Thus, management and trade union representatives may agree on a settlement that benefits their constituencies and simply pass on the cost of the agreement to the customers in the form of higher prices.

In international conflicts adversaries have often reached agreement at the expense of third parties. For example, Chamberlain and Daladier (for Great Britain and France) met with Hitler and Mussolini (for Germany and Italy) at Munich in September 1938 and agreed that the Czech government surrender a portion of its territory, the Sudetenland, to Germany. The participation of intermediaries makes it more likely that the interests of parties not directly involved in the negotiations will be represented. This is the important role played by government mediators in industrial negotiations and of U.N. official or agencies in international conflicts.

SUMMARY AND CONCLUSIONS

Intermediary roles vary greatly. In this chapter we have described the roles of enforcer, fact finder, trainer, and mediator. We discussed how each role varies in its degree of institutionalization and how the incumbents of the roles differ in their neutrality and the resources they control. We also examined how intermediaries interceded in different stages of a social conflict: to prevent its emergence, to limit its escalation, to hasten a settlement, and to sustain a lasting agreement. Intercession to limit escalation, we noted, was related to the degree to which the conflict was institutionalized, the integration between the adversaries, their degree of organization, and the balance of means available to them.

In this chapter, we focused on the many kinds of activities that mediators can and do perform. They vary in degree of intervention from providing a safe and neutral place for adversaries to communicate with each other to suggesting solutions to the conflict. In between are actions such as: (1) providing information about the nature of conflicts in general and about the views of the adversaries in a particular dispute, (2) reducing the emotional tensions and other interpersonal barriers to effective communication, (3) helping the negotiators think of new options for a settlement, (4) improving the negotiating procedures, (5) contributing resources to compensate for losses associated with an agreement, and (6) building support for the agreement among the negotiators and their constituencies.

Finally, we discussed the possible consequences of mediation, particularly in limiting escalation, speeding conflict resolutions, and even increasing the fairness of the agreements reached. On the whole, it does appear that mediators often significantly contribute to these consequences. Mediators can help adversaries accept agreements with less loss of face; they can loosen up the procedures so that new possibilities may be discovered; and they can introduce additional pressures and positive inducements for reaching an agreement. For all these possibilities, it is still necessary to recognize that mediation is constrained by the dimensions of the conflict itself. At any given time, the adversaries may be too antagonistic, too far apart in what they want, and still too hopeful of victory to allow mediators to play a meaningful role. In the Kochan and Jick (1978) study of labor negotiations, they found that the nature of the issue at stake was more important in determining the outcome of the mediation effort than were the actions of the mediators.

It is also worth noting, in conclusion, that the intercession of intermediaries in a conflict is not the only way to mitigate conflicts. The partisans themselves can limit a conflict. For example, they may utilize methods of pursuing their incompatible objectives so that escalation is self-limiting (Wehr 1979a).

Many questions, surround the intercession of intermediaries in conflict. For example, does the intervention of an intermediary make agreements more or less likely to be lasting? It might be argued, on the one hand, that mediator intercession results in relatively equitable agreements, and, therefore, the outcome should be more enduring. On the other hand, intermediary activity may be in the form of enforcer as well as mediator roles. In either case, the intervention may take the form of freezing the status quo or preventing parties from working out a stable resolution. As we saw in Table 6.2, intervention of intermediaries sometimes results in "frozen" conflicts. Frozen conflicts may be relatively unstable.

Another set of questions surround the effectiveness of different ways of interceding in a conflict and particularly different mediation techniques. We have seen that analysts differ about the value and effectiveness of mediators' intervening very actively. There also are dilemmas about many intercession choices. For example, if a trainer-mediator establishes workshops for representatives of adversary collectivities, the more removed the representatives are from policy making, the more able they may be to recognize what their opponents want and to create new possible solutions; but insofar as the representatives are removed from policy making, the greater will be the difficulty in transferring the ideas back into actual policies of the adversaries (Kelman 1977). Other dilemmas are related to the nature of the issues in dispute. Particularly intractable and profound disputes may be relatively amenable to mediation stressing the process of gaining mutual understanding. That emphasis requires extended time to be effective. When profound and intractable issues are in dispute, the fights may be particularly fierce and the desire for speedy action especially strong.

Undoubtedly, which techniques are effective varies with the issues at stake, the nature of the adversaries, the qualities of the intermediary, and the values being sought. We do not now know enough to specify those characteristics. We need to learn much more about the consequences of different ways of interceding in various conditions.

BIBLIOGRAPHY

BERMAN, MAUREEN R. AND JOSEPH E. JOHNSON (eds.), *Unofficial Diplomats* (New York: Columbia University Press, 1977).

BLOOMFIELD, LINCOLN P. AND AMELIA C. LEISS, *Controlling Small Wars: A Strategy for the 1970's* (New York: Knopf, 1969).

BOLLING, LANDRUM R., "Quaker Work in the Middle East following the June 1967 War," pp. 80–88 in Maureen R. Berman and Joseph E. Johnson (eds.), *Unofficial Diplomats* (New York: Columbia University Press, 1977).

BROOKMIRE, DAVID A. AND FRANK SISTRUNK, "The Effects of Perceived Ability and Impartiality of Mediators and Time Pressure on Negotiation," *Journal of Conflict Resolution,* 24 (June 1980), 311–327.

BURTON, JOHN W., *Conflict and Communication: The Use of Controlled Communication in International Relations* (London: Macmillan, 1969).

CROSS, JOHN G., *The Economics of Bargaining* (New York: Basic Books, 1969).

DOOB, LEONARD W. (ed.), *Resolving Conflict in Africa: The Fermeda Workshop* (New Haven, Conn.: Yale University Press, 1970).

DOUGLAS, ANN, *Industrial Peacemaking* (New York: Columbia University Press, 1962).

DOYLE, MICHAEL AND DAVID STRAUS, *How to Make Meetings Work* (New York: Playboy Press, 1976).

FISHER, ROGER WITH THE HELP OF WILLIAM URY, *International Mediation: A Working Guide* (New York: International Peace Academy, 1978).

FISHER, RONALD, "Third Party Consultation: A Method for the Study and Resolution of Conflict," *Journal of Conflict Resolution,* 16 (March 1972), 67–94.

GOLAN, MATTI, *The Secret Conversations of Henry Kissinger: Step-by-Step Diplomacy in the Middle East,* translated by R. G. Stern and S. Stern (New York: Bantam, 1976).

GOLDABER, IRVING AND HOLLY G. PORTER, "The 'Laboratory Confrontation': An Approach to Conflict Management and Social Change," pp. 122–123 in Arthur B. Shostak (ed.), *Putting Sociology to Work* (New York: D. McKay, 1974).

GOULDNER, ALVIN W., *Wildcat Strike* (Yellow Springs, Ohio: Yellow Springs Press, 1954).

HINCKLE, WARREN AND DAVID WELSH, "The Battles of Selma," pp. 100–109 in Walt Anderson (ed.), *The Age of Protest* (Santa Monica, Calif.: Goodyear, 1969).

HOLSTI, K. J., "Resolving International Conflicts: A Taxonomy of Behavior and Some Figures," *Journal of Conflict Resolution,* 10 (September 1966), 272–296.

INTERNATIONAL PEACE ACADEMY, *Coping with Conflict: A Review of the Work and Progress of the International Peace Academy* (New York: International Peace Academy, 1978).

JACKSON, ELMORE, *Meeting of Minds: A Way of Peace through Mediation* (New York: McGraw-Hill, 1952).

KELLOR, FRANCES, *American Arbitration: Its History, Functions and Achievements* (New York: Harper & Brothers, 1948).

KELMAN, HERBERT, C., "The Problem-Solving Workshop in Conflict Resolution," pp. 168–200 in M. R. Berman and J. E. Johnson (eds.), *Unofficial Diplomats,* (New York: Columbia University Press, 1977).

KERR, CLARK, "Industrial Conflict and Its Mediation," *American Journal of Sociology,* 60 (November 1954), 230–245.

KOCHAN, THOMAS A. AND TODD JICK, "The Public Sector Mediation Process," *Journal of Conflict Resolution,* 22 (June 1978), 209–240.

LAUE, JAMES, "Coping with Conflict: Understanding Strategies and Developing Skills," in *Coping with Conflict: Strategies for Extension Community Development and Public Policy Professionals* (Ames, Iowa: North Central Regional Center for Rural Development, Iowa State University, 1979).

LAUE, JAMES AND GERALD CORMICK, "The Ethics of Intervention in Community Disputes," pp. 205–232 in Gordon Bermant, Herbert Kelman, and Donald Warwick (eds.), *The Ethics of Social Intervention* (Washington, D.C.: Halstead, 1978).

LAUE, JAMES, H. AND DANIEL MONTI, "Intervening in School Desegregation Conflicts: The Role of the Monitor," pp. 187–218 in Louis Kriesberg (ed.), *Research in Social Movements, Conflicts and Change,* Vol. 3 (Greenwich, Conn: JAI Press, 1980).

PIVEN, FRANCES FOX AND RICHARD A. CLOWARD, *Regulating the Poor* (New York: Vintage, 1971).

RASKIN, A. H., "The Newspaper Strike: A Step-by-Step Account," *The New York Times* (April 1, 1963).

RUBIN, JEFFREY, Z. AND BERT R. BROWN, *The Social Psychology of Bargaining and Negotiation* (New York: Academic Press, 1975).

SCHELLING, THOMAS C., *The Strategy of Conflict* (Cambridge, Mass.: Harvard University Press, 1960).

SCHONBORN, KARL, *Dealing with Violence: The Challenge Faced by Police and other Peacekeepers* (Springfield, Ill.: Chas. C Thomas, 1975).

SHERIF, MUZAFER, *In Common Predicament* (Boston: Houghton Mifflin, 1966).

STRAUS, DONALD B., "Managing Complexity: A New Look at Environmental Mediation," *Environmental Science and Technology,* 13 (June 1979), 661–665.

WALTON, RICHARD E., "Interpersonal Confrontation and Basic Third Party Functions: A Case Study," *Journal of Applied Behavioral Sciences,* 4, no. 3 (1968), 327–350.

———, *Interpersonal Peacemaking: Confrontations and Third Party Consultation* (Reading, Mass.: Addison-Wesley, 1969).

WARREN, EDGAR L., "Mediation and Fact Finding," pp. 292–300 in Arthur Kornhauser, Robert Dubin, and Arthur M. Ross (eds.), *Industrial Conflict* (New York: McGraw-Hill, 1954).

WEDGE, BRYANT, "A Psychiatric Model for Intercession in Intergroup Conflict," *Journal of Applied Behavioral Science,* 7, no. 6 (1971), pp. 733, 761.

WEHR, PAUL, *Conflict Regulation* (Boulder, Colo.: Westview Press, 1979a).

————, "New Techniques for Resolving Environmental Disputes," pp. 63–82 in Louis Kriesberg (ed.), *Research in Social Movements, Conflicts and Change,* Vol. 2 (Greenwich, Conn.: JAI Press, 1979b).

WOLF, PETER, "International Social Structure and the Resolution of International Conflicts, 1920 to 1965," pp. 35–53 in Louis Kriesberg (ed.), *Research in Social Movements, Conflict, and Change,* Vol. 1 (Greenwich, Conn: JAI Press, 1978).

YOUNG, ORAN R., *The Intermediaries: Third Parties in International Crises* (Princeton, N.J.: Princeton University Press, 1967).

ZION, SIDNEY AND URI DAN, "Untold Story of the Mideast Talks," *The New York Times Magazine* (January 21, 1979).

8

Consequences
of Social Conflicts

Having mentioned several times that the development of a conflict is never completely anticipated by any party in a struggle, we now direct our attention to the unintended consequences of social conflicts. In this chapter, we examine the long-run and indirect consequences of specific social conflicts. The term *consequences,* not functions, is used so as not to imply that the effects of a social conflict account for or explain the prior emergence or persistence of a particular conflict or of conflicts in general and not to imply that conflicts arise and persist for the survival or equilibrium of a larger social entity.

We examine the consequences of social conflicts upon (1) each party to the conflict; (2) the relation of a conflict party to other parties; (3) the relations of the struggling parties; and (4) the system of which the adversaries are a part. We focus upon two sources of consequences: the means used in the struggle and the outcome of the struggle.

The interlocking of social conflicts, a recurrent topic, is involved in several aspects of this discussion. Each party to a struggle has constituent parts that themselves may be in conflict. Each pair of adversaries may, in a larger context, be allies against another adversary. Of special interest in this context is the possibility that external conflict causes internal dissension and division. There is even the possibility that internal discord produces conflicts with external parties or that domestic conflict inhibits external struggles. In assessing and specifying such possibilities, we will apply the concepts and propositions developed thus far.

We begin analyzing the consequences of struggles by considering their effects upon each conflict party. We examine the effects of the mode used and of the outcome achieved.

Consequences of the Mode

How a party pursues its goals affects the conflict group itself as well as its adversary. It affects the culture and social organization of the group and may affect the technology and general level of material well being. We will also analyze what influences it has on the emergence and expression of internal conflicts: whether or not external conflict produces internal solidarity and the lessening of discord.

Structure and Culture. One consequence of a struggle is increased innovation, at least in the means used in conducting the conflict. Such innovation is most obvious in the case of weapons technology in wartime. Allocating more resources to the development of means to coerce the enemy speeds the development of such techniques. This is also true of the development of such persuasive means as psychological warfare. In domestic struggles, too, innovation in the methods of waging the struggle increases in the course of a conflict, but it may be neglected or even stifled in areas unrelated to the conflict. Barbera (1973) examined the consequences of different degrees of nations' participation in World Wars I and II. He found that, on the whole, war activity among the more economically developed countries was associated with increased material development. Nincic (1980) found that the U.S. economy's growth surged during World War II, the Korean War, and the Vietnam War.

Also notable is the impact of manifest conflict and the coercive pursuit of goals upon the differentiation of each conflict unit. It has been asserted that societies at war become more centralized in power. Simmel (1955, pp. 87–89) has argued that war tends to promote the concentration of power in the highest levels of government. There is systematic evidence consistent with his idea. Lee (1978) studied developing countries in the 1960s and found that external conflict behavior (wars, military action, accusations) was followed by political repression. Cutright (1963) studied the degree of political development or democracy in nations of the world 1940 and 1961. Political development or democracy was measured by the number of years there was a parliament with more than one significant party and the number of years with an elected executive; let us assume that politically developed countries are less centralized. He found among countries of the Western Hemisphere and Europe that only 31 percent of the countries that had been invaded during war revealed political development gains, while 76 percent of the countries whose territory had not been invaded in war showed such gains. Naroll (1969) studied pairs of conspicuous states of several major world civilizations. He found wars somewhat correlated with political centralization. It is also possible, of course, that more centralized states were more prone to war. Ethnographic evidence from studies of preindustrial societies yield ambiguous results (Otterbein 1968; Abrahamson 1969). Certainly external conflict is only one among many other determinants of the level of political centralization.

Groups regularly engaged in conflict behavior within a society might also be expected to be hierarchically controlled. But struggles with adversaries also require constituency support and often widespread participation. This may result in granting benefits to relatively deprived states in order to gain their support. Faced with an external enemy, domestic minority groups, women, and members of the working class may gain new advantages (or promises of them). Furthermore, in struggles that involve general mobilization of the group's resources, those who were underutilized may become more valuable (Nincic 1980). In modern total wars, people who were previously excluded or only peripherally involved have been drawn into industrial employment. As a result, the overall inequality within a society may decline. This was the case in the United States for World Wars I and II and the Civil War (Kriesberg 1979, pp. 58–65). There was, however, no decrease in income inequality in the United States associated with the wars in Korea or Vietnam. The consequences of a war upon internal economic equality, then, vary with the war and the degree of mobilization of resources.

The costs of waging a struggle are not equally borne by all members of a conflict group. Clearly, in warfare, young men are particularly likely to pay the heaviest burden. Class and ethnic differences also exist in bearing the burdens of war. But as the discussion above indicates, the lower strata of a conflict group do not necessarily always carry that heavier cost. Thus, Winter (1977a) has found that in World War I, the British elite suffered heavy casualities—greater than the country as a whole. The sons of the elite, these graduates of Oxford and Cambridge, volunteered and served in military roles that had very high mortality rates. Furthermore, Winter (1977b) found that the health of the British working class improved during World War I, but this was not true for the working class in countries on the European continent involved in the 1914–1918 war.

Struggles also can bring defeats and adversity that promote dissension and, hence, weaken oligarchic control (Barbash 1967, p. 98). Under many circumstances, as the analyses of revolutions indicate, the weakness of the ruling group resulting from external stress facilitates successful challenges from subordinate strata.

Waging conflicts has diverse consequences for the internal structure of each conflict unit. Whether the use of coercion increases equality or hierarchical domination, or both, in different spheres, varies with many specific conditions. This variation may be the reason that Tannenbaum and Kahn (1957), in a study of four local unions, found no relationship between the amount of union-management conflict and the hierarchical distribution of power within the local unions.

Conflict per se does not determine the degree of centralized control within the contending parties. Whether or not struggling contributes to centralization depends upon the character of the conflicts and preexisting cleavages, for example, their degree of regulation, the nature of the adversary, and the relative power of the parties. Thus, a group engaged in a struggle with a much stronger adversary and seeking large changes tends to develop an ideology and strategy of conflict behavior that require great membership commitment. Such organizations also tend to develop centralized control and obedience (Coser 1956, p. 103). Revolutionary groups, such as those in czarist Russia, are illustrative of this structure (Nahirny 1962; Selznick 1952).

Andrzejewski (1954, p. 115) argues that if a society has a high rate of military participation by its members, then warfare will produce totalitarianism. The commitment and the allocation of resources in accordance with the way in which a conflict is pursued has lasting implications (Russett 1969). Herein lies one of the fundamental tragedies of social conflicts. In struggling for a particular end, the means used can preclude the attainment of the sought-for goals. Thus, "the types of personalities, as well as the forms of organization that usually emerge in a violent revolutionary struggle . . . are those which undercut the humanistic hopes of such endeavors" (Oppenheimer 1969, p. 71). Violence and the suppression of internal dissent inhibit popular participation even after "victory."

The means used in a struggle have enduring consequences for the self-conceptions of the users. This is, indeed, part of the argument some people give to justify coercive action and even violence (Fanon 1966). By such actions oppressed persons prove themselves to themselves. For example, some people have contended that American black men will achieve a greater sense of manliness by acting with courage and bravado. Of course, asserting one's claims for equality need not be done violently in order to demonstrate male or human liberation. In any case, the kinds of experiences that people have in the course of a conflict affect their views of themselves and of the world. It behooves us to examine what evidence there is about effects of the various experiences.

In a series of national public opinion surveys conducted in 1964, 1968, and 1970, a cross section of blacks and whites were asked to say where they would put various groups on a "feeling scale," ranging from zero (very unfavorable) to 100 (very favorable) (Campbell 1971, p. 141). In 1964 about half of the whites reported they were very favorable to whites, and this declined to 39 percent in 1968 and 30 percent in 1970. A higher proportion of blacks were very favorable toward blacks, and this proportion did not decline over this period, neither, however, did it rise (the percentage saying they felt very favorable was 65, 65, and 63 in 1964, 1968, and 1970, respectively). Obviously, the interracial conflict behavior is not the sole determinant of such assessments. But it probably contributed to the decline in white regard for whites, while it may have raised self-regard for some blacks and lowered it for others. A struggle and how it is waged has many consequences, and the meaning depends upon the interpretations and expectations people make as the struggle proceeds.

Since the political and social activism of the 1960s, many persons have speculated about and studied the consequences for the activists. Did they later become indistinguishable from others of similar position and background? Or did they remain committed to direct action and social change? Fendrich and Krauss (1978) analyzed data from a sample of U.S. whites and blacks who demonstrated in 1963 and student leaders in two universities about nine years later; they also studied a sample of Japanese students who several years earlier had been at universities where there had been large-scale political demonstrations. On the whole, they found that the activists of the 1960s tend to be more politically involved as adults than their student counterparts who were not active in protest politics. Lang and Lang (1978) studied a sample of persons who had been awarded a Woodrow Wilson Fellowship for graduate study. They used retrospective questions to examine changes through college and beyond for different age cohorts. They found that broadening experiences involving change in milieu, like going away to college, was a major influence in accounting for changes in political ideology. They also concluded that the liberalizing influence of the 1960s movement activities would persist in this academic elite.

It is important to study even longer run effects. Major conflicts can have a particularly strong impact upon the age group that reaches political maturity in the midst of it. This derives from the idea of political generations (Mannheim 1952; Heberle 1951, pp. 120–127). The conditions of social life, the salient issues, and the means used in settling them have enduring consequences. Thus the American depression generation is relatively more class conscious than other generations (Leggett 1968, pp. 90–91).

A detailed analysis of generational experiences upon foreign policy views was made by Cutler (1970) using survey data from 1946, 1951, 1956, 1961, and 1966. The data indicate that views of foreign policy vary with different age cohorts. Thus, the salience of foreign policy issues had tended to increase with each age cohort and is particularly high among persons who became eighteen years old between 1914 and 1918 and between 1934 and 1938. Advocacy of war in dealing with international crises is particularly low for those who became eighteen between 1919 and 1923 and between 1924 and 1928,while those who turned eighteen during World War I and World War II seem particularly likely to advocate war.

Kriesberg and Klein (1980) also examined possible generational effects of war experiences on opinions about U.S. military spending. They found that in 1973 and 1975 the Vietnam War generation was disportionally likely to say that the United States was spending too much on arms and the World War II generation was disportionally likely to say that the country was not spending enough. By 1978, however, generational effects were no longer clearly significant, holding age constant.

Internal Conflicts. External conflict might be expected to lead to the submergence of internal conflicts; in the face of a common enemy internal differences become less salient (LeVine and Campbell 1972; Coser 1956). It might be expected, however, that external conflicts aggravate internal divisions and induce more open expression of internal discord. Evidence of both tendencies can be cited. Rather than try to resolve this issue by asserting that external conflict induces or inhibits internal conflict, we need to specify the conditions under which each happens. Both may be occurring at the same time but with varying strength and for different segments of the population. In order to specify the effects of external struggles upon internal conflicts, we should be able to apply the mode of analysis already presented. We will examine how external conflicts affect the bases for conflict, the emergence of conflict awareness, and the ways in which struggles are conducted.

External conflict increases the bases for internal conflict in several ways. Generally, insofar as sacrifices are made to sustain coercive behavior against an adversary, a basis for conflict grows. Sacrificing to exert coercion means that the people have less of what they want than they previously had. Furthermore, the deprivations themselves can produce conflict insofar as there are inequities in the deprivations among the members of a conflict unit.

Conflict behavior, however, need not entail only sacrifices from constituent members. We saw in Chapter 4 that some conflict modes are gratifying to some people. Aside from such considerations, the mobilization of persons for a struggle gives importance to everyone who is being mobilized. People who had been relatively marginal or unimportant are now accorded more status and more equal access to other limited resources. For example in World Wars I and II, American blacks and women improved their positions in the labor market by entering occupations that had been previously closed to them. Such improvement, it is true, may be seen as a relative deprivation by whites and by men, and the invasion of their preserves of superiority may be resented. This might have played a role in antiblack riots, such as the 1943 Detroit riot (Brown 1944).

The possibility noted previously that conflict increases centralization of power may also be a source of deprivation and, hence, of dissent. Insistence upon unity and support for the struggle against an adversary may impose severe burdens upon significant groups.

External conflict may also markedly affect the emergence of internal social conflicts. Participation in an external struggle gives partisans an increased sense of their own rights and ability to attain them. Fighting one battle tends to give them the confidence to fight another. Veterans of wars may reenter civilian society with more militancy than they had prior to combat. At the officer level this sometimes engenders coups and at the rank-and-file level increased militancy in asserting old claims.

An external conflict may also affect the emergence of internal disputes by reducing the salience of internal dissension. Engaging in a common popular purpose submerges internal discord. For example, there is evidence that during civil rights campaigns aggressive crimes by blacks decreased (Solomon and others 1965). This can happen by absorbing energy and attention or by seeming to provide alternative ways of attaining sought-for ends. It can also happen by placing internal divisions within the context of fighting a common enemy. When the major basis for solidarity is a common enemy, then hostility toward that foe will strengthen solidarity. In this way, as the conflict with an adversary increases, military alliances have lessened internal dissension. This seems to be the case for NATO solidarity and Soviet-Chinese solidarity (Travis 1970; Holsti 1969; Hopmann 1967). Of course, this is relative to the deprivations arising from the adversary's hostility and coercion; at some point, external pressure places divisive strains upon internal solidarity. In general, however, collectivities organized in order to confront an adversary tend to show decreased solidarity when the threat from that adversary falls.

The balance between deprivation and presumed purpose helps explain the different internal consequences of limited and unlimited war. Smith (1971) analyzed domestic U.S. responses to World War II, the Korean War, and the Vietnam War. He studied changes in public attitudes about support for each war, changes in evasive draft behavior, and changes in protests and repression during each war. He found that during both the Korean War and the Vietnam War, but not during World War II, there were increasing disaffection and dissent. In the Korean War dissatisfaction and withdrawal of legitimacy contributed to the support of McCarthyism, conservatism, and repression of Communist and alleged Communist dissent. In the Vietnam War the dissatisfaction supported violent and nonviolent demonstrations in opposition to the war.

Let us see if we can interpret these finding using the ideas discussed in this book. First, the general mobilization of a total war, although entailing deprivations, is normally more equally deprivational than a limited war. Thus, in the United States there was a decrease in income inequality during World War II but no appreciable decline during the Korean War (Budd 1967). Second, the limited character of a war and the limited nature of its goals are less able to supersede domestic differences. That is, insofar as the struggle seems to be about issues that do not threaten the collectivity and its members, then it does not reduce the salience and awareness of internal struggles. Neither the Vietnam nor the Korean wars was viewed as involving the same threat to the nation that World War II was seen to have. The Korean War, however, was generally viewed as more justified and morally correct than the Vietnam War and yet more partisan (Smith 1971; Halberstam 1973; Mueller 1973). These differences may account for the variation in the direction of disaffection, dissent, and protest toward the two wars.

Finally, the conduct of the limited wars was not generally viewed as successful as was the course of World War II. Failure is reason enough to punish leaders and withdraw support. In terms of the analysis we have been making, however, failure has other implications for internal conflict. The leaders and authorities ordinarily are perceived as less competent, and, therefore, the chances of successfully challenging them is augmented. In other words, failure is a source of grievance; it does not compensate for deprivations; and it invites the assertion of previously submerged grievances against authorities.

External conflict affects how internal conflicts are pursued as well as their bases and emergence. Often there is an attempt to stifle or suppress overt conflict behavior that might interfere with the pursuit of the collectivities' external conflict. For example, during World War II, trade unions were induced by the federal government to pledge not to strike. Nevertheless, strikes increased with each year of the war except 1942. Presumably, the power of workers relative to management was greater in this tight labor market. This would be an inducement to strike, as noted in Chapter 4. Nevertheless, the great wave of strikes immediately after the war indicated that some stifling of labor disputes may have been accomplished. The upsurge after the war may also have reflected efforts to redress grievances by employers who felt they had been in a weaker bargaining position. At the same time, the inflation of the postwar period was another inducement for workers to strike.

How external conflict affects internal conflicts, then, might be expected to differ with the preexisting discord and the character of the unit (Coser 1956). In the case of nation-states, the political organization of the state significantly affects the degree and nature of any relationship between foreign and domestic conflict behavior. Wilkenfeld (1969) analyzed Tanter and Rummel's (Tanter 1966) data on internal and external conflict behavior in eighty-three nations between 1955–1957. He distinguished two dimensions of internal conflict: turmoil (riots, demonstrations, general strikes, assassinations, and government crises) and internal war (revolutions, purges, guerrilla warfare, and number killed in all domestic violence). He distinguished three dimensions of external conflict: diplomatic (number of ambassadors and other officials expelled or recalled), belligerent (number of antiforeign demonstrations and number of countries with which diplomatic relations were severed), and war (military clashes, number of wars, mobilizations, and people killed in foreign conflict behavior).

Wilkenfeld examined the relationship between external conflict and internal conflict in countries with three kinds of regimes: personalist, centrist, and polyarchic. Personalist regimes are dictatorial but less centralized than the centrist regimes; they are primarily Latin American countries. The centrist regimes are centralized dictatorships; half are socialist and some are Middle Eastern. The polyarchic regimes are in economically developed Western nations.

Wilkenfeld reports the relationship between external conflict in one year with internal conflict one year later and two years later. In countries with personalist regimes he found that diplomatic conflict behavior was somewhat related (.26) to internal turmoil a year later, and belligerency was related to internal war one year and two years later (.37 and .29, respectively). War was related, two years later, to both turmoil and internal war (.17 and .15, respectively). Presumably personalist regimes are generally neither able to suppress internal dissension nor conduct popularly supported external conflicts.

In countries with centrist regimes external conflict behavior is not related at all to subsequent domestic turmoil or with internal war (also see Wilkenfeld and Zinnes 1973). Apparently centrist regimes are able to control whatever dissension external conflict might induce. In polyarchic societies there is a small relationship between diplomatic conflict behavior and internal turmoil one and two years later (.21 and .19, respectively); there are also positive relations, although even smaller, between belligerency and war and subsequent internal turmoil. There is no statistically significant relationship between external conflict and internal war, however. There is some indication of a negative relationship; diplomacy and belligerency are negatively related to internal war two years later (–.15 and –.11). It appears that polyarchic regimes may permit the expression of dissent about external policies and about other issues, but this does not escalate to internal war. Indeed, for legitimate regimes waging relatively popular foreign conflict behavior, the chances of internal war may be reduced.

On the whole, in the contemporary world, the relative significance of internal conflict issues and the strains that result from conducting external conflict behavior are such that external conflict behavior is slightly *positively* related to domestic conflict (Tanter 1966). This is consistent with our observations about external stress and revolutions. Foreign provocative ventures generally would *not* lessen internal discord. But the major point is another one. Whether external conflict behavior makes internal struggles more or less likely and severe depends upon three kinds of possible effects. First, external fights may increase or decrease the underlying bases for conflicts within an adversary group; this varies with, for example, the equity with which the costs of waging a struggle are borne. Second, external conflicts may make potential internal conflicts more or less visible to domestic partisans, depending upon the nature of the goals in the external struggle and upon how the adversary defines the struggle and its antagonist. Finally, external conflicts tend either to foster or to inhibit the use of coercion in waging conflicts, depending upon the lesson experience teaches. People apply what they think they learned from the external fight to their pursuit of conflicting goals within their own group. Furthermore, leaders of a conflict group may be more or less permissive about the coercive expression of dissent during a fight. Ultimately, whether an external fight increases or reduces internal conflict behavior depends upon the balance of all these effects.

Consequences of the Outcome

The way a struggle ends, as well as how it is pursued, has consequences for conflict parties. We consider how the outcome of a struggle affects a party's future aims, the capacity to pursue them, and internal conflicts.

Future Goals. A conflict party's goals may be extended or contracted. The conflict party's view of the outcome as a victory or a defeat might be expected to affect importantly the expansion or contraction of future aims. But, victory may result in the expansion of aims or in the cessation of other demands; and defeat, too, may cause the abandonment of previous goals or their further expansion. For example, the victory of women's suffrage was more of a culmination than a stimulus for the women's movement of the time. The victory of the civil rights movement in gaining the passage of legislation making voting for blacks in the South more equitable was a stimulus for further demands rather than a culmination. Japan's defeat after World War II resulted in abandonment of previous imperial goals, but the defeat of France in 1870 did not make it relinquish its claim to lost territories.

Whether an outcome, regarded as victory or defeat, results in expanding or contracting aims depends upon how the outcome has altered the conditions that determine a unit's aims. The outcome may change the partisans in ways that markedly affect their formulation of goals. Particularly important are changes in the collective identity of the conflict group, changes in the magnitude of the group's grievance, and changes in the belief that the grievance can be redressed.

The self-conception of a partisan group can be significantly changed by a victory or a defeat. Victory may be viewed as imposing new grand responsibilities for others. Thus, a revolutionary party espousing nationalist goals, mixed with religious or political claims may increase the religious or political emphases upon victory. For example, a successful revolutionary struggle to overthrow a regime allegedly dependent on a foreign power may become transformed, upon the revolutionaries' gaining power, to one that claims to advance the new government's conception of socialism or Islam.

Victories that bring challenging groups recognition may also result in new self-conceptions that limit further claims. Having entered the establishment they had challenged, leaders may be co-opted into sustaining what had been won by ceasing to press for new gains. A new sense of identity will have emerged.

Collective self-conceptions also change after a fight is over because the coalition that waged the struggle inevitably changes. A successful challenge to a governing group, for example, requires the collaboration of diverse groups. Once a victory has been gained, the coalition tends to fall apart (Tilly 1978, pp. 218–219). Outcomes affect grievances in several ways. Defeat itself is often an additional grievance. For example, the shame of defeat seems to require another battle and a victory in order to vindicate honor and self-respect. This was the case for example among some Arab conflict groups vis-à-vis Israel (Peretz 1970; Harkabi 1970). In addition, the loss of territory or other resources may be part of the outcome.

Although new grievances may be added with defeat, changes in the social structure and the character of the collective identity may insulate or diminish the grievances. The defeat may be attributed to the now dismissed leaders; *they* bear the shame of defeat. Or the dominant group or class within a conflict organization may be overthrown, and the support for the former goals will not be continued by the newly dominant group. Therefore, victors sometimes try to alter the social structure of their defeated adversary. For example, efforts to democratize Japan and Germany after World War II by breaking the power of the military, large landlords, and industrialists presumed this strategy.

Conversions sometimes related to such structural changes also may lead to fundamental alterations in aims. For example, business managers may become convinced that trade unions are in their own best interests by reducing labor turnover and futher legitimatizing the distinctive managerial role.

Even a great victory may be the incentive for an expansion of goals. The fruits of victory often are disappointing. Having gained the long sought-for end, the victor may discover that it does not yield the anticipated pleasures. In that case, aims may be extended. The partisans realize that they had set their goals too modestly. For example, in a newly independent nation the leaders may find many problems remaining and believe that political sovereignty is not enough; economic liberation from neocolonialism becomes a new goal.

Finally, what has been won may become the basis for new claims. The level achieved is secured and accepted as background. Many social welfare gains in the United States and other developed countries have followed this scenario. Once contested strongly, after they became institutionalized the gains are taken for granted.

Whether future goals are expanded or contracted depends, finally, on the partisans' *beliefs* that grievances can be redressed. The apparent irreversibility of defeat is critical here. Thus, a defeat that seems irreversible would lead to the abandonment of former aims. The belief that the grievances cannot be redressed may follow from experiencing a clear and crushing defeat. For example, in 1941 Finland joined with Hitler's Germany to regain territory lost to the Soviet Union in the 1940 war between Finland and the Soviet Union. In ending World War II the Soviet Union obtained portions of Finnish territory. The Finnish leader, Urbo Kekkonen, however, told the Finnish people: "We must own our defeat to be final. The superior force of the Soviet Union is absolute and continuing; to harbor revanchist thoughts or indulge in open or secret scheming to regain lost territory means the destruction of our people" (Reston 1970).

The clarity of defeat is aided by institutionalization, otherwise the coercive force must appear to be totally overwhelming. The entire outcome and its context underlie the recognition of irreversibility. Germany and Japan abandoned former goals after World War II because their changed position within the international system made the goals clearly seem impossible. Similarly, in the case of the trade union movement, management's acceptance of employee rights to form trade unions and bargain collectively reflects the consequences of the outcome of a long struggle. That outcome includes legislative (and, therefore, governmental) support for collective bargaining and the power of employees organized in trade unions.

Capacity to Pursue Goals. A major component of a conflict group's expansion or contraction of aims is its belief in its ability to redress its grievances. That belief is largely dependent upon its capacities relative to particular adversaries. We now consider how outcomes affect the capacities of contending parties to wage future struggles.

Victory should strengthen a conflict group for new struggles, and defeat should weaken it. Victory, especially immediately afterwards, increases the commitment of marginal members of the conflict group; collective solidarity is increased and a sense of confidence strengthened. For example, following the Israeli victory in the Six-Day War of 1967, Jewish support from other countries increased. Contributions, immigration, and emotional involvement grew (Vocse 1971). Victory may also mean the creation of an increasingly effective organization for the waging of conflict and, hence, the search for new goals to which the capacity can be directed.

But victory does not always strengthen a group for new fights. We must also consider how victory weakens the capacity to pursue additional struggles. First, victory may entail burdens and costs that drain energy and other resources, making them unavailable for conflict. This can be variously exemplified. Student victories in gaining participation in the governance of universities then require searching for representatives, discussing positions, and attending what often seem like interminable committee and general meetings. Victory in international wars may also entail burdens of administering the gains that may not be fully compensated for by what is taken from the vanquished or what is available for exploitation.

A victorious outcome also may indirectly weaken the capacity to wage future conflicts. Fundamentally, the sense of grievance may be lessened by victory and, therefore, the drive for further pursuit of a conflicting goal reduced. In other words, if you get what you fought for, you do not need to fight on. Victory may even diminish collective solidarity in the long run, particularly in consensual conflicts about aggregate goals. Thus, an ethnic group, having struggled for equal opportunities for its members, may find that with equality members have lost some of their solidarity and sense of collective identity. In the United States successful assimilation of ethnic groups has meant such losses of identity. This need not be permanent and, indeed, we are witnessing a resurgence of collective ethnic identities through confrontation with other groups along ethnic lines.

Of course, victory always brings some disappointment, even bitterness. What was anticipated in the storm of a struggle must be purer and better than the ambiguous and complex reality of even a victorious outcome. Revolutionary leaders can look back nostalgically upon the purity of the struggle compared to the drabness and complexity of governing. For participants in an intense struggle, great hopes inevitably are not completely fulfilled.

Internal Conflicts. Outcomes as well as the conduct of a struggle may affect the emergence of conflicts within one of the units. Any conflict group is diverse enough that a particular outcome will benefit some members more than others and, perhaps, at the expense of others. For example, a collective bargaining agreement that gives all workers a fixed-sum increase will improve the relative position of the lower-paid workers, while an across-the-board percentage increase will be more of a benefit to the higher-paid workers than to those who already earn less. Either strategy pursued long or in an extreme form will create internal dissension, and the aggrieved category might come increasingly to oppose the union leadership and that portion of the members who support it. In a similar way, racial integration may adversely affect those blacks who had a protected occupational niche within a segregated labor market. For example, public school integration in the South threatened the jobs of black teachers in predominantly black schools when one system of evaluations of credentials was used. Of course, this implies that other outcomes could be imagined which would not be divisive to the black community. The attainment of such outcomes from the adversary, however, may be more difficult.

Victory, as we have noted, may itself arouse internal dissension when the hopes raised in the struggle are not realized upon gaining the prized outcome. Revolutions, national liberation, participation in governance, or equality of access to previously closed occupations or institutions may seem disappointing in the cold dawn of their attainment. Dissension and revolt, at least against the leaders, are possible responses. Systematic empirical data are lacking, however, on the extent to which conflicts are more likely after a victory than when the adversary was still engaged in conflict behavior.

Even without systematic data, it seems safe to suggest that defeat is more productive of internal discord than is victory. Not only does the defeated party suffer increased grievances, but the leaders are likely to be viewed as incompetent. Attacks against the particular leaders and sometimes against the stratum from which they come are likely after a defeat. In national societies the protests may take the form of coups or of social revolutions. The Egyptian army officers who overthrew King Faruq in 1952 were at least partly reacting to the defeat suffered in the 1948 war with Israel (Walz 1966, p. 79). Trade union leaders who fail to win benefits desired by their constituency are likely to face factional disputes and challenges to their leadership (Weir 1970).

CONSEQUENCES FOR CONFLICTS
WITH OTHER PARTIES

Conflicts between focal conflict parties also have effects upon each one's relations with many other parties. Heretofore we considered nonfocal parties largely in terms of their possible intervention in an ongoing social conflict. Now we ask: Will a party that is engaged in a struggle be more or less likely to engage another group in a fight? We present the various answers to the question and then try to reconcile the answers.

This discussion is limited to the ways in which internal conflicts may affect the emergence of external ones. We will not consider how one side in a conflict may be more or less likely to become embroiled in a struggle with other parties simply because it is in a conflict. We have already examined some aspects of this in the earlier discussions about the possible intervention of other parties, polarization, and coalition formation. All that needs to be added here are grounds for a partisan group to attack another party. As already suggested, conflict groups would be expected to avoid involving other parties as allies of their adversaries. Nevertheless, sometimes a conflict unit may attack another party in order to combat its main adversary more effectively. A prototype of this is the 1914 attack of imperial Germany against Belgium in order to fight France. This discussion also excludes the consequences of the outcome of conflicts. The outcome's implications for each party's future conflicts with other parties were implicit in earlier chapters, if we consider that the outcome affects each unit's conditions that in turn affect conflict awareness and pursuit.

Possible Effects

Several reasons why internal dissension induces external conflicts are noteworthy. One idea is that leaders of a collectivity, challenged by elements of their constituency or seeing a strife-ridden constituency, act aggressively or even provocatively toward an external enemy in order to rally support and achieve collective solidarity. From what we saw earlier, it is not at all certain that external conflict mitigates internal conflict, but perhaps leaders believe that it does and so use external adventures to get support from their constituency.

Internal disorders can result in external conflict by embroiling another party in hostile actions with one of the focal contending parties. Thus, foreigners and their goods may be hurt, damaged, or threatened by a segment of another country and so entangle the foreigner's group. For example, disorders or threats to corporate investments in one country may bring intervention from another to protect its citizens and their goods. This has happened in Latin America when the U.S. government and its agents have intervened to protect investments of U.S.-based corporations.

Internal factional disputes may also mean that a group is neglected by its purported representative, and consequently, it seeks its own redress of grievances against a third party. For example, trade union members may feel that the union leaders are insufficiently assertive and therefore will act independently against the management by initiating a strike.

It is also conceivable that internal conflicts stimulate feelings of hostility that are generalized, and bystander parties become targets for aggression. This, of course, is one kind of "unrealistic" conflict. Finally, it is possible that internal dissension so weakens a group that it is vulnerable to attack and, therefore, "invites" aggression.

There are also reasons to suppose that internal dissension can inhibit both the emergence of external conflicts and engagement in conflict behavior. First, internal struggles may so weaken a potential conflict group that it avoids confrontations with other groups. Second, internal dissension absorbs energies and resources that limit coercive efforts against outside parties. For example, a nation-state that is plagued by claims for more goods and services by generally submerged groups may find that foreign wars draw resources away from home. Finally, internal dissension reduces collective solidarity and support for collective goals against any adversary.

Specification

The effects of internal dissension upon external conflicts depend on the nature of the conflict unit, the degree and manner of internal dissension, and the state of relations with other parties.

In order to wage vigorous external conflict involving organized collective violence, as in wars, the conflict unit must have at least minimal solidarity and internal order. A variety of evidence is consistent with this idea (Broch and Galtung 1966; LeVine 1965). Wilkenfeld's (1969) analysis of internal and external conflict also gives evidence consistent with this interpretation. He found that in countries with personalist regimes, but not with centrist or polyarchic regimes, internal warfare was inversely related to external war one and two years later, −.15 and −.30, respectively. Internal war, however, was positively related to belligerence (antiforeign demonstrations and severance of diplomatic relations) one and two years later, .28 and .29, respectively. Presumably in countries that are relatively weak, internal disorders may stimulate leaders to act belligerently, but not to the point of entering into military clashes and wars.

In countries with polyarchic regimes internal war is not related to subsequent belligerence or external war. Perhaps internal war stimulates and inhibits external conflict behavior depending on additional considerations. Turmoil, however, is positively related to belligerence one year later (.19) and to war two years later (.32). It is possible that leaders in such regimes are willing to try to use external conflict to counteract internal dissension.

In countries with centrist regimes turmoil was also related to belligerence a year later (.28). But more strikingly, internal war was related to external war one and two years later (.32 and .43, respectively). In such regimes it may be that leaders become involved in external wars following internal dissension as a result of the regime's own provocation. It may also be that internal war invites external intervention, particularly in such societies. Furthermore, it is possible that internal war that is successful for the revolutionaries installs a more ideologically crusading regime and a more activist foreign policy.

In all these cases we are considering struggles that are hardly regulated. In more institutionalized conflict relationships, between parties organized for conflict, dissension within one of the parties stimulates more aggressive conduct if it is not so great as to weaken the party. Thus trade union factionalism generally does not lessen union militancy toward management (Seidman and others 1958). Indeed, union factionalism may lead to more external conflict than more quiescent memberships would (Ross and Irwin 1951). We have previously noted similar evidence indicating the same pattern within the civil rights movement (McWorter and Crain 1967).

The long-range results of different modes of waging struggles has been a matter of speculative assertions by many persons. Will waging a violent internal struggle make the group within which the struggle was fought more or less likely to use violence in relations with other parties? Again, we have only the beginning of systematic and comprehensive research. Dugan (1979) selected countries that have become independent since World War II and examined the consequences of varying amounts of violent and nonviolent actions preceding independence. She found a relatively strong positive relationship between violence before independence and later external belligerence.

In the course of a struggle leading persons and groups are particularly identified not only with the ends but also with the means of struggle. Furthermore, the group tends to become differentiated in terms of the conflict mode. In the case of society-wide struggles the emergence of armed groups gives military leaders particular salience in making policy and in influencing how that policy will be pursued.

The way in which a struggle has been waged also affects later relations with other parties. Given the interlocking character of all social conflicts, different forms of struggle are likely to involve alliances with different sets of other parties. Thus, an armed revolutionary struggle, if successful, generally requires external bases of support. Alliances so established may persist, and the enemies of the allies are potential adversaries. These factors contribute to explaining the complex set of antagonisms among the peoples and governments in Vietnam, Kampuchea, Thailand, China, Laos, the United States, and the Soviet Union.

CONSEQUENCES FOR RELATIONS
BETWEEN ADVERSARIES

One of the fundamental issues about any struggle is how it affects future relations among the contending parties. What are the consequences of how a conflict is pursued and of its outcome upon the continuing interrelations of the previous adversaries?

Consequences of the Mode

How each party tries to reach its goals affects the feelings the adversaries have toward each other. The exchange of violence tends to embitter relations, and this is particularly likely if the violence exceeds the conventional understandings of what is appropriate. Such feelings make a stable outcome less likely. While an outcome attained in large part through persuasion is more likely to be stable, those reached through explicit terminating processes and that are mutually and openly agreed upon tend to be more stable than outcomes that are only implicit.

The way in which a struggle is waged also affects how the parties will fight each other in the future. Whatever has happened becomes a precedent for its repetition. Having used violence once, it is easier to use it toward that party again. For example, the Israeli and Syrian governments are freer to resort to military violence against each other because they have done so in the past.

This is not to say that extreme coercion, if victorious, cannot so crush one party that the defeated one does not venture to contest the victor. When dealing with major social categories, however, even overwhelming defeats succeed only in demolishing particular organizations engaged in the conflict; new organizations emerge again. Thus, the American Railway Union led by Eugene Debs may have been crushed after the Pullman Strike of 1894, but railroad workers and workers generally went on to organize again and eventually to win political support to secure many of the goals they sought (Lindsey 1942).

The means used at one time may be a lesson about what is to be avoided as well as a precedent for the future. Which it is depends on the assessment the parties make about the results of the mode used.

Consequences of the Outcome

The outcome of every struggle is the basis for a new one. Whether or not that new conflict emerges into awareness, what the magnitude of the issues in contention is, and what the means used in the conflict are, however, vary with the outcome. We limit our observations here to the emergence of a new struggle. We ask: What about the outcome makes it more or less likely to endure?

Bases for Conflict. In the case of dissensual conflicts, outcomes that entail conversion may mean the disappearance of the bases for a perpetuation or renewal of the struggle. Thus, if the bases for conflict had been one party's insistence that the other hold the "right" ideas (namely, its own), then the adversary's conversion will cause the conflict to vanish. Similarly, if the party making claims upon another is convinced that the other's beliefs are equally valid, or anyway valid for *them,* again the basis for dissensual conflict has gone.

In the case of consensual conflicts outcomes may reduce the bases of conflict by reducing the disparities in what is valued. An outcome, however, may also entail the loss of what is valued by one side and its receipt by the other. A victor, indeed, is likely to impose terms of settlement that make the defeated, at least initially, worse off than it had been earlier. Presumably, that is an unstable outcome. The seeds of a new struggle are thus planted. Whether or not a fight breaks out, however, depends on the conditions that are relevant to the emergence of a struggle.

Integrative outcomes might be expected to be more permanent than one-sided ones or even than compromises. Yet, as in the study of conflict outcomes generally, there is a paucity of research. Schonborn (1975) examined intervention by peace-keeping forces in interpersonal, intergroup, interorganizational, intercommunal, and international conflicts. He categorized the intervention efforts as humanitarian (relying primarily on words, moral power, and social science expertise) and authoritarian (relying primarily on weapons and physical power). As noted in Chapter 7, humanitarian peace keeping was more likely than authoritarian interventions to result in intergration and compromise outcomes and less likely in domination ones. But, humanitarian interventions were no more likely than authoritarian ones to be permanent (requiring fewer repeated interventions).

It may be that integrative outcomes are preferred by more parties to a conflict than domination outcomes, but an imposed settlement may be equally stable.

Emergence of Conflict. One way in which an outcome affects the likelihood that a new struggle will erupt is that conditions are created that affect the sense of grievance and the belief that something can be done about it. We meet again with contradictory implications from the same event. The imposition of severe losses in status, power, or material resources is the basis of a grievance and a motive for instituting a struggle, but it also reduces the chances of redressing the grievance and, therefore, reduces the likelihood of entering a fight.

A reason that imposition of severe negative sanctions is conducive to later strife is that the imposition of losses gradually dissipates, leaving the side that suffered losses with increasing ability to redress old grievances. Or, if the conditions imposed lead to continuing deterioration, then struggles can occur from desperation. As Keynes (1920) wrote about the implications of the harsh terms in the treaty of Versailles ending World War I, "An inefficient, unemployed, disorganized Europe faces us, torn by internal strife and international hate, fighting, starving, pillaging, and lying" (p. 249).

Making changes that produce a basic grievance for the adversary must be compensated by other gains or involve sufficient reordering of strength so that redress based in conflict is viewed as impossible. Otherwise the losses and resulting grievance would be the basis for a new struggle, as they are in conterrevolutions. Half-won revolutions may be the foundation of new efforts to restore the status quo ante. As a revolutionary group attempts to smash the bases of strength of its adversary, it increases their grievance. While the revolutionary group often considers only the stability of an outcome, it must balance the grievance it is creating, the effective power to overwhelm efforts to redress the grievances, and the compensating gains to the aggrieved party in order to sustain the outcome. Without doing so, even constitutionally chosen governments seeking major social changes may be overthrown, as were the governments of Spain in the 1930s and of Chile in the 1970s. From the perspective of the challenged government, inadequate reforms or concessions may lead to more vigorous revolutionary challenges later (Skocpol 1979).

Outcomes that introduce major changes in only limited spheres of the relations between adversary parties are likely to be turned back. The emancipation of slaves after the American Civil War, for example, established legal rights for blacks but without effective economic and political power equal to those rights. The rights were reduced in practice as voting was restricted and Jim Crow laws were imposed by whites (Woodward 1957).

Sometimes outcomes involving changes in only limited spheres provide the bases for further changes that can occur without coercive conduct. This is more often true of aggregate goals. For example, blacks gaining more equal access to educational facilities in the 1950s are then more likely to enter occupations from which they had been barred by lack of credentials and by discrimination. Even the continuing discrimination, in the aggregate, is likely to be less effective. A changing occupational distribution of blacks then opens up other opportunities to use economic and political pressure, individually and collectively.

CONSEQUENCES FOR THE SOCIAL CONTEXT

In addition to the consequences of struggles for each adversary, relations between them and nonfocal parties, struggles also affect the entire system of which the adversaries are a part. The prevailing expectations, the basic rules for collective decision making, the relative position of major social groups, and nearly every other characteristic of any social system are affected by major struggles between component social groups. How the struggle is pursued and its outcome affect the social context within which the parties continue to exist. Conflicts are of primary significance in social change *of* and *within* a system (Coser 1967, pp. 17–35; Marx 1910; Dewey 1930).

Consequences of the Mode

The mode used in a struggle may affect the larger social system by establishing precedents for future struggles. Violence in one fight often makes it more likely to occur in another, even among different partisans in the same system. We noted in Chapter 4 the pertinence of models in the choice of means used to pursue conflicting objectives. Thus, in the United States in the 1960s demonstrations and nonviolent civil disobedience became ways of pursuing the objectives that a variety of conflict groups had adopted in the 1970s. Public support for what was previously regarded as unconventional politics increased (Hunt 1980).

But the modes used do not necessarily result in their continual repetition because they can be negative as well as positive models. Having seen the losses suffered by the use of a particular mode, potential users may shun the method. Following World War I, the revulsion with war and militarism seemed to affect many sectors of the French, English, and German populations as well as their governmental leaders for a generation. Following World War II, there was a turning away from militarism, especially in the defeated countries of Germany and Japan. Many Germans, for example, were sufficiently disgusted with war and nationalism to look for its avoidance by lessening national sovereignty within a united Europe.

One kind of evidence of such turning away from war as a result of experiencing it might be found in survey data. Earlier, we noted that analysis of public opinion surveys conducted in the United States over several years could be reanalyzed to discover if there were any generational effects. People who were young adults in World War I or in World War II showed no more tendency to be pacifists than other generations; rather, they were more likely to advocate war (Cutler 1970). Furthermore, this finding is not inconsistent with the evidence of a cycle in international violence. Denton and Phillips (1968) found evidence of an upswing in the level of violence about every twenty-five years. Singer and Small (1972) also examined the possible regularity of wars between 1816–1965. They found that although there was no regular pattern in the initiation of war, the amount of warfare under way reached peaks about twenty years apart. Perhaps the decision makers who had been in a war particularly wish to avoid a recurrence and know better how to do so. The next generation of leaders are more ready to see war as a possible means, perhaps even romanticizing it in retrospect, or are more prone to blunder into violence. But Singer and Small found the twenty-year cycle for the world, not for individual states. This suggests that the pattern is a result of the interaction of several systematic factors, including the size of wartime coalitions, the duration of wars, and the intervals between their onsets.

We need to know more about the extent to which experience with a particular means establishes a precedent for its recurrence or a warning that it be avoided. The consequences of the mode are in some ways inseparable from the consequences of the outcome. The disgust with war, for example, may be greatest among those who failed to get what they sought from the war.

The long-run effects of the mode are related to the meaning given to it. A particular effort is interpreted as having been a success or a failure and may have considerable consequences as a prevailing metaphor. For example, the way in which the English and French government leaders dealt with Hitler and the Nazis between 1933 and 1939 was generally regarded as appeasement and a disastrous failure. That interpretation played a role in the emergence of the cold war between the United States and the Soviet Union. It persisted and helps account for U.S. intervention in Vietnam, when the choice was viewed simply as between appeasement or military resolve (Hoopes 1969, pp. 7–16). It played a role in English and French leaders' dealings with Nasser that led to the British and French attack on Egypt in 1956. Other interpretations might have been constructed—for example, the need for collective solidarity and alliances even with such lesser evils as the Soviet Union; early recognition of the rights of others, such as German claims prior to the rise of Nazism; or the value of gaining time by allowing the adversary to prove it has unlimited aggressive aims (that is, the war against Nazism was more popular and perhaps more successful than an early attack upon Germany might otherwise have been). These rival interpretations enjoy little popular credence. A particular interpretation of past events often dominates alternative interpretations and then affects the interpretation of current and oncoming events. Imposing a simple analysis of a specific past case to a current one will inevitably produce errors.

The dominant interpretation of some events usually differs among the partisans. Blacks and whites tend to differ about the meaning and success of the urban riots in the 1960s. Students and administrators have their distinctive as well as shared ideas about the causes and consequences of particular conflict modes. These ideas and interpretations, as well as the events themselves, affect the working of the larger social system.

One other aspect of the conflict mode that has enduring systemic consequences deserves comment. Modes and their implementation vary in the extent to which people and groups are mobilized and form coalitions. Modes that involve large-scale popular participation may have enduring consequences for the system by having stirred people to become involved, and that leaves a residue of recurrent participation. More specifically, the set of groups that constitute the dominating coalition in the struggle establish the basic policy. In a revolutionary struggle, the relative balance of classes making up the triumphant revolutionary government shapes the government policy. For example, the urban proletariat in the Russian Revolution played a relatively large role comparable to that of the peasantry in the Chinese Revolution (Skocpol 1979). After the revolutions, the Soviets pursued policies more beneficial to the proletariat than to the peasantry; in the Chinese case, despite many shifts, there was relatively greater attention given to the interests of the peasantry.

Consequences of the Outcome

The outcome of a particular struggle or a series of struggles may alter relations and rules for reaching collective decisions in the social system at large. For example, when workers through collective bargaining and political action win representation in the management of industrial enterprises, the governance of the factories has been changed. It is also likely that the role of workers in the larger society has been changed, and it may even be that the rules governing other formerly less powerful groups will also be altered. Even without gaining managerial representation, the increased power of workers relative to managers has meant that they and their trade unions have more political power in the city and state governments and in the federal government as well.

The outcomes of major social conflicts have long-run indirect consequences. For example, if workers can increase their wages they increase labor costs to the employer, and this is a strong incentive for the employer to use labor more efficiently. Indeed, it is an incentive to replace labor by machinery. Labor leaders and economists have argued that unions contribute to the general economy by acting in ways that pressure management to introduce technical improvements and increase capital investments (Sufrin 1951; Coser 1967; Melman 1956; Levine and Geschwender 1981).

A fundamental question, asked particularly about revolutionary struggles, is whether victories are purchased at too heavy a price. We will not try to assign moral costs to humans killed in fighting, deprived of a better future, mistakenly repressed, or to humans' accepting subservience for themselves and future generations. Persons' entering or rejecting revolutionary struggles must make such moral assessments. The assessments are influenced by beliefs about the probabilities of collective gains and losses for partisans and nonpartisans in the struggle for the short and long term.

Evidence about the effects of revolutions is scanty and what there is is focused on economic effects. Lewis-Beck (1979) has described three views of such consequences: the conservative, Thermidorian, and Marxist. According to the conservative view (see, for example, Huntington 1968) revolutions disrupt productive forces and inflict enduring harm on a country's capacity to produce. According to the Marxist view, initial dislocation results in short-term losses, but these are more than offset by the improved capacity for greater production. The Thermidorian model stresses the return to "normalcy" that occurs after the fall in production immediately following a revolution.

Long periods of revolutionary turmoil may indeed produce significant and relatively long periods of reduced production. Skocpol (1979, p. 176) notes that France did not regain its prerevolutionary (1789) levels of foreign trade until well after 1815. The losses during and immediately following a revolution may seem to be an outcome in which nearly all contenders suffer significant losses.

Lewis-Beck (1979) examined the economic effects of the Cuban Revolution on sugar production and energy consumption. He concluded that none of the three models fit the Cuban experience. Rather, there was an immediate gain in aggregate production and a decline in growth later. Of course, the Cuban Revolution was not brought about through a long and devastating revolutionary war. The changeover was relatively swift, and the fundamental social changes were introduced from the top. Then, the economic ties with the United States were disrupted by the U.S. trade embargo. The subsequent decline in production might therefore be argued to be partially a result of U.S. sanctions, which could not be fully compensated for by the orientation of the economy to the Soviet Union.

From what we have seen in this book, we should not expect that revolutions would uniformly have major disruptive effects and then either result in decreased, increased, or unchanged rates of economic expansion. Revolutions, like all conflicts, are interlocked with many other fights. The implications of a revolutionary outcome within that set of interlocking fights will greatly affect societal economic developments. Foreign intervention may increase and prolong revolutionary turmoil, or it may assist some groups in their struggle against others in a coalition and in pursuit of one rather than another policy. In addition, revolutions may be waged in a variety of modes, and they will have varying consequences. Revolutions may include large components of nonviolent activities. They may have alternative organizational structures to which the populace give legitimacy, signifying that a new government has largely been formed before the old one was overthrown. Or revolutions may involve a relatively swift change in control of the government that unleashes a set of actions, with or without great coercion, to bring about fundamental social change. Many other characteristics of revolutionary struggles and outcomes affect the long-run consequences for a society.

SUMMARY AND CONCLUSIONS

Conflicts have long-lasting indirect consequences, often ones not contemplated by the partisans. Contenders struggle about their immediate goals and may give little heed to the long-term consequences for the various parties that may also be effected by the conflict.

We have seen how both the way a struggle is conducted and its outcome have consequences for each party to the fight, the future relations of the contending parties, other parties, and the system of which they are a part. We have especially discussed the relationship between one struggle and other possible ones. We have seen that external conflict may both increase and decrease internal conflict behavior. The consequences depend upon the characteristics of the external struggle and how they affect the bases of conflict within the group, the awareness of the conflict, and its pursuit by coercive means.

We have applied the framework developed in this book to study the consequences of conflicts. Thus, when we considered the consequences of one conflict for others, we analyzed how various aspects of conflict outcomes or various kinds of conflict modes would affect the underlying conditions, processes of emergence, and modes of conduct for other fights.

Conflicts are important stimulants for social change. But, just as conflict behavior does not alone determine the outcome to a struggle, neither do struggles alone determine the degree or course of social change. Competition, cooperation, and many other social processes underlie social change. Conflicts are essential, however, in changes pertaining to the reallocation of power and rules about how collective decisions are made.

BIBLIOGRAPHY

ABRAHAMSON, MARK, "Correlates of Political Complexity," *American Sociological Review,* 34 (October 1969), 690–701.

ANDRZEJEWSKI, STANISLAW, *Military Organization and Society* (London: Routledge and Kegan Paul, 1954).

BARBASH, JACK, *American Unions: Structure, Government, and Politics* (New York: Random House, 1967).

BARBERA, HENRY, *Rich Nations and Poor in Peace and War* (Lexington, Mass.: Lexington Books, 1973).

BROCH, TOM AND JOHAN GALTUNG, "Belligerence Among the Primitives," *Journal of Peace Research,* 1 (1966), 33–45.

BROWN, E., *Why Race Riots? Lessons from Detroit* (New York: Public Affairs Committee, Public Affairs Pamphlet No. 87, 1944).

BUDD, EDWARD C., "An Introduction to a Current Issue of Public Policy," pp. x–xix in Edward C. Budd (ed.), *Inequality and Poverty* (New York: W. W. Norton & Co., Inc., 1967).

CAMPBELL, ANGUS, *White Attitudes toward Black People* (Ann Arbor, Mich.: Institute for Social Research, University of Michigan, 1971).

COSER, LEWIS A., *The Functions of Social Conflict* (New York: Free Press, 1956).

———, *Continuities in the Study of Social Conflict* (New York: Free Press, 1967).

CUTLER, NEAL E., "Generational Succession as a Source of Foreign Policy Attitudes," *Journal of Peace Research,* 1 (1970), 33–47.

CUTRIGHT, PHILLIPS, "National Political Development," pp. 569–582 in N. W. Polsby, R. A. Dentler, and P. A. Smith (eds.), *Politics and Social Life* (Boston: Houghton Mifflin, 1963).

DENTON, FRANK H. AND WARREN PHILLIPS, "Some Patterns in the History of Violence," *Journal of Conflict Resolution,* 12 (June 1968), 182–95.

DEWEY, JOHN, *Human Nature and Conduct* (New York: Random House, 1930).

DUGAN, MAIRE A., "The Relationship between Pre-Independence Internal Violence and Nonviolence and Post-Independence Internal Violence, External Belligerency, and Internal Governmental Repressiveness," unpublished Ph.D. dissertation, Syracuse University, 1979.

FANON, FRANTZ, *The Wretched of the Earth* (New York: Grove Press, 1966).

FENDRICH, JAMES M. AND ELLIS S. KRAUSS, "Student Activism and Adult Left-wing Politics: A Causal Model Political Socialization for Black, White, and Japanese Students of the 1960s Generation," pp. 231–290 in Louis Kriesberg (ed.), *Research in Social Movements, Conflicts and Change,* Vol. 1 (Greenwich, Conn.: JAI Press, 1978).

HALBERSTAM, DAVID, *The Best and the Brightest* (Greenwich, Conn.: Fawcet, 1973).

HARKABI, Y., "Al Fatah's Doctrine," pp. 390–406 in Walter Laqueur (ed.), *The Israel-Arab Reader,* rev. ed. (New York: Bantam, 1970). Originally published in 1968.

HEBERLE, RUDOLF, *Social Movements* (New York: Appleton-Century-Crofts, 1951).

HOLSTI, OLE R., "External Conflict and Internal Cohesion: The Sino-Soviet Case," pp. 337–352 in Jan F. Triska (ed.), *Communist Party-States* (Indianapolis, Ind.: Bobbs-Merrill, 1969).

HOOPES, TOWNSEND, *The Limits of Intervention* (New York: D. McKay, 1969).

HOPMANN, P. T., "International Conflict and Cohesion in the Communist System," *International Studies Quarterly,* 11 (September 1967), 212–236.

HUNT, JOHN PHILLIPS, "Social Position, Political Consciousness, and Political Behavior: A Multivariate and Analysis," unpublished Ph.D. dissertation, Syracuse University, 1980.

HUNTINGTON, SAMUEL P., *Political Order in Changing Societies* (New Haven: Yale University Press, 1968).

KEYNES, JOHN MAYNARD, *The Economic Consequences of the Peace* (New York: Harcourt, Brace and Howe, 1920).

KRIESBERG, LOUIS, *Social Inequality* (Englewood Cliffs, N. J.: Prentice-Hall, 1979).

KRIESBERG, LOUIS AND ROSS KLEIN, "Changes in Public Support for U.S. Miltary Spending," *Journal of Conflict Resolution,* 24 (March 1980), 79–111.

LANG, KURT AND GLADYS ENGEL LANG, "Experiences and Ideology: The Influence of the Sixties on an Intellectual Elite," pp. 197–230 in Louis Kriesberg (ed.), *Research in Social Movements, Conflicts and Change,* Vol. 1 (Greenwich, Conn.: JAI Press, 1978).

LEE, HYOSUN, "The Impact of Interstate Conflict on Regression and the Political System in Developing Nations," unpublished Ph.D. dissertation, Syracuse University, 1978.

LEGGETT, JOHN C., *Class, Race, and Labor* (New York: Oxford University Press, 1968).

LEVINE, RHONDA AND JAMES A. GESCHWENDER, "Class Struggle, State Policy, and the Rationalization of Production: The Organization of Agriculture in Hawai," in Louis Kriesberg (ed.), *Research in Social Movements, Conflicts and Change,* Vol. 4 (Greenwich, Conn.: JAI Press, 1981).

LEVINE, ROBERT A., "Socialization, Social Structure, and Intersocietal Images," in Herbert C. Kelman (ed.), *International Behavior* (New York: Holt, Rinehart & Winston, 1965).

LeVine, Robert A. and Donald T. Campbell, *Ethnocentrism: Theories of Conflict, Ethnic Attitudes, and Group Behavior* (New York: John Wiley, 1972).

Lewis-Beck, Michael S., "Some Economic Effects of Revolution: Models, Measurement, and the Cuban Evidence," *American Journal of Sociology*, 84 (March 1979), 1127–1149.

Lindsey, Almont, *The Pullman Strike* (Chicago: University of Chicago Press, 1942).

McWorter, Gerald A. and Robert L. Crain, "Subcommunity Gladitorial Competition: Civil Rights Leadership as a Competitive Process," *Social Forces*, 46 (September 1967), 8–21.

Mannheim, Karl, "The Sociological Problem of Generations," pp. 276–322 in Paul Kecskemeti (ed.), *Essays on the Sociology of Knowledge* (New York: Oxford University Press, 1952). Originally published in 1928.

Marx, Karl, *The Poverty of Philosophy* (Chicago: Charles H. Kerr, 1910). Originally published in 1847.

Melman, Seymour, *Dynamic Factors in Industrial Productivity* (Oxford, Eng.: Blackwell, 1956).

Mueller, John E., *War, Presidents and Public Opinion* (New York: John Wiley, 1973).

Nahirny, Vladimir, "Some Observations on Ideological Groups," *American Journal of Sociology*, 67 (January 1962), 397–405.

Naroll, Raoul, "Deterrence in History," pp. 150–164 in Dean G. Pruitt and Richard C. Snyder (eds.), *Theory and Research on the Causes of War* (Englewood Cliffs, N.J.: Prentice-Hall, 1969).

Nincic, Miroslav, "Capital Labor and the Spoils of War," *Journal of Peace Research*, 17, no. 2 (1980), 103–117.

Oppenheimer, Martin, *The Urban Guerrilla* (New York: Quadrangle/The N.Y. Times, 1969).

Otterbein, Keith F., "Internal War: A Cross-Cultural Study," *American Anthropologist*, 70 (April 1968), 277–289.

Peretz, Don, "Palestine's Arabs," *Transaction*, 7 (August 1970), 43–49.

Reston, James, "The New Political Pragmatism," *The New York Times*, December 11, 1970.

Ross, Arthur M. and Donald Irwin, "Strike Experience in Five Countries, 1927–1947: An Interpretation," *Industrial and Labor Relations Review*, 4 (April 1951), 323–342.

Russett, Bruce M., "Who Pays for Defense," *American Political Science Review*, 63 (June 1969), 412–426.

Schonborn, Karl L., *Dealing with Violence* (Springfield, Ill.: Chas. C Thomas, 1975).

Seidman, Joel and Jack London, Bernard Karsh, and Daisy L. Tagliacozzo, *The Worker Views His Union* (Chicago: University of Chicago Press, 1958).

Selznick, Philip, *The Organizational Weapon* (New York: McGraw-Hill, 1952).

Simmel, Georg, *Conflict*, translated by K. H. Wolff (New York: Free Press, 1955). Originally published in 1908.

Singer, J. David and Melvin Small, *The Wages of War, 1816–1965: A Statistical Handbook* (New York: John Wiley, 1972).

Skocpol, Theda, *States and Social Revolutions: A Comparative Analysis of France, Russia, and China* (Cambridge, Eng.: Cambridge University Press, 1979).

SMITH, ROBERT B., *Some Effects of Limited War,* unpublished manuscript, 1971.

SOLOMON, F., AND OTHERS, "Civil Rights Activity and Reduction in Crime Among Negroes," *Archives of General Psychiatry,* 12 (March 1965), 227–236.

SUFRIN, SIDNEY C., *Union Wages and Labor's Earnings* (Syracuse, N.Y.: Syracuse University Press, 1951).

TANNENBAUM, ARNOLD S. AND ROBERT L. KAHN, "Organizational Control Structure," *Human Relations,* 10, no. 2 (1957), 127–140.

TANTER, RAYMOND, "Dimensions of Conflict Behavior Within and Between Nations, 1958–1960," *Journal of Conflict Resolution,* 10 (March 1966), 41–64.

TILLY, CHARLES, *From Mobilization to Revolution* (Reading, Mass.: Addison-Wesley, 1978).

TRAVIS, TOM ALLEN, "A Theoretical and Empirical Study of Communications Relations in the NATO and Warsaw Interbloc and Intrabloc International Sub-Systems," unpublished Ph.D. dissertation, Department of Political Science, Syracuse University, 1970.

VOCSE, TRUDIE, "24 Years in the Life of Lyuba Bershadskays," *The New York Times Magazine,* March 14, 1971, p. 88.

WALZ, JAY, *The Middle East* (New York: Atheneum Publishers, 1966).

WEIR, STANLEY, "U.S.A.: The Labor Revolt," pp. 466–501 in Maurice Zeitlin (ed.), *American Society, Inc.* (Chicago: Markham Publishing, 1970).

WILKENFELD, JONATHAN, "Some Further Findings Regarding the Domestic and Foreign Conflict Behavior of Nations," *Journal of Peace Research,* 2 (1969), 147–156.

WILKENFELD, JONATHAN AND DINA A. ZINNES, "A Linkage Model of Domestic Conflict Behavior," pp. 325–356 in Jonathan Wilkenfeld (ed.), *Conflict Behavior and Linkage Politics* (New York: D. McKay, 1973).

WINTER, J. M., "Britain's Lost Generation of the First World War," *Population,* 31 (November 1977a), 449–466.

——, "The Impact of the First World War on Civilian Health in Britain," *Economic History Review,* 30 (August 1977b), 487–507.

WOODWARD, C. VANN, *The Strange Career of Jim Crow,* rev. ed. (New York: Oxford University Press, 1957).

9

Essentials,
Settings,
and Implications

We have traced the full cycle of any specific social conflict—from its underlying conditions and emergence, to choosing how to conduct the conflict, to its escalation, deescalation, termination, and outcome, and, finally, to the longer run and indirect consequences of all that went on before. Now we can review the model of social conflicts as we developed it here. We can present the interaction and interdependence of stages more fully now that the whole possible sequence is before us. We will discuss, too, the peculiarities of social conflicts in different settings. We can also point out the special features of the approach presented here and consider its relevance for different kinds of conflicts as well as for social conflicts in general. Finally, some policy implications that derive from this analysis will be noted.

THE MODEL

This book is about specific conflicts—about struggles, revolutions, fights, strikes, campaigns, and wars. We have analyzed them in terms of a series of stages, or steps, and processes linking them. In a way, this approach may seem obvious. That does not make the approach valid, neither does it make it false. Other persons must use different evidence than that selected here to test the ideas. The general approach cannot be tested unless it is presented in a refutable form, but it cannot be phrased in neat propositions that might be proven wrong since the approach is too general. Nevertheless, two things can be done. First, the ideas can be stated clearly and precisely in an interrelated manner. Second, the peculiarities of the approach can be stressed so that alternative approaches will be salient enough to be compared with the one taken here. In addition, specific propositions have been presented throughout the book.

Summary Outline

In this approach, social conflicts move through a series of stages, although not every struggle goes through every stage. While each stage significantly depends upon an earlier one, expectations of and feedback from later stages also affect earlier ones. Specific struggles never revert to prior conditions exactly as they were. One struggle generally leads to another in an ongoing spiral of conflicts. In this summary, we review the stages of social conflicts, their interactive character, and their spiral continuity.

Stages. A full cycle in a social conflict consists of seven stages. First is the objective or underlying bases for a social conflict. Second is the emergence of a social conflict, when two or more parties believe they have incompatible goals. Third is the initial way in which the adversaries pursue their contradictory aims. The intensity and scope of the struggle escalates and then deescalates in stages four and five. Finally are stages six and seven in which the struggle terminates and there is an outcome. In addition, conflicts have consequences—indirect and unintended.

In discussing the bases of social conflicts, we distinguished two fundamental kinds of objective conflicts: consensual and dissensual. In consensual conflicts potential adversaries agree about what is valued and are so located that each believes that it cannot attain more of what is valued except at the expense of the other. In dissensual conflicts potential adversaries differ about what is desired or how to attain desired positions and find such differences objectionable. Note that these objective conflicts are between categories of people and are not within the minds of all people in a social system. We are concerned here with the bases for group conflicts, not the strains or role conflicts arising from cultural inconsistencies. It should also be kept in mind that the relations between possible adversaries need not (and indeed never are) purely conflicting. Common and complementary relations also exist.

A social conflict emerges when adversaries define goals that are opposed by each other. These aims are based upon a collective identity and sense of grievance and depend upon the underlying relations that constitute objective social conflicts. Only some of these conflicts become actualized. Whether or not a conflict emerges depends upon characteristics of the units involved, their interrelations, and their social environment.

Once the adversaries are in conflict, they select ways of contending with each other. Three fundamental ways of inducing the other side to yield what is desired can be distinguished: coercion, persuasion, and reward. One conventional meaning of conflict requires that coercion, especially nonlegitimate coercion, be used in pursuit of the incompatible goals. According to the approach taken here a conflict exists apart from how it is conducted. Furthermore, attention is directed at noncoercive ways of pursuing conflicting aims. This is possible because in any concrete struggle many struggles are interlocked and the parties have common and complementary relations as well as conflicting ones. We analyzed how the mode used is affected by the issue in contention, the characteristics of the adversaries, their relations with each other, and their social environment.

Once a conflict party has begun to pursue its goal in opposition to an adversary, the struggle between them usually escalates before the fight ends. Escalation means increased magnitudes of conflict behavior either in scope or in the way in which the struggle is conducted. But conflict behavior also deescalates. Deescalation usually precedes conflict termination. In an extended struggle escalation and deescalation can recur many times. Movements toward escalation and deescalation result from processes internal to each adversary and processes which pertain to the adversaries' interrelations. Whether the processes result in escalation or deescalation depends on the mode of conflict, characteristics of the adversaries, the interaction of the antagonists, the issue in contention, and the general context of the conflict parties. What is particularly important to recognize is that escalation is not inevitable and endless. Furthermore, the processes that result in escalation are dependent on certain conditions; other conditions would halt or reverse the movement toward escalation.

The processes of escalation and deescalation bring combatants to the termination stage. Termination is implicit or explicit; if explicit, it may differ in the particular rules governing the terminating processes and in their degree of institutionalization.

After termination the last stage is reached: the conflict's outcome. We noted that outcomes have both distributive and integrative dimensions. We considered outcomes in which one party gained at the expense of another and outcomes in which adversaries all gained (or all lost). In any specific conflict outcome, these dimensions are combined. It is important to keep in mind that the outcome of a conflict is rarely, if ever, the simple imposition of one party's will upon its adversaries.

Perhaps it needs to be reiterated: A particular struggle may end and the objective conflict remains or is changed only a little. Furthermore, the outcome may be the starting ground for a new conflict, while many other struggles between the adversaries continue. Nevertheless, it is necessary to consider how specific fights end and what the result is at that time and subsequently. The partisans often make such assessments and, therefore, we must understand where the partisans think they are. As analysts, we must make such assessments even if the partisans do not. Such assessments help us understand what has happened, what is happening, and what is likely to happen.

Although it is useful to analyze conflicts as a sequence of stages, the sequence is not fixed. Actions may be taken by subgroups for a variety of purposes, and afterward meaning is given to those actions by leaders of conflict parties or by other interested persons. For example, a riot or hostile attack may lead to a response that adds a meaning to the events they previously lacked. Based on that interaction, goals for the riot may be retroactively proclaimed. The partisans then seek an underlying conflict to justify their conduct.

Recursions. The discussion of stages and the general approach might be viewed as one in which conflicts flow like a stream through a number of locks, waterfalls, and pumping stations. The image of such a stream may be helpful, but it can be terribly misleading. It is necessary to consider the many ways in which the stages are interconnected and how "later" stages may affect "earlier" ones. One reason for the interconnections is the interlocking character of social conflicts; each struggle is part of a larger one and each one is accompanied by several others. In each case, adversaries in the focal dispute are at a particular stage in that struggle, but located at other points in other fights. Where they are in other fights must affect the developments of each struggle.

Our discussion of how later stages affect earlier ones, however, is largely confined to a single focal conflict. Such apparent reversals of sequences or backward flow of influence may occur in two ways: by feedbacks and by anticipation. Let us see how each operates through various stages. The links are diagrammed in Figure 9.1, a more complicated version of the figure presented in Chapter 1. First, let us consider how the mode selected to pursue a goal may affect the awareness of conflict. One way is by anticipation. Thus, the conflict mode partisans think they will be able to use affects the formulation of their goals. For example, in the Kennedy administration the development of counterinsurgency capabilities contributed to forming the goal to prevent the Viet Cong guerrilla forces from overthrowing the Republic of Vietnam government in Saigon (Halberstam 1973).

Collective identity and the sense of grievance will be affected by the kind of behavior adversaries expect to use in trying to attain their ends. In addition, the actual choice of mode affects the members' sense of grievance and identity by feedback processes. That is, members' experiences when initially choosing a mode then affect the sense of identity, grievances, and formulation of aims. For example, people who demonstrate for the first time and experience physical violence from police are likely to feel more solidarity with the other demonstrators. Of course, continued escalation of such confrontations may frighten away some demonstrators unless the aims increase in importance to make the losses acceptable.

Similarly, the anticipated escalation or deescalation of conflict behavior affects the initial selection of the mode. Expecting that the use of a particular conflict mode will lead to much escalation may inhibit its utilization. It may also facilitate calling in intermediaries to serve as mediators. Anticipation of the outcome certainly affects the initial choice of the way to pursue a goal and influences movements toward escalation and deescalation. Anticipation of the outcome even affects the emergence of a conflict. As we noted, insofar as members of a group believe they can redress their grievances, everything else being equal, they will try to do so. Undoubtedly, anticipations do not as strongly affect the formulation of goals, the choice of ways to pursue them, or the degree of conflict escalation, compared to more contemporaneous factors. The anticipated future is more easily distorted to be consistent with current circumstances than are current circumstances vulnerable to reinterpretation in the light of expectations of the future. Of course, this is not unreasonable: The future is even more uncertain than the ambiguous present.

Feedback is the other way in which later stages affect earlier ones. Since conflicts are continuous and interlocked, events at a later stage in one conflict provide information to partisans who are also at an earlier stage in another related struggle. Thus, a subgroup of partisans escalates its dispute with an adversary

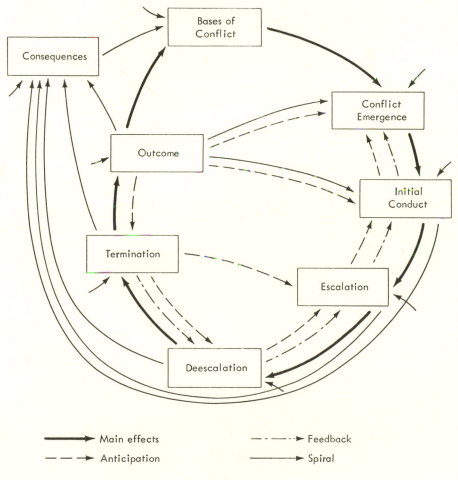

Figure 9.1

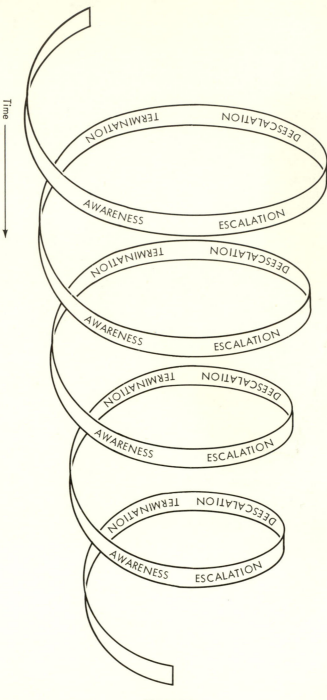

Figure 9.2

subgroup; the response of the adversary provides information to the larger entity of partisans who then escalates or deescalates the struggle further. Similarly, once terminating processes have begun, their course provides information which can effect escalation or deescalation.

Spirals. The outcome of every conflict is the possible basis for another struggle. But no struggle returns to exactly the same condition that existed before it began. Conflicts are interlocked in a continuous series. Even when they go through a full cycle of stages and then begin again, they do so at a somewhat different level (see Figure 9.2). An outcome, even in the case of a withdrawal of demands, does not signal a complete return to the conditions prior to the assertion of the demands. A failed effort provides information and alters expectations of all parties to the struggle.

In the preceding chapter, we discussed the variety of long-run consequences of the outcome of a conflict and how the outcome was pursued. We saw how the consequences affect the relations between the adversaries and the possible emergence of a new struggle. Such spiral effects are also included in Figure 9.1. Thus, the outcome of a struggle has implications for the collective identity of the adversaries, their sense of grievance, and the formulation of new aims. For example, an outcome that yields a conflict group many of its goals may increase its hopes for further benefits and strengthen support for new conflict-behavior efforts. Furthermore, how a conflict has come out has implications for how another one is likely to be pursued. The conflict group has strengthened or weakened confidence in the mode it used depending upon the outcome of its use, as the group interprets the mode's effects. For example, the "lesson" people in the United States draw about "war" differs when we compare the World War II and the Vietnam War generations.

In an important sense, the emergence of a new struggle helps explain what the previous one was really about. That is, if the adversaries define their goals as being relevant to the major objective conflicts, the outcomes may alter the conditions underlying the conflicts in ways that significantly reduce the probability or intensity of new struggles. For example, the increased job control and security won by trade unions have modified the objective conflict between labor and management. Some issues persist, for example, regarding wages and fringe benefits. Other issues may even become more salient, for example, dissatisfaction with work activities that lack inherent meaning and gratification.

Some outcomes that appear to be victories turn out to be unsatisfactory or inadequate even to the victors. Presumably, insofar as the victors attain their ostensible goal and yet their grievance remains, their struggle was unrealistic. They were striking at a scapegoat or they otherwise misdiagnosed their plight and either sought redress from an adversary who could not provide what they really needed or they sought the wrong concession from the adversary. Actually, victorious leaders rarely admit they made a mistake. If victory does not yield a satisfactory result, the goal is likely to be expanded. Thus, if national liberation does not change socioeconomic conditions as desired, economic independence from the former colonial power must be sought as well as political independence. The previous struggle is then regarded as a necessary step, but inadequate alone.

Some rank-and-file members of a partisan group, a rival adversary group, or an analyst may insist, however, that the conflict was indeed unrealistic since the goal's attainment did not yield the desired results. Thus, many U.S. groups during the 1960s sought to reduce poverty, racial discrimination, and sexism. Adversary groups pursued specific goals to serve these general purposes. Many of the specific goals were attained, but many of the gains seemed to have very limited effect. For example, radical feminists or blacks may argue that ending gross and obvious forms of discrimination are palliatives that do not alter the fundamental exploitive class relations that sustain sexism and racism.

Fundamentally, analytic assessments of the degree of realism and unrealism in a conflict depend on the consequences of a fight's outcome. The conflict's outcome and the adversaries' relations with each other after the struggle has ended provide a basis for judging the appropriateness of the adversaries' contending goals and their means of promoting them.

Unrealistic conflict has two major dimensions: (1) What the parties are apparently struggling about is not what "really" divides them, and (2) The level of conflict behavior is more extreme than is warranted by the sought-for goals. In the former case one or both sides may be misinformed, misled, or otherwise inaccurate in their assessments of what divides them. The latter case is often a matter of conflict behavior escalating in a mutual interaction of fear, injury, and animosity. In both cases, assessments can be most adequately made only after the consequences of a struggle are discerned.

Emphases in the Model

Sound and convincing as the model presented in this book may seem, its value can be estimated only compared to alternative models. Therefore, it is important to stress the peculiarities of this approach compared to other possible approaches. Five aspects of the approach deserve particular attention: the purposefulness of adversaries in conflict, the mixed character of each struggle, the importance of interaction, the significance of nonfocal parties, and the variety of means by which conflicts are conducted.

Purposefulness of Adversaries. The approach taken here assumes that conflict partisans are purposeful and, in some senses, rational. Rationality is an elusive concept. Without attempting a discourse on the topic, we should consider some meanings of rationality and in what sense this model embodies an analysis of conflicts as rational.

First, the approach stresses that the partisans act in order to reach goals and think they are rational. As analysts, we must pay attention to what the partisans think they are fighting about because their interpretations affect how they pursue their goals and how the conflict will be terminated. If we become too subtle and devious in our analyses, we can err seriously in understanding the development of a struggle. At the subjective level for each party, then, the partisans try to be reasonable. They try to calculate costs and benefits and try to interpret and justify their actions so they are consistent with their avowed purposes.

But each party's trying to be rational does not guarantee a rational outcome. That is, none of the parties gets what it most prefers. An observer may note that the parties are not pursuing policies that make their goals likely to be reached. And, in fact, they may not for two fundamental reasons. First, the development of a struggle depends on interaction among adversaries, and none alone determines the course of a fight. Second, parties may be misinformed and lack crucial information; therefore, they do not pursue their self-interest in what the analyst would judge to be a rational way. Such partisan misjudgments, furthermore, may well be the consequence of emotions, of fears, hates, and loves. This does not deny, however, that the partisans are trying to make as good judgments as they can within the limits of their abilities. Nor does all this reject the possibility of analyzing how emotions play a role in defining goals and the ways of pursuing them.

This brings us to another way in which this model assumes what might be called the purposefulness and, even, rationality of social conflicts. Fights are about something. Conflict awareness, by definition, involves incompatible goals. But more than that, the notion of objective conflict presumes that there are bases for struggles even before partisans are aware of them. If we as observers could make such assessments accurately, we would have a powerful predictive capacity. The framework for analysis presented here should increase the likelihood of successful predictions, but it is not sufficiently detailed to readily yield the numerous predictions anyone might wish to make.

In this approach, then, there is a presumption that objective grounds of conflict underlie an emerging struggle. Such underlying conditions continue to be pertinent when we want to understand the course of a fight and its outcome.

The term *rational* is loaded with too many connotations and implications for easy communication. The main points of this discussion may be better summarized without using that word. We presume that an observer can make sense of the course of a social conflict. In doing so, it is helpful to consider that partisans are trying to be reasonable and even calculating in what they are doing. Due regard should be given to the partisans' view regarding which of their conflicts they believe to be the focal one. In trying to explain the course of a conflict, an observer should also take into account the conditions facing each party that affect how the partisans feel, think, and act. In this way, we may understand how the adversaries, each of whom reasonably seeks particular goals, may individually or jointly find themselves in situations they would wish to avoid.

Mixed Character of Conflicts. No specific social conflict is purely conflicting. The problem is that the word *conflict* is generally used in two different senses. In one sense, we refer to a struggle, fight, confrontation, or other form of opposition between adversaries' believing they have incompatible goals. In the other, we refer to a quality or aspect of a social relationship. In other words, the relations between any two groups have conflicting, cooperative, accommodating, and many other qualities. We may abstract from that totality those aspects that are conflicting. We may also abstract a sequence of events that are regarded by the groups as a struggle or fight. In this book, specific social conflicts refer to those sequences of events we call revolutions, wars, strikes, or demonstrations. Such sequences of events are between groups that have a whole range of relations, not all of which are purely conflicting. For example, during the extended student occupation of the University of Chicago administration building, some students slipped out, attended class, and returned to continue the sit-in.

The mixed character of conflicts also reflects the degree to which specific fights are interlocked. We have distinguished six ways conflicts are interlocked: (1) serial or nested in time, (2) converging or nested within each other in social space, (3) superimposed or issue-linked, (4) cross-cutting, (5) internal, and (6) concurrent. Partisans give primary attention to one conflict, but shifts in the focal conflict are crucial in conflict escalation and deescalation (Kriesberg 1980). The existence of many interlocking conflicts also provides the basis for mixing persuasion and rewards in trying to gain one's goals against an adversary. Thus, noncoercive inducements are particularly useful in efforts to divide the adversary or prevent united actions by a coalition of adversaries. For example, peace initiatives were launched by President Sadat of Egypt in part to weaken the solidarity between the Israeli and U.S. governments (Kriesberg and Klein 1980) and the Soviet premier, Khrushchev, launched his competitive but peaceful coexistence campaign in part to reduce the solidarity among Western European governments and the U.S. government (Kriesberg 1981).

Interaction among the Adversaries. The emergence, development, and termination of a struggle are not determined by the internal characteristics of a conflict unit. They depend predominantly on the interaction among the adversaries. Neither party can alone determine the course of a social conflict. This is one reason why, even if each party is purposeful, the outcome for the two of them may be undesired by both. We saw how this could be the case for an arms race, in Chapter 1 and Figure 1.3. Each country, acting reasonably to prevent its being at a military disadvantage to the other, increases its arms. Consequently, they are both in a worse position than if they had agreed to limit arms. This is true, granted the relative values of the cells in the payoff matrix of Figure 1.3.

The importance of interaction in determining the development of a social conflict may be seen, too, in the way each party helps to determine the identity of the other. The shape and character of any adversary always is somewhat problematic. Even in international conflicts, the governments cannot be certain who their constituency is. The opponent helps shape that, as in the case of the Nazi-Soviet war.

The interactional character of conflicts also helps provide a means by which outside parties and contextual influences affect the course of a struggle. Each adversary is exposed to many aspects of the larger social context to which the other is exposed. Consequently, just as one party may model itself upon counterparts to act in a particular way, its opponent may expect such actions because it can also see how its adversary's counterparts are acting. This helps account for the sudden contagion in conflict modes. For example, when university students are demonstrating, the students at another university may think it is appropriate that they, too, demonstrate. Furthermore, the administrators at that same university may even expect that their students will demonstrate. Such shared expectations may increase the probability of the event's occurring, unless the expectations result in negotiating or conceding what is anticipated from the events.

Nonfocal Parties. Together with the emphasis upon the interactional character of social conflicts, the model stresses that the interaction occurs within a social context. That context importantly includes other parties who are audience, potential allies, adversaries, judges of the means and ends of the parties to the conflict, and potential beneficiaries of the losses suffered by both parties in the fight.

Of the many nonfocal parties we considered, we examined intermediaries in particular. Intermediaries cannot be neutral or without influence in the course of a conflict. The very expression of disinterest communicates a judgment of the issues at stake and the acceptance of the likely outcome. More generally, nonfocal parties help shape the terms by which adversaries define who they are, what they are striving for, how they should pursue their goals, and their expectations about the likely outcomes. Intermediaries play special roles in mitigating the costs of conflicts. They may serve as enforcers, fact finders, trainers, and mediators.

Alternative Means. Finally, a peculiarity of the approach taken here is the attention given to noncoercive inducements. We have argued that persuasion and positive sanctions are used to pursue aims in a struggle. They are blended together with coercion in a variety of mixtures. This blending is related to the presumption that no struggle is purely conflicting. Furthermore, we have stressed that the conflict modes vary in their degree of regulation and institutionalization. This, however, is generally noted in writings about social conflicts.

SETTINGS FOR SOCIAL CONFLICTS

At the outset, we stated our intention to analyze all kinds of social conflicts. We argued for the advisability of avoiding conventional distinctions among types of disputes. Rather, we outlined several dimensions of conflicting relations and of conflict units. It was then possible to consider what were the significant aspects of the differences and similarities among particular struggles.

In this concluding chapter, it is useful to consider specifically the implications of various settings within which conflicts occur. Now we will utilize conventional categories, such as international conflict, organizational conflict, community conflict, and class conflict. The attention is directed to the implications of struggles in settings as various as organizations, communities, societies, and world systems. Four dimensions of each setting will be examined: the nature of the social relations within it, the degree of organization of the whole system, the rules about conflict within the system, and the autonomy of the setting.

Community

The community as a setting for social conflicts refers to any territorially limited, relatively dense, residential area. Thus, cities, towns, villages are all communities. This list also suggests that the term is restricted to territories with a governmental structure and, thus, exclude neighborhoods within a city or town. Community conflict conventionally refers to disagreements in which partisans contend with one another using means that exceed the usual and legitimate ones (Coleman 1957). We shall continue to use the definitions of social conflicts developed in this book, but the conventional meaning of community conflicts indicates some of the peculiarities of this setting for struggles.

Peculiarities. We first discuss the important characteristics of communities that are relevant for social conflicts, before considering their implications for the spiral of conflicts.

Within communities people interact with one another in multiple roles when compared, for example, with the segmental and specialized role relations of members of most organizations. In addition, interactions are extensive and cross-cutting, and they involve large components of nonconflicting relationships.

Communities generally have some degree of organization and differentiation in the handling of conflicts—more than in the world as a system of states, more than in many organizations, but less than in most countries. The rules for conflict regulation usually restrict the means to nonviolent ones and to nonphysical coercion; there are usually even limits to verbal abuse. Communities, like organizations and unlike societies, have relatively little autonomy. Consequently, the social environment within which they exist can have important consequences for the course of social conflicts.

Implications. These features of communities have implications for each stage of community conflicts. The underlying bases for conflicts are innumerable, but none is inherently salient. The multiple cross-cutting relations and the availability of means for reaching collective decisions tend to keep most conflicts from emerging.

This makes problematic the emergence of struggles and the mobilization of partisans. Changes in relative numbers or power of particular categories of community members are often related to the emergence of community conflicts. Thus, rapid immigration of young urban families into a village-becoming-a-suburb may require readjustments that the old decision-making mechanisms are unable to provide without high levels of controversy which the citizens regard as conflict behavior. Furthermore, the existence of differentiated structures for collective decision making, as in the form of governments, often makes governmental leaders the targets for one side in the conflict. The struggle then may take on the form of a challenge to the authorities. It is also worth noting that the lack of autonomy of communities means that conflict awareness may be speeded and conveyed among communities by society-wide leaders, writers, agitators, and others representing a segment of people in many communities.

The conflict modes used are generally nonviolent and, even if coercive, have high admixtures of persuasion and reward. This is partly because there are collective decision-making structures and institutionalized rules for handling conflict, which constrain the means used and inhibit escalation. Moreover, the lack of community autonomy means the superordinate collective decision-making structures and possible outside intervention further inhibit and often enforce limits to escalation.

Organizations

When we speak of organizations as settings for social conflicts, we refer to large formal organizations, such as armies, prisons, industrial plants, government agencies, universities, professional associations, and churches. There is specialized literature on each of these kinds of organizations and also attempts to analyze organizations comprehensively (Caplow 1964; Hall 1977).

Peculiarities. We briefly note characteristics of organizations that have implications for the course of social conflicts. Social relations within organizations are generally more segmental than within communities. That is, persons relate to one another predominantly in terms of their organizational roles. It is true that some organizations entail extensive involvement of members and relations covering a wide sphere of activities, and, as these become extensive, the organization merges or turns into communities or societies (Diamond 1958). Even with segmental relations, there is often mutual dependence of categories of members. Such complementary and common interests that may exist, however, should not lead to any assumption or proof-by-definition that organizations have common purposes shared by all members.

Organizations vary in the degree to which there is differentiation and structures for collective decision making. All organizations have such structures even if they are informal and minimal. Frequently, the basic form this takes is hierarchical: Decisions are made by those with higher authority. This authority may be more or less clearly delegated by a larger constituency of owners, contributors, or citizens, or even by the totality of members.

Organizations often lack rules for handling conflicts, aside from the procedures for reaching collective decisions. A few organizations have procedures by which individual members may appeal decisions (Scott 1965), and there may be institutionalized conflict regulation mechanisms, as in collective bargaining. But most organizations lack any devices for handling group conflict internal to the organization.

Finally, organizations have relatively little autonomy. Not only are members' relations segmental, but the members also conduct only a portion of their lives within the organization. Organizations are generally dependent upon the social environment. Usually any given organization is not the sole alternative for its members; people can look for other organizations in which to conduct their affairs.

Implications. Several implications for objective conflicts flow from these organizational peculiarities. On the one hand, the segmental character of relations and the hierarchical nature of decision making produce relatively discernible objective conflicts. Demarcations are simpler than in circumstances in which multiple and cross-cutting relations predominate. On the other hand, the existence of alternatives may make possible a variety of self-selection and turnover patterns that tend to reduce conflicts. Thus, persons are recruited into, and remain within, particular organizations to some extent only insofar as they accept the terms of membership. For example, ideologically oriented voluntary organizations tend to select and be selected by similarly minded persons.

When it comes to emergent conflict, the existence of clear categories makes lines of cleavage relatively salient. Collective identity is more easily developed. In general, mobilization is less problematic than within communities. Given the common hierarchical structure, opposition is often directed across that line of cleavage, as in the frequent case of subordinates' seeking redress of grievances against their superordinates. Struggles often take the form, then, of challenges to those in authority.

Given the power differences and the usual modes of reaching collective decisions, objective conflicts often do not become actualized. If they do, the mode used will often involve persuasion (appeal to the organizational charter and rules of fairness). The interdependence also means that exchange of rewards, on bargaining, is likely. This may be done collectively or individually (and hence on an aggregate basis). Furthermore, individuals can act on a private basis by withdrawing from the organization, insofar as there are reasonable alternatives. Such aggregate rather than collective actions are another way of inducing change and redressing grievances, aside from the use of group conflict (Scott and others 1963).

When alternatives are limited and the grievances severe, then the absence of institutionalized regulations regarding group conflict may mean the occasional eruption of high levels of coercion, as happens in prison riots and naval mutinies.

Yet, there are limits to the escalation of violence that are set by the more encompassing societal agencies and organizations.

Society

Given the lack of autonomy of both communities and organizations, a country or society often appears to be the ultimate setting of most social conflicts. Struggles within organizations or within communities cannot be understood and their outcomes explained without recourse to outside parties and the social environment generally. This is less true for society-wide conflicts based upon general cleavages, such as race, sex, age, ideology, religion, and class.

Peculiarities. Societies, like communities, are settings in which people are implicated in multiple relations with one another. Cross-cutting bonds and cleavages are inevitable. But, categories of people are large enough that such relationships are not interpersonally enacted. They depend upon intermediaries, interpersonal communications, and symbolic identifications (Blau 1964).

Societies generally have the most elaborate collective decision-making structures among the settings we are discussing. These structures are typically the governmental ones. A government's claiming sovereignty over the society is a predominant condition. Within each society, there are generally elaborate institutionalized rules about conflict. Finally, societies are relatively autonomous. The bulk of interactions are conducted within each society, and governments act to preserve societal boundaries. Nevertheless, societies are not completely autonomous: There are extensive movements of people, goods, and ideas across societal boundaries (Angell 1969; Kriesberg 1968).

Implications. The diversity of persons and the multiplicity of activities conducted within societies mean that major objective conflicts abound. The predominance of certain institutions helps determine which ones are particularly salient. Generally the existence of government makes relative political power a fundamental cleavage. Furthermore, the considerable autonomy of societies makes struggles among component parts seem more like zero-sum contests: The separateness of a society implies that allocations of what is valued must be made within the confines of the society.

The number of persons within various categories is sufficiently large to make possible a sense of collective power and solidarity and to help provide a basis for the differentiation and the history needed to develop ideologies, which help make conflicts emerge from underlying conditions. Governments, either as arbitrators or as direct partisans, are likely to be the focus of conflicting aims. Some of the peculiarities of societies, however, makes conflict less likely than is true of other settings. The autonomy and existence of other societies, who may be rivals or adversaries, and the often long socialization and indoctrination in societal identification, all contribute to a sense of common interest with others in the society. In addition, the elaboration of rules for handling conflict may reduce struggles so they appear to be games rather than fights. For example, political elections in some countries allow for the transfer of power in almost a routine fashion.

For similar reasons, persuasion and the trading of rewards are possible and likely modes of conducting struggles. The existence of collective decision-making structures and the institutionalization of rules about conflict behavior generally limit escalation and help restrict the level of coercion. Nevertheless, if the issue is one that does not readily fit into the extant understandings, fights may assume much less limited dimensions. This is particularly likely to be the case on moral issues. The relative autonomy of societies leaves the possible escalation open-ended, as in some civil wars. Outside intervention cannot readily impose a settlement. If intervention does not occur, the domestic adversaries may be free to fight it out; that is, escalation may occur until one side is fundamentally defeated. If intervention does occur, it is likely to be partisan and itself be the source of additional escalation.

The World

The setting for interstate conflicts is the world. The world can be the setting for other kinds of conflict as well: religious, racial, and ideological. Although the whole world is rarely involved in a particular conflict, we must consider it the context within which struggles are waged.

Peculiarities. First, the world is not highly integrated. Neither governments nor countries, neither cross-cutting identities nor associations are worldwide in scope. Societies and cultures are diverse, and most interaction occurs within rather than across their boundaries. The autonomy of countries allows each one to develop coercive means in response to domestic pressures, with relatively little attention to the threats such developments may engender in other countries. Government leaders are basically dependent upon domestic support to sustain their leadership.

There are few institutionalized collective decision-making processes available at the world level, although some rudimentary procedures do exist (Aron 1966). Governments presume sovereignty and mutually support this conception. The rules for regulated conflict are not highly institutionalized, even when and where they exist (Kaplan and Katzenbach 1961). Supranational structures, where they exist, are regional or restricted in spheres of activity (Etzioni 1965; Haas 1965; Kriesberg 1960).

The world is socially autonomous. Most world struggles are conducted, however, in only a portion of the world, and that part is not fixed. Any struggle may expand to involve the rest of the world.

Implications. Major objective conflicts between parties at the world level may be less numerous than between adversaries in other settings. The lack of integration and of organized collective decision-making structures means that many of the things groups value and desire cannot be given by other groups. In a system that lacks highly institutionalized collective decision making, however, conflicts can be intense, and the importance for many people of their nation-state identification promotes struggles over such matters as the scarce resources that one country lacks and another has. The solidarity citizens tend to have with their country means that mobilization of the constituency is often taken for granted, although in actuality mobilization is problematic (Kriesberg 1956; Grodzins 1956).

Within the contemporary world system, national governments are likely to view other governments as allies or as adversaries. Adversaries confront each other at least defensively and with fear. The prospect of efforts at aggrandizement by one or another party seems omnipresent.

The lack of integration and cultural diversity limits the use of persuasion as a way to pursue conflicting goals. The minimal integration also reduces the possibility of exchanging rewards in trade-offs. These conditions and the lack of institutionalized ways of reaching joint decisions makes coercion seem essential to the pursuit of conflicting aims. The lack of rules for regulating conflict behavior and the autonomy of the system make violence and the escalation of violence likely. What makes such circumstances additionally frightening and frightful is the immense power of contemporary weapons.

Leaders dependent upon domestic support are relatively free to express hostility against a foreign adversary. The foreigners can be blamed for domestic troubles, and the foreign enemy has little leverage to gain even reasonable concessions.

POLICY IMPLICATIONS

In a book about social conflicts, I feel an obligation to make some observations about the implications for policy of the approach taken in the book. It may be helpful to state explicitly my analytic orientation. Social life is constantly changing because of the complex interplay of many social processes. People construct their own worlds. They strive and contend as individuals, groups, movements, classes, and societies. In most relations, they cooperate, exchange, accommodate, assimilate, and engage in conflicts with others. This welter is not without order and some stability, but it is an order that is not controlled or even fully predictable by any of the participants.

The analysis made in this book is intended to account for how people act in conflicts. It does not purport to state normative laws asserting how people should act or "natural" laws asserting that their actions are determined. Presumably a fuller and more accurate understanding of how processes interact and how conditions result in particular consequences can affect the courses of conduct people follow. Adversaries often act as if they forgot what they were fighting for (Iklé 1971); but the approach taken here attempts to explain this. Partisans are not willfully unreasonable. They follow courses that seem best among the alternatives they believe available. Consider the use of violence. It often seems counterproductive and very costly for what is gained, but it is frequently resorted to out of a sense of desperation. I assume that a more accurate and comprehensive view of social conflicts by the partisans will make their actions, even in retrospect, appear more reasonable, rational, and efficient than they otherwise would be.

One other aspect of the general view assumed in this book should be noted. This book is about social conflicts, but I do not wish to imply that conflict is the paramount social process or that specific conflicts are the only way in which change occurs or more equity attained. First, many kinds of dissatisfactions are not amenable to solution by any conflict behavior; they are part of the human condition, at least under existing circumstances. Thus, natural disasters, many illnesses, ultimately death cannot be prevented—but their costs and probabilities may be variously distributed. Social life and equity may be improved in many ways aside from conflict. Cooperation among persons and the cumulative developments of material goods and of ideas may profoundly affect the human condition.

The perspective taken in this analysis has many implications for policy for people in conflict relationships and a few will be singled out. But the implications rest on values as well as on empirical regularities. It is impossible to suggest policies without recognizing the ends to be served. In making suggestions here, I presume not only the desirability of mitigating the costliness in human lives and anguish of waging conflicts, but also the desirability of maximizing the improvement in human conditions that struggles may produce. In any specific case, people may differ about the priorities of these and other values. The implications I note are based upon my values and my interpretations of the empirical regularities.

It seems to me that people should not deny the existence of conflicts or seek to end all of them, since such efforts are often refusals to recognize the interests of other groups. Objective conflicts are omnipresent. If they are not manifest, it may be out of the hopelessness of the aggrieved party rather than because of the irrelevance of the conflict.

Seekers after justice should also not believe that coercive behavior is the only way to attain what they seek. Even if coercion is applied, however, partisans should consider using persuasion and possible rewards. Some combinations may be more effective for particular aims than the use of coercion or violence. The long-run consequences may also contribute to maximizing other values.

There is another important reason to consider carefully the choice of means to pursue conflicting goals: The course of a struggle and of its outcome are problematic and, in fact, are ultimately unpredictable. Therefore, it is risking much to justify harsh means by pointing to a desirable end to be attained. Since the final outcome and indirect consequences will be unknown, the way chosen in trying to reach a goal should be minimally harmful.

Although the outcome of a struggle is unknown, it is important for the partisans to consider the likely outcomes and, indeed, that there will be one. Keeping in mind that fights end and there will still be a future should make partisans more sensible in the course of a struggle. Throughout a fight, partisans should keep in mind the broad spectrum of possible consequences presented here, the variety of possible outcomes, and of alternative ways in which they may be attained. In considering outcomes and consequences, partisans should assess those they do not want as well as the desired ones. Giving attention to unsatisfactory consequences would suggest ways that might minimize those consequences without reducing the desired ones.

In formulating goals for fights it is well to seek ones that are attainable (and, perhaps, also attainable by acceptable means). Partisans should keep in mind that there is a fundamental relationship between means and ends. Thus, deterrence is effective if the demands are not too severe. The more stringent the goals as far as the adversary is concerned, the more coercion is necessary to attain them. This is one reason that autonomy *from* others is a more attainable aim than domination *over* others.

Generally, considering the interactional nature of social conflicts, it is wise to imagine the role of the adversaries as the struggle develops. Sometimes failure to do so, perhaps out of passion, may enable one party to pursue its aim further than it might otherwise do. Putting oneself in the role of the adversary may temper ruthlessness and even faith and conviction in one's own goals, but, usually and in the long run, taking into account how the opponents view a struggle will decrease the chances of mistakes and disasters. The outcome will be more stable, and, from the perspective of the larger system of which the partisans are constituent parts, benefits are more likely to be maximized.

Means and ends that have as consequences the furthering of conflict regulation and its institutionalization should be considered especially attractive. Since partisans are members of a larger system of relations and since other fights will occur after each is settled, conflict regulation is important in the long run for all participants. But the content of the rules regulating conflict tend to favor some parties more than others. Therefore, attention should be given to the equity of the regulations. This in part will reflect the equity of the conflict's outcome.

Peace and universal solidarity may be wished for, but they are unattainable. People will strive collectively against one another. Such contentions are not without benefits to one or even to all adversaries in the long run. Neither, however, are they without costs and often great pain and anguish, and too frequently much death. We cannot escape the inherent strife of social life, but human knowledge and wisdom can help reduce its pain and increase its benefits. Let us try to contribute to such knowledge and wisdom and act in accord with them.

BIBLIOGRAPHY

ANGELL, ROBERT C., *Peace on the March: Transnational Participation* (New York: Van Nostrand Reinhold, 1969).

ARON, RAYMOND, *Peace and War* (New York: Doubleday, 1966).

BLAU, PETER M., *Exchange and Power in Social Life* (New York: John Wiley, 1964).

CAPLOW, THEODORE, *Principles of Organization* (New York: Harcourt, Brace Jovanovich, Inc., 1964).

COLEMAN, JAMES, *Community Conflict* (New York: Free Press, 1957).

DIAMOND, SIGMUND, "From Organization to Society," *American Journal of Sociology,* 63 (March 1958), 457–475.

ETZIONI, AMITAL, *A Comparative Analysis of Complex Organizations* (New York: The Free Press, 1961).

———, *Political Unification* (New York: Holt, Rinehart & Winston, 1965).

GRODZINS, MORTON, *The Loyal and the Disloyal* (Chicago: University of Chicago Press, 1956).

HAAS, ERNST B., *Beyond the Nation-State: Functionalism and International Organization* (Stanford, Calif.: Stanford University Press, 1965).

HALBERSTAM, DAVID, *The Best and the Brightest* (New York: Fawcet Books Group-CBS Publications, 1973).

HALL, RICHARD H., *Organizations: Structure and Process,* 2nd ed. (Englewood Cliffs, N.J.: Prentice-Hall, 1977).

IKLÉ, FRED CHARLES, *Every War Must End* (New York: Columbia University Press, 1971).

KAPLAN, MORTON A. AND NICHOLAS DEB. KATZENBACH, *The Political Foundations of International Law* (New York: John Wiley, 1961).

KRIESBERG, LOUIS, "National Security and Conduct in the Steel Gray Market," *Social Forces,* 34 (March 1956), 268–277.

———, "German Leaders and the Schuman Plan," *Social Science,* 35 (April 1960), 114–121.

———, "U.S. and U.S.S.R. Participation in International Non-Governmental Organizations," pp. 466–485 in Louis Kriesberg (ed.), *Social Processes in International Relations* (New York: John Wiley, 1968).

———, "Interlocking Conflicts in the Middle East," in Louis Kriesberg (ed.), *Research in Social Movements, Conflicts and Change,* Vol. 3 (Greenwich, Conn.: JAI Press, 1980).

———, "Noncoercive Inducements in U.S.-Soviet Conflicts: Ending the Occupation of Austria and Nuclear Weapons Tests," *Journal of Political and Military Sociology,* 9 (Spring 1981),

KRIESBERG, LOUIS AND ROSS A. KLEIN, "Positive Inducements in Middle East Peace Efforts." Unpublished manuscript, Syracuse University, 1980.

SCOTT, W. H., ENID MUMFORD, L. C. MCGIVERING, AND J. M. KIRKBY, *Coal and Conflict: A Study of Industrial Relations at Collieries* (Liverpool: Liverpool University Press, 1963).

SCOTT, WILLIAM G., *The Management of Conflict: Appeal Systems in Organizations* (Homewood, Ill.: Richard D. Irwin and Dorsey Press, 1965).

Author Index

Subject Index